Beyond American Hegemony

BEYOND AMERICAN HEGEMONY

The Future of the Western Alliance

DAVID P. CALLEO

A Twentieth Century Fund Book

Basic Books, Inc., Publishers   New York

The Twentieth Century Fund is an independent research foundation which undertakes policy studies of economic, political, and social institutions and issues. The Fund was founded in 1919 and endowed by Edward A. Filene.

Library of Congress Cataloging-in-Publication Data

Calleo, David P., 1934–
  Beyond American hegemony.

  "A Twentieth Century Fund book."
  Includes index.
  1. North Atlantic Treaty Organization. 2. Europe—
Defenses. I. Title.
UA646.3.C24   1987   355'.031'091821   87–47506
ISBN 0–465–00655–8

For Gertrude Crowe Calleo

Happy he
With such a mother!
—TENNYSON, *The Princess*

CONTENTS

FOREWORD

SIGNS ABOUND that the post–World War II era, which was marked by American domination of both its wartime allies and its former enemies—with the exception of course of the Soviet Union and its satellites—has ended. Witness the fashionable and facile predictions that the end of American hegemony will be followed by a continuing American decline, similar to the decline of British power in the late nineteenth and early twentieth centuries. Yet the differences between the United Kingdom then and the United States now are far greater than the parallels. To begin with, we are geographically a continental country and not a small island. And though we may have lost our supremacy in various industrial sectors, just as the British did earlier, we remain far ahead of all other countries in much of the technology that characterizes the so-called post-industrial society.

This is not to say that the United States can do without a substantial industrial base. Nor is there any assurance that the United States can maintain its superpower status and at the same time be in debt to the rest of the world. (The Soviet Union, though, can hardly claim to be gaining on us.) Even if we use the leverage that a big debtor can sometimes exercise, it is difficult to conceive of a superpower that is dependent on other nations for financial support. Yet it does not follow that the loss of our position as world hegemon necessarily means a breakdown in the international system that has been built up in the postwar period.

Will there be a vacuum to be filled now that the United States is no longer *the* dominant economic power in the world? If so, who will fill it? And does the loss of overwhelming economic prowess mean that our military might will also be weakened? What kind of foreign policy should we have in a period of transition? What can be done to adjust our current institutional arrangements to new conditions? These are among the questions considered by David Calleo of the School of Advanced International Studies at Johns Hopkins University, an especially thoughtful student of American foreign policy. In this book for the Twentieth Century Fund, Calleo looks first at the Atlantic Alliance, the frequently attacked but nevertheless enduring pillar of American leadership in the postwar period, and then proceeds to a wide-ranging and provocative analysis of our foreign policy—its strengths, its weaknesses, its pretensions, and its practicability. He argues for maintaining an American presence in Europe, but he suggests that we can do so only if there is also a new pluralism in world affairs, one that encourages and permits sharing the burdens with our major allies.

The Fund is grateful to David Calleo for his challenging book. Unlike some of the pessimists now being heard, he makes a convincing case that fresh and imaginative new approaches can lead to a stronger and even more resilient alliance. These changes will take leadership and political will, here and abroad, but as Calleo's masterful critique of current policy makes clear, we are inviting trouble if those qualities are not exercised in formulating a new set of policies to take us into the next century.

M. J. ROSSANT, *Director*
The Twentieth Century Fund
April 1987

ACKNOWLEDGMENTS

A BOOK covering so many subjects, each with its own particular expert knowledge, needs a good deal of help from others. Fortunately, a series of willing and talented researchers have been available from among my students at the Johns Hopkins School of Advanced International Studies (SAIS). Dana Allin has seen the book through its final stages over the past year and a half. Others have helped along the way—Proctor Reid and John Paul Shutte, and also Thomas Rogers, in the early stages in Paris; Witek Radwanski, while a student at our Center in Bologna, made important contributions to chapters 2 and 11; Malcolm DeBevoise, Catherine Farry, Alexander Hittle, Christopher Johnson, David Rowe, and Stephen Soper helped put everything together in Washington.

I have also had wise counsel and expert criticism from a series of colleagues, friends, and acquaintances. Among those who reviewed parts of the manuscript at various stages were Benoît d'Aboville, Hedley Bull, Steven Canby, Harold van Buren Cleveland, Henry Ergas, Robert Grey, Warren Nelson, Dimitri Simes, Robert Skidelsky, Ronald Steel, Susan Strange, and Warren Zimmerman. A grant from the German Marshall Fund made it possible to organize a series of meetings at the Johns Hopkins Center in Bologna, which brought forth a series of helpful critiques from my friends and colleagues John Harper, Giorgio La Malfa, and Douglas Stuart. In Paris, my friend Dominique Möisi presided over a meeting on the Franco-German chapter at the Institut français des relations internationales. I also had the benefit of a series of conversations with Jonathan Alford and a number of his colleagues at the International Institute for Strategic Studies in London. Parts of chapter 2 were presented at a conference at the Royal Institute of International Affairs. Several of my SAIS colleagues in Washington have commented on various parts of the manuscript. I should particularly like to thank Michael Harrison, whose own book on French military policy stands as a major study in postwar alliance relations. I am also grateful to my wife, Avis, for her expert advice and gentle encouragement.

The great bulk of financial support for the project has come from the Twentieth Century Fund. I have very much enjoyed working with its director, Murray Rossant, who, along with Theodore Draper, has given careful commentary and unobtrusive good advice on the various drafts, as well as constant encouragement.

While the book was being written, I was also a NATO Fellow and received a

Fulbright grant, the latter for a study of comparative budgetary policies that found its way into chapters 6 and 7.

I hope my advisers will find some satisfaction from what has resulted. Obviously, their good counsel was not always taken, and they cannot be held responsible for the views I have finally adopted.

PART I

The NATO Question in Context

1

NATO and American Foreign Policy

SINCE 1949, the Atlantic Alliance has been the nucleus of the postwar international system. Bound together in the North Atlantic Treaty Organization, North America and Western Europe have given the postwar world its vital center of military stability and politico-economic order. The world around NATO, however, has changed dramatically, while the alliance itself has been relatively static. Militarily, it remains as it was in the beginning—an American nuclear protectorate for Europe.

This book deals with two fundamental questions: Can the Atlantic Alliance remain viable in its present form? And, if not, is there an alternative form that could be viable?

The issues involved are complex and multifaceted, and they have been studied, at least piecemeal, many times. If pursued in earnest, they do not easily lend themselves to categorical affirmations. Nevertheless, this work reaches certain strong conclusions, and it is useful to state them briefly at the outset.

The NATO alliance today is essentially an American protectorate for Europe. As such, it is increasingly unviable. The reasons spring not so much from particular mistakes as from a fundamental global trend of recent decades. Since the middle of the century, when NATO's present arrangements took form, the world's distribution of resources and power has evolved in a more plural direction. Economic wealth, military power, and political initiative are far more evenly distributed around the world than they were in the years immediately following World War II. While still immensely powerful, the United States is nevertheless markedly weaker in relation to its own allies, the Soviets, and the rest of the world. As a result, attempts to perpetuate America's old role increasingly damage the international system and the United States itself. Thus, even if the fundamental common interests of the United States and Western Europe dictate a continuation of the Atlantic Alliance, as I believe they do, the old hegemonic arrangements cannot continue without becoming self-destructive.

The trend that condemns the present arrangements also presents their alternative. A more plural world offers the United States and Europe new opportunities and advantages; it creates the opportunity to preserve NATO by reshaping its internal character. The transformation will require a reasonable degree of political leadership on both sides of the Atlantic—above all, from the United States, France, Germany, and Britain. Before such leadership is likely to come forth, however, publics and their leaders must understand more fully why change is both essential and possible. This book hopes to jog the lagging evolution of such understanding. The first half considers whether NATO can remain viable in its present form; the second addresses possible alternatives.

The analysis begins by scanning the broad case for and against change and by attempting to place the NATO question in its proper context. This chapter sketches the arguments and relates them to the fundamental issues of American foreign policy. Chapter 2 discusses the broader global context.

The case for the status quo is a powerful one. Every decade the alliance has managed to meet serious challenges without making fundamental changes. NATO's long success, in spite of the serious differences that have always existed between Europe and America, naturally engenders a certain complacency about its future. In the military sphere, Europeans have worried about the reliability and dangers of American deterrence for Europe. Americans have worried about the dangers that their European commitment might pose to themselves and have fretted over the inadequacies of Europe's own contribution to deterrence.

Beyond military issues, the transatlantic allies have had broader diplomatic and geopolitical differences. Disputes over how to manage relations with the Soviets have surfaced periodically. While America's Soviet policy has regularly oscillated between confrontation and détente, Western European governments have had a more tenacious interest in a relaxed *modus vivendi*, particularly within Europe itself. Moreover, since the alliance's earliest days, important differences over Third World policies have led to bitter disputes.

Many of these political and military differences are so serious and deep-seated that, if ever pressed to their logical conclusions for policy, the Atlantic Alliance would have trouble surviving. Fortunately, Western diplomats have grown skillful at papering over their national disagreements.

The decade from the mid-1970s to the mid-1980s illustrates both the typical and recurring transatlantic differences and the processes by which they have been contained. Starting in the mid-1970s, the Americans moved away from détente toward rearmament and confrontation with the Soviets. The Europeans were willing to follow, but only selectively. Even though by and large they welcomed America's rearmament, they refused to accelerate their own. As America turned from diplomacy toward hostility to the Russians, Europeans were diffident about cutting back their own diplomatic and cultural ties with the East. They refused to help enforce a sort of economic quarantine on the Soviet Union, not even as punishment for its behavior in Eastern Europe, let alone in the world at large. Europeans believed that détente in Europe should be insulated from Soviet-American confrontations elsewhere. American policy was therefore not at all to their taste. Not only did it injure various European economic interests, but it threatened, they believed, a perceptible if fitful amelioration of conditions in Eastern Europe. Forcing the Soviets back to greater autarchy would impose terrible hardship on Eastern Europe while reinforcing the Eastern siege mentality that opposes any movement, however desperately needed, toward a more open, flexible, and efficient politico-economic system.[1]

American policy was based on a sharply different view—both of the Soviets and of Western Europe's proper role in the alliance. The Carter and Reagan administrations believed that because NATO was America's major military investment and the Europeans were America's major allies, Europe should not be a safe zone for détente (as the Europeans seemed to wish), but a pressure point where the Soviets could be punished for bad behavior elsewhere. Since the Soviets had come to depend on European trade and investment, America's allies should use their economic leverage in the common task of containing Soviet power globally. Behind these views lay the assumption that heavy rearmament and economic pressure would threaten the Soviet regime's stability enough to force it to moderate the arms race and sharply curtail its ambitions for world power. Détente, in other words, could wait until the Soviet Union had first been thoroughly chastened by the strain of competition with an aroused and determined West.[2]

By the mid-1980s, U.S. policy appeared to be moving into a more conciliatory phase. Public fear of nuclear war had threatened to become a major political force both in Europe and America. The large American budget deficit implied cutbacks in future defense spending. Accordingly, by 1985, the Reagan administration, having long denounced earlier arms talks, entered an unprecedentedly broad and comprehensive arms negotiation.

This policy switch, however, is merely the latest in a series of cyclical fluctuations that have characterized America's Soviet diplomacy and security policy since World War II.[3] Moreover, experience suggests that a new series of transatlantic tensions is likely to follow this conciliatory turn. Europeans are no less wary of the détente phases of American policy than of the confrontational. When Soviet-American détente is in vogue, Europeans shift their concern from whether the United States is too provocative to whether it is strong and determined enough to maintain a military balance. They also worry that Americans and Russians are moving toward a superpower condominium at Europe's expense. In short, European reactions almost inevitably counterbalance American oscillations. Ultimately, Europe helps drive American policy back to its opposite phase.

Such swings in policy are firmly rooted in the American political system itself. American policy has never been sufficiently committed to confrontation or détente to follow either to its logical conclusion. On the one hand, American political opinion has never been willing to sustain the cost of all-out rearmament and confrontation for very long. Sooner or later, even the most anti-Soviet administrations have returned to arms control, summit meetings, and all the other paraphernalia of superpower détente. On the other hand, the system has proved equally unwilling to pay the political price of accommodation. Rather than accept the Soviet Union as a geopolitical equal and a global comanager, the United States periodically returns to rearmament. Hence, American policy alternates between a hostility that stops short of genuine confrontation and a détente that stops short of genuine accommodation.

This assessment suggests a rather complacent model for Soviet-American-European relations. Many professional analysts accept such a model, which explains why they remain relatively unperturbed by transatlantic quarrels. The oscillating pattern of Soviet-American and American-European conflicts appears to have its own self-limiting stability, not only because the stabilizing limits have been demonstrated so many times, but also because the pattern seems to be in everyone's real interest. Periodic American alternation between détente and rearmament can be seen as the carrot-and-stick required for reasonable superpower relations. Oscillation also seems to keep transatlantic relations in balance. The shifts help prevent the allies either from drifting too close to the Soviets' embrace or from taking America's protection too much for granted. A more consistent American policy would, sooner or later, force a break with some or all of Western Europe.

This complacent view of NATO's disputes implies confidence that Europe and America will continue to have enough tolerance and resilience to react responsibly to the other, and that there is, on all sides, a general satisfaction with things as they are. For Europe, such satisfaction might seem doubtful because the status quo is a bipolar world that has divided Europe into American and Soviet spheres. Nevertheless, Western Europe is widely believed to be no less satisfied than America. Europe fears the Soviets and needs an alliance to contain them. Better a divided Europe than a Europe dominated by Russia. Beyond the perceived Soviet threat, Europe needs both the Americans and the Russians to solve its own German problem. If there were no bipolar division of Europe, it is said, the old problem of continental hegemony would almost certainly revive from within. If Germany were reunited and Russia were out of Eastern Europe, Western Europe's postwar comity would very likely vanish, to be replaced by the old French, German, and British competition, the principal cause of this century's two world wars.

From this perspective, the Atlantic Alliance is unlikely to break down because no major government, including the Soviet Union, desires such an outcome. To remain viable, the present Atlantic-European system needs only to be reasonably well-managed. America's oscillating policy must be kept from flying out of its proper orbit—from becoming too weak or too confrontational. Similarly, the Western Europeans must not become so preoccupied with developing their Eastern ties that they neglect their military balance, their American connection, or their own solidarity. A close Atlantic Alliance ensures prudent management. Each side of the Atlantic helps limit the excesses of the other. Europe moderates America's enthusiasm for either détente or confrontation. American caution tempers European zeal for Eastern accommodation but also underwrites European détente by foreclosing Soviet ambitions for domination. NATO thus embodies a kind of transatlantic constitution. American and European elements generally help stabilize their own relations as well as those of East and West.

Even from this complacent perspective, however, the present order has obvious imperfections. The arms race wastes enormous resources, distorts economic, social, and political institutions, and poses a perpetual risk of nuclear war—high costs that everyone pays to some degree. Some countries, Poland for example, pay a particularly heavy price for stability. But to a great many professional observers, Soviet, American, or European, the present bipolar order, particularly within NATO, is the best arrangement that can be imagined without presupposing utopian or apocalyptic changes.[4]

Has the complacent view of NATO, which has prevailed for a long time, become any less valid today? What changes threaten the stability of a system that seems so universally beneficial? To answer in a single sentence: While the issues that bedevil NATO are mostly familiar, the context within which they must be managed has changed for the worse.[5] This changing context forms the subject of the next several chapters.

NATO's military problems are not new, but they seem to have grown more serious, primarily as the result of changes in the overall strategic balance between the superpowers. Whereas strategic parity was merely hypothetical in the 1950s and 1960s, by the late 1970s it had grown real. With the United States now as vulnerable as the Soviet Union, the difficulties of extended deterrence are obviously much more complex.

Long-standing diplomatic and political problems in NATO also seem to have advanced to a more serious stage in the 1980s, again because of important changes in the global context. The diverging paths that America and Europe favor in their political and economic relations with the Soviet Union have always posed a potentially serious problem for the alliance. But during the prolonged détente of the 1970s this division intensified as Europe's direct relationships with the Eastern bloc grew more varied and extensive than America's. The French, the Italians, and above all, the Germans became deeply committed to rebuilding some sort of pan-European network of special relationships with Eastern Europe and even with the Soviet Union. In effect, European détente policy has become linear. American détente policy, however, remains incurably cyclical. Transatlantic reconciliation over Soviet policy can therefore be expected to grow more difficult in the future, as illustrated by the bitter disputes of the early 1980s over Western Europe's trade with the East.

The 1970s also saw European-American differences take on greater significance as the global context itself changed rapidly. Third World countries grew more important, and Europeans took an independent approach to dealing with them. Particularly after the oil crises, Europe's independent line reflected not only distaste for particular American policies, but also the fear that the United States could no longer protect Europe's own global interests and was less and less inclined to try. American power seemed to be serving a narrower definition of its own national interest, less identified with the welfare of its allies or the health of the global system in general.[6]

America's economic policies increasingly lead Europeans to the same conclusion. Economic differences between Europe and America have always existed, but in the 1970s they coincided with a growing economic malaise.[7] With Europe's long-range economic prospects becoming more troubled each day, differences with America grow ever more central. If the broad economic deterioration continues, domestic imperatives for economic relief will almost certainly combine with familiar political and military dissatisfactions. This combination is likely to be profoundly unsettling for American-European-Soviet relations.

A wide spectrum of public opinion, in America as well as abroad, places heavy responsibility for international economic decline on America's own economic policies, in particular its monetary policy. Already a major source of discord in the 1960s, monetary difficulties worsened throughout the 1970s and into the 1980s when an unstable dollar unquestionably burdened the international economy. Many Europeans, like many Americans, interpret the dollar's gyrations as a symptom of economic mismanagement in the United States—the sign of a fundamental disequilibrium in the American economy that American policy appears to exacerbate rather than control.[8]

For many Americans, however, European criticism of American economic policy has a hollow ring. The American fiscal and monetary policies that Europeans deplore are not unrelated to the American military protection to which Europeans still cling. The most obvious link is America's persistent budgetary deficit, widely thought to be in itself a major source of the world's economic disorder. But America's fiscal deficit can easily be explained by noting its comparatively large military expenditures—mandated, in turn, not only by the continuing strategic and global rivalry with the Soviet Union but also by the requirements of America's hegemonic obligations within NATO.[9]

Such obvious military-economic linkage reveals, incidentally, the shortcomings of a too-specialized view of transatlantic relations. The Atlantic Alliance is not merely a set of political and military connections between Europe and America; it is also the centerpiece of a global economic system. The viability of any set of military arrangements depends not only on their military efficiency but also on their economic consequences. To address military and political problems while ignoring critical related economic ailments is analogous to a doctor setting a broken bone while his patient lies dying of a snakebite.

These phenomena—the qualitative change in the military balance, the unequal progress of détente, the growing power of the Third World, and the economic malaise—constitute significant alterations in the postwar global framework. As a result, NATO's disputes of the 1980s are qualitatively different from those of the past, whatever the superficial similarities. At the very least, these systemic changes suggest that the complacent view of NATO needs serious reexamination.

In many respects, the global changes that exacerbate NATO's particular difficulties may be summarized in terms of one fundamental change: the decline of American power in relation to the rest of the world. Militarily and economically, the United States has lost the ample edge it held at the end of the Second World War. One result has been a "Great Debate" in the mind of the American body politic over what to do about this decline, a debate that has been going on, often only half-consciously, since the late 1960s. The question of NATO's viability is, in effect, a special part of that debate.

What seems remarkable is not that such a debate has occurred, but rather how incomplete and provincial it has been. Logically, two broad courses suggest themselves: reaffirmation or devolution. The former calls for rejuvenating and reasserting America's role as the world's preponderant leader; the latter, for consciously transforming the global system into a more plural structure. Thus far, however, the debate has essentially been between what may be called rival formulas for reaffirmation. The focus has been so narrow because the broader issue has seldom been properly posed.

Since the Vietnam debacle, it has been fashionable to read the changes in the transatlantic and global system not so much as a relative decline of American power, but as a decline of the United States itself. After Vietnam, it is argued, an America obsessed with guilt and self-doubt rejected patriotic discipline, allowed its military prowess to decay, retreated from its world obligations, and grew bemused by the possibilities of superpower détente. The view is obviously not without some foundation. And since the early 1960s, America's power to control events in the world has certainly seemed to decline. The United States has grown militarily weaker in relation to the Soviet Union and economically weaker compared with Western Europe and Japan.[10] Its capacity to shape events in the Third World has been much reduced. Moreover, an international system still structured around American power has shown many signs of disintegration.

To describe these worldwide developments as a decline of the United States alone, however, seems too simplistic and parochial a perspective. From a broader, more cosmopolitan view, America's strength has not so much declined absolutely as it has fallen proportionally. America is not sinking; the rest of the world is rising. Furthermore, America's relative decline should surprise no one. An America that generously promoted the revival of Western Europe and Japan should hardly have been taken unawares by the predictable consequences. Recovery for the desolated Europe and Japan of 1945 could only mean a relative diminishing of America's overwhelming superiority. A policy of encouraging rapid global development, moreover, was bound to bring about a stronger and more independent Third World. Nor should the subsequent rise of Russia have been a great shock. American policy never sought to destroy the Soviet Union, but merely to contain it. Peaceful containment for forty years was almost bound to mean a stronger Russia than in 1945. American power, in short, has become the victim of its own generosity. From this cosmopolitan perspective, America's decline is not absolute but relative, not the result of failure, but of success in rebuilding a peaceful and prosperous world.

The difference between these "national" and "cosmopolitan" interpretations is more than a semantic quibble over whether American decline is relative or absolute. Whether American policy is informed by one perspective or the other tends to make a great difference in the prescriptions that follow. The national view sees the decline essentially as the result of America's own failings and therefore prescribes reversing the decline with leadership that infuses new patriotism and discipline and spends a great deal of money on arms. From the cosmopolitan perspective, however, such a prescription, even if partially beneficial in itself, is fatally inadequate as the basis for any longer-range strategy. For while the United States should not allow its national strength to decay through internal weakness, its decline relative to the rest of the world cannot be reversed. If its affairs are reasonably well managed, the United States should long remain the world's most powerful nation, but it will never regain the global preponderance it enjoyed after World War II. From this perspective, yoking American policy to regaining its influence spells the formula for national disaster. If followed, it will put the United States on that long list of declining hegemonic powers who lacked the wisdom to consolidate their resources and, as a consequence, destroyed themselves by overextension.

While such criticism of reaffirmation may grow more convincing as the Reagan experiment with it continues, the real task is to define and propose a broad geopolitical alternative. But simple renunciation, the obvious counterpoise to reaffirmation, is not a policy that suits the American temperament or the realities of the late twentieth century. What is needed is a strategy not for retreat from responsibility but for sharing it, a strategy not of renunciation but of devolution. By failing to consider such an alternative, America's Great Debate has, for years, suffered from intellectual malnutrition.

The theoretical case for a new American policy of devolution is easily made. Postwar American policy, it may be argued, has never been sure how to respond to its own predictable consequences. Having created a plural world, the United States has never been able to proceed to the next logical step. The enlightenment that led us to assist in the recovery of Europe and Japan has not yet been matched by equal imagination in harnessing their new strength. Within the Atlantic Alliance, American policy is frozen—unable either to keep or to renounce its old position. Similarly, the prudence that led the United States to contain rather than attack the Soviet Union has not been followed by a successful formula for coaxing a more powerful Russia into a more cooperative role. In short, while the world balance of forces has changed, the United States has not found the way to transform the postwar international structure from one based on an overwhelming U.S. strength to one based on a more pluralistic balance.

This cosmopolitan interpretation of America's predicament might be entirely accurate, but it does not necessarily follow that a policy of devolution would work. Devolution of the American role requires others who are able to take or share that role. Even if the United States can no longer sustain its role, there may be no other way to run the world. Certainly, no attractive new candidate for hegemony has appeared on the political horizon. Few would find the Soviets a congenial or probable replacement for the Americans. Those with hopes for détente would at least like to see the Soviets brought into a more cooperative relationship. But with their relentless military buildup, their inept and brutal conservatism at home, and their taste for meddlesome adventure abroad, the Soviets still seem unpromising partners for world collaboration.

By far the least disturbing version of devolution calls for a more plural arrangement, with America's renascent allies taking a greater share in the burdens of sustaining the international system. In particular, the allies might begin by taking the lead in providing their own regional defense. America's role in NATO could then change from Europe's hegemonic protector to its supporting ally. Even though devolution of this sort would be desirable, many observers find it unfeasible.

European states, they argue, express little inclination either to renounce the benefits of American hegemony or to pay the real price of greater independence, even if they do increasingly resent and resist American leadership.

So long as the NATO allies remain complacent about the status quo and the United States remains able to carry out its role, a policy of transatlantic devolution is neither possible nor necessary. And if devolution cannot succeed in NATO, it is unlikely to succeed anywhere. In this respect, the American Great Debate ultimately turns to the NATO question—the long-range viability of NATO's traditional arrangements and the prospects for some alternative. On the one hand, any policy of hegemonic reaffirmation must carry the alliance rather than alienate it. On the other, the allies' reaction will determine whether a policy of devolution can succeed or must fail. Either way, if NATO ceases to be viable, and no substitute can be found, the postwar *Pax Americana* cannot endure.

Neither America's debate nor NATO's prospects can be considered apart from the rest of the international system. While NATO is essentially a military pact, its current viability and historic significance rest on the broader political, cultural, and economic relations that form the postwar Atlantic Alliance. But that alliance, or "Atlantic system," is part of a more general "world system." The next chapter takes a broader look at the evolving structure of that global system and NATO's place within it.

2

The Atlantic Alliance
and the Global System

TO CONCEIVE of anything so abstract as a world system calls for imagination of a specialized nature. The teeming complexity of international relations has to be squeezed into some sort of conceptual model—giving, at best, a highly selective approximation of reality. Such a model invariably reflects the vantage point and preoccupations of the analyst. Its usefulness depends on whether it helps separate superficial happenings from the deeper forces that shape events. Insofar as it does, past and present scenarios may be more clearly understood and future events may be anticipated or even shaped.

From an American perspective, it is the all-pervasive role of the United States that distinguishes the world system after World War II from what preceded it. Since 1945, the United States has clearly been the leading power over much of the world and, in many spheres, has acted as a sort of managing director of the international system. So central has the American role been in creating, conceptualizing, and sustaining the postwar global order that this order may reasonably be described as a *Pax Americana*, with the United States playing the role of hegemonic power.[1]

To call a system hegemonic, however, is not to indict it as coercive or exploitative.

Many styles of hegemony exist among nations, just as many fashions for leadership can be found among individuals. Elements of exploitation and coercion necessarily exist in any international system, but the question of who profits and who pays is generally complex. Sustaining its world role in the present system costs the United States a great deal. To some extent, America's allies are free riders on the benefits of that American effort. In that respect, it is they who exploit the United States.[2]

Determining coercion is no less problematic. Even in the Warsaw Pact—NATO's Soviet counterpart, where the disparity of power between the hegemon and its allies is enormous—Russian leadership involves considerable persuasion and concession. NATO reveals hegemonic leadership in a far subtler mode. Several of America's Atlantic allies are themselves important political, economic, and military powers. When they accept American leadership, they do so because, on balance, it seems in their own interest. Their own strength, as well as the variety and intricacy of transatlantic entanglements, compel discussion and bargaining. Multi-lateral institutions are natural structures for regulating such relationships. If the United States has played the leading role in many of the postwar multilateral institutions, it has by no means always had its own way. In short, to call an international system hegemonic means that one power generally takes the initiative in structuring and managing. It does not necessarily mean that the role results in exploitation or springs from coercion.

Not only is America's hegemony strongly qualified—even among countries with whom it has the most intimate connections—but its weight varies greatly from one region of the globe to another. This postwar international system, even if viewed as a *Pax Americana*, is extremely diverse in its parts and is probably becoming more so. The system's overall character depends on the relationships among these diverse parts, and the relationships have been changing significantly.

For convenience, it has grown customary to divide the postwar system into three broad state groupings, or "worlds." The United States, together with the other NATO states, the rest of "Free Europe," Japan, and the white British Commonwealth make up one obvious grouping: a core of liberal, democratic, advanced industrial states that are closely linked to each other. This First World forms what can be called the Near Empire of the *Pax Americana*. Aside from the United States itself, the most important part of this inner core is Western Europe, and the most important relationship, upon which the whole structure depends, is the Atlantic Alliance.

Beyond the pale of the *Pax Americana* is the alien Second World of the Soviet sphere—initially limited to a vast continental bloc including Eastern Europe and China. The Russians, attempting to rival the Americans, have extended their influence and have become entangled with a variety of other far-flung clients. Meanwhile, the Chinese defection has removed a giant chunk from the original Eurasian empire.

While the Soviet role in the postwar system has often been described as a threat to be contained, the relationship between Second and First worlds is clearly more complex than that description would imply. The Russians and their allies are increasingly entwined in the general international system. Eastern Europe and even the Soviet Union itself have been drawn into a nascent pan-European system of growing economic, cultural, and political significance. At the same time, Soviet strategic rivalry with the United States has become rather structured over the years, particularly through the arms limitation agreements.

Finally, everyone speaks of a Third World of highly diverse states in Asia, Africa, and Latin America. Many of these countries were once parts of Europe's formal or informal colonial empires. Many are still military clients or economic dependencies of the Americans or Western Europeans. A few—Cuba, North Korea, Vietnam—are Soviet clients. The biggest states—China and India—are militarily nonaligned.

Most Third World states are poor by Western industrial standards, although several have immense natural resources and some have had remarkably rapid industrial growth. With the exception of vast and still autarchic China, most Third World states are closely integrated into a world political economy that depends heavily on conditions and policies in the United States, Western Europe, and Japan. Hence, if Europe, America, and Japan are the Near Empire of the *Pax Americana,* the Third World is the Far Empire.

The international system has not only distinct geographical parts but also distinct functional dimensions. To name the most obvious, the *Pax Americana* has both a military and an economic dimension. Even if these realms are more related than is often believed, particularly by those expert in one and uninformed about the other, each is usually analyzed by discrete sets of experts and managed by distinct bureaucracies. Each has its own set of multilateral institutions through which international relations are structured.

Within these separate military and economic institutions, the political relationships between the United States and its allies are markedly different. NATO's formal organization, for example, is forthrightly hegemonic. In many respects, Western Europe seems an American military protectorate. All members, even those with nuclear deterrents of their own, depend on the American strategic deterrent to balance the immense Soviet nuclear force. Most, including the Federal Republic of Germany, have no other strategic defense. In addition, NATO vests the United States with organizing and leading Europe's territorial defense. Thus an American general is NATO's Supreme Allied Commander (SACEUR), and an American ground force of ten divisions is either stationed in West Germany or waiting to be sent there if needed. A large American tactical air force guards European skies, and a large American fleet is permanently stationed in the Mediterranean.[3]

As Europeans have grown stronger, they have not supplanted the Americans within NATO so much as developed independent national military capabilities outside it. Among the major European states, France has gone the furthest in this direction. France has a completely independent national nuclear deterrent and has formally withdrawn its armed forces and territory from the American-directed NATO command. France remains, however, within the alliance and still cooperates selectively in military arrangements. Moreover, geography ensures that France, like the rest of Western Europe, will continue to enjoy the advantages of American protection.

Thus while NATO preserves the forms of American hegemony, the reality has grown more complex, with a substantial part of Europe's own military strength outside the NATO framework.[4]

In the multilateral institutions that seek to organize economic relations in the First World, the formal pattern is far less hegemonic. The most obvious institutional difference lies in the establishment, in 1958, of the powerful European Economic Community (EEC), where Europeans meet without Americans not only to regulate the intimate and interdependent economic relations within Europe but also to try to form a common position for dealing with the rest of the world.

This differentiation between military and economic relations can be seen as a sort of transatlantic compromise. As the Europeans recovered from the war and grew stronger, they built their own independent organization for economic relations but chose to remain militarily dependent within an American-dominated alliance. Thus, while Western Europe remains an American protectorate militarily, it has organized itself into an economic bloc that has become not only America's biggest single customer but also its biggest industrial and financial rival. As is often said, Europe has become an economic giant while remaining a military dwarf.

The tensions of such an ambivalent dual relationship have been rising in recent years. Trade and monetary relations have grown highly political. The United States has become increasingly inclined to invoke its military role while demanding economic concessions.[5] While the "affluent allies" have grown more critical of American economic "mercantilism" and "mismanagement," Americans have increasingly resented European free riding on their heavy defense spending, a burden that weakens the American economy while protecting the physical security of its principal competitors.

Japan illustrates the consequences of this dual pattern of military dependence and economic competition even more sharply than does Europe. After the war, the Japanese renounced not only nuclear weapons but also any kind of substantial military establishment. Japan's singleminded pursuit of civilian industrial prowess has yielded a rich harvest of economic success, but the country's continuing military dependence has also left it open to an increasingly blatant use of American hegemony to exact economic concessions. Japan's recent moves toward rearmament, while presumably prompted by American demands for sharing the military burden, may well result in growing economic resistance and diplomatic independence.[6]

Relations within the First World are closely affected by the separate and increasingly distinctive American, European, and Japanese relations with the other worlds. Chapter 1 noted diverging American and European relations with the Soviet and Third Worlds, primarily for the effect this conflict has on NATO's own durability. Such divergences have often been reactions to changes in the global context, changes that alter relations among the three worlds and then reverberate back to affect relations within the First World.

American relations with the Second, or Soviet, World are mostly with the Soviet Union itself and are primarily concerned with security matters. Attempts to develop Soviet-American economic relations have foundered on recurring American efforts to bargain trade for political concessions or fears that trade would strengthen Soviet war-making capabilities. The Russians themselves have a natural tendency to emphasize the military relationship. It is the only sphere where they are, in any sense, equal to the Americans. In commercial weight or cultural prestige, they are notably inferior to the United States as well as to the major European states and Japan.[7]

This bilateral Soviet-American preoccupation with security questions reinforces a tendency in both to see world politics in military terms and, as a result, to exaggerate each other's role in shaping world events. In Washington as well as in Moscow, international politics can still be seen as a global duel—a zero-sum game where all events are significant only insofar as they represent a gain for one or a loss for the other. Since bipolar competition is thought to be the underlying reality, conflict in one geographical region is seen as tied to conflict in another. Such "linkage politics," or "horizontal escalation," is a characteristic tendency of American policy.

One consequence is the manic-depressive American reaction to détente diplomacy, the latest round of which was discussed in chapter 1. Those inclined to blame the Soviets for most of the world's troubles tend to overestimate the likely gains from more cordial diplomatic relations. They are equally ready to react strongly when détente brings no significant diminution in the world's revolutionary turbulence or in Russian attempts to take advantage of it. For all its fixation on duopoly, however, American diplomacy has never been willing to offer the Soviets the equal global status they presumably crave. But while the United States has never been willing to appease Russia by acknowledging it as a comanager of the international system, neither has it been willing to persist with confrontation. Each time the Americans turn in anger from détente, the consequent political, diplomatic, and economic strains eventually return them to it. Hence, the continuing cycle of fresh hope and fresh disappointment that characterizes Soviet-American relations.

The Western Europeans have broader and, in many respects, more intimate relations with the Second World, the Eastern European states in particular, than do the Americans. European détente diplomacy has concentrated less exclusively on military questions than on trade, investment, cultural communication, travel, and emigration.[8] Such relations tend to penetrate more deeply and directly into the societies and economies of the Eastern bloc.

Behind Europe's détente diplomacy lies a basic geopolitical strategy for gradually reconstituting a pan-European system, but without accepting Soviet hegemony, renouncing American protection, or constructing an indigenous European balance of power. The strategy builds on Western Europe's own anomalous position as a group of highly advanced states, loosely linked together, which remain simultaneously military dependents and economic competitors of the Americans.

As loyal American allies in NATO, Western Europeans enjoy a certain collective anonymity in their military dealings with the Russians. Their national diplomacy with the East can therefore focus on more promising economic, cultural, and diplomatic relationships. The low politics of trade, investment, and cultural exchange thus serve the high politics of promoting pan-Europeanism. The Russians, it is hoped, can gradually be led out of their paranoiac isolation into a prosperous and liberal European family. The process may also persuade the Russians to loosen their grip on the other states of Eastern Europe.

Few Western European governments expect, or probably want, sudden or dramatic success from this strategy. Many have seen perceptible progress over recent years, and few see any alternative approach. Pan-Europeanism poses considerable practical difficulties, however, for the Atlantic Alliance, as well as provocative long-range implications for the international system in general.

In the opinion of many analysts, however, these long-range implications are likely to remain merely theoretical, for Europe's strategy is hamstrung by too many drawbacks. Progress in opening up the Eastern sphere tends, for example, to revive old divisions among the major Western European states themselves. The more the Western states succeed in their Eastern strategy, the more they tend to quarrel among themselves. Recurring French nervousness about supposed German tendencies toward Finlandization is a perennial symptom.[9] And the more the Europeans are divided among themselves, the more their détente strategem risks becoming an invitation to Soviet hegemony.

A second drawback to Western Europe's Russian strategy lies in the very rigidity of Soviet hegemony and the domestic incompetence of most communist regimes, not least that of the Soviet Union itself. A Western European policy based on promoting peaceful liberalization through prosperity is forever stymied by national communist bureaucracies too inflexible to permit the freedom needed for economic prosperity and often unable to govern at all without brutal and alienating repression. The greater the popular discontent, the more the heavy-handed Soviets can be counted on to block reform. The problems of Poland are an obvious illustration.[10]

Periodic confrontation between the superpowers also upsets Western Europe's détente strategem. The experiment requires making the continent a sort of safe zone where pan-European relations can develop while insulated from East-West conflicts elsewhere.[11] For obvious reasons, America's manic-depressive détente cycle, combined with the tendency toward linkage politics or horizontal escalation, is a particular threat. The détente phases of American policy raise fears of a super-power condominium, cemented by a shared desire to keep Europe divided and subordinate. American enthusiasm for détente also generally corresponds with less-ened military spending, which leads to deterioration of the bipolar military balance, either at the strategic level or in the European region itself. Western Europe's strategy depends on being able to operate from a position based both on Europe's own economic and political superiority and on military strength borrowed from the Americans. When American military protection falters, Europe's comfortable détente strategy falters with it. In short, Europe's policy requires a delicate balance between deterrence and cooperation, and America's oscillations inevitably cause unwelcome reverberations.

Aside from the difficulties of managing so delicate a strategy, there is the longer-range danger that Europe will be so drawn into the Soviet embrace as to lose or abandon its American protection. Unable to borrow America's military strength, Europe would become Finlandized. Its resources would fall under Soviet hegemony, and the *Pax Americana* would end. Such a view assumes that Europe would be unable to produce its own substitute for American military protection. Here, the greatest danger is probably not any dearth of Western European military capabilities, nor illusions about dealing with the Soviets from a position of military inferiority. Rather, it is the internecine conflicts that would arise if the Western European states began building a military coalition of their own. Such a coalition would require a major strengthening of West Germany's forces and would raise the question of Germany's nuclear protection. Rather than face these issues, European govern-ments have much preferred that military problems be handled via an American protectorate organized through NATO, an arrangement that sustains a military balance at minimal economic and political cost to themselves and, despite increasing American protest, still leaves their hands relatively free for conciliatory and pro-ductive economic relations with the East. Insofar as this military dependence grows more delicate and discordant, as the next several chapters indicate, the triangular American-European-Soviet relationship becomes a point of vulnerability not only for the Atlantic Alliance but for the postwar order in general.

Differing American, European, and Soviet relations with the Third World add another complex dimension to the postwar system. A far more diverse category than either the Atlantic or Soviet worlds, the states of the Third World offer a bewildering variety of climates, cultures, religions, races, internal conditions, and international relationships. Except for China and the handful of states in the Soviet orbit, such as Cuba or Vietnam, most Third World states are caught up in varying degrees of economic and political dependence on the United States and its major allies of the Near Empire. These relationships reflect the economic and political patterns that have succeeded the old imperial systems that died in World War II.

Through diverse alliances, subsidies, and indirect as well as occasionally open interventions, the United States took the early lead in shaping this postwar Third World. American policy promoted rapid decolonization and an open international economy.[12] In its theory, the American formula for decolonization was not unlike that championed by the British Liberals of the last century. All nations were to have formal political independence, but within an international economic system that opened their raw materials and markets to trade. Advanced manufacturing nations would continue to enjoy economic access to the world's less developed regions, but would have no direct political or administrative control over them.[13] Like the nineteenth-century British Liberals, twentieth-century Americans believed that if comparative advantage were permitted to work its beneficial magic, the global economy could be expected to prosper. With trade open to all, the world could also avoid these mercantilist wars over economic access that, as Adam Smith taught long ago, were as unnecessary as they were destructive.

Critics often call this formula "free-trade imperialism," the natural ideology of countries so advanced that they fear no competitors. Protectionism, by contrast, has typically been sought by developing industrial countries, like Germany or the United States in the mid-nineteenth century, trying to shield their infant industries from the rigors of superior competition—at that time, British. Classic protectionist theory did point ultimately to free trade among equally developed economies: in other words, to a pluralist liberalism. Britain's free-trade imperialism, however, was seen as a premature and hegemonic form of liberalism, really a mercantilist ideology for perpetuating Britain's historical advantage.[14]

Colonialism came to be defended as a sort of systemic analogue to domestic protectionism. Unable to compete in an open world system, where another power is still dominant, an industrializing state seizes and directly controls some portion of the non-Western world, thereby guaranteeing itself access to the raw materials, markets, or profitable investments it needs for its own development. A world thus divided into several colonial empires can be said to reflect a plural balance within the international system, with no single dominant economic and military power. The theory was amply demonstrated in practice. As other industrial powers rose to challenge Britain in the later nineteenth century, they turned to imperialism as well as protectionism. Free trade was abandoned, and the scramble for colonial empires began. Britain did better than other countries in the scramble, but to have to annex territory hitherto dominated informally was, in itself, a sign of Britain's decline from world hegemony.

The United States after the Second World War occupied the same overwhelming economic and military predominance as Britain had in the mid-nineteenth century. A policy of liberal free trade and anticolonialism thus came naturally to the Americans. In an open system, with weakened European and Japanese competitors ejected from their privileged colonial sanctuaries, America would predominate. From such a perspective, commonplace in Europe, America's decolonization seemed merely an ideological cover for replacing Europe's colonial empires with America's new global hegemony.[15] In some circles, European bitterness was considerable and still has not been entirely forgotten. But since the cause of reestablishing Europe's colonial empires could not generate sufficient moral, political, or military force to defeat the forces of Third World nationalism, decolonization had to be accepted, gracefully by the British, painfully by the French, Dutch, Belgians, and Portuguese.

Americans had little sympathy. Europe's best interest lay in rebuilding its own domestic economies to compete successfully in the open world America was fostering. Europe's lingering colonialism was hopelessly out of step with the insistent nationalism that the war had triggered everywhere in the Third World. Americans feared Europeans would embroil themselves in a series of militarily hopeless and morally indefensible wars opposing Third World independence. European attempts to link the defense of their empires to the containment of communism were countered by American fears that the Russians would be made to seem champions of national independence. The irresistible nationalism of the Third World would thus be linked with the Soviet model for national development. The great challenge, as the Americans saw it, was to join the Third World's nationalism to political and economic liberalism rather than to totalitarian and protectionist communism. Hence a liberal-national model for Third World development became vitally important in postwar American policy.[16]

Creating a development model to suit Third World nationalism extracted serious concessions from America's free-trade liberalism. Third World countries, sensitive about free-trade imperialism, wanted not only formal political independence but also modernization. This meant developing an indigenous industrial economy rather than merely providing food and raw materials for the industrial West. Soviet and Chinese communism offered a mercantilist autarchic model for achieving that industrial goal. In response, American development theory, although continuing to stress free trade and private multinational investment, quickly came to encompass a substantial degree of state planning, subsidy, and trade concessions. European development theories generally have gone even further in this direction.

As in the Near Empire, multilateral institutions and international bureaucracies have managed much of the system's business. Institutions like the World Bank, the General Agreement on Tariffs and Trade (GATT), and, later, the United Nations Conference on Trade and Development (UNCTAD) became the contexts within which American, European, and Third World interests have played out and reconciled their competing claims. For the United States to remain the predominant global power, it has had to adjust its ideas to the increasingly assertive and effective demands from both Third World countries and its own Western and

Japanese allies. Where it has lagged, its hegemony has grown less acceptable.

In many respects, this Far Empire of the *Pax Americana* has been a notable success. Despite the immense transformations and dislocations bound up with decolonization and modernization, many countries in the non-Communist Third World have achieved remarkable economic growth.

Success in the Third World has also tended to reinforce ties within the First World. While disputes over the colonial legacy continued to sour transatlantic relations in the 1950s, European states, while losing their colonial domains, gradually realized that the economic objectives of the old empires could be achieved far more cheaply within the more universal system of the *Pax Americana*. Japan's postwar position presents the most striking illustration. For Japan, losing the Second World War meant giving up an Asian "coprosperity sphere" but gaining access to a much wider range of markets throughout the whole world, including the American domestic market.

Under the broad mantle of the *Pax Americana*, Europe and Japan have refashioned something of their old global influence. For Third World countries, leery of too-intimate patronage from a superpower, Europe and Japan have been alternative sources of capital, markets, and arms. Through its various trade and aid policies, the Common Market has been a powerful instrument of European diplomacy. Both France and Britain, moreover, have maintained a substantial military capability in various regions, legitimized by a range of alliances, including constitutional links with former colonies.

In the 1950s, and occasionally thereafter, French diplomacy vainly sought to structure an American-British-French global directorate—presumably as a way to exert greater leverage on American global policy.[17] From time to time, NATO has sought to coordinate "out of area" policy. While formal attempts at structured cooperation generally have failed, American and European policies toward the Third World, even where competitive, came to terms easily enough through most of the 1960s. Europeans, like Americans, wished to limit Soviet global influence. Since the late 1960s, however, transatlantic consensus on global matters has been undermined by wars in Vietnam and the Middle East and, in the 1970s, by the oil crisis. Europeans, while demanding consultation, have often distanced themselves from particular American policies toward the Third World.

As the United States has grown less able to control events in the Third World, Europeans have increasingly sought their own special relationships and arrangements, often in rather ostentatious disagreement and competition with the Americans. This has been particularly noticeable since the oil crisis of 1973.[18] A secure flow of cheap energy was a major benefit of the early *Pax Americana*. With the United States seemingly less able to guarantee that flow, American prestige suffered while Europe and Japan grew more aggressive in preserving their own positions. Just as American success in the Third World had reinforced transatlantic interdependence, its diminishing sway beyond Europe provoked transatlantic separation.

Surveying this postwar system in its various elements gives rise to somewhat conflicting reactions. America's postwar leadership, and the Atlantic partnership that has sustained it, has given the world a prosperous peace of impressive duration. For all its obvious blemishes, this postwar order has been a dazzling success. Few governments seriously want to overturn it, even if many would prefer a more favored position within it. But there are now strong trends undermining the system's stability, not least within the Atlantic world itself.

To suppose the present international system incapable of rejuvenation seems premature. Among the states with the most to lose are those of Western Europe, which have enjoyed a prosperous security unprecedented in this century. Whatever the accumulating irritations, the Atlantic Alliance still has a powerful geopolitical logic, reinforced by compelling cultural bonds and roughly four decades of institutional cooperation. The United States, with its enormous wealth and vitality, not to mention an impressive heritage of civic decency and self-discipline, is unlikely to be thrown over by the Europeans in favor of adventures with the Soviet Union or the Third World. The Alliance's underlying strength has long been so obvious that its tensions have been complacently pushed aside. But looking at these tensions within the larger context suggested here leads to a more troubling evaluation, particularly when the economic dimension is considered alongside the military and political. The next five chapters examine these tensions as they have arisen and evolved over the postwar decades.

PART II

The Alliance's Evolving Problems

3

The Founding Cycle:
NATO from 1948 to 1960

MUCH OF NATO's internal history reflects the influence of American security policy toward the Soviets. Since American policy tends to be cyclical, NATO's history also embodies a certain cyclical pattern.[1] Events in the alliance's first three decades coincide with two broad cycles of American security policy and European reaction. A major American rearmament and energetic reassertion of leadership mark the start of each cycle, and a phase of declining American defense spending, with strong interest in arms control and détente, signals its end. A third cycle, which began in the late 1970s, has yet to play itself out.

Each round of American policy provokes countercyclical European policies. As Americans rearm and grow more confrontational toward the Russians, Europeans tend to resist further military buildups and to promote diplomatic negotiations. As Americans move toward arms reduction and détente, Europeans complain about American weakness, question the reliability of American deterrence, and suspect the superpowers of accommodation at Europe's expense.

The first cyclical pattern in the history of NATO began around 1948. This "founding cycle" commenced as a transatlantic security treaty was first proposed and continued through the Truman and Eisenhower years. This early period reveals a number of the alliance's enduring features: most interesting, perhaps, is how much conflict and diffidence over NATO existed within the American government. The early history also reveals the initial motives of the major European states in establishing NATO as well as their critical role in stilling American opposition. Moreover, even at this early stage the persistent military dilemma of the American protectorate is evident: the reluctance of either Americans or Europeans to bear the costs. The reliance on nuclear weapons was the logical consequence.

The greatest struggle that attended NATO's birth took place within the American government itself. The hesitations were not so much over whether to have a security treaty with Europe but over its form.[2] Two of the State Department's most experienced and influential diplomats, Charles Bohlen and George Kennan, strongly resisted establishing a highly structured, American-run military alliance. They preferred a European alliance backed by an American security guarantee. Bohlen and Kennan were opposing what amounted to a significant shift in the substance and style of American policy toward Europe.

With NATO, America's European policy moved out of its Marshall Plan phase, which had emphasized economic recovery and European initiative, and into a new phase that featured massive rearmament and direct American leadership. This was the second major shift in American policy in less than three years, for the Marshall Plan itself had been a shift away from the "Wilsonian" policies of the Roosevelt administration—policies designed to co-opt the Soviets into the United Nations and to reconstitute a world economy based on free trade. Kennan and Bohlen helped engineer the shift to the Marshall Plan phase but resisted the shift to the NATO phase.

Kennan explained his position in a series of internal memoranda. He based his opposition on his views of the Soviets, on the one hand, and of the Europeans, on the other. Those views were tolerably embodied in the Marshall Plan phase of American policy, but not in the earlier Rooseveltian phase, nor in the subsequent NATO phase. Kennan's views expressed one side of the running argument within the Truman administration over the character of the Soviet threat and the proper American response in Europe. Although he had achieved his reputation by calling attention to the inherently hostile and aggressive nature of the Soviet regime, and hence to the impracticality of expecting to co-opt it, Kennan strongly discounted the danger of an actual military invasion in Europe.[3] As he saw it, Stalin's regime, like the czarist regime throughout most of Russian history, was repressive at home and paranoid abroad. Since genuine cooperation was impossible with the Soviets, hopes for partnership through multilateral machinery were unrealistic. Left to its own preferences, Stalin's Russia, like that of the czars, would be persistently but cautiously expansive.

Kennan was not prepared, however, to see Stalin as another Hitler. Having inherited an immense and self-sufficient territorial empire, Stalin was not driven by Hitler's fear that his authority would collapse if he did not expand. Thus, Kennan argued that Stalin could be contained by firm barriers. Such barriers, he thought, required not so much direct American military force as the political rejuvenation of Russia's neighbors. However hostile, Russia was in no condition to pursue military aggression against a United States armed with nuclear weapons. But Stalin would certainly exploit Europe's domestic misery and chaos with external intimidation, thereby reinforcing internal subversion.

For Kennan, the real problem lay in Western Europe's own political and social demoralization, a weakness reflected in the presence of large and vigorous communist movements in France and Italy.[4] Without some significant boost to morale, Europe's economic and political recovery might not get started, and its revolutionary domestic forces would grow stronger. While an American military guarantee against external aggression would certainly be useful, America's greatest service would be to initiate a dramatic program to increase the material flow to prime Europe's pumps. A major military rearmament would simply divert European and American resources from the real task at hand.[5] Moreover, militarization of the West would serve to emphasize the only sphere in which the Soviets had some competitive advantage.

Kennan also saw long-range diplomatic objections to NATO. A formal military alliance, involving a major buildup of conventional forces, would militarize Europe's territory around a superpower confrontation. It would thus prevent the political and diplomatic flexibility needed for a later European settlement. Once European territory came to be seen in a confrontational military perspective, the Russians could never withdraw from positions they might otherwise come to see as undesirably overextended.[6]

Kennan particularly opposed the rearmament and further militarization of Germany. It would make the country's division inevitable, he argued, and thus lock both Americans and Soviets in a permanent military confrontation across the face of Europe.[7]

Kennan's concern over the diplomatic costs of militarization also led him to prefer a strictly limited membership in the alliance. Under no circumstances, he argued, should the notion gain credence that only countries formally incorporated within NATO would be defended if attacked. Otherwise, any country not explicitly included would be presumed abandoned. A sort of diplomatic frenzy would result, followed by a ponderous system of formal military treaties linking the United States inflexibly to every part of the free world.[8]

Behind Kennan's positions regarding NATO lay a more general vision of how the postwar system should evolve. He looked to the restoration of a plural world, where a crowd of other powers—the European states in particular—would dilute the nascent U.S.–Soviet superpower confrontation. Such a configuration would offer more diplomatic opportunities for adjusting to the changes inevitable in the postwar era; in this more plural and flexible world, the United States could avoid becoming a new Rome. Kennan feared the costs of any such hegemonic role for America's future economic prosperity and stability. Above all, he doubted whether the United States was politically and culturally suited for such a part and feared the consequences for the nation's internal political balance and vitality.[9]

Kennan's concern for a pluralist reconstruction prompted his insistence that aid to Europe be given in a way to promote political revival and economic self-reliance. Even after congressional and European pressure had made a formal military alliance inevitable, he still sought to place the primary responsibility for managing Europe's defense on the Europeans themselves.[10]

Kennan's emphasis on European independence was built into the Marshall Plan phase of American policy, whereas it was contradicted in both the Roosevelt and NATO phases. Although Roosevelt's Wilsonian vision, which saw America co-opting the Soviets to run the world, had scant interest in a powerful independent Europe, the generous economic aid of the Marshall Plan carried a strong emphasis on gaining European cooperation and building European self-reliance. While American leadership was certainly not absent from the Marshall Plan, the United States self-consciously attempted to hand over its planning initiative to the Europeans themselves, on the condition that they strive to create a closely integrated European economy. Economic integration, it was hoped, would lead toward some sort of federal union that could be a bulwark against the Soviets as well as a way to domesticate those ancient rivalries that had led to so many wars.

American enthusiasm for European federalism was not without its own ambiguous ambitions, as Charles de Gaulle was to make clear in later years. Kennan's support, at least, clearly reflected a more modest view of America's future world role than that held in Roosevelt's time. A restored and united Europe seemed desirable because it would release the United States from having to maintain a permanent European protectorate to contain the Soviets. Such a Europe could be the second pillar of a liberal democratic world order. America would no longer have to be the world's Atlas, and the rest of the world would no longer have a blank check on American resources. Once having completed its special responsibilities for postwar reconstruction, the United States could participate more selectively in global affairs.[11] The Marshall Plan phase of American foreign policy, then, reflected a more pluralist vision of the postwar world than did either the Roosevelt or the NATO phases.

Although the Marshall Plan phase was to have lasting effects in Europe and would never disappear as a strain in American policy, it was quickly superseded by the NATO phase, which followed only two years later. Both, of course, were products of the Cold War disillusionment with the Soviets. Fear of the Soviet threat was a strong stimulus for the unprecedented rush of American aid to rebuild the European "allies." But whereas the framers of the Marshall Plan phase viewed the Soviet threat primarily as economic and political and tried to pass the initiative for response onto Europe—the NATO architects saw the Soviet threat as military and established an American-run protectorate.

The military focus did not prevail in American policy until after the Korean War seemed to confirm the danger of direct Soviet military aggression. But the struggle between economic and military emphases had begun several years before that war, as Americans grew increasingly concerned with the military balance in Western Europe. Plans for a massive American rearmament were discussed as early as 1946. The Truman Doctrine, promulgated in 1947, combined economic and military aid to two countries, Greece and Turkey, with universalizing rhetoric about an American commitment to defend national freedom everywhere.

The tide turned decisively against views like Kennan's in Truman's second term. The rationale and implications of the shift toward rearmament are most fully embodied in the celebrated *National Security Council Memorandum 68*, adopted formally in 1950.[12] By the late years of the Truman administration, the military perspective of NSC-68 clearly predominated in the formulation of American foreign policy.[13] NATO established a militarized transatlantic connection and plans to rearm Germany began to be drawn. Thus, not only was containment militarized but it also became the rationale for a closely integrated Western alliance under American direction. The dumbbell model for transatlantic relations, with Europe at one end and America at the other, gave way to an American-directed NATO.

While Kennan is sometimes called the father of containment, his version of containment implied a fundamentally different course from what eventually evolved. His arguments were employed by others in a highly selective fashion to support a policy he did not intend.[14] The notion of an insatiable Soviet aggressiveness, derived from internal flaws and requiring firm limits, was universally accepted. Europe's need for economic and political reconstruction was also accepted. But the deliberate policy of playing down the military aspects of containment, or emphasizing European self-reliance, was not. Thus, containment became the rationale not only for moving from the first to the second phase of American policy, as Kennan had intended, but also for the kind of *Pax Americana* that Kennan wished to avoid. Containment became the basis not for a plural world, but for an American empire.

The shift in American policy can be charted in NATO's own internal evolution— from the North Atlantic Treaty itself, signed in April 1949, and the subsequent North Atlantic Treaty Organization, set up in 1950. The treaty established the commitment to consider an attack on one member's home territory an attack on that of everyone else, although it left each to respond with whatever means that member deemed appropriate. It also called for a standing political council of all members, a secretary general, and a standing military committee of the Big Three (Britain, France, and the United States). The actual "organization" that followed, however, also brought Europe an American supreme commander in December

1950, along with integrated staffs and a heavy commitment of American troops. This evolution of NATO's arrangements led to de Gaulle's later claim that France could remain true to the treaty, with its traditional diplomatic pledge of mutual aid, while renouncing the subsequent military organization, which put Europe's armies under American command.[15]

From the perspective of American security policy, the shift from the Marshall Plan approach to that of NATO and NSC-68 can be seen as a move from selective to general containment or, as some analysts call it, from "asymmetrical" to "symmetrical" containment.[16] With the switch, the United States embarked on a course of directly countering Soviet power at every level and blocking Soviet advances in every region. Kennan's opposition to NATO was, in effect, opposition to the switch from selective to general containment.

Behind the competing formulations of containment or the successive phases of American postwar strategy lay fundamentally different visions of the postwar order. Kennan's containment policy, with its emphasis on economic and political reconstruction, conjured up a dream of a plural world restored. His historical imagination seemed to yearn for the traditional balance-of-power models of Europe after 1815. NATO, by contrast, seemed inspired by the idea of a *Pax Americana*, a more hierarchical transatlantic system under American hegemony. Kennan's objections to NATO were, in effect, objections to that hegemonic vision. Each viewpoint obviously implied a different role for the United States. Whereas in the Kennan vision the United States would act as a balancing power, intervening to prevent Soviet hegemony while Western Europe's traditional great powers recovered from the war, that of NSC-68 implied a permanent American role as the system's sustaining workhorse.

In envisioning a leading role for America and a subordinate role for Europe, the militarized Cold War perspective of NSC-68 and the Wilsonian perspectives of early postwar policy had much in common. Roosevelt's postwar plans were infused with the ancient liberal vision of an integrated global political economy, so prominent in his own world view and that of his secretary of state, Cordell Hull. If that Rooseveltian outlook showed less concern about the Soviet threat than did Kennan's containment policy, it also had a far more ambitious view of America's postwar role. The United States was to build and manage a new, liberal, global political economy to replace the wreckage of the last century's disintegrated Europe-centered order. This grand Wilsonian ambition can be found not only in Hull's tireless promotion of free trade, ultimately embodied in the GATT, but especially in the international monetary arrangements negotiated in 1944 at Bretton Woods, arrangements that created the International Monetary Fund.[17]

The liberal economic perspective underpinning Roosevelt's policy had traditionally carried strong hegemonic overtones. The coming *Pax Americana* was to be a rebirth of the collapsed *Pax Britannica*. From this perspective, restoring Europe to its prewar status risked blocking the American grand design. What Kennan saw as the return to the normal power balance seemed a return to the interwar interregnum. It was an independent Western Europe, after all, that toppled the *Pax Britannica* and its beneficent global order. The United States had fought two world wars with Germany, not with Russia. Not only was a revived Germany likely to threaten a *Pax Americana*, but so would a revived France or a rejuvenated imperial Britain. It was with London, after all, that New York had long struggled for mastery of the world's banking system.[18] It was the British who had built and still maintained the world's biggest trading bloc.

Whatever its merits, this perspective was indisputably widespread in the American political imagination, particularly among Wall Street bankers and lawyers, from whose ranks so much of the postwar foreign policy elite was recruited. Nor is it difficult to grasp how this vision, confronted unexpectedly by a powerful and menacing Soviet Union, could rapidly evolve toward confrontational bipolarity. Anticommunism became the means for rallying American domestic resources for world leadership and for yoking foreign allies into a liberal *Pax Americana*. Thus, the first phase of American postwar policy transformed itself quite easily into the third, for both pointed to American world hegemony. In between these visions of economic and military hegemony, and opposed to both, stood Kennan's plural vision.

In contrast to most of his countrymen, Kennan fixed his imagination not on the American Century and the coming marvels of multinational capitalism, but on the old-fashioned European balance of power. His nineteenth-century vision was not the worldwide *Pax Britannica* that enchanted so many other American analysts, but continental Europe's post-Napoleonic balance of 1815. Kennan's judgments as a diplomatic historian suggest the character of his imagination as a policy planner and, in particular, his apprehensions about a hegemonic *Pax Americana*. In Kennan's interpretation of history, the wise statesman is careful never to transform a temporary advantage into a permanent offense against the balance of power. Kennan admired Bismarck, for example, for trying not to disturb Europe's general equilibrium even while unifying Germany.[19] Clumsy successors, lacking Bismarck's measured restraint, extended Prussian pretensions to continental hegemony and world empire. Their extravagant ambition ruined Germany and Europe together.

In retrospect, Kennan's early criticisms of NATO appear to stand up rather well. He was probably more right than wrong about Russia's actual military weakness in the early 1950s. Certainly, European and American fears now seem to have been excessive. Kennan's fears of the tendency toward an excess of formal commitments seem fulfilled in the Dulles era. His apprehensions about the diplomatic costs of rearming and militarizing Europe must seem prescient to those pursuing a European settlement through superpower disengagement. His fears of a deformation and overloading of America's political institutions and economy should also strike today's analysts with considerable force. So, too, should his fear that an American protectorate would make European states excessively dependent and sap their political self-confidence to the point where they could no longer hold their own in any European or global balance.

All this being said, Kennan was probably a better prophet than policymaker. His principal conclusion for his own time seems mistaken. The objective conditions for a plural world system did not exist in the decade after World War II. Kennan underestimated both the exuberant strength of the United States and, above all, the weakness of the Western Europeans.

The reasons may well lie in his relative unconcern for the geopolitical implications of international economic power. Kennan was, of course, highly sensitive to the importance of Europe's economic recovery: hence, his intimate involvement in promoting the Marshall Plan. Economic rejuvenation was necessary, he believed, to revive domestic morale and cohesion—essential preconditions for restoring national power and hence diplomatic weight. But Kennan, like many traditional diplomats, or diplomatic historians, seems to have been less sensitive to the direct significance of economic power projected into the international political economy.

In the arena of international economic power, the weight of the United States was overwhelming in the late 1940s, above all in the monetary sphere that was critical to European recovery. The need for dollar credits made Europe, including Britain, utterly dependent on American largesse and likely to remain so for the foreseeable future.[20] America's economic preponderance was industrial and commercial, as well as monetary. Multinational business was already becoming the game of the future as American corporations were immeasurably stronger and more confident than their European counterparts. As a result, Europe was about to absorb a major invasion of American firms.[21] Kennan seems to have been heedless of this explosion of economic power, perhaps because he disliked what it meant for both European and American culture. But the Wall Street foreign policy elites were not so fastidious, nor were the Europeans any more so.

However much Kennan was out of sympathy with the ambitions of his countrymen, he was even more out of tune with the European governments at the time, all of whom firmly opposed his views on NATO. They, above all, insisted on a hegemonic American alliance. Each country had its own particular reasons, but all sought to borrow American strength to further their individual national purposes.

The British were Europe's leading power. They were determined to engage the Americans firmly with the responsibility for Europe's territorial defense. British observers feared that the Marshall Plan's enthusiasm for European unity was only a more subtle form of traditional American isolationism, and in some respects it was. In any event, European union had little to recommend it to the British. They had no desire to dilute their own independence in a European construction with former enemies and defeated friends. Nor did they wish to see their influence with the Americans supplanted by some continental coalition. Nor, finally, did they want to tie up their extremely stretched resources in defending the continent at the expense of their already overstretched global role. NATO seemed an ideal solution. With American commanders and forces taking primary responsibility for European ground defense, no question would remain about America's willingness to come to Europe's aid. Britain could reserve for itself those military and naval commands needed to retain control over its own national defense.[22]

French governments of the time matched Britain's enthusiasm for an American protectorate. American forces seemed doubly useful. They would contain both the Soviets and the Germans. French resources could thereby be liberated for reconstructing the domestic economy and bolstering the colonial empire, already faltering in Indochina and soon to be challenged in North Africa. Through NATO, France could hope to penetrate the old Anglo-American special relationship. American power could thus be directed toward defending France's vital national interests—globally as well as in Europe.[23]

Konrad Adenauer's Germany was no less interested in encouraging a strong American role in NATO. While Social Democrats and some Christian Democrats feared NATO would preclude German reunification, the West German chancellor saw neutralist reunification as an illusory and probably undesirable goal. NATO's need for a new German army, foreseen from the early stages of the alliance, could be the lever for regaining sovereignty for West Germany—within a context, moreover, that bolstered its democratic forces and economic recovery. Adenauer followed the same strategy in staunchly supporting European economic integration and the European Defense Community, always on the condition that West Germany be treated as an equal partner.[24]

NATO's other European partners were equally enthusiastic about America's taking charge of the alliance. Individual national interests combined with a general fear of the Soviets. Among the smaller countries, American protection seemed both more reliable and less onerous than a system dominated by their own bigger neighbors. In short, with Britain and France not at all eager to assume responsibility for balancing the Soviets, only Americans like Kennan, it seemed, wanted a more genuinely independent Europe. Thus, even Americans reluctant to support a *Pax Americana* began to see an American protectorate as the only alternative to Soviet hegemony, a dilemma that has bedeviled American policy ever since.[25]

What can explain this European craving for dependence in 1948? The answer lies not only in the weakness and ambitious reconstruction that followed the Second World War but also in the lessons widely drawn from the two decades preceding it, when the Europeans had failed, despite Germany's defeat, to restore that continental balance so valued by Kennan. The history of their interwar failure strongly suggests why European powers preferred outright American hegemony after World

War II. Contrary to the popular cliché, American power was never isolated from Europe in the interwar period but was felt in all spheres and was decisive in several. Through the 1920s, for example, most European economies depended on American credit. But America's power, however omnipresent, was also highly unpredictable. Credit that was generously extended in the early 1920s was abruptly withdrawn in 1928. The same pattern was characteristic of the military sphere. American troops intervened to decide World War I. Thereafter, calculations of the European balance could hardly omit the American factor. Without support from the United States, the British and French victors were ultimately highly vulnerable to a renewed German bid for continental primacy. But with U.S. strength backing Britain and France, Germany could not reasonably expect to establish its own hegemony. America's volatile behavior fed the miscalculations on all sides that helped make another war inevitable.

This interwar experience does much, no doubt, to explain European behavior after World War II. Europeans had no desire to enter once more into the phantom pluralism of the interwar era. If the conditions for the restoration of the old indigenous continental balance did not exist before World War II, they could hardly be expected after it. Germany's second defeat had further ruined Britain and France, left America more predominant than ever, and opened the way for a new and stronger Russia. Hence, Europe's policy was to yoke America firmly to a responsibility for continental leadership. With America's power thus domesticated, each European state could proceed to maneuver for its best position within the American hegemony. European initiatives might include building a European bloc or cultivating détente with the Soviets. Neither effort, however, was so much a substitute for American hegemony as it was a strategy for increasing European leverage within it.

While Kennan's pluralist vision was out of phase with the perspectives prevailing in both Europe and America, and about to be swept aside in Truman's second administration, the seeds nourished by the Marshall Plan nevertheless continued to grow, and American hopes for Europe's geopolitical revival never died out completely. Despite the transition to a more overt hegemony, the pluralist form and style of American leadership cultivated in the Marshall Plan phase remained. In contrast to the rather brutal anti-Europeanism of the Hull era, American leadership in NATO has always been tailored to suit an underlying European self-esteem.

By and large, the tone of transatlantic relations was set by relatively cosmopolitan Americans. Even if inspired by the vision of a *Pax Americana*, they shared Kennan's admiration of European civilization and respect for its sensibilities. Postwar American leadership thus developed a characteristic style that clothed the realities of hegemony in the trappings of pluralism. The decline and demotion of Britain was cushioned by its "special relationship" with the United States, while an American military protectorate for Western Europe was packaged in the multilateral hocus-pocus of NATO. But these relationships could not embody the plural alliance Kennan desired: a European defense of Europe with the Americans assisting.

Supporting the idea of European federal unity was one way for Americans to ease their misgivings about their hegemonic commitment to Europe. The heavy American role would be only temporary, because Europe, at American prodding, was moving toward a federal union of its own. European economic integration was paving the way to political union while offering advantages to American investors and guarding against a return to nationalist mercantilism. Federal unity would resolve the murderous internecine struggles that had formerly made Europe such a menace to the world and to itself. In due course, a European Defense Community would have ample resources to balance the Soviets and replace American military hegemony. Meanwhile, NATO's protectorate would give the United States a continuing strong influence in shaping the new Europe in a liberal direction. By ardently supporting European federal union, Americans, and like-minded Europeans, had the best of both worlds. They could favor a more balanced transatlantic relationship in principle, but make it depend upon a political program with dubious chances of success.[26]

Reservations about America's NATO commitment were hardly limited to the upper reaches of the Foreign Service. Fears of geopolitical overextension were widely shared in Congress, on both left and right. Republican skepticism over open-ended European commitments had been a major inducement for the Marshall Plan's emphasis on European initiative and ultimate self-sufficiency. The shift to NSC-68, along with NATO's integrated command structure and heavy deployment of U.S. forces, awaited the seating of a Democratic Congress in 1949 as well as the gradual spread of anticommunist fever on the right itself. When the Korean War finally triggered the huge buildup of arms presaged in NSC-68, strong reactions soon developed in the American political system and, under Eisenhower, forced reversal.

The conservative congressional views of the late 1940s and 1950s are often dismissed as "neo-isolationist" and therefore unworthy of serious attention. In retrospect, the congressional critics, at their best, shrewdly anticipated the likely consequences of the Truman administration's definition of America's world role. Senator Robert Taft was probably the most distinguished and perceptive of the conservative skeptics. The senator's father, President William Howard Taft, had been defeated for a second term by Woodrow Wilson and Theodore Roosevelt in the election of 1912. The elder Taft had then become a law professor and ultimately chief justice of the United States; the younger Taft was himself a major contender for the Republican presidential nomination in 1948 and 1952.

Taft does not easily fit the isolationist stereotype. He was anything but a primitive provincial, ignorant or uninterested in the rest of the world. On the contrary, it was a substantial knowledge of history and politics that fed his worry about America's impulses toward moral pretentiousness and economic overextension. Like Kennan, Taft was skeptical of how well the American political system was suited for an imperial role. He saw clearly how it would increase the importance of the government sector in the economy and in society, as well as the importance of the presidency in the constitutional balance. His writings display a deep, albeit tranquil, patriotism as well as a cosmopolitan reluctance to claim special virtue or wisdom for the United States. Like many conservative isolationists after World War I— the elder Henry Cabot Lodge, for example—Taft understood the importance of maintaining a balance of power but was skeptical of grand Wilsonian schemes for a world order managed by the United States. Like Kennan, he believed the United States should play a selective rather than universal role in sustaining a world balance, one dictated by a prudent definition of national interest. Echoing Lodge and other imperialists at the turn of the century, Taft favored a maritime strategy that avoided continental commitments. The United States should, he believed, concentrate on a powerful navy and air force and eschew a large standing army.

Nevertheless, Taft reluctantly supported the NATO Treaty and accepted the need for American troops on the continent until the Europeans could recover more fully. But he was dismayed at the elaborate organization that followed in 1950 under General Eisenhower, arrangements that clearly implied a long-range American protectorate. Such a commitment, Taft feared, would put the United States on a permanent war footing, distort the economy by creating industrial dependence on military orders, and alter, for the worse, the traditional balances of American politics. The country risked institutionalizing militarism and profligacy. Its political system would grow more and more vulnerable to the manipulations of imperialist adventurers. Such a course seemed a graver peril than any likely Soviet aggression.

Taft's writings also reveal how impotent he felt to resist this course. Again and again he envisages the unfortunate consequences of some step in America's progress toward world hegemony, but then he supports it.[27] Taft's situation reflects that of many American conservatives throughout the postwar era. Their fierce ideological hatred of Soviet communism, which Taft shared but did not exaggerate, led them to support policies that had the domestic effects they most feared. What is striking about Taft is the degree to which he recognized his own dilemma but was unable to escape it. The reasons, of course, lay not only in his passionate anticommunism but also in the weakness of a world, Europe above all, that called out for American hegemony. Like Britain's power in the nineteenth century, America's strength was irresistibly drawn into a global vacuum. In the end, Taft's forebodings were no more effective that Kennan's.

Neither gave support to the other. The anti-imperialists in the State Department and the conservatives in Congress never seemed to grasp the significance of the other's message. Kennan despised Congress for its windy rhetoric, but his fear that America might be overreaching itself was shared far more by the Congressmen he disdained than among his ambitious friends in the bureaucracy. Kennan's ideas had scant reception in the conservative circles that might have found the greatest use for them. Perhaps the respective prejudices and misunderstandings between a Europeanized, somewhat alienated scholar-diplomat like Kennan, and the mid-western conservatives in Congress, even of so aristocratic and educated a variety as Taft, left too great a gap for mutual comprehension. For whatever reasons, the various strands of opposition to an American imperial role were never able to forge a common view. Much of the moral appeal of the conservative position was lost in the hysterical anticommunism, shameless prejudice, and disgraceful illegality of the McCarthy era.

Although NSC-68's push for heavy rearmament could not be prevented, its consequences soon provoked a strong reaction. The Korean War demonstrated the public's opposition to using American forces in prolonged confrontations in parts of the globe having only peripheral interest to Americans, a lasting drawback for any policy of sustained symmetrical containment. The public's reaction helped bring the Republicans to power in 1952 for the first time in twenty years. Ironically, it was not the so-called isolationist Taft who reaped the harvest, but the interna-tionalist Eisenhower. The general won the Republican nomination after resigning as the first Supreme Allied Commander of NATO. He ran, he said, to preempt Taft and thus prevent the dismantling of America's world role.[28] No sooner was Eisenhower elected than his secretary of state, John Foster Dulles, initiated a rash of new security treaties and regional organizations that girdled the Soviets and extended America's formal commitments.[29]

Eisenhower's subsequent policies, however, illustrate the basic realities that reg-ularly push postwar American policy back and forth between hard and soft lines. Even if he was dedicated to preserving America's global commitment intact, political and economic pressures made him eager to reduce the costs. In due course, he abandoned the ambitious rearmament of NSC-68, drastically cut military spending and forces, and turned toward détente and arms control.

What drove Eisenhower was, above all, his fear of economic inflation. Truman's fiscal conservatism had been one of the major obstacles to rearmament. Without wartime taxes and controls, fiscal balance seemed incompatible with the mobilization of resources needed for the sort of world role NSC-68 presupposed. To overcome Truman's scruples, the authors of NSC-68 had artfully blended imperial politics with Keynesian economics. In the conditions of the late 1940s, they argued, the federal spending needed for the arms buildup would greatly expand American output. Rapid growth, full employment, and burgeoning tax revenues would be the happy result.[30] The initial deficits would be investments in a prosperous future.

By the time Eisenhower came into office, the Korean War had temporarily discredited this imperial version of Keynesian economics. And the controls and taxes actually needed to contain the inflationary pressures were unpopular with the public and anathema to Republican politicians and their business supporters. Eisenhower also grew increasingly troubled at how the enormous wartime bureaucracy was perpetuating itself and how the military establishment and its economic allies— the "military-industrial complex"—were weighing more and more heavily on the American political economy. After a life in the army, Eisenhower had few illusions about the military's capacity to discipline itself and fewer inhibitions than most presidents about overruling military advice that ran contrary to his broader political and economic strategy. He therefore abandoned both the vast military buildup of NSC-68 and the economic policies that were its analogue. He was not, however, prepared to reduce America's global commitments to the same degree. His problem, therefore, was how to reconcile a conservative fiscal policy with an internationalist foreign policy.

Technology provided the solution. Thanks to America's undoubted superiority in nuclear weapons, NSC-68's rearmament could be abandoned. To meet its commitments, the United States no longer needed to match the Soviets "symmetrically" at every level of warfare and in every geographical region.[31] No longer would the U.S. be bled in conventional wars in Asia or try to match Soviet manpower in Europe. If the Russians or their allies attacked American allies, they could expect massive retaliation from American nuclear weapons. The Russians had nuclear weapons as well, but since the United States had ringed the Soviet Union with air bases and the Russians had little capability for attacking the United States directly, massive retaliation seemed a reasonable strategy. To succeed it seemed to require only precise commitments and an American government apparently willing to use its nuclear weapons to defend them. Dulles wrote the commitments and did his best to convince the world that American nuclear weapons would be used. In due course, low-yield battlefield nuclear weapons, able to stop mass attacks from superior conventional forces, made deterrence more selective and thus more credible.[32]

Aside from its moral liabilities, which alienated substantial parts of the public in both Europe and America, Eisenhower's nuclear strategy had another major vulnerability. It was useless against subversive guerrilla movements.[33] Eisenhower apparently drew the consequences. For the most part, he continued to stress traditional anticolonialism and carefully avoided major confrontations with revolutionary forces in the Third World.[34] Where the United States was able to use minimal conventional forces and covert operations to control local situations, it did so, most notably in Guatemala and Lebanon. But it carefully stayed out of France's wars in Indochina and Algeria and opposed the Anglo-French occupation of the Suez Canal.

Eisenhower's strategy, like Kennan's, could be called asymmetrical containment. The United States sustained its commitments without NSC-68's crushing expense of matching the conventional arms of the Soviets, their allies, or all the other hostile and revolutionary forces in the world. But Eisenhower's asymmetrical deterrence was based on technology rather than balance-of-power diplomacy. In other words, he was not following Kennan's policy of selective intervention to shore up indigenous local balances maintained by local powers. On the contrary, Eisenhower's policy depended on ironclad American territorial commitments, combined with direct American military control over the defended territory. Relying on battlefield nuclear weapons to stop a conventional attack against NATO, for example, meant keeping American generals in direct command of European defense. NATO forces were furnished with American nuclear weapons only under arrangements that gave the United States a veto over their use.[35] The logical alternative was nuclear proliferation to the allies—never a popular policy, although the United States was ultimately constrained to accept independent British and French nuclear arsenals.

Eisenhower's military doctrine enhanced rather than reduced America's military hegemony in NATO. European states got used to having the Americans provide territorial security. This led some nations to prolong their unrealistic global and colonial pretensions and led most to keep their conventional military forces and spending well below the point needed for defending themselves.[36] Eisenhower, in short, offered the first version of hegemony on the cheap. Technology, in this instance America's nuclear superiority, was called on to reconcile extended commitments with shrinking resources.

Eisenhower's solution was rational enough so long as the Americans possessed a monopoly of effective nuclear deterrence. It was undermined when the Russians began to acquire a reciprocal capacity. Once large numbers of Soviet rockets could reach the United States, a NATO strategy to defend Europe through American massive retaliation grew less credible and therefore more dangerous—the lesson quickly drawn in 1957 when the Soviets launched Sputnik.[37] Even the use of local or battlefield nuclear weapons grew problematic against opponents who had similar weapons. The consequence was a new doctrine—"flexible response"—which reverted to NSC-68's symmetrical deterrence and called, logically, for a second round of massive rearmament. Once such thinking regained ascendancy, Eisenhower could be faulted for neglecting military preparedness.

By the end of his second term, Eisenhower's policies were beginning to suffer from these accumulating military contradictions. Meanwhile, his fiscal conservatism had meant less inflation but also a more sluggish economy. Eisenhower thus left office under criticism both for neglecting military defense and for failing to achieve full employment.

The succeeding Kennedy administration proposed the familiar solutions of NSC-68—a major arms buildup combined with a Keynesian fiscal deficit. American policy had come full circle, and a new cycle had begun. While Eisenhower was in power, however, his strategic formula had temporarily resolved his fiscal-military dilemma. Unfortunately, it also created what proved to be ineradicable bad habits among the United States and its allies. Americans grew used to hegemony on the cheap; Europeans grew addicted to importing defense from the Americans.

Some aspects of Eisenhower's policy did look beyond the period of facile American nuclear deterrence. Thanks to American pressure, Germany once more became a military power, despite French displeasure and desperate Soviet maneuvers. The sovereign and rearmed Federal Republic that emerged was, in the longer term, a critical precondition for a more self-sufficient Europe in the future.[38]

Eisenhower's negative reaction to the Anglo-French Suez intervention gave a further push to European independence. Britain and France both nourished hopes that American power could be borrowed for use in the Third World as it had been borrowed in Europe. Eisenhower had disappointed the French in Indochina in 1954, and the Suez crisis of 1956 was also a bitter letdown for the British. Not only did the United States do its best to sabotage Anglo-French retaliation against Nasser for seizing the canal, but it actively condemned the intervention when it took place and even refused to guarantee the allies against the Soviet threats that followed.

Each ally drew a different lesson. The British, concluding that they had become dangerously isolated from the Americans, redoubled their efforts to cement a special relationship. The French, disillusioned about the prospects for manipulating the Americans, turned decisively toward building a European bloc.[39] France's reaction helped carry through the 1956 negotiations for the European Economic Community, which formally came into existence in 1958.

By brutally disappointing European pretensions to manipulate American Third World policy, Eisenhower made a major American contribution to European integration. If the French saw support for European integration as anti-American, the Eisenhower administration did not. On the contrary, it did everything possible to encourage the new EEC, ostensibly with the hope that a federal Europe might someday permit the United States to withdraw from commitments that stretched its resources.[40]

Finally, Eisenhower also opened a new phase in American relations with the Soviet world. Initially, his administration had indulged itself with the heightened Cold War rhetoric fashionable in the McCarthy era, including conservative fantasies about "rolling back" the Soviets, hopes cruelly exploded when Eastern Europe actually rose in rebellion in 1956.[41] Meanwhile, Western plans for German rearmament led to Russian initiatives for some sort of European settlement. The administration remained deaf to these overtures until after the German rearmament question had been settled.[42] Thereafter, encouraged by the British as well as by Soviet signals, Eisenhower began to explore the possibilities for a Soviet agreement. Although the 1960 Paris Summit with Khrushchev came to an unfortunate dénouement, it did break the Cold War's diplomatic impasse and legitimized later initiatives toward détente.[43]

President Eisenhower's reputation has risen greatly in recent years. In an age of economic gimcrackery and inflation, he stands out as a president who refused to believe a state could safely spend more resources than its political system was willing to provide.[44] In this respect, he shared the basic conservative outlook of both Kennan and Taft. But he could not adopt their solution of a reduction in America's hegemonic role and a more pluralist conception of world order. Instead of reducing the geopolitical commitments that permanently unbalanced the American political economy, Eisenhower used nuclear strategy for a cheap but transient resolution. In short, his prudence depended a good deal on luck. While this strategy lowered the economic cost of America's geopolitical role for at least a decade, it also greatly increased the difficulties in store for the future.

Once America and its allies grew accustomed to hegemony on the cheap, it became virtually impossible either to increase federal resources to meet the real cost of the geopolitical commitments or to readjust those commitments to fit the revenues the public would actually provide. Meanwhile, as Kennan had feared, Europeans grew increasingly comfortable in their dependence. And as Taft and Eisenhower himself had feared, the strains and distortions induced by America's imperial overextension became a permanent feature of its national life.

4

The Second Cycle: From Kennedy to Ford, 1961–1976

WHEN the Kennedy administration came to power in 1961, America's nuclear invulnerability seemed to be ending. The strategic consequences made the American protectorate for Western Europe more expensive and international politics more complex. Americans, now vulnerable to nuclear attack at home, wondered if their commitments abroad endangered their own domestic safety. Europeans questioned the reliability of the extended nuclear deterrent for Europe. American nuclear retaliation was meant to deter conventional as well as nuclear attacks. That a vulnerable United States would initiate a nuclear war to stop a conventional attack on Europe seemed implausible to many Europeans and frightening to some Americans. In short, the new administration confronted the strategic dilemmas that have bedeviled NATO ever since.

The Kennedy administration tackled these problems rather more urgently than was necessary. Contemporary estimates of Soviet rocket strength and conventional superiority were usually greatly exaggerated.[1] Real strategic parity was more than a decade away. But whatever the short-range remissions, the long-range dilemmas were clear enough.

Logically, the end of American invulnerability suggested a devolution of the American commitment to the Europeans. If the Europeans could put together adequate forces of their own, including nuclear forces, the burden would no longer fall on the Americans, at least not exclusively. Europeans had always talked about this option, and Britain and France did build nuclear deterrents. But hopes for a collective European federal army, let alone a nuclear force, remained stillborn. In short, Europe was unable or unwilling to take over America's European commitment.

The Kennedy and Johnson administrations, moreover, were not interested in relinquishing that commitment. On the contrary, the Kennedy administration was bent on a vigorous reassertion of American world leadership. Devolution thus remained only a hypothesis among analysts rather than a practical goal for policymakers. Analysis and policy focused not on how America might divest itself of its European commitment, but on how the American protectorate might be made more convincing to Soviets and Europeans and less dangerous to Americans.

The Kennedy administration pressed forward with a new NATO strategy of "flexible response." Unlike the earlier Eisenhower strategy that emphasized theater and tactical nuclear weapons, the new doctrine ruled out any automatic nuclear response to a conventional attack, let alone an automatic massive retaliation.[2] Henceforth, NATO was to meet any attack with the lowest level of violence sufficient to thwart it. Should one level fail, there would be a carefully controlled escalation to the next. A continuing dialogue with the enemy would facilitate agreement as soon as possible and thus keep military force from running beyond rational political control.

Logically, flexible response reinforced the need to centralize control of all NATO forces under an American Supreme Allied Commander. Since the American president had ultimate say over using NATO's nuclear weapons, and these weapons were indispensable for a process of precisely graduated responses, it seemed more appropriate than ever before that NATO's national forces be centralized under an American SACEUR. And since the new strategy required close communication with the enemy, it implied a consolidation of diplomatic communication to parallel the consolidation of command.

Flexible response also called for major rearmament. Containment at a nonnuclear level required a great expansion of conventional forces. If the Americans were to remain in charge, they would have to provide a major army for European defense. The Kennedy administration began adding new forces for Europe as well as special new troops for global intervention. At the same time, a major upgrading of strategic nuclear forces was undertaken to ensure a continuing American superiority, even if the old invulnerability were lost.

While the Europeans welcomed additional troops, they grew increasingly displeased with the economic consequences of America's rearmament (see chapter 6), as well as with the new military strategy itself. Flexible response was clearly an American strategy reflecting American preoccupations; several of its features were difficult for the European allies to accept.[3] Whereas the Americans wanted to minimize the likelihood that the U.S. defense of Europe would lead to nuclear war between the superpowers, Europeans believed their safety depended on convincing the Soviets that an attack on Europe would quickly escalate into an all-out nuclear war with the Americans, a war that would not spare the Soviet Union's own territory. For Europeans, the object of deterrence was not to limit a war, but to prevent one. The more any war seemed likely to spread, Europeans reasoned, the less likely it was to break out. Their nightmare was a war in which the superpowers confined their attacks to each other's part of Europe.

The American enthusiasm for conventional forces in Europe was also unwelcome. Emphasizing conventional forces implied that NATO's nuclear force might not be used and almost seemed to invite Soviet military incursions into Western Europe. Europeans professed to be almost as frightened of a conventional war as of a nuclear war. The danger that any military thrust meant nuclear war was, they reasoned, the principal guardian of European peace.

A buildup of conventional arms had other negative features in European eyes. After the low demands of massive retaliation, substantial increases in military spending and conscription would be highly unpopular. Forces on a scale to match those of the Russians meant mass British and French armies in Europe, which would curtail their domestic goals as well as their military reach beyond Europe. Preserving their global roles had been a prime motive for Britain and France to enter NATO in the first place. Nor was any further buildup of the West German military popular among Europeans generally or in Germany itself.[4]

Both the British and the French developed alternative military strategies reflecting these views.[5] They pressed on with building their own modest nuclear forces, despite American displeasure. Whereas America preached the dangers of nuclear proliferation in general and the specific dangers of a dispersion of decision-making authority in NATO, France and Britain argued the advantages of multiple deterrents, particularly when small national forces might be expected to trigger a superpower duel. Instead of flexible response, French strategic doctrine called for a massive nuclear strike on Soviet cities whenever the French national *sanctuaire* was under attack.

While the British smoothed over their differences with the Americans, Franco-American relations openly deteriorated. Under President de Gaulle, the French seemed to delight in carrying their theories to extreme, if logical, conclusions. De

Gaulle took drastic steps to ensure France's independence from American military direction: French forces withdrew from NATO's integrated command, and NATO forces were denied automatic use of French territory and air space. The French did not, however, denounce the Atlantic Treaty. They merely withdrew from the integrated organization established to carry out its purposes. The French were not leaving the American protectorate; they were redefining its terms.

As numerous angry commentators kept pointing out, French arguments against the reliability of the American deterrent for Europe also applied to any putative French deterrent for Europe. Strictly speaking, such criticism was irrelevant, since France's deterrent was intended solely for its own national defense. The French never claimed to be trying to supplant the Americans or to cover their European neighbors. Aside from occasional vague statements about holding their deterrent in reserve in case a unified European coalition should emerge, the French scrupulously avoided offering nuclear guarantees that were, in any event, never requested. As signatories of the NATO treaty, with its bold requirement to treat an attack on one as an attack on all, they were obliged to assist their allies in whatever fashion seemed appropriate. And by withdrawing from SACEUR's control, the French made it clear that they would decide for themselves what was appropriate.

The French did continue to keep an army in Germany and eventually equipped it with the capability of using short-range rockets with nuclear warheads. Under what circumstances these might be used remained a mystery to everyone except the French military planners themselves. As French strategic doctrine put it, nuclear deterrence depends on uncertainty. France's contribution to deterrence in Germany lay in the uncertainty created by its independent nuclear status and the fact that its army was stationed on German soil. The French believed that their nuclear weapons could stop a Soviet land invasion before it reached French territory— without attacking Soviet territory directly. In effect, a nuclear-armed French army in Germany constituted France's own version of flexible response.[6]

France, therefore, had every reason to want Germany to remain an American nuclear protectorate. With the Americans there, France was shielded. The *force de dissuasion* was additional insurance, according to French doctrine; it augmented the credibility of America's deterrent for Germany while lowering its political price for France.

While it is easy to see why such arrangements appealed to the French, or indeed the British, they were highly damaging to the Kennedy strategy. By creating a separate nuclear trigger, France directly increased the nuclear risk to the United States that flexible response was designed to limit. France's nuclear force, unlike Britain's, was built without any American help, so the United States had no comparable leverage over its use.[7] The French, moreover, emphasized their independence by not participating in NATO planning.

French military policy was equally distressing to other Europeans, the West

Germans in particular, although they shared French doubts about the reliability of the American deterrent. According to the logic of the French position, the highly exposed Federal Republic should also have had its own nuclear deterrent. Officially, of course, the French found such a development unthinkable because, among other things, the Soviets would be violently opposed to it for historical reasons, which the French said they understood and, in fact, shared. In any event, German disquiet expressed itself officially not by seeking a national nuclear force, but by demanding a firmer coupling of the American deterrent to Europe.[8] Nevertheless, fears of possible German nuclear ambitions helped inspire plans for some sort of separate collective European or distinct NATO nuclear force.

Of these options, only the last was seriously pursued.[9] A federal European deterrent remained only a theoretical solution, with negligible prospects. Nor were the French or the British willing or able to offer West Germany a credible nuclear guarantee. But the Kennedy and Johnson administrations, as well as the British, did float schemes for a separate multinational nuclear force, the Multilateral Force (MLF), within NATO. An armada of surface ships was to be equipped with medium-range nuclear rockets, manned by mixed crews from several NATO states and commanded by the SACEUR.[10] Each participating nation, including the United States, was to have veto power over its use. In strict military logic, the MLF was superfluous; American national forces could cover the same targets. With an American commander and an American veto on firing, the MLF seemed to critics no more convincing a deterrent than a regular American national force.

While the MLF project was ultimately abandoned, the substantial number of American medium-range rockets stationed in Europe under the "two-key" system did constitute a NATO deterrent of sorts. The SACEUR commanded these weapons, but the United States or the host country could veto their use.[11] In addition, the SACEUR controlled some seven thousand battlefield nuclear weapons installed under American control during the Eisenhower era.

The Kennedy and Johnson administrations also sought to meet demands for "coupling" the American deterrent to Europe by offering the NATO allies a structured role in nuclear planning. The Nuclear Planning Group was set up in 1967.[12]

These arrangements had notable success in assuaging concerns about the reliability of American deterrence while dampening demands for a German national deterrent. Nevertheless, as strategic parity between the superpowers, hypothetical in the 1960s, approached reality in the 1970s, the basic issues of America's extended deterrence kept returning in one form or another.[13] To this day, Europeans remain worried that the American deterrent is not credible or that Soviet-American rivalry elsewhere will spark military confrontation in Europe. Concern about credibility leads to recurring demands for more American missiles to be placed on European soil. Concern over superpower rivalry elsewhere leads to recurring contrary demands to remove the American nuclear weapons already there. Americans, in turn, continue to worry about being dragged into an intercontinental nuclear war for Europe's sake. The need for nuclear escalation to stop a conventional attack on Europe continues to hang as a major threat to the security of America's heartland. Measures taken to reassure uneasy Europeans inevitably create uneasy Americans.

For most Americans and many Europeans, stronger conventional defense has long seemed the logical way to reduce the risks of nuclear escalation. A more credible conventional deterrent was one of the prime objectives of the Kennedy-Johnson flexible-response strategy.[14] The ensuing problems helped reveal the enduring difficulties.

The rearmament pursued under Kennedy and Johnson strengthened America's European forces substantially, at least until the war in Vietnam drew the forces away. Europeans, principally the West Germans, also increased their manpower and financial contributions.[15] But what the Germans added to conventional deterrence with forces and money, they subtracted with the implacable political imperatives that they imposed on NATO strategy. German sensibilities about ceding territory to an attack imposed a "forward defense" strategy designed to stop a Soviet attack at the border, as opposed to a mobile defense in depth. At the same time, German sensitivity toward ratifying the country's postwar division proscribed serious fortifications along the intra-German border. The combination of forward defense with an unfortified frontier was a grave handicap to serious military planning, especially since NATO, as a defensive alliance, had to wait for the Soviets to initiate an attack. German domestic pressures also kept American forces from being properly stationed to cover the zone they were presumably defending. Diplomatic considerations, moreover, resulted in assigning manifestly inadequate Belgian and Dutch troops to critical sectors of the central front.[16] In short, it was difficult to believe that Europeans took conventional defense seriously. Conventional forces remained only symbols of American determination and of European burden-sharing.

France's withdrawal from NATO in 1966 was the gravest blow of all. Without either French forces or French territory, conventional defense against a Soviet attack on West Germany became an unpromising task.[17] After France's defection, the conventional aspect of flexible response strategy was condemned to remain what it had hitherto always been—a pause to decide whether Europe was worth a nuclear confrontation.[18] At best, NATO forces might deny the Soviets the assurance of a quick and easy victory with conventional weapons. A major battle would prolong matters and make the use of nuclear weapons highly probable. In short, the defense of Germany continued to depend primarily on the American nuclear deterrent.

Ironically, NATO could not agree to accept flexible response as its formal strategy until 1967, just after the Gaullist defection had made the doctrine's larger goals improbable.[19] To describe flexible response as a failure would, however, be a great exaggeration. If it could not resolve the problems inherent in extended deterrence, it at least addressed them energetically. NATO's conventional capabilities were certainly strengthened, and American credibility was reinforced.

By the end of the 1960s, then, NATO's strategic problems seemed less acute than at the beginning of the decade. Diplomatically, détente was replacing the earlier mood of confrontation. Militarily, Kennedy's rearmament, combined with more realistic estimates of Soviet strength, assured the Americans of several more years of comfortable nuclear superiority, if not invulnerability. While the Russians followed the Kennedy buildup with a major strategic rearmament of their own, the strategic balance did not change until the mid-1970s. The old problems of extended deterrence would then return with a vengeance and provoke, once more, a new cycle of rearmament.

The struggle in NATO over flexible response highlighted not only the fundamental military problems of the alliance but also its major diplomatic vulnerability. Along with upgraded conventional defense and centralized military command, flexible response called for close communication with the Soviets. A precise control of military escalation required an efficiently conducted dialogue during the battle itself, and in a language whose concepts were already familiar to both sides. Such a dialogue implied an established relationship between the superpowers, with rules of the game thrashed out in advance. The avoidance of dangerous crises called for confidential political consultations, with tight control over allies to prevent local crises from triggering unwanted confrontations with the other superpower.

This diplomatic corollary to flexible response reflected the natural implications of the military evolution toward strategic parity. In an environment of "Mutual Assured Destruction," negotiation was an essential part of any strategy. Eisenhower had already concluded that a more vigorous effort to stabilize superpower relations was an imperative American concern. Negotiations, moreover, seemed necessary to placate rising popular fears of nuclear war in Europe and America. Rearmament could then be defended as a prerequisite to détente—from which might follow arms control, trade, political settlement, and, ultimately, disarmament itself. There was also some hope that détente might liberalize Soviet society internally and make Russia less aggressive externally. Greater economic interdependence might inhibit the Soviets from disturbing the global system, lest their own prosperity be affected.[20]

Hopes of this kind began to circulate during the Kennedy years and peaked in the Johnson and Nixon eras. The rearmament cycle turned toward détente, and the United States sought to extricate itself from Vietnam and from escalating military costs in general.[21] American détente diplomacy emphasized the special responsibility of the superpowers in maintaining world order. Its bilateral focus recalled the first phase of America's postwar diplomacy, with Roosevelt's dream of incorporating the Soviets into the *Pax Americana*.

The Europeans viewed détente from a different diplomatic perspective. While welcoming the decreased tension between the superpowers, they firmly resisted the notion of an American monopoly over Western diplomacy. The major European states, with de Gaulle's France again in the lead, vehemently refused to permit the United States to negotiate for them in settling the European issues outstanding from World War II. Thus, in addition to deep differences over military strategy, the 1960s had a parallel transatlantic quarrel over Soviet relations.

As de Gaulle saw it, Kennedy's diplomacy was merely seeking a new Yalta, where the superpowers would confirm their earlier partition of the continent while reducing the inconvenience and danger of their confrontation along the consequent East-West border. In practical terms, this meant consolidating the status quo in Europe, including the division of Germany. De Gaulle argued that Europe's own long-range interest was radically different, that it lay in creating a new, more autonomous continental system. Only in such a context could some form of unity for Germany be realized and the wounds of two world wars finally be healed. It was essential, therefore, to deny the Americans hegemony over European diplomacy and for the European states to open their own dialogue with the Soviets. De Gaulle approached the Soviets with his own rather elusive formulation of a "Europe from the Atlantic to the Urals."

De Gaulle's diplomatic formula was a sort of modernized and enlightened version of the diplomacy of the *ancien régime*. Democratic Europe was to rediscover the family diplomacy of royal cousins. The national states, each guarding its own self-determination, would organize and balance themselves through a complex series of diplomatic linkages, reinsurance treaties, and intergovernmental institutions. At the system's core would be France and Germany, bound in a special relationship to produce and sustain a European confederation. Perhaps Britain would eventually join them. Such a confederation would form the needed counterweight to both the Russians and the Americans. It would be the core of a "Europe made up of free men and independent states, organized into a whole capable of containing all possible pretension to hegemony and establishing between the two masses the element of equilibrium without which peace will never come about."[22]

In de Gaulle's vision, Europe would keep its military alliance with the United States as a needed balance against Soviet militarism but at the same time would seek a closer relationship with the Russians. Europe's interest required keeping in check American as well as Soviet pretensions. In particular, Europe could not let its economic life be dominated by America—a greater and greater issue in the late 1960s as American inflation began to spread its effects worldwide. Soviet cooperation was also essential for resolving Europe's old German problem. A tacit Franco-Russian reinsurance treaty, which would silently guard against any overbearing German domination, would also create the context that could ease the way for some form of German national union.

De Gaulle was hardly an enthusiast of Soviet communism, nor was he heedless of Russia's aggressive militarism. But he tended to discount the lasting effects of Communist ideals and to see the Soviet Union as a modernized version of czarist Russia. Since that old Russia seemed essential to an internally balanced Europe, de Gaulle kept encouraging it to reappear. China's reinvigoration and the fermenting racial nationalism of Russia's own Asian subjects would, he hoped, greatly accelerate Russia's evolution toward becoming a manageable European power. Accordingly, de Gaulle was among the first to signal the importance of the Sino-Soviet conflict.

Ironically, de Gaulle's France was widely accused of being anti-European, partly because de Gaulle lost few opportunities to deflate the supranational pretensions of the European Economic Community. But it was Gaullist France, in fact, that infused the EEC with the political will to preserve its identity against American, British, and even West German efforts to drown it in some larger Atlantic construction. France was also Europe's spearhead in the battle to bring American monetary hegemony under some kind of collective control.[23] De Gaulle's brutal sarcasm toward the facile rhetoric of European integration did offend many "Good Europeans." But not the least of his European contributions was to challenge the fantasies of the European federalists and Brussels bureaucrats and to demand that Germany, and ultimately Britain, begin seriously to readjust their national perspectives and strategies to accommodate each other within a European bloc.

De Gaulle's diplomacy was naturally of great interest to the Germans. Chancellor Adenauer grew sympathetic to de Gaulle's larger views and believed his policies were useful to German interests. He therefore eagerly accepted the Franco-German Treaty of 1963, billed as the nucleus of European political confederation.[24] Announcement of the treaty was coupled with de Gaulle's rejection of Britain's bid to join the Common Market, underscoring the general's long-standing animus toward the Anglo-Saxons.

The new Franco-German arrangement alarmed the Americans and outraged Atlanticist opinion in Germany and elsewhere in Europe. In October 1963, Adenauer was finally maneuvered out of office. His replacement was Ludwig Erhard, leader of a rival faction within the Christian Democratic Party, a man whose fervent liberal Atlanticism had previously led him to oppose the Common Market.[25] Relations between France and Germany quickly grew strained, although the treaty continued to institutionalize their interdependence.

But Erhard also felt the need for a more independent national policy toward Eastern Europe. Under his aegis, a rather aggressive new German *Ostpolitik* offered economic blandishments to several Eastern neighbors, while ignoring Moscow and East Berlin. This policy displeased both the French and the Soviets.[26] By 1966, Erhard and the liberal Atlanticist Free Democrats were maneuvered out of office by a "Great Coalition" of Christian Democrats, Bavarian Christian Socialists (CSU), and Social Democrats (SPD), a feat of political legerdemain engineered by the so-called German Gaullists.[27] The SPD leader, Willy Brandt, became the Great Coalition's foreign minister.

By 1970 Brandt had become chancellor in a new Socialist-dominated coalition with the Free Democrats, and *Ostpolitik* took on a more imaginative character. German diplomacy formally accepted, "step by step," the postwar status quo, ultimately including a separate East German state. In return, the Federal Republic increased its economic, cultural, and political access to the Eastern countries. In effect, by formally accepting the territorial status quo, the Germans put themselves in a better position to change the postwar order. The Federal Republic's enormous economic attraction began to pull much of Eastern Europe into a German economic, cultural, and even political sphere. Brandt was careful to cultivate intimate relations with the Soviets themselves, to minimize suspicion that Germany was seeking to isolate the Soviets from their own empire. As a non-nuclear power whose standing military forces were completely absorbed in NATO, the Federal Republic could present itself as a state that posed no distinct military challenge.

NATO was essential to Brandt's *Ostpolitik*. Had Germany been an independent military power, or been required to seek security through some genuine military alliance with its Western European neighbors, military considerations could not have been so conveniently insulated from Eastern diplomacy. In effect, Brandt's Germany was flirting with a form of neutralist diplomacy between East and West, a policy enhanced and insured by the fact that Germany was an American nuclear protectorate rather than an independent military power.[28] By the early 1970s, with both the Americans and the rest of NATO avidly pursuing détente, Germany's diplomatic promiscuity no longer seemed incompatible with its military dependency.

The Johnson administration was still in office when the Great Coalition began to set Germany's new Eastern policy. The United States was itself seeking better relations with the Soviets, partly in the belief that the solution to Vietnam lay through Moscow. Since Kennedy's experience in the Berlin Crisis of the early 1960s, the Americans had sought an agreement to eliminate the danger of direct superpower confrontation over Germany. Realistically, Soviet-American agreement over Europe would require the Americans to stop supporting the Federal Republic's claims to prewar boundaries and exclusive legitimacy. For Kennedy, therefore, Adenauer's obdurate diplomacy seemed a major obstacle to Soviet-American agreement. Having the West Germans themselves legitimize the territorial status quo paved the way for a Soviet-American-European agreement, while relieving the United States of the embarrassment of abandoning its ally.[29] Thus, while American misgivings over Brandt's *Ostpolitik* were considerable, so were the immediate advantages for American diplomacy. Moreover, by Johnson's time the quarrel with Gaullist France had suggested the futility of trying to prevent European states from making their own diplomatic initiatives toward the Soviets. The United States, preoccupied with Vietnam, was in no position for a second major quarrel within NATO.

By 1967 the United States and the European powers reached a formal *modus vivendi* on détente diplomacy, embodied in the NATO Council's so-called Harmel Report.[30] It was agreed that NATO would proceed on a double track: while assiduously protecting the military balance, its members—individually and collectively—would seek better relations with the Soviet sphere. The allies, however, had to be careful not to weaken the alliance by bidding against each other for Russian favors. A loose policy coordination was therefore desirable. But each partner, the United States and the European powers alike, could proceed along parallel lines to cultivate its own détente.

Conditions for such a policy were increasingly favorable. As Vietnam turned more and more into a domestic nightmare for the Americans, entering the conciliatory phase of their military-diplomatic cycle grew all the more imperative. The Soviets, too, appeared ready. Even their 1968 invasion of Czechoslovakia seemed genuinely hesitant, and they went out of their way thereafter to reassure Europeans and Americans of their continuing interest in a broad European settlement.[31]

As Brandt proceeded, however, the increasing tempo of *Ostpolitik* began to exacerbate French and American apprehensions. De Gaulle had proposed a sort of collective European neutralism between the superpowers. His successors, weakened by the economic problems following the troubles of 1968, found Brandt's *Ostpolitik* too German and not sufficiently European.[32] French concern over German neutralism promoted a degree of reconcililation with Britain, which was finally allowed to join the European Communities in 1973. The Nixon administration was also growing uneasy. A Franco-American reconciliation of sorts blossomed even in 1969, de Gaulle's last year in power. Relations with France improved while those with Germany worsened. Henry Kissinger became openly critical of Germany's drift to neutralism,[33] but as his own pursuit of Soviet détente grew more ardent, he could hardly hope to prevent the Germans from following a parallel course.

In effect, European détente permitted Germany the same liberty within the American protectorate that Britain and France had always enjoyed. Détente legitimized *Ostpolitik*, while America's hegemonic military protectorate provided freedom rather than constraint for German national policy. NATO enabled the European nations to take the military balance for granted and, to a great degree, to insulate it from the rest of foreign policy.

Reconciling Brandt's *Ostpolitik* with Germany's membership in the alliance stands as a notable accomplishment for American and European statesmanship. Potentially, the German question had constituted a profound vulnerability for both transatlantic and Western European solidarity. By accommodating Brandt's *Ostpolitik*, NATO managed for a decade to quiet a major source of unease in the

West. That accommodation depended on a convergence of Western Europe's ambitions for a pan-European settlement and America's cyclical need to substitute diplomacy for rearmament. For several years, moreover, both European and American détente were underwritten by the strategic superiority purchased by Kennedy's rearmament. Consequently, transatlantic trouble over détente in Europe was not to reappear until the late 1970s, when the Americans, believing their own weakness to have disturbed the strategic military balance, denounced détente and turned to a new cycle of rearmament.

By the late 1960s, American and European diplomacies had reached a certain reconciliation in Europe, but they remained far apart in the Third World. By and large, Europeans opposed America's war in Vietnam, its policy in the Middle East, and its general strategy for development. In these areas, détente brought little improvement. On the contrary, American and European global perspectives diverged throughout the 1970s.

The incoming Kennedy administration was probably as self-conscious about its Third World strategy as about its military strategy. The administration's view of the developing world was greatly influenced by the "take-off" theory of development promulgated by the economist Walt Rostow—one of the more creative and controversial figures of both the Kennedy and Johnson administrations.[34] Rostow taught that once developing market economies reached a certain stage in their evolution, they would take off into rapid and self-sustaining economic growth. Invariably, however, the dislocations, inequalities, and hardships that would accompany progress carried the risk of a political reaction. If unchecked, such a reaction could halt the economic growth prematurely. Zealots and politicians could always be found with plausible formulas to justify self-defeating controls over growth. These varieties of mercantilist, fascist, or communist illiberalism constituted, in Rostow's view, the adolescent diseases of development. If they were not avoided, a growing economy was unlikely to reach its otherwise natural maturity. Development policy should therefore couple open trade and generous subsidies with precautions against the communism or fascism to which developing economies are politically susceptible. Development, in other words, had a military as well as an economic aspect.

Kennedy's Third World policy reflected Rostow's thinking. Liberal American economic assistance was bolstered with new counterinsurgency forces and military tactics designed to hold illiberal predators at bay. The Peace Corps and the Green Berets were thus complementary aspects of Kennedy-Johnson development policy.[35]

Europeans viewed America's new vigor in the Third World with considerable misgiving and jealousy. France, Britain, and Germany also had very substantial national aid programs. The Common Market had an ambitious development strategy of its own, oriented initially toward French Africa and the Mediterranean. The EEC stressed bilateral arrangements with mutual trade concessions—anathema to the liberal purists in the State Department, who saw such arrangements as nascent neocolonial blocs. The Americans pushed the Europeans to abandon reciprocal advantages but could do little to blunt their impulse toward establishing geographic zones of influence.

Disagreements over American military interventions were more serious. Having frequently failed to block left-wing revolutions in the Third World, the Europeans had learned to live tolerably well with them. To Europeans, America's preoccupation with counterinsurgency and anticommunism seemed dangerously out of tune with the emerging political cultures of the Third World itself. In particular, the war in Vietnam was highly unpopular in Europe, a reaction tinged with a certain *Schadenfreude*. Not only did European governments refuse to help with token forces, as they had in Korea, but some openly attacked the American role.[36]

Differences also widened over the perennially vexatious Arab-Israeli dispute. The 1967 War, in which Israel crushed the Arabs and occupied the West Bank of the Jordan, aroused much opposition to Israel and general misgiving about American policy. De Gaulle took a highly critical view of the Israeli annexations, an outlook increasingly shared by the other European states.[37] In short, American and European diplomacy was already seriously divided over the Middle East well before the spectacular crises of the 1970s.

This brief analysis of alliance problems in the Kennedy-Johnson period should not end without a passing reference to the West's economic differences. Throughout the 1960s an escalating transatlantic quarrel over trade and monetary policies formed the economic counterpart to the quarrels over military and diplomatic policies. By 1968, for example, the postwar structure of the international monetary system was near collapse. These economic problems were, moreover, closely linked to the differing military and diplomatic positions of America and Europe. Since the subject seems too large and complex to fold into the military-diplomatic narrative, it is examined in detail later (see chapters 6 and 7). In fact, however, the economic, diplomatic, and military quarrels were not isolated but were mutually reinforcing.

In 1968, the Kennedy-Johnson era came to an ignominious end. Its history amply demonstrates the characteristic transatlantic strains during an upswing in the American security cycle. The Nixon administration, by contrast, marks the recessional phase. Nixon's situation in 1969 was not unlike Eisenhower's in 1953. The country, having sustained a major rearmament for many years and having involved itself in a frustrating war in the Third World, was ready for détente and disarmament. Nixon's recessional phase, however, gradually created urgent transatlantic problems of its own. As he set about repairing the financial and commercial ravages of a decade of overextension, Europeans found sharing the burden of defense not at all to their liking. They began to suspect that their interests were being sacrificed for good relations with the Soviets and started to complain about America's military weakness.

Nixon's most urgent task lay in extricating the country from Vietnam, a goal that proved far more traumatic than ending the Korean War. While much of the world, including a substantial and vociferous part of the American population, clamored for American withdrawal, a viable regime could not be created in South Vietnam. It was difficult to disguise departure as anything other than an inglorious defeat.

The effects of the Vietnam debacle on American opinion strongly constrained the Nixon administration and those that followed in the 1970s. The recessional phase of the security cycle came on with a vengeance, for the public had developed a profound antipathy toward any commitment of American troops in the Third World. A Congress strongly predisposed to cut military spending blocked further development and emplacement of antiballistic missiles, refused to fund a new bomber to replace the aging B-52, and balked at building the new land-based intercontinental MX missile to replace the ten-year-old Minuteman. Funds for conventional forces and weaponry were also cut, but most significant of all, conscription was allowed to lapse as the United States converted to a professional army. While the sums spent on defense were still gigantic, an all-professional military meant a much higher proportion for manpower costs. The American military, demoralized and disoriented, was slow to develop a new mix of forces, weapons, and strategy appropriate to the changed conditions.[38]

Nixon also faced the accumulated economic problems of the 1960s. Here again, his difficulties were similar to Eisenhower's but more acute. After the ambitiously expansive Kennedy-Johnson civilian and military programs, plus the war itself, stagflation had become endemic in the domestic economy and the dollar was fatally undermined abroad.[39] The dollar's impending collapse threatened to become America's economic Vietnam.

Like Eisenhower, Nixon searched for a formula that would reduce the strain on American resources without undermining the postwar international system or American hegemony within it. In other words, Nixon's broader strategy called not for a reduced American role, but for a less costly way to manage it. Eisenhower, with a similar brief, was fortunate to have had an easy strategic and technological solution: massive retaliation. America's technological superiority in strategic weapons set a balance of commitments to costs that enabled America to continue sustaining its world role out of its own resources, even while significantly reducing military spending. Nixon, lacking such an easy military solution, turned instead to diplomacy. He found in Henry Kissinger the brilliantly active diplomat that such a strategy required.

Nixon's options and choices may be expressed in a somewhat more theoretical vein. Like Eisenhower, he faced a populist revolt against NSC-68's formula for American world hegemony. Like Eisenhower, he therefore needed some new military or diplomatic formula to permit the United States to sustain its international position on the cheap. Logically, there may be said to have been three theoretical options—one military and two diplomatic: (1) a new military technology or formula to provide cheap superiority; (2) a new relationship with the Soviet Union that could reduce costs; or (3) a new relationship with America's allies and clients that could share costs.

Since no cheap military option was available, Nixon fell back on his two diplomatic options. His diplomatic strategy concentrated on building détente with the Soviets and on cultivating allies in the Third World to act as America's regional surrogates. His détente diplomacy had a specific military aim: to negotiate arms ceilings low enough to permit the United States to hold its own against the Soviets, despite Congress's manifest unwillingness to spend money on the arms race.

As Kissinger often pointed out, such a policy had clear limitations. A strategic superiority that Congress was unwilling to finance could not be sustained by diplomacy alone. By the early 1970s, however, America's former strategic supremacy was very likely unsustainable in any event. In the later 1960s, that ascendancy had been based on being about five years ahead of the Soviets in developing MIRVs (multiple-headed rockets, each capable of independent targeting). MIRV technology permitted a remarkable expansion of American warheads, from 2,490 in 1971 to 7,290 in 1983. By the early 1970s, the Russians had built their own MIRVs and were bound to multiply their warheads accordingly.[40] Realistically, negotiations could not freeze the former U.S. superiority but could only hope to agree on a parity low enough not to require improbable new expenditures from Congress. The Strategic Arms Limitation Treaties, I and II, by and large succeeded in accomplishing this.[41]

The "SALT Process," however, was encumbered by very ambitious political overtones, reflecting the more radical possibilities of a new Soviet-American relationship. Cooperation in limiting arms was half-expected to lead toward cooperation in maintaining world stability in general. Agreements to set parity were half-expected to blossom into a broad world settlement. Cooperative superpower diplomacy rather than strategic power might henceforth contain the Soviets.

In pursuing such ambitions, the superpowers found their diplomacy hamstrung by a fundamental incompatibility in their aims. While the Soviets wished to become America's geopolitical equal, the United States was determined that they should not. Nixon's diplomacy was the means chosen to sustain American world hegemony, not to give it up. Thus, while the United States was willing to negotiate arms agreements on the basis of strategic parity, it was not willing to accept the Soviet Union as a geopolitical equal that had the right to be consulted on issues around the globe. Instead, American détente diplomacy aimed not only to stabilize the arms race at a manageable level but also to contain the Soviets within their own regional boundaries. The Soviets could not reasonably be expected to accept such a bargain unless the United States, or some combination of powers, was in a military position to hold them to it.

The American military position, however, was clearly deteriorating, not merely in its strategic forces but above all in the strength of its conventional arms. As strategic parity was becoming a reality, conventional forces were naturally growing more significant. Traditionally strong in their army, the Soviets had for a long time been building their naval forces as well. With declining American strength, the Soviets might reasonably be expected to probe the world for places to demonstrate their new status. Assuming it could not regain its old strategic superiority, the United States had three options: it could strengthen its conventional forces, encourage others to develop the military power needed for various regional balances, or try to accommodate some Soviet global ambitions in return for limiting others. Some combination of all three was the obvious course. In the end, the Nixon-Kissinger diplomacy was never able to pursue any of the three seriously.

Congressional opposition and military disorientation ruled out conventional rearmament. As for accommodation, no serious effort was ever made to test the Soviets as partners in some regional arrangement. The Middle East was one obvious place to try. Given the geographical proximity of the region, the Soviets had strong claims to a vital interest in it. Any durable settlement of the Arab-Israeli dispute was improbable without their cooperation. In the 1973 War, during the supposed heyday of détente, the United States pressed every advantage to eject the Soviets from the region even though, by Kissinger's own account, the Soviets had played a responsible role. Had any Soviet leader been inclined to take seriously American hints of a common policy of shared global responsibility, the experience of American-Israeli maneuvering in the 1973 War and its aftermath must have been sobering. Instead of trying to build a broad international consensus behind a settlement, Kissinger seized control of the negotiations and ultimately ejected not only the Soviets but also the Europeans.[42]

Despite the American performance in the Middle East, Kissinger professed to be outraged at what he called a betrayal of détente when the Soviets moved a few years later to establish client regimes in Angola and the Horn of Africa. The Soviets might be forgiven for finding his reaction unreasonable. Here, as elsewhere, the Soviets were behaving with their usual cautious but relentless aggressiveness, not unlike other great powers in history. American diplomacy had every reason to counter these moves, but not to claim a betrayal that discredited détente. American diplomacy had never offered to move from arms control to a broader geopolitical settlement—at least not on any terms short of Soviet renunciation.

In theory, help to the Soviets in the economic sphere might have been an alternative to American geopolitical concessions. Progress in this domain was effectively blocked by the congressional penchant for meddling in Soviet internal affairs on behalf of Jewish dissidents. As early as 1974, the Senate's Jackson-Vanik Amendment sought to make economic relations and détente dependent on the Soviets' changing their internal policies to permit a great increase in Jewish emigration.[43] As a result, closer economic relations, once envisioned as an incentive toward détente and global cooperation, never developed—or developed with Western Europe rather than with the United States. The one exception—the grain trade—was soon highly politicized and proved vulnerable to pressure groups and volatile shifts of the American political mood.[44] With this experience, the Russians could hardly have been expected to allow their economy to grow more dependent on trade with America.

In short, American détente policy, once it moved beyond arms control, was predictably headed for disappointment. The Soviet Union may be exceptionally aggressive externally, and it is undoubtedly extremely unattractive domestically. But it is also a great power. If American policy hoped to substitute détente diplomacy for military spending during the 1970s, it was not realistic to expect the Soviets to renounce any overt strategic and geopolitical challenge without, in compensation, appeasing their long-standing desire to be accepted as a world power. It was equally unrealistic to plead with the Soviets for mutual cooperation to sustain world order while elbowing them out of the Middle East. And it was self-defeating to saddle trade policy with blatant and insulting interference in Soviet internal politics.

Arguably, a diplomacy of accommodation would not have been morally justifiable or politically realistic. But insofar as the United States was not prepared to appease the Soviets, it should logically have been willing to pay the military and political price needed to resist them. As a practical matter, strategic parity was bound to lead to greater pressure on conventional forms of deterrence. Even a deliberate and consistent policy of limited appeasement, to be kept within acceptable bounds, would have required strengthening conventional forces. A détente diplomacy with no concessions was hardly a substitute.

The limitations of its détente diplomacy spurred the Nixon administration into its only other option: sharing the burden of defense with its allies. If America could not strengthen itself sufficiently through its own resources, it could try to mobilize the strength of others. While this was clearly a major goal of the Nixon-Kissinger diplomacy, its realization suffered from the same condition that hampered détente diplomacy. Nixon's diplomacy was designed to preserve America's world role, not to devolve it to others. Under these circumstances, burden-sharing became a policy designed to shore up hegemony rather than share it. Instead of having American power sustain the system, the system was to contribute to sustaining American power. Burden-sharing was conceived not as a divestiture of hegemony but as a greater taxation of its beneficiaries. It meant not so much reducing the leading role of the United States as leaning more on others to support that role.[45]

In its early days, the Nixon administration seemed to promise a more radical departure from the traditional hegemonic policy. Early official explanations stressed how Nixon's diplomatic strategy was anticipating a more plural world, dominated by five great powers or groupings of powers: the United States, the Soviet Union,

China, Japan, and Western Europe. American diplomacy's new grand design was to coax these powers into cooperative relationships able to sustain regional balances and resist destabilizing changes.

Opening relations with Communist China, or discovering a "China Card," was the policy's greatest accomplishment.[46] But its application in Western Europe was seriously flawed. Ironically, Europe was the region where the potential for success was greatest. Had the administration been seriously interested in promoting and taking advantage of a more pluralistic world, devolving America's hegemonic military role in NATO would have been a prime place to begin. Had the Western Europeans managed at least their own conventional defense, a fundamental and favorable improvement would have followed in the balance between American commitments and capabilities. In reality, however, American policy held tenaciously to NATO hegemony, perhaps for the economic reasons to be discussed later. Indeed, with the ill-fated Year of Europe in 1973, the United States, seeking a veto within the policymaking apparatus of the European Community, tried to extend its military hegemony into the economic sphere.[47] As Kissinger's own account makes clear, the Europeans had no interest in arrangements that reduced their independence while increasing their burdens. Instead, they were busy pursuing their own version of Soviet détente and increasingly preoccupied with their relations with the Third World.

Failure to achieve devolution in Europe during the superpower détente of the 1970s had one particularly unfortunate consequence. It encouraged European détente policies that, although they had quite different goals from those of the Americans, counted on an indefinite continuation of American military protection. The problems foreshadowed in the Gaullist rhetoric of the mid-1960s began to materialize. Europe's own pursuit of détente, legitimized by the Americans themselves, set loose a chain of divergent policies that could be expected, sooner or later, to highlight the essential differences between the geopolitical positions and interests of Europe and America. The danger was less that Western Europe and the Soviet Union might reach a pan-European accommodation, but that the process had begun before Western Europe had consolidated itself sufficiently to sustain an indigenous pan-European balance. The United States was thus left with the task of protecting a Europe whose geopolitical interests were growing ever more divergent from its own.

The American diplomatic energy that could have been expended on the critical European front, where the objective conditions for a stable devolution of power and responsibility might have existed, was instead invested in the Middle East, where they did not. At the time, however, the Middle East seemed an ideal hunting ground for "surrogates." Regional powers were to be armed, preferably at their own expense, to assist the United States in sustaining the status quo against Soviet incursion or revolutionary destabilization. To its familiar client, Israel, the United

States added Iran, Saudi Arabia, and finally Egypt. The United States adroitly made itself exclusive broker for the Egyptian-Israeli settlement of the 1973 War. Kissinger then promoted an Israeli-Syrian settlement of the Golan Heights dispute and took on the hopeless West Bank and Gaza questions. American diplomats seemed everywhere at once, eagerly grinding away at the region's most intractable problems.[48]

The Middle East revealed the Nixon policy in its true colors: hegemony based on hyperactive diplomacy. The United States was more involved than ever before. But while the perpetual whirl of diplomacy seemed to be leading the United States from triumph to triumph, its actual position was growing more precarious.

According to the rationale for surrogate diplomacy, allies were substitutes for America's own faltering strength. The relationship generally involved a heavy arms buildup and a large American presence. Both often proved a source of weakness for the regime itself and ultimately a drain and embarrassment for the United States as well.

The Pahlevi regime in Iran was the classic case. As a barrier to Soviet penetration southward, the Shah was supposed to be protecting Western interests in the Persian Gulf. The more intimate the Shah's involvement with the United States, however, the weaker he grew. Hectic modernization and militarization, prompted by the American connection and accompanied by an ostentatious influx of foreigners, helped undermine the regime. Its survival required more and more smothering of popular disaffection. American involvement in this repression was ambivalent and hesitant enough to blunt its effectiveness, but extensive enough to fuel the hatred of those who would eventually come to power. In the end, the Iranian relationship proved not a source of American strength, but of American vulnerability. The United States was deeply exposed but too weak to protect its interests. A policy designed to conserve resources left the United States more overextended than ever.

In the best of circumstances, the Shah's contribution to American interest was not altogether clear. His status as surrogate did not impede his enthusiastic role as a major organizer of the 1973 oil embargo or the revolution in oil prices brought about by the Organization of Petroleum Exporting Countries (OPEC). Thereafter, Iran's abundant new wealth brought large military and civilian contracts to American industries and large deposits of capital to American banks, but this could hardly compensate for the damage done to the international economy in general and to America's European allies in particular.

The oil crisis was itself a major event in the chronicle of alliance relations and points up the ever more vital American-European differences over Third World policy. The oil shock of 1973–74 endangered Europe far more directly than it affected the United States. (The economic consequences are addressed in chapter 6.) Politically, the oil crisis suggested the limits of America's ability and willingness to guard Europe's vital interests in the Third World—even in a region where the

Americans were ostensibly more predominant than ever before. That such predominance partly reflected Europe's exclusion from Arab-Israeli diplomacy did not, of course, improve alliance relations. The embargo, moreover, was in retaliation for America's unswerving support for Israel, a policy that many Europeans had already grown to dislike.

Kissinger's reaction to the crisis tended to exacerbate transatlantic differences still further. Initially, Americans talked of forceful intervention to break the oil embargo and roll back the price. Europeans were skeptical about using force and resigned themselves instead to higher energy costs. Economically much more dependent on Middle Eastern oil than the Americans, Europeans looked for some long-range accommodation. In the short run, they did everything possible to bolster their exports and to attract OPEC capital. Their national strategies emphasized the advantages of an enduring structured relationship between the oil suppliers and their customers. Economically and politically, the situation put them in competition with the Americans.

Kissinger, meanwhile, was trying to yoke the Europeans and the Japanese into a collective organization—the International Energy Agency (IEA)—to mount a common response. The United States would naturally play the leading role. The European reaction followed the familiar pattern. The French denounced the arrangements as hegemonic and refused to participate. The rest of Europe went along with the Americans, but only after stripping the arrangements of their rigor. The French participated indirectly and enjoyed whatever benefits there were, but without even the minimal commitments that bound the others. IEA headquarters were actually located in Paris.[49]

Transatlantic differences in the oil crisis set a pattern for American and European reactions to the Third World's growing assertiveness. OPEC's success prompted broad demands for a New International Economic Order. Europeans were scarcely united among themselves, but their high dependence and involvement prompted a more accommodating reaction, even if well short of enthusiasm for any wholesale redistribution of world income.

Some European differences with Americans were mostly rhetorical. European states proved quite willing to intervene with military force when it seemed feasible and beneficial. Nevertheless, Europe was more inclined to see the Third World's new weight and assertiveness as inevitable and to welcome the greater opportunities to maneuver. Europeans, of course, remained happy to borrow American strength when it suited their purposes. They were quick to sound the alarm, moreover, when American "weakness" appeared to be attracting Soviet military power to Africa. But they showed little inclination to leave their own Third World interests in American hands or to follow the American lead in setting their own policies.[50]

Transatlantic divergence over the Third World was thus not healed by the end of American involvement in Vietnam, or by Kissinger's departure in early 1977. Instead, it reflected a more fundamental European and American reaction to America's declining capacity to control global events.

In its heyday, the Nixon-Ford era seemed the zenith of postwar American diplomacy. In retrospect, this period's greatest accomplishments were in liquidating the most egregious liabilities inherited from the Kennedy-Johnson era. Nixon and Kissinger got the United States out of Vietnam and successfully managed the dollar's decline. Their superpower détente, moreover, clearly did contribute to global stability. Despite the declining defense budget, arms agreements helped sustain a strategic nuclear balance. In addition, American diplomacy assuredly enjoyed some brilliant tactical successes, which helped sustain morale and prestige in a difficult period. Dealing itself a China Card gave American diplomacy further leverage. And Soviet influence was eclipsed in the Middle East, even if replaced, in the end, with something even less manageable.

The consequences of American overextension and military weakness could not, however, be conjured away forever. The failures of the Carter administration were implicit in the situations Nixon and Kissinger had left behind.

Like Eisenhower, Nixon looked for a formula to continue the American world role while radically reducing its domestic costs. Eisenhower relied on a technological military advantage bound to be transitory, while Nixon relied on a diplomatic prestige whose foundations were crumbling. Neither Eisenhower nor Nixon tried seriously to cut back America's geopolitical commitments. Neither was prepared for appeasement—a broad geopolitical settlement with the Soviets—or for devolution—a new division of labor with Western Europe. Both administrations were ultimately criticized for letting the United States grow dangerously weak relative to its commitments. In each case much of the military criticism was overdone. Kennedy's "missile gap" was illusory, and so, finally, was Reagan's "window of vulnerability." Nevertheless, hegemony on the cheap turned out, in every case, to be a perilous policy.

One difference between Eisenhower and Nixon is probably more significant than all the parallels. Eisenhower did rein in the bounding acceleration of federal spending. When he left office, public finances were sound and inflation was no longer the problem it had been in 1952. The same could hardly be said for Nixon or Ford. Despite cuts in the arms budget, fiscal policy was never brought into balance. As a result, the Carter-Reagan military buildup had a far more precarious economic base than Kennedy's. That fundamental change in economic conditions is likely to remain significant for the alliance long after the diplomatic quarrels and triumphs of the 1970s have been forgotten.

5

The Carter-Reagan
Turnaround, 1977–1983

EVEN IN RETROSPECT, the Carter administration seems curiously indefinable. It rode to power on the popular outrage against Vietnam and Watergate but, once in office, was pulled down by the military, diplomatic, and economic policies set mostly by its predecessors. Trying to catch a second popular wave—the conservative backlash against America's inflation and geopolitical decline—the administration alienated old supporters without gaining new ones. But the policies developed in the process—initiating rearmament, abandoning détente, and imposing monetary stringency—set the course for a new cycle of American security measures that had profound effects on transatlantic relations. These effects were greatly magnified by the succeeding Reagan administration.

By the time President Carter took office in 1977, the decline in America's military forces that had begun after Vietnam appeared dangerous for both the global and the European balances. Following Kennedy's rearmament, the Soviets had been steadily strengthening their forces. As they belatedly acquired MIRV technology, their proportion of warheads to launchers began to climb rapidly. At the same time their long-standing buildup of launchers continued unabated. As a result, they were beginning to approach the long-anticipated strategic parity with

TABLE 5.1

Growth of U.S. and Soviet Strategic Arsenals[a]

	1964 ICBM/Total	1971 ICBM/Total	1976 ICBM/Total	1980 ICBM/Total	1984 ICBM/Total
U.S.					
Launchers	925/2035	1054/2070	1054/2163	1054/2026	1037/1803
Warheads	925/2665	1254/4230	2154/9406	2154/8708	2137/9509
USSR					
Launchers	200/330	1510/2090	1527/2817	1398/2557	1398/2522
Warheads	200/330	1510/2510	2339/4036	3154/5530	7460/9345

[a] This table includes those nuclear systems defined as strategic under SALT I, such as ICBMs, SLBMs, and Long-Range Bombers.
SOURCE: *The Military Balance 1964–65; 1971–72; 1976–77; 1980–81; 1984–85* (London: International Institute for Strategic Studies, 1964, 1971, 1976, 1980, 1984), 3, 5, 22, 23, 36; 55, 57, 58; 5, 73–75; 5, 88–98; 130–36.

the United States. Indeed, the Soviets were well on their way to numerical superiority in land-based intercontinental warheads (see table 5.1).[1]

Some observers began speaking of America's "window of vulnerability." The Soviets, they said, would soon be able to destroy all of America's land-based missiles in a first strike. Popularizations of the consequent dangers frequently ignored the rest of the American triad—the submarine-based missiles and the huge bomber force. In both areas the United States remained superior to the Soviets.[2] Nevertheless, the Carter administration felt constrained to restore the balance in land-based forces; it proposed the giant MX missile, which Nixon had tried to have built earlier. Despite its huge size, the MX was mobile. Carter's scheme called for moving the missiles around a gigantic maze of subterranean tunnels and launching sites, meant to frustrate a Soviet first strike. The plan, scheduled to take up a large portion of the state of Utah, met stiff opposition in Congress and was never carried out.[3] Meanwhile, Carter delayed submitting the SALT II Treaty to the Senate.[4]

In Europe, uneasiness about the intercontinental strategic military balance revived the usual fears about American decoupling. The Soviets, moreover, paralleled their intercontinental buildup with a rapid increase in the number of new intermediate-range nuclear missiles (SS-20s) aimed at Western Europe. German Chancellor Helmut Schmidt began pressing the Americans to counter by deploying in Europe some intermediate-range missiles of their own.[5] As the Americans reluctantly agreed, European public opinion remembered old fears about Europe's being dragged into a nuclear war over superpower conflict elsewhere or being the battleground because the superpowers would not dare to attack each other's home territories.

Carter's growing reputation for impetuous diplomacy fed these fears. Long-dormant peace movements began stirring in Northern Europe, most importantly in Germany and Britain. NATO governments began to wonder whether they could go through with deployment.[6] At the very least, they wished to appease their various national publics by prior Soviet-American negotiations to demonstrate Western good faith.

NATO's attempt to resolve the situation, the so-called Two-Track Decision of 1979, proposed negotiations, combined with a firm schedule for initiating deployment should the negotiations fail.[7] The deadline was set for the end of 1983. By then, the Reagan administration was in its third year, and the Euromissile question had ballooned into a serious political crisis in Europe with significant reverberations in the United States. America's deteriorating strategic superiority revived the traditional transatlantic conflicts inherent in America's extended nuclear protectorate for Europe. As Europeans resurrected their traditional worry about superpower nuclear confrontation confined to Europe, dissident strategic experts in America, concerned over an unwanted nuclear escalation originating in Europe, began calling for a NATO "No First Use" policy. Instead of relying on nuclear weapons, they argued, NATO should develop a credible conventional deterrent.

Establishing such a credible conventional alternative, however, seemed further away in the late 1970s than ever before. NATO's manpower remained well below the level needed to avoid a quick resort to nuclear weapons.[8] The Carter administration had tried to lock NATO into a sustained strengthening of conventional forces, and in 1977 the allied governments pledged budgetary increases of at least 3 percent annually.[9] While most European governments stopped meeting the target after the deep recession of 1980, NATO's conventional defense continued to receive greater attention from all parties. Indeed, European armies had been developing new conventional tactics and organization throughout the 1970s.[10] In due course, the American army began to stir. By the late 1970s the SACEUR, General Bernard Rogers, was promoting a new tactical doctrine, the Air-Land Battle, designed to create a conventional deterrent around new non-nuclear weapons, including missiles that would strike behind the front and disrupt an enemy attack.[11]

NATO's increased attention to conventional forces fed a new round of transatlantic recriminations over arms procurement. Americans deplored the alliance's lack of standardized equipment; Europeans deplored America's unwillingness to buy their weapons. The Carter administration tried to promote both standardization of weapons and more equitable procurement. These familiar goals faced familiar difficulties. Neither Congress nor the Pentagon was eager to buy European equipment, and European governments had no intention of abandoning their armaments industries. The furor did, at least, appear to prompt a certain intensification of joint European efforts.[12]

While Carter's initiatives may have helped reverse the alliance's military decline, political relations between Europe and America continued to deteriorate. Transatlantic friction grew partly from military issues but was greatly intensified by parallel diplomatic and economic developments. The administration's turnaround in security policy was hastened by the rapid disintegration of Kissinger's earlier diplomatic edifice. In Carter's hands, both surrogates and détente proved weak supports for holding up America's declining world position.

The disintegration took a particularly dramatic form in the Middle East, the scene of so many of Kissinger's triumphs only a few years before. In 1978 Carter capped Kissinger's Arab-Israeli peace process with the Camp David settlement between Israel and Egypt. However, it gradually became apparent that no accord on the West Bank would follow. Apart from the usual Arab intransigence and disunity, the Israeli government's annexationist policy made a Palestinian settlement impossible to negotiate. American diplomacy produced an endless succession of plans with all the familiar rodomontade of shuttle diplomacy and White House meetings—with few results.[13]

The reality of the violent revolution in Iran in 1979 could not be ignored either. Kissinger's prize surrogate was swept away on a populist upheaval that revealed the depths of frustration and anger at Western predominance and modernization. The United States became the focus of a century of Persian resentment. The cruel drama of the American hostages acted out the hatred and left the United States painfully exposed and powerless. Although sympathetic, few European policymakers admired Carter's handling of the hostage crisis. Moreover, European governments were reluctant to join in severe sanctions against Iran. They found it prudent to keep communications open with the new regime and its sympathizers elsewhere. To do otherwise, they feared, would sweep away Europe's influence together with America's, to the possible advantage only of the Russians.[14]

Iran's bloody revolution was terrifying to its fellow surrogate, Saudi Arabia, and to the rich and vulnerable Gulf States, all traditional regimes who supplied vital oil to Western Europe. Iran, already armed to the teeth by the Americans, seemed a serious military threat to them. Neither the United States nor anyone else in the West had a deployable military force on such a large scale. Ironically, the principal obstacle to Iranian expansion proved to be Iraq—a revolutionary regime, armed and cultivated by the Soviet Union and France and hostile to the United States.[15]

In late 1979 the Soviet Union invaded Afghanistan, a step that further inflamed American apprehensions. But it also enabled American policy to resolve the baffling complexities of domestic Middle Eastern politics into the familiar patterns of the Cold War. The Carter administration professed to see the invasion as the first step toward Soviet domination of the Persian Gulf. The president declared himself brutally disillusioned with détente.[16] Heavy economic sanctions followed, including cancellation of the Soviet-American grain contract. The administration dropped any pretense of trying to get the Senate to ratify the SALT II Treaty. Instead, apparently acknowledging the window of vulnerability, Carter pressed for the new MX missile. Plans for conventional rearmament accelerated, especially for a Third World Rapid Deployment Force. The "Carter Doctrine" proclaimed a new American protectorate for its allies around the Persian Gulf. In short, a new American security cycle was launched.[17]

After all the fears about American weakness, Europe welcomed Carter's rearmament. His diplomacy, however, filled many Europeans with dismay. It seemed to combine simplistic principles and confused perceptions with a disquieting propensity for mercurial and unmeasured reactions. European governments, even though they deplored the Afghan invasion, nevertheless saw it as a defensive Soviet move to preserve its traditional ascendancy in Afghanistan itself rather than as a first step toward dominating the Persian Gulf. Western policy, they believed, should maximize Soviet costs within the region: arms should make their way to the rebels, and Moslem outrage and fear should be exploited. The invasion might provide a golden chance to rebuild relations with revolutionary Iran.

But Europeans thought the wider-scale American reaction to Afghanistan disproportionate and self-defeating.[18] Denouncing détente and imposing broad sanctions against the Soviets threatened to escalate a regional conflict of slight relevance to NATO interests into a major confrontation endangering political and economic stability in Europe itself. The costs seemed incommensurate with any conceivable gain. Europe, not America, would pay the principal economic price for anti-Soviet trade sanctions, and a serious deterioration of pan-European political relations could bring Europe's physical security into question. Wiser diplomacy, Europeans believed, would seek to contain the crisis rather than spread it to other regions. Above all, it should not be allowed to spread to Europe itself.

In this mood, Europeans began to have substantial reservations about Carter's new Rapid Deployment Force. The administration was suggesting an increase in European forces within NATO in order to free American troops for a new role in the Middle East. Europeans were diffident about any such division of labor, or the close identification with American Middle Eastern policy it implied.[19] Thus, Americans who found themselves humiliated by their weakness in the Third World and criticized for being unable to protect vital Western interests there, also found Europeans uncooperative about strengthening the American position.

Behind this exasperating situation lay not only Europe's traditional "freeloading" but also its skeptical view of American Third World policy and its particular disapproval and jealousy of the U.S. position in the Middle East. Europeans had little confidence that American policy would preserve their global interests. They much preferred to cultivate their own relations, often by emphasizing their differences with the United States. The prospect of a mobile American military force, using European bases for quick drops into Middle Eastern or African trouble spots, did not reassure them. Where military intervention might still be effective, as in Africa, they preferred to do it themselves. If they still relied on American security to counter the Soviets—in the Middle East as in Europe itself—they sometimes seemed to prefer a Soviet-American rivalry closely enough balanced to permit European fine tuning. Such a view, needless to say, did not endear European governments to the Carter administration.

By Carter's last year in office, the principal occasion for transatlantic diplomatic conflict had moved to Europe itself. Poland seemed on the verge of a populist revolution. Solidarity, the Polish workers movement, had translated deep popular discontent into demands for far-reaching economic and political reform, but Soviet pressures combined with the Polish military to repress further liberalization. The Americans again turned to economic sanctions, for Poland had become increasingly dependent on the economic relationships of détente. By jeopardizing these relations, the United States intended to force the Soviet and Polish Communists to permit liberal reform.[20]

European governments grew uneasy. Although popular outrage at the suppression of Solidarity was widespread, American policies seemed too extreme, volatile, and public to be effective. Partisans of détente, particularly in Germany, believed nothing was to be gained by abandoning the process of bridge-building to the East. Solidarity, moreover, was insisting on truly revolutionary changes—workers' control of factories, for example—that would have been firmly resisted even in Social Democratic Western Europe, not to mention capitalist America. That so militant a mass movement could arise was perhaps a tribute to the efficacy of European-style détente, but it was also a warning of its dangers. Long-run success depended on not alarming the Soviets with changes too abrupt for political and social stability in Eastern Europe or in the Soviet Union itself.

True friends of freedom, it was felt, would caution rather than incite the Polish reformers. The West should offer steady but gentle attractions, while stressing the inevitability of setbacks and bitter disappointments in the quest for economic, social, and political change. While it was important to show sympathy with the struggling Poles, foreign politicians were not to inflame the situation so that violent repression became inevitable. If the West openly exploited Poland's anti-Soviet feeling, it would only discredit the process of détente that had nourished Poland's fragile reflowering of liberty. Above all, domestic reform in Eastern Europe should never be linked with a challenge to Soviet military hegemony.[21] In short, a successful détente policy took steadiness and a clear head, two qualities Europeans could not find in Carter's diplomacy.

Between Carter's diplomacy and such European views, serious friction was inevitable. Prodded by the Americans, NATO adopted a series of threats to retaliate against Polish repression. Nevertheless, when martial law was imposed, European enforcement of sanctions was highly selective. Americans grew disgusted with European "spinelessness" while Europeans grew alarmed at America's "crude posturing." Behind these different reactions lay a growing divergence in geopolitical interests in détente. America, caught up in its own cyclical rhythm, was dropping détente and turning sharply to rearmament and confrontation. As de Gaulle had foreshadowed in the 1960s, Europe was following a different path.

General European disapproval of American diplomacy was paralleled by an almost universal European disdain for American economic policy. European discontent in this sphere was hardly new. In economics, as in defense and diplomacy, Carter inherited Nixon's policies as they were approaching bankruptcy. Here too, as it happened, Carter set the new course for the 1980s. The next chapter focuses on these economic questions, but it is important to remember them at this point in the discussion as they were part of the general atmosphere of acrimonious transatlantic disillusionment.

By the time Carter left office, he had revised most of the broad military, diplomatic, and economic initiatives of the Nixon years. Unfortunately, his changes struck the public as insufficient, tardy, vacillating, and amateurish. Carter's style seemed to reflect all too faithfully the weak position he had inherited. The popular reaction forced him from office before his changes could reap their own reward. There was arguably a certain rough justice in his fate. Carter came to office as the beneficiary of Nixon's mistakes at home; he left it as the scapegoat for Nixon's mistakes abroad.

Ronald Reagan assumed the presidency with a pledge to restore America's global might and to halt its domestic inflation. The intellectuals of the New Right promised a Reagan revolution in both security and economics. Unfortunately, the two revolutions had contradictory aims. While economic and strategic conservatives shared certain common dislikes, their goals proved difficult to reconcile. No lasting formula could be found to combine opposition to a big free-spending government with dedication to strategic superiority and global hegemony, a contradiction that went back to the days of Taft and Eisenhower. When Reagan actually had to decide, the empire won out over the economy. As a result, Reagan parlayed Carter's rearmament into a carnival of indiscriminate military spending, which brought out all the more clearly the fundamental vulnerabilities in America's geopolitical position—above all, those that stemmed from continuing to offer extended deterrence for Western Europe.

Within four years, President Reagan had increased American defense spending in real terms by roughly one-third. The buildup in arms took place, however, without any notable increase in military manpower. No attempt was made to restore the draft; the emphasis was on new weapons. Like Eisenhower, Reagan turned to technology rather than manpower. But this time the policy could scarcely be described as hegemony on the cheap. The Pentagon displayed an astonishing escalation in the cost and complexity of American military technology.[22] Most striking was the gargantuan growth of the surface navy, which included building or restoring huge surface ships long thought obsolete. A rejuvenated navy was supposed to give the United States much greater ability both to intervene globally and to protect the sea lanes in any prolonged European war.[23]

By contrast, Reagan's early steps in the strategic nuclear sphere were more cautious than might have been expected, given the administration's worries about arms control and the window of vulnerability, and its general restiveness over the Mutual Assured Destruction of traditional deterrence theory. The administration honored the much-maligned SALT II agreement, and while Reagan resuscitated the campaign for the MX missile, his proposals greatly reduced Carter's number of missiles and dropped his idea of tunnels.[24] With congressional opposition to the MX still strong, Reagan sent the issue to a commission headed by President Ford's national security adviser, retired General Brent Scowcroft. Its report deprecated the argument of a window of vulnerability and constituted, in effect, a reaffirmation of traditional deterrence theory. America's nuclear deterrent, it noted, was a triad. Destroying one leg, even if theoretically possible, would not deprive the United States of its capacity to devastate the Soviet Union many times over. The commission's suggestions were for a much reduced MX deployment, essentially a bargaining chip to be negotiated away for Soviet concessions. For the longer term, it recommended a much smaller and more portable missile with a single warhead—the logical solution, the commission believed, to the vulnerability of land-based missiles.[25]

The Scowcroft report was as conventional as it was sensible. After an electoral campaign so critical of the standing strategic doctrine, its acceptance by the administration appeared a welcome if surprising dénouement. By endorsing the commission's report, the administration seemed to be accepting the fact that strategic parity was unavoidable. Reagan's more radical strategic bent did not emerge until 1983, halfway through his first term, when he called for a new "Strategic Defense Initiative" (SDI). It would involve an antimissile defense in space that, if completely successful, would restore American strategic invulnerability.

Meanwhile, the administration had also been pursuing its ideas about limited nuclear wars, which it believed were increasingly probable. The war envisaged was a limited regional conflict involving the combined use of conventional and nuclear forces. The administration seemed to believe such wars could be waged successfully, given effective strategy and careful preparation, and that the United States was consequently obligated to prepare a nuclear war-fighting capability. Some sense of this was expressed earlier by the Carter Pentagon, but with nothing like the same determination.[26]

While planners often imagined these limited wars escalating into precisely limited, "surgical" nuclear exchanges between the United States and the Soviet Union, a view made popular by advocates of the window-of-vulnerability thesis, the whole concept seemed to apply most plausibly to a superpower struggle over some external region, like the Middle East. In effect, nuclear war-fighting doctrines were an effort to flesh out an actual scenario for making good on a pledge of extended deterrence, but with a less than all-out strategic war. Focusing public attention on these questions—given Reagan's massive buildup, deteriorating superpower relations, and the impending missile deployment—naturally had important reverberations in Europe, where Reagan had inherited NATO's Two-Track Decision of 1979. By 1983 the Soviet-American arms-control negotiations were stalling, and this development meant meeting the year-end deadline for deployment. Linking the emplacement of new weapons to a confusing and probably unmanageable set of arms-control negotiations for the European theater began to seem a serious political error. Missile deployment required approval of the host parliaments, and major domestic political battles were shaping up in several European countries. Worse, the Germans, having initially requested U.S. missiles, decided not to receive them unless joined by three other NATO partners.[27]

Fear of nuclear war ignited throughout Europe, and neutralism, often linked to vigorous new environmentalist movements, grew into a significant political force in several countries.[28] Soviet propaganda played its role, but the most effective material for the antinuclear campaign seemed to come from the loose-talking Reagan administration itself. Reagan's extravagant anti-Soviet rhetoric, which was thought to have deeply offended Soviet leaders, thoroughly alarmed the jittery Western Europeans. They noted the administration's massive arms buildup and bellicose tone and concluded it was callous to the horrors of nuclear war, not serious about arms talks, and spoiling for a fight all over the globe.

As the administration began to feel the cost of its rhetorical self-indulgence—traditional in the right-wing American circles from which it had sprung—its spokesmen grew more sensitive to the public's fears. By the election of 1984, Reagan was in the midst of a peace offensive of his own. This included his revolutionary Strategic Defense Initiative and the scheduling of comprehensive new arms talks for 1985. Apprehension was temporarily allayed, and by the end of 1984, NATO had begun to deploy American missiles in Europe.

Successfully carrying through the two-track decision of 1979 was, in fact, a great victory for the alliance and for the Reagan administration. The German general elections of 1983 proved decisive. Schmidt's coalition with the Free Democrats had disintegrated, and the CDU, which unequivocally favored the missiles, returned to power. The SPD, with Schmidt no longer its leader, had turned against deployment, and the issue became a major factor in the election. Fortunately, Soviet propaganda proved clumsy enough to remind the Germans of why they needed American arms in the first place. NATO received unexpectedly forceful support from France, with President Mitterrand addressing the Bundestag directly and urging deployment in the name of Franco-German solidarity. Nevertheless, the drift of the German Social Democrats into outright opposition to a NATO policy initiated by their own chancellor was a troublesome sign for the future.[29] The Peace Movement remained a formidable if protean force in several European countries.

The missile debate in Europe also had disquieting reverberations in America. Antinuclear sentiment had been aroused by the arms buildup and fanned by the same bellicose administration rhetoric.[30] But American and European critics were not necessarily on the same wavelength. The character of the debate on both sides revealed not only how unchanging the problems of extended deterrence were but also how they might be growing even more intractable. The debate, moreover, was important in understanding Reagan's more radical strategic initiatives.

Positions in the missile debate developed little that was unfamiliar on either side of the Atlantic. Analysts from the European peace movement feared American missiles because they seemed to imply a Soviet-American nuclear war confined to Europe, a fear reinforced by the Reagan Pentagon's apparent enthusiasm for limited nuclear wars. American critics fell into two broad categories: those like the Catholic bishops, who questioned the morality of nuclear deterrence itself, and those who accepted nuclear deterrence but questioned the wisdom of continuing to extend deterrence from America to Europe. For the latter group, European complaints that American missiles threatened Europe seemed an insolent inversion of the truth. The missiles were being deployed to couple Western Europe's defense with America's strategic deterrent. Rather than insulating the American continent from a European war, they acted as hair triggers ensuring that any European war would set off a general conflagration that included America. While deploying missiles may have substantially increased the credibility of America's extended deterrence for Europe, it also greatly increased the danger to the United States itself. The Soviet Union was unlikely to endure any nuclear attack on itself without retaliating against the United States directly.

These fears were spelled out in a widely publicized series of articles written by a distinguished group of American analysts: McGeorge Bundy, George Kennan, Robert McNamara, and Gerard Smith, all of whom had held high offices in previous administrations. The articles dwelled explicitly on the dangers presented to the United States by its European nuclear protectorate. American missiles were necessary in Europe, the authors argued, because the Europeans had never bothered to develop an adequate conventional defense of their own. In particular, NATO's inadequacies in conventional forces made the use of nuclear weapons almost mandatory in response to any Soviet thrust.

The authors suggested instead that if Europeans were worried about American missiles precipitating a nuclear war in Europe, NATO should adopt a No-First-Use strategy wherein nuclear weapons would be used only in retaliation to a Soviet nuclear attack.[31] Europeans could then be certain that the Americans would not start a nuclear war in Europe. For such a strategy to succeed, however, the alliance needed to build an adequate conventional defense so that the American nuclear deterrent would no longer have to substitute for an insufficient NATO army. This course would increase American as well as European security, since the United

States would not be forced into a nuclear war as the only alternative to an otherwise inevitable European conventional defeat.

The idea may have been timely, but it was hardly new. European governments had opposed it since the early days of flexible response. They had always preferred to rely on NATO's nuclear strategy rather than find the resources for a conventional balance. Within the logic of this position, as superpower parity began to sap the credibility of America's extended nuclear deterrence, Europe should have acquired an independent nuclear deterrent of its own. But European governments never seriously confronted the technical and political problems of a collective European nuclear force. Instead, Britain and France had developed national deterrents that initially acted more as triggers than as substitutes for the American deterrent. Even with a major upgrading planned for the 1990s, they would still be national forces; as such, they would not guarantee a nuclear cover to West Germany.

No-First-Use arguments raised the fundamental strategic and political issues that had bedeviled the alliance since *Sputnik*. Soviet-American arms talks were likely to raise the same questions in any event. The Soviets insisted that British and French nuclear forces could be counted in NATO's totals, while the British, and particularly the French, adamantly objected. Counting their forces together with the Americans would imply that one was substitutable for the other. As a practical matter, it would logically result in a formula where increased French or British nuclear forces would imply corresponding cuts in NATO's American nuclear forces. For obvious reasons, the British and French had no desire to be maneuvered into such a position. With each superpower sporting several thousand warheads, it seemed preposterous that their few hundred warheads should be singled out for urgent reduction.

The Anglo-French stance reflected their privileged position as selective users of American military strength as well as their reluctance to assume further responsibility for Europe's security. Even in the aborted Geneva talks of 1983, the Anglo-French position had roused considerable resentment among NATO governments and publics. If the status of their arsenals were ever to obstruct an otherwise desirable arms control agreement, the delicate fabric of transatlantic strategic compromise would, at the very least, be greatly strained.[32]

In retrospect, critics of nuclear deterrence may well have had a less significant impact on public opinion than on President Reagan. For eventually the most serious assault on traditional deterrence doctrine, as well as on NATO's traditional arrangements, came not from the peace movement, or the Soviets, but from the Reagan administration. Within less than a year after new American missiles began to be positioned in Europe, the president was pressing forward with his Strategic Defense Initiative, the implications of which constitute a revolution in strategic doctrine.

With SDI, the Reagan administration proposed using new technology to build a shield, partly in space, against missiles poised for attack. At a minimum, SDI promised to help protect American missiles—closing the window of vulnerability without adding new offensive weapons. At best, SDI would form a shield to protect American cities. Should such a comprehensive defense ever be developed, the president suggested, it could be given to the Soviets and used to cover Europe. In theory, the consequences would be a strategic revolution. Offensive nuclear weapons would become useless. With an absolute defense, nuclear deterrence would disappear.[33]

Reagan's initiative provoked a diffuse strategic debate in the United States and Europe and came to dominate negotiations with the Soviets. Much of the debate was highly speculative. Most people believed the "Star Wars" project would absorb incalculable expenditures, and many arms experts were deeply skeptical about its feasibility. The minimal program, improving defense of missile sites, could certainly be achieved technically. But Soviet counteractions, such as building more missiles or decoys, would probably prove relatively easy and far less costly than the defense itself. As for the maximum goal, nearly all experts discounted the probability of ever achieving an absolute civilian defense. Even if, by some unforeseeable technological twist, it proved feasible for the continental United States, it would never be feasible between Europe and the Soviet Union.[34]

Despite the skepticism of the experts—and formidable congressional opposition—some kind of program was bound to go forward. The administration was not proposing deployment, but research. Congress could not easily deny the funds, particularly since the Soviets had themselves been developing antiballistic systems as well as laser and space weapons.[35]

The existence of such a research program, its significance magnified by an apocalyptic debate launched by the president himself, posed serious problems for the Europeans as well as the Soviets. As Reagan's program went forward in a blaze of publicity, they could not ignore it. Insofar as it succeeded, the strategic balance would be affected and perhaps radically destabilized.

For the Soviets, keeping up with the Americans would mean huge new expenditures. For the Europeans, American offers of cooperative research carried numerous pitfalls. Failure to participate could mean being left out of technology that might be of great importance to civilian industrial development as well as to military prowess. Participation could mean becoming a subordinate part of the American military-industrial complex and permitting further American control over European technological trade. An obvious case existed for broad intra-European cooperation. France proposed Eureka, a European civilian counterpart to participation in SDI. Although the British, German, and Italian governments gave it strong rhetorical support, individual European countries and firms—unevenly developed in their capabilities and jealous of each other—often thought they might do better by striking a deal with the Americans. European governments would have great difficulty in maintaining a common front.[36]

However remote the prospects for SDI's success, its long-range strategic implications could hardly be ignored. Insofar as a U.S. strategic defense became more effective, the Americans would be regaining their old superiority. The Soviets would feel compelled to build more missiles and race ahead with their own strategic defense systems. The arms race would continue. Within the Reagan administration, one influential theory held that an accelerated technological arms race might strain the Soviet system to a breaking point.[37] Other analysts, however, cited the temptation for the Soviets to launch a preventive war if they found their position on a gravely deteriorating curve.

For the Europeans, the long-range strategic implications of SDI were scarcely less disquieting. For geographical reasons, strategic defense could never be as effective for Europe as, in theory, it might prove for the United States—or even for the Soviets vis-à-vis the United States. If the Soviets developed a strategic defense, the British and French deterrents might be devalued and Europe thus pressed to maintain a more plausible conventional balance, a policy European governments had long resisted. In general, U.S. allies were highly satisfied with the traditional deterrence doctrine. They believed no rational government, the Soviet Union included, would initiate a nuclear war. Without nuclear deterrence, Europeans believed their security would lose its moorings.

Reagan's SDI implied an end to that deterrence. It seemed ironic to the Europeans that they should be dealt this blow by the Americans, just as the traditional postwar deterrence doctrine was winning an overwhelming victory in getting European political systems to support the deployment of U.S. missiles. Deterrence doctrine, defending itself successfully from pacifism on the left, was suddenly ambushed from the right. Reagan's America was trying to regain a superiority that was unneeded and, ultimately, unattainable. As it unfolded, Reagan's rearmament, however well-intentioned, was beginning to seem a greater threat to Europe's security than the Soviet Union itself.[38]

Along with traditional and new differences over military strategy, European-American relations were strained as well by traditional and new differences over diplomatic policy. As the Reagan administration vastly augmented Carter's rearmament, it also proceeded more vigorously and systematically against all forms of détente. Whereas the Carter sanctions were specific reactions to specific events, Reagan adopted a consistent and relentless opposition to détente in all its forms. The administration was particularly concerned about transfers of Western industrial technology, and powerful elements within the administration appeared committed to long-term economic warfare. Although control of technology was ostensibly designed to slow the development of sophisticated Soviet armaments, its broader aim seemed to be to stunt Soviet industrial development. As some administration experts argued publicly, if the Soviet politico-economic system were sufficiently threatened, the USSR might cease its perpetual global probing. Genuine détente could then follow: that is to say, détente based on Soviet renunciation.[39]

Such views were obviously incompatible with long-standing European diplomatic strategy. Europe's détente policy had been built on hopes that a gradual strengthening of economic and political relationships would break down the barriers between Europe's Soviet and Western halves. By the 1980s, the European governments had only modest expectations. Under the best of circumstances, normalizing relations with the Soviet sphere would take a long time and doubtless suffer many reverses. Despite rhetorical differences, European leaders, analysts, and publics all seemed to have reached a broad consensus. Détente was still Europe's only sensible policy. While it had to be pursued with prudent regard both for Europe's military balance and for the Soviet Union's limited flexibility, détente had already brought about some significant changes in the East and could not be abandoned.

Such divergent European and American perspectives made it difficult for the alliance to reconcile the technology issue. Whereas the Europeans could not condone selling vital military technology to the Soviets, they were inclined to pursue economic interdependence for its own sake. Unusually generous financing had grown characteristic of much Eastern bloc trade, and many Eastern countries, notably Poland, Hungary, and Rumania, were highly overextended debtors to Western banks. Carter's insistence on trade sanctions over Soviet behavior in Afghanistan and Poland had already caused serious transatlantic friction.

In the early 1980s, a long-simmering dispute over the projected natural gas pipeline connecting several Western European countries and Siberia brought the Eastern trade issue to a head. Like so many other difficulties of the Reagan era, it began in the Carter administration. Europeans had agreed to finance the construction and to sign a long-term contract for the gas. Eventually the pipeline was to supply around 5 percent of Europe's energy. Europe would thus diversify its energy sources and reduce its dependence on the volatile Middle East. Since alternate sources could easily be found, the Soviets would not gain any serious leverage over Western economies and, in fact, would grow more dependent on them. Selling the gas would give them a stake in Western prosperity. More hard currency would translate into greater Western trade, thereby breaking down Soviet economic isolation and self-sufficiency. Conversely, in the depressed conditions of the early 1980s, the exports would be highly welcomed by Europe's beleaguered steel and capital goods industries. The project, moreover, was a step toward gaining access to the huge Siberian treasure house of raw materials.

The Reagan administration took a very different view. Hard currency from the gas would permit increased purchases of technology vital for military purposes. Instead of helping to squeeze the Soviets into submission, America's allies were giving concessionary financing to develop Soviet natural resources and prop up the decrepit economy. Western Europe's greatest asset, its economic strength, was serving not the common defense but the common enemy. Yet the Americans were expected to go on defending Western Europe.

To prevent the deal, the U.S. government tried to extend its regulatory authority to include European subsidiaries of American corporations, European companies manufacturing products under American licenses, and even European manufacturers using American components. European companies were blacklisted for honoring their contracts with Eastern Europe. These policies raised a hornet's nest of angry jurisdictional disputes. European governments were adamant about going ahead with the pipeline, and by 1984 the Americans had retreated. But the technology issue was still smoldering as the Pentagon kept pressing the allies and trying to extend its control.[40] This discord formed part of the background for the frictions over military procurement and cooperation for SDI.

Behind the technology and trade issues lay Europe's long-standing tendency to insulate economic and even diplomatic questions from security matters. The transatlantic compromise of the 1950s had permitted a hegemonic military relationship to coexist with a pluralistic economic relationship. By the 1960s the coexistence was already strained. The Europeans were asserting their independence in diplomacy, and the Americans were trying to reassert their hegemony in the economic sphere. While détente had soothed NATO's military conflicts in the 1970s, transatlantic conflicts had intensified over economic and Third World issues. The end of Soviet-American détente revived the old transatlantic quarrels over NATO's military arrangements and Europe's Soviet diplomacy—without, however, diminishing frictions over economic policy.

European-American differences over strategic and trade policies were supplemented, as usual, by differences over the Third World. Reagan's first term was spared the drama of Carter's various global crises, but the Third World nevertheless had high priority in the administration's military plans and diplomatic initiatives. Along with a vast buildup of conventional naval power, Reagan expanded Carter's plans for an amphibious and airborne Rapid Deployment Force. With such forces, it was contended, America's global role would no longer depend so much on surrogates as on its own military and naval power.

With the defense buildup came a renewed taste for intervention. American forces were sent to eject a Castroite revolutionary regime on the tiny Caribbean island of Grenada and to support a friendly government in Lebanon. Reagan accelerated Carter's shift from wary tolerance of Nicaragua's Sandinista regime to all but direct military intervention. As in the early days of the Vietnam conflict, American "advisers" were training local troops, and American weapons were abundantly available. The Central Intelligence Agency was reported to be busy with guerrilla campaigns and political intrigues. American naval and military forces promoted and joined large-scale regional exercises. Despite congressional critics and public hostility, the predilection for intervention was evident, and European governments openly disapproved.[41]

In the Middle East, Reagan witnessed the further collapse of America's long-standing but ill-conceived diplomatic initiatives.[42] A comprehensive Palestinian settlement more remote than ever, the United States was apparently unable to prevent Israel's 1982 invasion of Lebanon. Reagan then staked American prestige on establishing a national Lebanese government and arranging the mutual withdrawal of Israel and Syria. American marines arrived to encourage a truce and to supervise the expected withdrawals; British, French, and Italian contingents were induced to join the effort. Predictably, the initiative failed, and beleaguered Western forces withdrew with unseemly haste, the Americans leading the retreat.

The administration's enthusiasm for intervention again manifested itself when, in 1983, Libyan troops entered the neighboring state of Chad. The French had maintained an uneasy hegemony for nearly three decades, despite civil wars, numerous changes of regime, and several Libyan invasions. The United States professed to see the newest incursion as a Cold War challenge. American planes and ships were sent to the Libyan coast, along with highly publicized offers of full support for French intervention. The administration thought its pressure was needed to keep France from succumbing to the "European disease," in which case it would abandon Africa to chaos and the Soviets, leaving the United States with the burdens. In the French view, American pressure merely complicated a routine exercise in sorting out local factions, any of which were more or less acceptable. Chad was only one aspect of France's tangled relationship with Libya. The Americans suffered from a dangerous and counterproductive bias toward ideological oversimplification, public posturing, and premature force. The French reaction was widely shared among other Europeans, who generally found the Reagan approach to Third World problems unsympathetic and maladroit.

Such differences were hardly new but had grown more important as the Third World itself had grown more significant. While no great Third World crisis had tested Western solidarity during Reagan's first term, European-American cooperation seemed at a low ebb.

By the end of the Reagan administration's first term, the broad character of its foreign policy was already clear enough. The policy amounted to a forthright effort to rebuild and reassert American world power. Finding the consequences of hegemony on the cheap unacceptable, the administration astonished the world with its scale of military spending.

Reagan's attempts to reaffirm American hegemony have had, at best, highly ambiguous results. The administration has prided itself on regaining the international prestige that seemed to slip so badly during Carter's presidency. But prestige, particularly prestige based on power, is an elusive and intangible asset. If Reagan's

America gained new respect for its formidableness, it may also have made its enemies more numerous and determined. Whether the balance is favorable remains to be seen. Much probably depends on whether the power is ever tested in a serious way. In his first term, Reagan, unlike Carter, seemed remarkably lucky in avoiding those humiliating confrontations that reveal the impotence of even a superpower.

Reagan's second term has been less lucky. Sending the marines to Beirut was a fiasco. The meeting with the new Soviet leader, Mikhail Gorbachev, at Reykjavik revealed a radical volatility in American arms-control policy and shook confidence in Reagan's leadership at home and especially abroad. Subsequently, the Soviets have been able to use the arms-control negotiations at Geneva to exploit European-American strategic differences. The combination of diplomatic incompetence and domestic skulduggery revealed in the Iran-contra affair devalued Reagan's prestige still further.

No one can say what adventures lie in the future. Prestige aside, in any fundamental and long-term calculus, the actual fruits of Reagan's policies do not look very impressive. Rearmament has only marginally improved America's effective military power, while Reagan's strategic doctrine has threatened to intensify the arms race with the Soviets, and his arms-control diplomacy has threatened to give new life to old quarrels within the alliance.[43] All in all, it seems difficult to argue that Reagan's efforts to bolster a waning American primacy have made the international system fundamentally more stable. Instead, the requirements of continuing American hegemony seem, in themselves, to be increasingly destabilizing to the *Pax Americana*.

Any assessment of Reagan's effort grows still more disturbing when the economic aspect of the world system is taken into account. America's global and Eurasian military role has always had powerful indirect consequences for the international economy. The scale of Reagan's geopolitical reaffirmation has made those consequences clearer than ever before. For whatever its other military and geopolitical effects, Reagan's effort has cost a great deal of money. Financing the cost of hegemony was, in itself, threatening to make the international system unworkable. The means, in other words, were coming to devour the ends.

6

The Atlantic Alliance
and the World Economy

SINCE THE 1960s, the problems of America's extended geopolitical posture have found a ready parallel in the strains of its international economic position. The similarity is hardly surprising. The Atlantic military alliance and the global economic system are complementary parts of the same *Pax Americana* and often affect each other directly. Cycles in America's military spending have had major consequences for the world economy. The Truman and Kennedy-Johnson rearmaments, for example, each culminated with a worldwide inflationary boom, exacerbated by a war. Particular policies in one sphere often have a close parallel in the other. Kennedy's flexible-response strategy, which called for greater American control over European defense, had its parallel in his economic Grand Design, which pressed for greater transatlantic economic integration. Similarly, de Gaulle paired his anti-hegemonic policies in NATO with an attack on the dollar's role in the international monetary system. Curbing the dollar, the general hoped, would help keep American military power and geopolitical ambition within the limits he preferred. Success and failure in one sphere reverberate into the other. In the early days of the alliance, economic ties and military solidarity reinforced each other; in recent years, politico-military divergences and economic quarrels have compounded one another. But the alliance's economic stresses, perhaps even more than its political and military differences, have a cumulative as well as cyclical character.

At the heart of Europe's economic grievances lies the belief that the Americans have been manipulating the world economy for two decades in order to compensate for their own internal disorder. To Europeans, America's economy seems in a perpetual disequilibrium, the effects of which are regularly exported to the rest of the world. By the later 1970s, some knowledgeable European observers, not at all unfriendly to the alliance, were counting the effects of this exported disequilibrium a greater threat to Western solidarity than the Soviet Union itself. What is the nature of this American imbalance?

In economics, as in diplomacy and morals, equilibrium is a highly abstract concept. Indicators to measure it are correspondingly elusive. Internationally, a persistent balance-of-payments deficit seems the most obvious sign of fundamental disequilibrium. A country with a basic deficit, that is, a deficit on goods, services, and long-term investment, is, in effect, taking more from the world outside than it earns from it. To finance its deficit, such a country must use its own reserves or else attract foreign capital. When the country is no longer able to do either, impending bankruptcy forces a change in habits. It will no longer be able to take from abroad more than it provides.

In an ever-changing world, there can never be equilibrium all around. Not everyone can be in surplus or deficit at once, and nearly every country oscillates around equilibrium, according to the interaction of its own cycles, policies, and general stage of development with world conditions. A surplus or a deficit sets in motion a chain of reactions that leads toward its opposite. The United States, however, has managed to run a chronic basic balance-of-payments deficit since the end of World War II.[1] These deficits, originally welcomed in the interests of European and Japanese recovery, have continued unabated for nearly four decades—quite a remarkable record. No other developed country could have behaved in this fashion for as long. Only America's unique position in the postwar system has made such a perpetual imbalance possible. Thanks to its position, the United States has been able, directly or indirectly, to pass much of the burden of financing its deficits to the rest of the world economy. American policy, moreover, has grown utterly dependent on this international solution. Without it, the United States would have to change drastically its postwar mix of foreign and domestic policies.

While this American dependence on manipulating the international economy has existed at least since the 1960s, the method of doing so has changed significantly. Broadly speaking, American manipulation has employed three formulas: the Bretton Woods formula that lasted through the 1960s, the Nixon formula of the 1970s, and the Reagan formula of the 1980s. All three have depended on the dollar's position in the international monetary system. Exploring these formulas in technical detail cuts across a wide range of contentious economic issues, a task I have tried to take on in an earlier book, *The Imperious Economy*.[2] Here, a brief history may help illustrate how the economic formulas have worked.

The postwar monetary arrangements codified at the famous conference at Bretton Woods in 1944 were not fully in effect until European currencies became convertible in 1958.[3] Technically, the system was a gold-exchange standard, similar to the system that followed World War I, except that an International Monetary Fund was to manage the arrangements, in particular to provide credit and discipline for those countries experiencing a temporary deficit. The guiding rules were free convertibility of national currencies and stable, if occasionally adjustable, exchange rates. The dollar was the *numeraire*. Every other currency had a fixed value in relation to the dollar, a value that its government was supposed to defend and that could be changed only by agreement in the IMF. The dollar, in turn, was freely convertible both into other currencies and into a fixed amount of gold. The dollar was thus the fixed point against which other monies were measured. As seemed only natural under the circumstances, the dollar was the principal reserve currency held and used by foreign central banks to cover their external debts. It was also the principal currency for private international transactions and reserves. With such arrangements, the stability of the world monetary system was uniquely dependent on the stability of the dollar and, hence, on the economic conditions and policies of the United States.

It was presumably the duty of the United States to manage its economy so that the dollar kept a steady value. Since the United States had accumulated most of the world's gold, it also seemed rather important to provide enough dollars to finance the rest of the world's postwar recovery and steady growth thereafter. Politicians and economists regularly warned of a dollar gap that would throttle both.

As it happened, the American economy proved not at all reluctant to provide the liquidity the world demanded. United States balance-of-payments deficits have persisted since 1945. Initially, this flow had a salutary effect on the world economy. Marshall Plan aid helped Europe to rebuild. In the 1950s, continuing U.S. military and economic aid, heavy American private investment, and the growing American appetite for imports and tourism all helped stimulate and stabilize world prosperity and development.[4]

By the Kennedy-Johnson era of the 1960s, the American outflow began to seem excessive. The Bretton Woods system, based as it was on stable exchange rates and free convertibility, presumably never envisaged that any one country could run a balance-of-payments deficit regularly from one decade to the next. Technical and political factors made it possible for the United States to do so. The dollar's reserve-currency status meant that foreign countries were legally able to accumulate the exported dollars in their central banks. Since the United States was also their military protector, the allies felt constrained not to refuse.

For Europeans, the French in particular, the situation grew into a major grievance against the Americans. The accumulating dollar balances in the central banks of Europe and Japan were seen as little better than forced loans, sometimes to finance activities that many Europeans opposed, like the Vietnam War, or that even seemed directly inimical to their own interests, like the heavy influx of U.S. corporations. In short, the United States was seen to be abusing its position as a reserve-currency country.

The abuse seemed not only politically unjust but also economically damaging. According to de Gaulle's favorite economist, Jacques Rueff, American payments deficits were a relentless source of world inflation.[5] Thanks to the dollar's role in the gold-exchange standard, the gold standard's mechanisms of adjustment failed in the case of American deficits.

In the end, the world's currency markets did bring down the Bretton Woods system. Since it was a gold-exchange rather than a pure dollar standard, the dollars were supposed to be convertible into a fixed amount of gold and into foreign currencies at a fixed rate of exchange. As the American balance-of-payments deficit continued year after year, central banks increasingly demanded repayment, and American gold and foreign currency reserves dwindled in relation to American foreign obligations. Private holdings of expatriate dollars accumulated in an immense offshore or Eurodollar capital market. Speculation against the dollar grew more possible and more logical. Kennedy and Johnson both tried to control capital flows and to convince other countries to help defend the dollar's parity, and Johnson used heavy political pressure. But such efforts could not control the private currency market; in the end, the policies adopted were unable to save the dollar's fixed exchange rate. By 1971, Nixon had to float the dollar and then formally devalue it. As the dollar continued to fall, a further devaluation followed in 1973. Still the dollar could not be stabilized, and it continued to float downward through most of the 1970s. The United States could no longer sustain its hegemonic obligation to maintain a stable value for the dollar. A de facto floating-rate system had begun, not formally ratified until the Jamaica agreements of 1976.[6] By then, Bretton Woods was clearly dead, and the United States was well into a new formula for spreading its disequilibrium to the world.

The Kennedy and Johnson administrations had not wanted events to evolve this way. Both had desperately tried to reverse the dollar's growing weakness. Why had they failed?

The immediate cause seemed obvious enough. Neither administration had succeeded in controlling America's persistent balance-of-payments deficit. The United States, it was clear, was suffering from a basic payments disequilibrium vis-à-vis the world economy as a whole. Instead of the permanent dollar gap that had once been feared, there developed an apparently permanent dollar glut.

The causes were never firmly grasped, mainly because the most sensible explanation pointed to conclusions that were universally unwelcome. Two explanatory schools developed among policymakers. The first, popular in the 1960s, focused on particular items from the so-called basic balance of payments. This balance tried to measure only flows from the "real economy"—goods, services, and long-term investments—and thus ignored short-term capital flows. Such measurements invariably indicated that whereas American trade in goods and services was always in surplus, combined outflows for overseas U.S. military forces, aid, long-term corporate investment, and tourism regularly turned the balance into a deficit.[7] The payments deficit thus seemed essentially political. It was an imperial balance-of-payments deficit. Overseas government spending and even corporate investments could be counted the expenses of running a *Pax Americana*. The hegemon's overseas costs were not being met by its overseas income. Now that the European and Japanese allies had manifestly recovered, the obvious solution seemed some form of burden-sharing, as well as an end to any remaining discrimination against American products.

A second explanation for the weakening dollar came from monetarist economists, American and European. From their perspective, any analysis based on singling out particular items in the basic payments balance was economically illiterate. Instead, they argued, overall monetary conditions determined payments balances.[8] When a country had more expansive monetary conditions than the norm in the international system, its excess money tended to flow out as a payments deficit. The increasing internationalization of business, of capital markets in particular, lent weight to monetarist analysis. The dollar was actually brought down, for example, not by the inability to finance the relatively small basic balance-of-payments deficits, but by great waves of speculation in the currency markets.[9] These waves were financed from the enormous pool of dollars available in the Eurodollar capital market. Speculative movements of this sort had nothing directly to do with the American basic balance of payments but were movements of short-term capital, or "hot money," responding to international monetary conditions. They therefore required a monetary explanation.

According to the monetarist model, the United States ran a payments deficit because its monetary conditions were relatively abundant compared to the norm for other countries in the international system as a whole. To diminish the deficit, the U.S. money supply would have to diminish comparatively. While a money supply is an elusive concept whose measurement is difficult within one economy, let alone comparatively, the monetarist model nevertheless has always had great logical force. In effect, it held the United States to be more inflationary than the international norm. The payments deficit meant, logically, that the United States was creating money excessively in comparison to the growth of money elsewhere. But the dollar's international role ensured that America's domestic price inflation did not necessarily reach a rate higher than in the rest of the world. Instead, the

United States could export at least part of its surplus money supply. Instead of pushing up prices at home, that part flowed outward as a balance-of-payments deficit, swelling the money supplies of other countries and promoting price inflation abroad.

Why, however, was American monetary policy so expansive—too expansive, in the end, to be compatible with a stable dollar?[10] American monetarists tended to suggest incompetence at the Federal Reserve, or the Fed's lack of institutional and political support. More fundamentally, they blamed neo-Keynesian growth policies that kept the economy stimulated beyond what they called its natural level of unemployment. Foreign monetarist critics, the French particularly, also saw the United States overstretched in its overseas ambitions, as well as tempted into over-extension by an international monetary system that permitted the dollar too much leeway. In strict economic logic, American overextension could not be attributed to either external or internal policies and aims, but rather to their combination. Somehow, America's combined goals were too great for its available resources.

Relating an external disequilibrium to excessive political goals requires looking beyond the balance-of-payments deficit to the country's overall macroeconomic conditions and, in particular, to the role of government in shaping those conditions. The government not only tries to shape monetary conditions but is itself a very large consumer. In other words, alongside monetary policy there is fiscal policy. And aside from a perennial payments deficit, a perennial fiscal deficit seems an obvious symptom of overstretching and general disequilibrium. Starting in 1961, an unbroken string of federal fiscal deficits ran through the boom years of the 1960s until 1969, resumed without interruption through the 1970s, and is certainly fated to continue at least through the 1980s. Each decade, moreover, seemed to bring a quantum jump to the size of the average deficit.[11]

It seems scarcely accidental that this string of fiscal deficits first grew up in tandem with the Kennedy-Johnson cycle of rearmament, combined as it was with their equally ambitious program to develop America's human resources. Nor was it accidental that the dollar's external difficulties first grew serious as the rearmament cycle and the Great Society began to gather momentum.

Kennedy and Johnson were able to win domestic support for their ambitious goals because, while reasserting NSC-68's military posture, they also adopted its congenial neo-Keynesian fiscal principles. The unbalanced fiscal policy of the 1960s could not, of course, be blamed on military and space spending alone. The upgraded domestic program proved even more costly. Logically, it was the combination that fueled the great increases in federal spending. The fiscal deficit, moreover, could not be blamed only on increased spending. The proportion of federal taxes to the gross domestic product had also dropped. Thus, according to the analyst's vantage point and policy preferences, deficits could be blamed on military or civilian spending, insufficient taxes, or, indeed, insufficient overall growth of the economy.[12]

In any event, peacetime fiscal deficits were scarcely novel. Since Roosevelt's time, successive administrations had regarded Keynesian counter-cyclical deficits as inevitable and beneficial during a recession. Eisenhower had countenanced record deficits during the recessions of the 1950s.[13] The Kennedy administration, however, greatly expanded the range of economic conditions in which deficits were regarded as legitimate. The neo-Keynesian arguments justifying full-employment budgets were officially adopted and promoted.[14] Fiscal deficits were thereby justified whenever the economy was working at anything less than full capacity. If sufficiently appealing new expenditures could not be found, taxes were to be cut. Kennedy proposed the first full-employment tax cut in 1963, and Congress passed it in 1964, soon after Johnson came into office. The shift in doctrine and practice marked a new phase of American fiscal policy; deficits grew more severe in relation to their general economic context.

Fiscal deficits, of course, need not result in inflation, unless monetary policy also expands to finance or accommodate the deficit. Instead of loosening money and credit in the face of a deficit, central banks can hold steady. Under such conditions, the government bids in the capital market against private borrowers for the extra credit it needs. The government's deficits are then financed by real savings rather than by newly created money. The consequence is not inflation, but high real interest rates that may crowd out investments from the market and dampen economic growth. High interest rates may also encourage a higher level of domestic saving, or an inflow of foreign savings. In any event, so long as monetary policy remains firm, no inflation need follow. Any such sustained tight monetary policy, familiar by the 1980s, was, however, nearly unthinkable in the political and economic conditions of the Kennedy administration. When, for example, the Federal Reserve did begin tightening monetary conditions in 1966, both Congress and the Johnson administration vociferously objected.

Monetary stability was not high on the agenda of the 1960s. Kennedy arrived in office with an ambitious set of domestic and foreign programs. He realized that the resources for these programs could be found only in a period of rapid growth. His gradual conversion to neo-Keynesian growth policies followed. Kennedy was already convinced that the United States had been asleep in the Eisenhower era, its economy stunted, he believed, by a pusillanimous conservatism. As a result of America's slow growth, its industry was losing competitiveness, long-needed domestic programs were blocked, racial conflict was threatening, military superiority had been allowed to decline, and development in the Third World had been left to languish.

A full-employment fiscal policy, the neo-Keynesians promised, could easily achieve the growth needed to reverse this decline. More inflation might result, but, as the Phillips Curve indicated, moderate inflation could be traded for more rapid growth and higher employment. Tight monetary policy, however, would frustrate such a growth policy. Sustained monetary stringency thus seemed intellectually and politically unacceptable, even after high employment was actually reached and the Vietnam War was adding substantially to the federal deficit. As a result, both Kennedy and Johnson opposed using tight money to save the dollar. Its defense was left instead to various ad hoc policies, such as temporary capital controls or taxes designed to insulate domestic monetary conditions from the world capital market.

The first major reversal came in 1968. The progress of American inflation had seemed so alarming that Johnson and Congress finally accepted a tax increase. Fiscal 1969 is, consequently, the only year after 1960 when the federal government did not run a deficit. Meanwhile, the Federal Reserve finally nerved itself to sustain tight money. With fiscal and monetary tightening thus abruptly combined, inflation turned to stagflation. As Richard Nixon came to power in January 1969, the country was heading into its most serious recession since the Second World War.[15]

Recession did help to bolster the dollar. But tight money, higher taxes, and severe recession were unpopular with the voting public, and the 1970 congressional elections registered a sharp defeat for the Republicans. Nixon and the Federal Reserve had already begun to foster a reflation. By the spring of 1971, the dollar was again in crisis. Pressure built up until, on August 15, Nixon officially suspended the dollar's convertibility. Nixon also imposed a substantial surcharge on imports and froze domestic wages and prices. By December of 1971, America's "affluent allies" had formally accepted a dollar devaluation. Bretton Woods might thereby be resurrected, they hoped, and the new dollar parity defended successfully.

The administration followed a different policy. Seconded by the Federal Reserve, Nixon pushed a vigorous economic expansion through his successful bid for reelection in 1972.[16] Victory was celebrated by dismantling not only wage and price controls, but also the capital controls left over from the Johnson administration. As Nixon's boom continued, the dollar's new parity began slipping. The administration had no serious intent to defend it. A second official devaluation followed in 1973. Bretton Woods had clearly broken down. With floating rates, the United States had found a new formula for financing its disequilibrium.

The new Nixon formula proved highly successful both in relieving the more egregious problems of the old Bretton Woods system and in permitting the United States to continue to run regular balance-of-payments and fiscal deficits.[17] Under fixed exchange rates, America's habitual inflation had become a twin disability. It had pushed prices of domestically produced goods higher in relation to foreign goods, and it had encouraged American capital to go abroad rather than to invest in modernizing production at home. By the late 1960s, the American trade balance was turning sharply negative for the first time since the nineteenth century. Protectionist pressure from domestic-based industries and their labor unions was growing unmanageable. At the same time, internationally oriented business—multinational corporations and banks—chafed at the capital controls made necessary by the U.S. defense of the inflated dollar's parity.

A floating dollar pleased both groups. With the dollar depreciating substantially and repeatedly, domestically produced goods grew more competitive. Exports in certain key industries, like capital goods, enjoyed remarkable rejuvenation. Pressure for protection subsided. Floating also permitted an end to capital controls, which made managing multinational enterprises easier and effectively fused the domestic and international capital markets. American banks profited greatly as their international earnings grew rapidly and began to equal their domestic business.

Nixon's success was not entirely fortuitous or unplanned. The transformation to floating had been anticipated with an elaborate rationale. By the later 1960s, declining American trade had provoked great disquiet in thoughtful industrial and academic circles.[18] Europe and Japan seemed to be surpassing the United States in industrial competitiveness. Out of this anxiety came a systematic American case against its rich allies, the counterpart to Europe's complaints about America's exported inflation.

This case rested on the assumptions that America's declining competitive position should be blamed on an overvalued dollar, and that the overvalued dollar, in turn, should be blamed on the Bretton Woods monetary arrangements. In this view, a weakening dollar was entirely predictable and not America's fault. It had come about because early in the postwar era the United States had generously permitted its war-devastated competitors to peg their currencies at an undervalued level. Several had managed to devalue their currencies still further. After their recovery, they refused to make the obvious adjustment. The Bretton Woods rules imposed no sanctions to force the rich allies to revalue but made it theoretically impossible for the dollar to devalue. Under such circumstances, American analysts concluded, the United States had no obligation to defend the dollar's distorted exchange rate. Instead, these experts argued, the United States should adopt an attitude of benign neglect. If the needed parity changes could not be negotiated voluntarily, the market, left to its own devices, would eventually bring currencies into a more reasonable relationship. If Bretton Woods collapsed, the fault would lie with America's rich allies, who had proved too irresponsible to share the burden of managing a fixed-rate system.[19]

Benign neglect carried overtones of a broader political case. American analysts began to see the United States being exploited by its own allies. Europeans and Japanese were not only mercantilist chiselers, squeezing commercial advantage by refusing to adjust an outmoded monetary system, but also free riders enjoying cheap military security at America's expense.[20] Nixon's secretary of the treasury, John Connally, pointedly observed how America's basic balance-of-payments deficit tended to approximate, year after year, the exchange costs of American troops stationed overseas, mostly in Western Europe.[21] As an economic explanation for the payments deficit it may have been shaky, but its political logic was all too clear. Taken in a larger framework, moreover, Connally's economic point was more than plausible. Thanks to its protector's role, the United States did carry a much heavier military burden than those rich allies who were also America's major economic competitors. That extra military burden could not easily be ignored in explaining America's fiscal imbalance, its relatively expansive monetary climate, and the dollar's consequent chronic weakness.[22] In effect, item-by-item explanations for the payments deficit, which tended to focus on America's imperial costs, and monetarist explanations, which emphasized inflation, could easily be merged. Together they provide a comprehensive and convincing, if unwelcome, rationale for the dollar's weakness. Imperial costs, combined with the nascent welfare state, promoted an unbalanced fiscal policy and a too-expansive monetary policy: hence, the weak dollar.

The same explanation, however, also makes clear why floating rates were unlikely, in themselves, to cure the dollar's instability. For if the comprehensive imperial-monetarist analysis is correct, the dollar's problem was not merely a historical mal-adjustment of parity, brought on by European and Japanese recovery, but rather a fundamental and continuing American disequilibrium, brought on by the cost of America's combined foreign and domestic objectives. So long as the United States could not find the resources to finance those objectives without inflationary fiscal and monetary policies, American monetary conditions were likely to remain looser than those in Europe or Japan. As a result, no once-and-for-all adjustment of the dollar's parity could, in itself, cure America's disequilibrium—or the dollar's weakness, which was its consequence. With floating rates, repeated depreciation would be the dollar's normal state, interrupted by exceptional periods of domestic monetary and fiscal stringency but resuming whenever the economy returned to expansion, as in 1971. In short, Nixon's formula—domestic expansion and floating rates— meant not merely one or two belated adjustments of a distorted parity, but repeated depreciation and perpetual instability.

The Nixon administration would doubtless have preferred a more genuine cure for America's disequilibrium. Even while trying to promote a boom for 1972, the administration also sought to cut government spending, arms spending in particular. Nixon and Kissinger's elaborate diplomacy of détente and surrogates was designed, among other things, to find a way to back off safely from the budgetary costs of the Kennedy-Johnson rearmament. But while U.S. military expenditures did fall in the wake of Vietnam, the rapid growth of domestic social services more than offset that decline. Johnson's Great Society had developed momentum of its own. Consequently, the Nixon administration managed only a change in the mix of military and civilian expenditures rather than a drop in the overall total.[23]

What is more, Nixon's foreign policy almost ensured that his reductions in military spending would prove only temporary. Cuts in military means were not accompanied by any genuine reduction in broad geopolitical commitments. As a result, the American military grew more and more overstretched, a situation greatly aggravated by the switch to a volunteer army in 1973. This lack of equipoise between commitments and forces was bound to prove unstable, despite the apparent success of Soviet-American détente. Once détente faltered, a strong rebound in military spending was predictable. But even while détente flourished, no administration was able to achieve fiscal equilibrium, thanks to the sharp growth in civilian expenditures. The Ford and Carter administrations continued to witness a depreciating dollar.

The Nixon formula of expansion and depreciation was far more popular at home than abroad.[24] With the collapse of the Bretton Woods formula, it was simply a new way of passing to the world economy the consequences of America's own domestic disequilibrium. For Europeans and Japanese, the Nixon solution posed a serious dilemma between unemployment and inflation. As the dollar fell, their products would grow increasingly less competitive. This, they reasoned, would mean higher unemployment and lower investment in their export industries—a sector far more vital to them than to the United States. If, to avoid these trends, they supported the dollar in currency markets (dirty floating), or otherwise kept pace with American monetary expansion, they risked an inflation that would also undermine their competitiveness and upset their social order.

As the years passed, the unfavorable consequences of the Nixon formula began to be felt strongly at home as well as abroad. Renouncing the obligation to defend the dollar's parity did more than pass on the effects of American inflation; it removed a major barrier against further price augmentation. As inflation mounted precipitously after 1971, the consequences, exacerbated by volatile shifts in Federal Reserve policy, eventually produced a severe recession in 1974. A return to the Nixon formula of reflation and depreciation in the Ford-Carter period brought on even greater inflation in the later 1970s and a still more severe recession in 1980.

As the cyclical oscillations grew worse at home, their effects worsened abroad. The year 1973 saw record price inflation worldwide, much of it exported by an ebulliently expansive American economy.[25] Global inflation naturally had unsettling effects on world commodity prices. Food prices skyrocketed throughout the year, and by the year's end, OPEC was able to engineer an astonishing fourfold increase in oil prices. Much of the subsequent monetary disorder of the 1970s has been blamed on these food and oil shocks. In retrospect, however, such shocks seem not merely exogenous events but also reflections of long- and short-term world economic and political conditions, which American economic policy did much to determine and often to magnify.[26]

The oil price shock, for example, is often blamed for the severe recession of 1974. But in the United States that recession was under way months before the effects of the higher oil prices could be felt. It was a highly exaggerated cyclical downturn, reflecting, above all, the reaction to the inflationary excesses of Nixon's election boom.[27] It was made worse by the sharp rise in oil prices, but not caused by it. Once the oil shock had occurred, moreover, America's inflationary policy persisted in magnifying its unsettling consequences. Logically, the vastly increased oil prices implied a secular shift in the terms of trade between oil and manufactures. In one stroke, the oil prices, which had declined relative to industrial prices since the end of World War II, recaptured their lost ground.[28] Since Western Europe and Japan imported most of their oil, to regain external equilibrium they had either to earn more from exports or to use less oil. Logically, government policies in such a situation would strive to conserve energy, dampen domestic demand, and promote exports. Nearly all advanced industrial countries, except the United States, followed such a course.

America's exceptionalism was not so apparent while the recession lasted. By the election year of 1976, however, the Ford administration had succeeded in reflating the economy, while it had still failed to push through any effective program to conserve energy. Instead, domestic American subsidies and controls continued to keep domestic American fuel prices well below world levels.[29] The obvious consequences followed: U.S. energy imports soared and the trade and current-account balances recorded unprecedented deficits. The same conditions continued through the Carter administration. In effect, the United States greatly delayed adjusting its real economy to higher oil prices.

Profligacy with energy resources, combined with comparatively inflationary macroeconomic policy, weakened the dollar still further, particularly since Europe and Japan, trying to adjust their real economies, continued to restrain domestic demand in order to promote exports. As in the Nixon years, a repeatedly depreciating dollar proved to have many advantages. American exports remained competitive abroad despite inflating prices at home. And since world oil was traded in dollars, inflation and a depreciating dollar meant, if oil prices were not raised to compensate, a lower real price for oil—particularly for holders of strong currencies, but also for Americans. After their initial sharp price increase, OPEC countries dared not raise their prices to keep up fully with American inflation and the falling dollar. World recession and energy conservation had glutted the oil market. The United States, with its enhanced hegemonic role in the Middle East, seemed in a strong position to lean on its Saudi and Iranian clients. In short, Nixon's solution to the weak dollar, perpetual dollar depreciation, became also the American solution to the oil crisis.

America's exported inflation also had profound effects on international finance.[30] The huge and unrepentant balance-of-payments deficits channeled a flood of dollars to the oil-rich states. In many instances, their economies could not absorb it. Since no alternative international currency was in sight, and the large holders could not dump their dollars without enormous loss, the surplus dollars continued to accumulate in the Eurodollar market.

The oil shock produced not only a new flood of surplus capital, but also an eager crowd of borrowers. Even countries taking strong measures to adjust to the new oil prices often needed heavy borrowing to finance the transition. For many other countries, particularly in the Third World, adjusting their real economies meant scrapping long-range industrial plans or accepting an intolerable drop in living standards. Like the Americans, they refused to adjust. Unable to print internationally acceptable money themselves, they found bankers eager to lend them surplus dollars. In a climate of general and accelerating inflation, borrowing seemed simpler than facing severely disruptive changes in their economies. Although international agencies tried to manage this financial recycling, private commercial banks were less officious and hence more inviting to borrowers and lenders alike. As the United States gradually ended capital controls and banking regulations, overseas and domestic capital markets grew increasingly integrated. Large American banks, no longer blocked by controls, accumulated an increasing share of the swelling international debt. Thanks to the ardent enterprise of the banks, borrowing was easy and seemed painless. Credit seemed unlimited, and the general level of world debt grew to hitherto astonishing heights. With the exception of the underpopulated OPEC states and a few rich industrial states, nearly every nation ran deficits and lived by borrowing. As in the 1920s, most of these international loans were short-term. With such practices widespread, and with banks competing eagerly for paper profits, the world's financial structure grew more and more fragile.[31]

On the surface, the United States appeared to be doing well in the mid to late 1970s, certainly better than the Europeans. The Nixon solution had permitted Ford's reflation in 1976, despite the recession in the rest of the world. The boom lasted through most of the Carter administration. With a depreciating dollar, domestic inflation did not automatically make domestically produced American products less competitive. American protectionism receded. With no concern for defending the dollar, the painful implications of the energy crisis could be ignored. With capital controls ended, American banks could reap huge profits from the great expansion of credit in the United States and the urgent need for it elsewhere.

The principal losers from this policy were the OPEC countries, who saw their stunning 1973 price increase erode considerably within a few short years.[32] Next came the Europeans and Japanese, who were seriously trying to adjust their real economies. Their competitiveness was menaced by the dollar's depreciation, and their stability by American monetary expansion. From their perspective, the floating monetary arrangements constituted as great an abuse of hegemonic privilege as the decayed Bretton Woods system of the 1960s. The United States was able to get away with so generous a policy of credit creation because of the dollar's special role in the international economy. In economic terms, the Nixon solution constituted a use of "money illusion" on a world scale. In relations with both Europe and the oil producers, the illusion was reinforced by power. Rather than exercising their hegemony to guide and stabilize the monetary system, the Americans were exploiting it.

Economically and politically, the Europeans could find no easy way out of their Nixon-imposed dilemma. Floating had not meant that the dollar would give up its preponderant role in the international economy. The dollar was still the world's principal reserve currency, even if many European countries were holding an increasing proportion of their reserves in gold. The dollar was also the main currency for international transactions. Most raw materials were traded in dollars. The United States remained the world's largest economy, intimately tied to others through trade and capital flows. To replace the dollar would require some new international money with a political backing sufficient to make it credible. A new international currency was difficult to envision, except in the long run, and then probably only after some destabilizing catastrophe. Neither the Germans nor the Japanese wanted their currencies to have a greater international role, with all the attendant dangers for domestic stability. Collectively, the Europeans may have had the economic resources, but they lacked sufficient political will and common interest to support a common currency. Attempts at even a limited European Monetary Union were notably unsuccessful until the end of the 1970s.

Behind the technical role that the dollar played in the world economy lay the geopolitical hegemony of the United States. To challenge the dollar's role would have required the major European powers to unite for an economic confrontation with the United States, possibly involving capital controls and trade barriers—a course not easily compatible with their posture as American protectorates. The disaffection engendered by being placed in such a dilemma was part of a growing general awareness that their American protector, also a tough commercial and industrial rival, was increasingly inclined to take shortcuts in securing its own economic interests—even, if necessary, at the expense of the international system it claimed to be guiding.

From an American perspective, U.S. economic policy could easily be justified as merely forcing the free-riding Europeans and Japanese to pay indirectly some of the cost of their own security. No administration was willing to contemplate returning to the orthodoxy of Bretton Woods and fixed exchange rates, a framework that had seemed to guarantee America's domestic decline to the profit of those allies whom it was defending. In economic policy as in security policy, the United States had grown determined to exercise its hegemonic role in a fashion that augmented rather than reduced its own national welfare. Economically as well as militarily, America's diplomatic primacy would increasingly substitute for the abundant force that had once flowed from within.

The Carter administration, having lived off the Nixon legacy, was fated to cope with its bankruptcy. Carter came into office inheriting Ford's reflation of 1976. The consequent boom fitted the Nixon formula. Responding to the combination of domestic stimulation and unrestricted oil imports, the economy expanded, the trade balance deteriorated, and the dollar began a new round of rapid depreciation. The administration nevertheless stimulated the boom further. As was to be expected, debate over transatlantic economic policy grew increasingly polemical. Each side had its characteristic arguments. When the Europeans complained of American inflation and mercantilist exchange-rate policy, the United States was ready with its "locomotive theory" of world recovery. Strong economies, according to the Carter administration, were supposed to pursue expansive policies to offset the oil shock, to permit poorer countries to sell exports, and, in general, to pull the world out of its slump.[33]

By 1979, the days of the Nixon solution appeared numbered. Europeans had revived their project for a European Monetary System and had finally begun to create a European currency bloc. A mechanism was coming in place to permit Europe, in extremis, to cut loose from the dollar. The European Community was thus in a better position to bargain. Meanwhile, reactions against inflation in the capital and currency markets began to force a change in American economic policy. By 1979, foreign and domestic reactions came to a climax. An accelerated deterioration of the dollar, combined with a spectacular rise in gold prices, brought money markets to near panic. America's domestic bond market seemed close to collapse as soaring interest rates anticipated runaway inflation. OPEC, worried by declining revenues and deeply shaken by the Iranian revolution, imposed the first major real price increase since 1973.[34] This conjuncture of events in currency, gold, oil, and capital markets constituted an international and domestic revolt against the Nixon economic formula. Europeans, Arabs, and domestic holders of capital reacted together against a policy of deliberate inflation and depreciation.

The collapse of the Nixon formula in the economic sphere paralleled the degeneration of the Nixon-Kissinger formulas in the diplomatic and military spheres. Nixon's dollar policy and détente policy faltered together. Both had been designed to continue America's traditional world role with strained resources. By 1979, the Soviet invasion of Afghanistan had brutally punctured any remaining hope that détente could counterbalance Soviet power in the Third World. It had also steadily grown apparent that arms-control negotiations could not succeed, by themselves, in maintaining American nuclear superiority. Americans could not sustain by negotiation a strategic position they were unwilling to back up with arms. Enthusiasm for SALT II gave way to fears about a window of vulnerability. As the military balance seemed to decline, European fears of decoupling revived, with fresh demands for American nuclear missiles and a populist rebirth of European neutralism. As strategic parity made European conventional defense more significant, and the

United States began to plan new forces for the Third World, quarrels over burden-sharing intensified. Meanwhile, the policy of relying on surrogates contributed to the humiliations of the Iranian debacle. The Carter Doctrine pronounced a formal American commitment to defend the Persian Gulf, and the United States found itself more entangled than ever in the Middle East.

With this accumulation of defeats and apprehensions, the United States clearly lacked the military strength to sustain its geopolitical role. As Iran demonstrated, a vulnerable United States had become the target of widespread resentment without the means to compel respect.

If the Carter administration cannot be said to have handled these inherited breakdowns with conspicuous skill, it nevertheless did set the path for a new cycle of American policy. By the middle of Carter's term, a mood of confrontation was replacing détente; military budget cutting and hegemony on the cheap were giving way to a Kennedy-style rearmament.[35] But Carter's rearmament cycle was inaugurated under very different economic circumstances. Kennedy had had the great advantage of succeeding the thrifty Eisenhower; Carter followed Nixon and Ford. Both had imitated Eisenhower's parsimonious military policies, but rising domestic expenses had robbed them of Eisenhower's fiscal success. Thus, both the Nixon and Ford administrations, despite their conservative rhetoric, had continued and intensified the neo-Keynesian macroeconomic policies of Kennedy and Johnson. By the end of the 1970s, both the American political system and the world in general were in revolt against the inflation that followed. In short, while one political mood was bent on rearmament, another was ripe for disinflation. The result was worsening schizophrenia in American policy.

Reconciling rearmament with economic restraint posed a political and intellectual challenge of great complexity. The Carter administration tried fitfully to prune its fiscal budget into balance but was soon defeated by military needs. Truman had met a similar challenge through new taxes plus wage and price controls. Carter faced a wave of public opinion demanding not only an end to inflation but also lower taxes and more liberal markets. Under such circumstances, tight monetary policy emerged as the only solution. If the central bank refused to expand credit, fiscal deficits would have to be financed from real savings, at the expense of private borrowers. Rearmament would then mean not inflation but a credit squeeze. The formula had long been used in the Federal Republic of Germany, which had managed for half a decade to combine substantial fiscal deficits with low inflation.[36]

When Carter appointed Paul Volcker as chairman of the Federal Reserve in 1979, American monetary policy resolutely took on its thankless task.[37] Money in America grew tighter than ever before in living memory. For the United States and the world, the coming cyclical downturn developed into the major recession of 1980–82, more severe even than the Nixon-Ford recession of 1974–75.[38] At the same time, the world's ramshackle financial structure faced an international debt crisis more serious than anything experienced since World War II.[39] In short, rearmament, stringent monetary policy, and a deep recession were Carter's legacy to the 1980s.

While the incoming Reagan administration embraced rearmament and tight money, it found a formula to escape from recession. This Reagan formula, like the Bretton Woods and Nixon formulas, relied heavily on manipulating the international economy.

The history of the Reagan administration provides a striking demonstration of the persistent dilemma of postwar American conservatism. On the one hand, the administration strongly supported maintaining America's world role. Many of its prominent members and backers had vociferously warned against declining American military strength and had been notably unimpressed by détente diplomacy. True to his convictions, Reagan pushed through a military budget designed to restore American power. At the same time, the Reaganite platform also opposed heavy government spending, high taxes, inflation, wage and price controls, and big government generally. The administration was particularly determined to cut taxes in order to reverse the bracket creep that kept biting into middle-class wealth. It pushed through the largest tax cut in postwar history. Combining these defense and tax policies led predictably to very large fiscal deficits, an anomalous outcome for a conservative administration ostensibly opposed to big government and inflation.[40]

Like most governments with irreconcilable goals, the Reagan administration sought refuge in political and economic fantasy. Fiscal balance, it kept saying, could be reached by cutting the government's civilian expenditures. But though dismantling the welfare state was a goal with rhetorical appeal among conservatives, budget cuts large enough to right the fiscal balance would mean major reductions in Social Security and Medicare, proposals that would alienate a sizable segment of Reagan's conservative constituency. The president refused even to contemplate such cuts.[41]

Fiscal balance through efficiency was another Reagan bromide. While studies showed how "business methods" could save billions, the administration was notably unsuccessful in translating these familiar observations into actual practice. Indeed, the rapid increase in the size of the arms budget made efficiencies in the egregiously wasteful military sector more elusive than ever. The administration also had a more novel version of efficiency. It proceeded to discard a good deal of environmental and safety regulation and to dismantle much of the accompanying inspection system. It also deregulated a large part of the banking and transportation industries, a policy already under way in the Carter administration. But whatever their intrinsic merits, these initiatives clearly could not generate the revenues or savings needed to plug Reagan's enormous fiscal gap.[42]

The manifest unreality of its budget-cutting proposals suggested that the administration had put its real faith elsewhere. Like the Kennedy administration when it was bent on rearmament, the Reagan administration ended up embracing the NSC-68 fiscal formula. In other words, spending would create its own resources. Since Truman's time, the formula had evolved from spending more without raising taxes to spending more while cutting taxes. The full-employment tax cut, passed in 1964, had been a major step toward the inflation that followed. The Reagan growth model merely decorated the old neo-Keynesian fiscal formula with supply-side rhetoric to make it acceptable to conservatives. Rather than promoting growth through a redistribution of income to poorer consumers, the Reagan model counted on high profits to vigorous entrepreneurs and provident rentiers.[43]

By the time Reagan came to power, however, there was one major difference in the macroeconomic climate. The traditional easy monetary policy had come to an end. The market, the public, and even the economists had grown fed up with inflation.[44] Volcker's monetary policy enjoyed powerful support within Reagan's conservative coalition. Under the circumstances, the administration found itself committed to a tight monetary policy at the same time as its fiscal policy required lower taxes and higher defense spending.

Logically, so bizarre a combination appeared to be self-defeating. Tight money would throttle inflation, but large fiscal deficits combined with tight money would also abort recovery. Certainly that was Volcker's oft-stated view, but despite his misgivings, the Fed went on performing its appointed role. The credit squeeze of 1979–80 brought, not unexpectedly, a dramatic rise in real interest rates and triggered the worst recession since the end of World War II. By 1982, price inflation had dropped sharply while unemployment had risen to 11 percent.[45] Recovery would follow, the Fed hoped, because recession would reduce the demand for money and real interest rates would fall. Continuing monetary stringency, reassuring investors, would sweat the "inflation premium" out of lending rates. Low interest rates, plus low inflation, would help the cyclical recovery grow into a genuine boom, based more on a capital investment for growth, the Fed hoped, than on inflated neo-Keynesian consumer demand.

The Fed's scenario was difficult to reconcile with the administration's huge fiscal deficits. The administration, in any event, had its own scenario. Supply-side tax cuts, deregulation, and, ultimately, tax reform would spark the recovery. The consequent entrepreneurship, investment, and saving would generate the resources needed to eliminate the fiscal deficit.

Events took a different course altogether. By 1982, despite deep recession and a dramatic fall in price inflation, real interest rates refused to come down.[46] As Volcker himself never tired of observing, the reason was not obscure: the government's huge fiscal deficit was the principal culprit.[47] Financing the deficit preempted market funds and kept alive inflationary expectations. As monetary tightness and the deep recession persisted, many analysts began to fear a major depression, possibly set off by a general collapse of the international banking system. Much of the domestic credit industry was also shaky, in particular the huge savings and loan sector.[48]

Faced with these dangers, the Federal Reserve, having tried vainly to get the administration and Congress to bring the fiscal deficit under control, finally returned to easy money. From roughly the middle of 1982 through much of 1984, the money supply increased sharply, in several quarters at a rate apparently exceeding even the pre-inflationary binges of the early and mid-1970s.[49] There followed the Reagan recovery of 1983, a familiar neo-Keynesian consumer boom.[50] Domestic production expanded rapidly, and, for a time, high public and private consumption was matched by a major investment boom. But while credit was abundant, real interest rates still continued at record high levels, as many investors apparently feared history was repeating itself and that a major inflation would follow, particularly with 1984 a presidential election year. From this view, Reagan's boom looked to be merely a somewhat eccentric version of the ever more inflated business cycles common since the mid-1960s.

Even before the end of 1983, the Federal Reserve, alarmed by the bounding speed of the recovery, was thought once more to be trying to restrict credit. With the government's huge financing needs, many analysts, including Volcker and many of Reagan's own economic advisers, feared their monetary tightening would bring sharp increases in the already record real interest rates. An abrupt end to the Reagan recovery was the probable consequence.

Had the United States been a closed national economy, high interest rates would almost certainly have throttled the recovery. But while investment, which grew rapidly in late 1983, had slackened by the middle of 1984, personal consumption and government spending continued to rise strongly. As the boom continued and the U.S. economy moved toward full employment, America's inflated demand was met increasingly by goods imported from abroad. This helped stifle price inflation but also led to unprecedentedly large and rapidly growing trade and current-account deficits.[51] Once more the world economy came to the rescue of America. Throughout the period, American monetary conditions were characterized by a very large net inflow of international capital. Thanks to the capital inflow, the record current-account deficit was financed without difficulty. Indeed, the dollar kept rising.[52]

Why, with its multiple deficits, had the United States become such a magnet for foreign capital? Analysts credited the unusual pairing of Volcker and Reagan policies. Volcker's apparently steadfast monetarism seemed to promise a continuing strong dollar and a low inflation rate. Imports, in fact, kept domestic prices down. Meanwhile, Reagan's huge government deficits kept real interest rates up and resulted in very high levels of return for investors. The capital influx, as it financed the swelling current-account deficit, also pushed up the dollar's exchange rate. By 1983, the floating dollar had regained and surpassed all that it had lost since 1971. For foreign holders, returns from the dollar's high interest rates were topped by profits from the dollar's appreciation. Meanwhile, the Fed's 1982–83 reflation had sparked a stock market boom, itself a major magnet for foreign capital.

The dollar was also thought to benefit from Reagan's psychological reflation of the American image. Investors seemed to accept the administration's view that its boom was the just reward of its virtue. As the administration's supporters explained its success, America had put itself firmly in the hands of a vigorous conservative government, highly appreciative of the beneficent consequences of entrepreneurship, profit, and deregulation. No wonder the country was booming! Reagan's macroeconomic policy had found a magic formula to stem inflation while stimulating growth. Europe, enmeshed in socialism, welfarism, and highly restrictive market practices, was said to be still following traditional deflationary policies to restrain inflation. Unlike Reagan's America, it had not learned to stimulate and liberate its entrepreneurs.[53] Consequently, while America was booming, European growth remained sluggish and unemployment was at its postwar record. Many commentators recorded a severe bout of Europessimism about the old continent's long-range economic prospects and its general socio-economic climate.

For European governments, the contrast to Reagan's ebullient America was both painful and exasperating. America, they believed, was flourishing not from the vaunted economic merits of Reagan's outlandish policy but because that policy constituted a new and highly successful formula for exploiting the rest of the world. After the Bretton Woods and Nixon formulas had come the Reagan formula. With the mammoth net capital inflow to the United States, the languishing world economy was supplying the savings needed to finance America's boom. Thanks to that inflow, America's long-awaited credit squeeze had failed to develop, despite tight money and the huge fiscal deficit. Meanwhile, the unfolding of Reagan's macroeconomic formula, which led to the dollar's unnatural strength, stymied Europe's own efforts at reflation, most notably in France, where the newly elected socialist government was attempting its own neo-Keynesian boom. Depreciating European currencies, while helping to make European exports more competitive, also greatly raised prices for Europe's imported raw materials, generally factored in dollars. Analysts were speaking of Europe's "third oil shock." Further depreciation of European currencies against the dollar threatened to rekindle inflation. In short, from a European perspective, American prosperity was being achieved at Europe's expense. American monetary and fiscal policies were sucking capital from Europe, and the consequences were blighting Europe's domestic prosperity. Europe's monetary interdependence with America was, as usual, leading to highly unsatisfactory results.[54]

Reagan's macroeconomic policy also seemed increasingly dangerous for the world economy in general. Monetary and trade problems aggravated each other. Reagan's policies almost inevitably fed protectionism on both sides of the Atlantic. American manufacturing firms and their workers were increasingly devastated by the effects of an overvalued dollar on their competitiveness. They naturally pressed for limits on competing imports. Europe, with its prolonged recession and high unemployment, grew more and more allergic to competition from Japan or the newly industrialized countries. The dollar's record real interest rates greatly increased carrying charges for the world's debtors—most notably Third World and Eastern European countries that had borrowed heavily and short-term from commercial banks during the Nixonian period of abundant liquidity. The Reagan policy made their interest burden much heavier and dramatically revalued their capital costs.

Their trade opportunities threatened in Europe and America, many Third World debtors already were finding it difficult, despite record exports, to earn the extra dollars needed to finance the greatly augmented carrying charges on their debts. Several major borrowers required rescheduling and several leading American banks were overstretched. Fear of defaults and a general banking crisis threatened to dry up credit still further. The main central banks, the IMF, and the World Bank all grew more and more entangled in what seemed a haphazard, hectic, and perilous series of rescues.[55] Debtors tended to blame not their own imprudence but the fickleness of American monetary conditions that made long-range development planning nearly impossible. Above all, they blamed American fiscal policy, whose deficit financing would apparently require a large part of the world's available savings for the foreseeable future. To many it seemed highly unnatural, not to say obscene, that the world's richest country should also be its biggest borrower.

Along with its moral and political deficiencies, Reagan's prosperity seemed both fragile in the near term and damaging in the long term. With America's borrowing needs so high, and its savings rate traditionally so low, Reagan's prosperity had come to depend on a perpetual net influx of foreign savings. But so long as it lasted, the consequent strong dollar was having predictably disastrous effects on the international competitiveness of the U.S. real economy. By the end of 1984, U.S. trade and current-account deficits were already on a scale scarcely imaginable a few years earlier.

By 1985, these external deficits were themselves beginning to blight the Reagan recovery, despite the continuing net capital inflow. Growth of the gross national product sputtered as the inflated public and private demand was increasingly met not by domestic production but by cheaper imports. While imports had helped repress inflation, at least in the tradeable-goods sector, they also began to reduce profits and investment. The latter had fallen off in 1984, and the former in 1985. The Reagan-Volcker chain of high, inelastic credit demand, high interest rates, huge capital inflows, high exchange rates, high trade and current-account deficits, and depressed prices was strangling the real economy. In effect, the United States seemed headed into a supply-side recession. As far as the real economy was concerned, both profits and real investors were disappearing. Instead, capital was attracted to high-yielding government and bank paper, or else into grandiose takeover bids reflecting the depreciated valuation of real assets. Many firms were reported to be making severe cuts in their domestic operations.[56] As in the late 1960s, fears of an irreversible decline in American manufacturing grew widespread.

Such circumstances greatly restricted the options open to U.S. monetary policy. Congress, to be sure, had been talking a great deal about reducing the budget deficit, which would certainly have given the Fed greater leeway. But success was problematical, particularly as a new recession began to be widely feared. At best, several years would be needed to bring the fiscal situation under control. Faced with the apparently inelastic demand for public credit, the international debt crisis, the severe strain in private domestic financial institutions, the heavy load of corporate and consumer debt, and a slowing economy, the Fed was naturally under great pressure to expand the money supply in order to reduce interest and exchange rates. Monetary conditions did grow easier after mid-1985. The already anomalous foreign confidence naturally began to erode, and the dollar started to fall rapidly.

Reversing capital flows and a sharply falling exchange rate presented a new dilemma. Without monetary accommodation from the Fed, Reagan's fiscal deficits, if unchanged, almost certainly would bring the long-awaited credit squeeze and a deep new recession, with all the financial dangers of which the Fed was all too painfully aware. But insofar as the Fed monetized the swelling budget deficits, the dollar would fall faster and another inflationary cycle would be in the making.

Even with the generous monetary policy of 1986, however, the American economy remained discouragingly listless. For a time, much was expected from rapidly falling oil prices, which OPEC's disarray had pushed to extreme lengths. But while this course guaranteed at least a temporary respite from price inflation—and seemed to promise lower costs and hence greater profits for industry generally—its deflationary effects on profits and investments in oil and banking were severe, as were its consequences for a number of leading Third World debtors and their American bankers. At the same time, some reflux of oil prices seemed probable, since the Saudis were unlikely to continue indefinitely to depress the market to such an extreme degree.

Much was also expected from the favorable effects that the depreciating dollar might have on trade. But these effects, normally delayed in any event, were particularly slow in coming to America, a phenomenon that supported fears of a structural decline in domestic industry.

While no one could predict the precise course of events, signs of great disquiet were everywhere to be seen. That the later 1980s might well witness an acute new crisis for American economic policy and the world economy in general seemed all too probable.[57] Monetary policy was unlikely to be able to compensate indefinitely for so radically unbalanced a fiscal policy. As in the late 1960s with Bretton Woods, and the late 1970s with the Nixon solution, Reagan's formula for using the world economy to resolve America's national imbalance seemed to be reaching its inherent limits.

The basic similarity of the three postwar monetary formulas is worth noting. The Kennedy-Bretton Woods formula was, in effect, a way to borrow money by running balance-of-payments deficits. These became, de facto, inconvertible obligations to foreign central banks and overseas capital markets. The Nixon or floating formula allowed the dollar outflow and external indebtedness to continue, even though exchange-rate depreciation was repeatedly reducing its value. In both the Kennedy and Nixon formulas, the inflationary money supply was first created by monetary policy at home, then exported abroad through balance-of-payments deficits. Finally, the Reagan formula used America's swelling fiscal debt as a magnet to attract the exported dollars back home. America's present borrowing was financed by its past borrowing. Meanwhile, the basic balance-of-payments deficit, or external disequilibrium of the real economy, remained at record levels.

As the Reagan formula eventually breaks down like the others, what new American formula will emerge for exploiting the international economy? If the past simply repeats itself, an acceleration of American monetary inflation and a radical depreciation of the dollar seem the most probable outcome. Domestic and foreign debt crises have already created a powerful constituency for easy credit. A cyclical downturn, probable in the normal course of things, would swell the ranks. The Fed would be unlikely to stand in the way, even if it so desired. For a time, renewed easy money would probably spark a new boom, and low oil and other commodity prices might mitigate the tendency toward renewed price inflation. Almost certainly, the dollar would depreciate rapidly, and all the onerous public and private debt factored in dollars would go down with it—including, of course, America's huge new debt to Europe and Japan. As in the Nixon-Ford-Carter era, the locomotive theory will become the official American ideology. But even more than before, any turnaround in trade adequate to compensate for America's inner and outer disequilibrium would be catastrophic for industry elsewhere in the world. For that reason, it is extremely unlikely to occur. Others will inevitably protect themselves.

Again, if history repeats itself, the new policy will work well enough to give some relief to American industry and to prevent a financial collapse and a real depression. The international system will adjust without radical mutation in basic economic or political relationships. America's allies will complain, but manage. The past, in other words, supports a complacent perspective toward the *Pax Americana*'s long-standing economic problems, just as it encourages complacency about the alliance's military and political problems. The postwar system's economic arrangements have been at least as resilient as its political and military arrangements.

Nevertheless, the economic difficulties of the 1980s do seem to have a cumulative and accelerating quality. American manipulation of the international economy appears increasingly disruptive, damaging, and resented. Changes in the underlying context of international economic relations seem to have seriously threatened Europe's prosperity for the first time since the early 1950s. In addition to the monetary disruptions that began in the 1970s, the world economy has witnessed a sort of twin revolution. On the one hand, cheap, efficient, and increasingly high-quality manufacturing has been developing rapidly in the Third World. On the other hand, high technology has been creating new industries while sometimes drastically transforming old ones. Thanks to this twin revolution, all the old, rich, industrial nations have seen their postwar prosperity challenged. Europe and the United States have followed divergent responses. Since the late 1960s, American prosperity has continued to depend heavily on being able to manipulate international monetary conditions. Since Europeans could not, or would not, finance disequilibria by developing reserve currencies, and since their economies depend far more on trade than does America's, they have been driven to protect their competitiveness through strict macroeconomic policies to control domestic inflation. As a result, starting in the mid-1970s, economic conditions and policies in Europe grew somber and penitential—characterized by high real interest rates, relatively slow growth, and high unemployment.[58] High unemployment, in turn, greatly increased the cost of Europe's generous welfare systems. The consequent fiscal problems tended to mean higher employment taxes, leading to even higher unit labor costs and even more labor-saving investment. Productivity soared but unemployment worsened. With the recession of the early 1980s, unemployment reached frightening levels not seen since the depression of the 1930s.[59]

The capital outflow to America, along with the strong dollar, made tight monetary conditions essential to control inflation. But tight money precluded reflation to reduce unemployment and discouraged the investment needed to keep Europe's high-cost labor competitive. Capital was short to transform old industries threatened by Third World competition or to build up new high-technology industries in which the Americans and Japanese already held a lead. While export industries aimed at the American market were thriving, the rise of American protectionism and the strong dollar's fragile base made investment based on such exports hazardous. By the 1980s, with the Third World threat to old industries combining with a revived American challenge in new industries, and with slow growth, financial weakness, and monetary and trade quarrels inherited from the 1970s, Europeans had grown self-consciously embattled about their own economic situation and highly critical of American policy, a mood that helped explain their adamant resistance to American efforts to restrain growing pan-European economic ties.

Signs of a feeble European cyclical revival came in the mid-1980s, hastened by America's huge trade deficit. But European employment was not reviving in proportion. As the dollar began falling rapidly, Europe's industries began to feel threatened and defensive in the face of competition not only from the United States, but also from all the newly industrialized countries tied to the dollar. The falling dollar merely intensified the long-range threat—both from American high technology and from Third World industrialization. Joblessness seemed likely to remain a severe problem so long as Europe's wage costs, above all its welfare charges, could not be cut substantially. Europe, in short, faced a major structural adjustment that went to the very heart of its postwar civilization. At issue was whether its highly successful compromise between welfare and capitalism could be preserved in a more competitive and straitened world. Immediate prospects were troubling and long-range industrial planning extremely difficult, thanks in good part to the irregular and extreme oscillations of American monetary policy.

America's domestic conditions and policies were the very reverse of Europe's. The Nixon administration eschewed macroeconomic restraint and reflated. The Ford and Carter administrations followed suit. Until the end of the 1970s, a depreciating dollar sustained competitiveness. Instead of Europe's high investment, high productivity, and stagnant employment, America's booming economy had low investment and low productivity, but rapidly growing employment. Much of America's new growth sprang up in labor-intensive services, where foreign competition was scarce and American labor costs were often relatively low—partly because low-skilled labor was abundant, but also because welfare benefits and payroll taxes were lower. The less-structured American business climate also favored the proliferation of new firms built around high technology. But while employment was growing in new industries and services, productivity throughout the economy hardly grew at all. Under these conditions, the depreciating dollars of the 1970s became a drug to compensate for declining industrial efficiency. Predictably, when Volcker's tight money ended the Nixon formula and made the dollar appreciate, much of American industry was severely stricken and began to clamor for protection.[60] Japanese-American trade relations grew embittered to a degree that began to preoccupy political leaders on both sides. Meanwhile, old and new trade quarrels with Europe proliferated.

Predicting the long-range consequences is hardly easy. Until the 1980s, Europe's economic difficulties, however troublesome, were contained without seriously affecting the high level of general prosperity. By the mid-1980s, the continuing record unemployment, even after an upturn, was pointing to a grimmer future and more adventuresome politics. In the 1930s, fierce international competition and high unemployment led to radical domestic politics, protectionist blocs, and widespread cartelization. In the economic circumstances of the 1980s, the prospect of similar consequences naturally comes to mind. Protectionist sentiment is already rampant, if not yet triumphant, and predictions of a gradual transatlantic economic estrangement are easily supported. Broad trade patterns are shifting from the transatlantic axis—European-American trade has declined relatively for twenty years. The Common Market itself is already the world's largest trading bloc—reaching out to the Middle East, Africa, Eastern Europe, and the Soviet Union. America's Pacific trade is already greater than its European trade, and it is still growing rapidly. Much of America's trade with Europe, moreover, is agricultural, while Europeans have troublesome agricultural surpluses of their own.[61]

Against these centrifugal trends, however, are the undoubted countertrends toward international integration. Production is certainly more global in its organization than before World War II. Given existing investments, habits, and expectations, attempts at a serious reversal would meet fierce resistance, not easily overcome without some catastrophic financial breakdown. Just such a breakdown occurred, of course, in the 1930s. The economic dislocations since the 1970s have clearly made states more mercantilist—more assertive in promoting and protecting national industries. International trade and investment have thus grown highly political. So far, this has seemed to work mostly to America's advantage. But the advantage is likely to prove transitory and superficial. The American hegemony we have been describing is more a form of exploitation to compensate for weakness than a real supremacy—more buccaneering than domination. The long-term trend, after all, has been a steady weakening of the United States's economic competitiveness, despite its capacity to manipulate the world monetary system.

In the long run, neither America, Europe, nor Japan seems likely to have the economic weight and political power to dominate the world economy that appears to be developing. In its economic sphere, as in its political and military spheres, the world system will grow increasingly plural—with a proliferation of important actors, including states determined to safeguard their national prosperity. Taken altogether, these conditions and trends point, if anything, toward a new age of cartels—a web of agreements that permits competition but limits the damage. Some such organized competition would be the most rational and humane outcome and perhaps the only way to preserve the fabric of an open world economy in the face of so many destabilizing changes.

Perfecting the arrangements for an organized plural system will necessarily require a great deal of time and mutual forbearance. Prospects for a nontraumatic transformation will be very different if the old system simply collapses. It is therefore extremely foolish to underestimate the risks inherent in this present period of malaise and redirection. As a politico-economic system, the *Pax Americana* is showing severe strain in its economic sphere. For America's international as well as its domestic interests, squaring macroeconomic policy with hegemonic responsibility for maintaining world monetary stability seems an increasingly urgent priority. Without this long-delayed overhaul of American macroeconomic policy, Europe will either have to accept an increasingly damaging instability or be driven to cut itself off from the thrashings of the American monetary machine. To be sure, an indefinite passive resignation is one possible European response, but probably not the most likely. It seems to be in no one's interest to find out.[62]

What chance is there for the United States to achieve an external equilibrium? In theory, every administration since Eisenhower's would have liked to bring the American economy and the world economy into balance. Powerful forces have nevertheless continued to work against equilibrium, and America's balance-of-payments deficits have relentlessly continued to grow. One of the most obvious obstacles has been America's long-standing fiscal deficit. By Reagan's time, that internal disequilibrium was self-evidently linked to external disequilibrium and both were threatening to escape rational political control entirely. Prominent among the reasons for the fiscal imbalance were, on the one hand, the enormous expense of the Carter-Reagan rearmament and, on the other, the overriding popular pressure that led Reagan to a major tax cut. The coexistence of these contrary policies was not merely fortuitous. It was only one more demonstration of how America's postwar geopolitical role has grown out of harmony with the internal dynamics of its domestic political economy. All hegemonic world powers have probably felt the same tension. Most have ultimately been undone by it. In America's case, as the next chapter seeks to elucidate, the problem may be less intractable than it seems.

7

America's Budgetary Dilemma: Fiscal Deficits and Geopolitical Strategies

FEDERAL DEFICITS are an old story in American politics. In thirty-two of the forty years from 1946 through 1985, the federal government finished its fiscal year in the red. Since 1962, only one year has ended in surplus. In the 1980s, however, federal deficits rose to a new order of magnitude. Fiscal 1983 officially recorded a $207.8 billion shortfall; fiscal 1984, one of $185.3 billion. The new figures frightened businessmen and unnerved many economists. Without major changes in tax rates or spending, heavy deficits seemed certain for the rest of the 1980s.[1]

Deficits on such a scale could not be blamed merely on current economic conditions. As the president's budget report for fiscal year 1984 noted, two-thirds of America's fiscal deficit was not cyclical, but structural. In other words, with existing tax rates and spending commitments, even a return to near full employment would leave two-thirds of the colossal deficit intact. Eliminating the remaining two-thirds would require fundamental changes in the basic patterns of government spending and taxation.[2]

What was the cause? Why was so rich a country habitually unable to keep federal

TABLE 7.1

Current Disbursements/Receipts of Government (as a percentage of GDP)

	1962[a]	1972[a]	1982[a]	1983[b]	1984[b]
United States	26.4/27.0	30.3/30.0	36.3/32.0	36.9/31.7	—
Japan	13.4/21.6	15.5/21.5	27.3/30.2	27.5/29.8	27.1/30.3
Germany	29.5/36.6	35.1/39.8	44.8/45.3	44.4/45.2	44.2/45.6
France	32.9/36.3	34.2/38.2	47.5/46.9	48.9/47.7	49.4/48.4
United Kingdom	31.1/33.1	34.4/36.8	44.6/43.7	44.2/42.4	44.9/42.9

SOURCE: [a] OECD Economic Outlook (December 1984), 172, 174.
        [b] OECD Economic Outlook (December 1986), 162, 164.

expenditures in rough balance with federal income? Why had the chronic deficits reached such extravagant dimensions by the 1980s?

At heart, the American fiscal deficit has always been a political problem. The American public has not paid taxes equal to the combined civilian and military ambitions of its government. The public is not necessarily opposed to these ambitions—at least not enough to vote out of office those who support them. But the same political system that votes the spending is unwilling to vote the taxes.

A look at what might be called America's fiscal profile suggests some reasons for this imbalance, particularly when American spending and taxation are compared to those of the rich democracies of Western Europe, those countries most like the United States. Probably the most relevant comparisons are with France and Germany, both large, advanced democracies with important military roles and with per capita GNPs roughly equal to America's.[3] Like the United States, both France and Germany ran deficits in their combined central and local government budgets during the recession of the early 1980s. The U.S. federal deficit, however, was the most severe of the three in relation to the overall size of its economy. America's accumulated debt was also proportionately the worst.[4]

An even more striking difference among the three countries lies in the combined level of public spending and taxation at all levels. The United States, despite its larger deficit and debt, has had proportionately lighter expenditures as well as lighter taxes. In other words, relatively speaking, the public sector in America both spends and taxes much less than it does in either France or Germany (see table 7.1).[5]

From a French or German perspective, the United States has fiscal deficits not because it spends too much, but because Americans pay too little. Compared to Europeans, Americans seem to have an extraordinary aversion to paying taxes, a distaste expressed not only by electing a president in 1980 who pledged drastic tax reduction, but also by numerous local tax revolts throughout the country. American fiscal politics seem a never-ending Boston Tea Party.[6]

Part of the explanation for America's low taxes doubtless lies in its particular capacity to share domestic imbalances with the rest of the world. Since the international monetary system imposes relatively few sanctions on the United States, fiscal deficits have remained a relatively painless option for American policy.[7]

Comparing the ways in which American, French, and German governments raise and spend their money suggests, however, a further and more complex interpretation. While international comparisons of fiscal spending and taxation can never be very precise, and comparative statistics are surprisingly difficult to come by, certain broad differences between American and Franco-German fiscal patterns are striking.[8] The differences may be grouped under three headings: civilian spending, methods of taxation, and military spending. The following comparisons are for government at all levels, regional and local as well as central.

In Europe, welfare benefits and civilian spending generally are proportionately much higher than in the United States. Studies for the late 1970s showed that in both France and Germany, income maintenance—which includes pensions, sickness benefits, family allowances, and unemployment compensation—was nearly double the proportion of GNP that it was in the United States. In 1979, for example, overall government spending on income maintenance was 17.4 percent of GNP for France, 15.2 percent for Germany, and 8.6 percent for the U.S.[9] In Europe, moreover, the benefits, while comparatively generous to the poor, also extended more significantly to the middle class. European pension benefits depended much more on previous income, and top pensions were much higher.[10]

European political systems also seem more generous with merit benefits—items like education, health, and housing—which not all citizens consume equally and for which the individual consumer might otherwise have to pay a larger share of the cost. For merit benefits in 1979, the French government channeled roughly another 15 percent of the GNP, the German government 13 percent, and the United States only 9 percent.[11]

The ways governments distribute money for education and health also seem to differ significantly. While government in the U.S. spent roughly the same portion of the 1979 GNP for education as did the French and German governments (approximately 6 percent for each), American government spending covered much less of the total cost of education (78 percent in the United States versus 93 percent in France and Germany).[12] In other words, American students pay a substantially higher proportion of the total cost of their education directly. This is most notably true of higher education, the particular preserve of the middle class. Whereas university fees in France and Germany are minimal and students are directly subsidized, even American public universities, particularly the better ones, now charge a substantial tuition. Thus, although American higher education has proportionally twice the enrollment, individual American students pay a good deal more themselves. Even at the university level, the American middle class seems much less directly benefited by public money spent on education.[13]

Health care shows a pattern with similar consequences for the individual American

TABLE 7.2

Main Tax Sources as Percentage of Total, 1983

	Income and Profits	Social Security	Payroll	Property	Goods and Services	Other
U.S.	42.6	28.7	—	10.6	18.2	—
France	17.7	43.9	2.4	3.7	28.9	3.2
Germany	33.4	35.6	—	3.4	27.5	.02
U.K.	38.5	17.6	1.4	12.7	29.7	.03
Italy	36.8	35.9	—	2.8	23.4	1.1

SOURCE: *Revenue Statistics of OECD Member Countries 1965–1983* (Paris: Organization of Economic Cooperation and Development, 1985), 85.

taxpayer. American public spending on health care, though expanding rapidly, has traditionally been well below European levels. Like education, health care costs the economy more in America but the government pays a lesser share. The patient, like the student, pays a substantially higher proportion of the system's costs.[14]

If pensions, education, and health are considered together, a certain pattern emerges. In European countries, taxpayers get more direct benefits from the state than in America. They receive not only higher pensions in their old age, but also less expensive education in their youth along with far more security from the financial costs of illness throughout their lives. The transatlantic difference is compounded by comparing not only the relative generosity of European civilian benefits, but also their relative extent throughout the population. The welfare state in America is still seen mainly as charity for the poor. In Europe, its clear purpose is to provide security and comfort for the middle class.

The same pattern extends to the way benefits are financed and taxes are raised in general. Not only are European taxes higher, but the proportions raised from various types of taxes show considerable differences. In brief, the United States relies more on direct taxes on income; Europe, more on indirect taxes on consumption (see table 7.2).

Consumption taxes give a relative advantage to those able and disposed to save. Direct income taxes, invariably progressive, fall more heavily on the middle than the poorer classes. High real estate taxes fall most heavily on the American middle class. In other words, American taxes hit the middle class more directly and personally.

Putting the American pattern of tax consumption and tax payment together, and comparing it with that of France and Germany, makes middle-class America's comparative aversion to taxes not altogether surprising. In America, the middle classes, who pay the largest share of taxes, appear to get substantially fewer benefits in return: hence, logically, one reason for America's relative lack of a middle-class constituency for the public sector.[15]

In this perspective, America's aversion to taxation loses much of its mystery. Why should the American middle-class taxpayer accept European-level taxes without a more generous and coherent program of public services for those who supply the bulk of the revenue? Why, it might be asked, should Americans pay European taxes if the United States will still lag far behind rich European states in subsidizing education and health care—not to mention that whole range of public amenities, like clean cities, efficient public transport, or safe streets, which Europe's urban dwellers take for granted? Why is the solution not as obvious as the cause?

Even in periods when they have been disposed to it, American policymakers have never been able to develop a European-scale welfare state. Why? American society may be too heterogeneous. A higher proportion of unemployable poor or widespread immigration may result in financial or administrative strains that effectively limit our capacity for a middle-class welfare state. America's economic culture may be more individualistic. American middle classes may simply prefer lower taxes to public benefits or amenities. The tax system itself may affect these preferences. Europe's heavier emphasis on payroll and consumption taxes may be inherently more acceptable to taxpayers than income or property taxes. Americans may be more litigious as well as more individualistic. Thus, in the American tax structure middle-class benefits may be found in the complex system of deductions and income shelters rather than in positive government programs. Tax reform that severely restricts these exemptions might, of course, ultimately change middle-class attitudes toward spending. European benefits may also be more obvious and direct. Certainly few benefits in the United States can compare, in this respect, with Europe's universal family allowances.

In one expenditure, defense, America far outdistances Europe. In 1984, for example, defense spending as a percentage of GNP was 6.9 percent in the United States, 4.1 percent in France, and 3.3 percent in Germany. Per capita, Germany spent $334 on defense in 1984, France $367, and the United States, $1,057.[16]

Under the circumstances, America's inability to match Europe's welfare benefits is not surprising. United States civilian spending is more crowded by military spending. And, although military spending has its own strong constituency, the overall American mix of civilian and military spending, or direct and indirect taxation, does not, it seems, generate a constituency sufficient to sustain taxation at a European level, or even at a level sufficient to cover the United States federal government's actual expenditures; hence, the perpetual American deficit, with all its troubling geopolitical consequences.

To suggest that America's fiscal imbalance is linked to its comparatively outsized defense spending is not to prove the huge military budget undesirable or unnecessary. The Reagan defense buildup had many ardent defenders and was voted by a Congress whose lower house was controlled by Democrats.[17] The Carter administration had already started on the same path. A major buildup seemed essential to sustain

TABLE 7.3
U.S. National Defense Outlays as a Percentage of GNP

1950	4.7
1955	11.0
1960	9.5
1965	7.5
1970	8.2
1975	5.7
1980	5.0
1983	6.3
1984	6.2
1985	6.4
1986, est.	6.3

SOURCE: 1950: U.S. Bureau of the Census, *Statistical Abstract of the United States 1985* (Washington, D.C.: U.S. Government Printing Office, 1985), 331; 1955–86: U.S. Bureau of the Census, *Statistical Abstract of the United States 1987* (Washington, D.C.: U.S. Government Printing Office, 1987), 317.

America's worldwide military position against the Soviets or other adversaries. While Reagan's budgets were raising defense spending to new heights in absolute terms, they were still well below the proportion of defense spending to national income common in the 1950s and 1960s (see table 7.3).

Meanwhile, the Soviets had strongly augmented their industrial capacity and were thought to have vastly increased their military spending. The Carter years appeared to demonstrate how inadequate American military power had become, and how the Soviets and revolutionary forces everywhere had grown contemptuous of American power.

The Reagan administration occasionally drew a parallel between its position and that of the Kennedy administration. Each followed a decade where American policy, without abandoning commitments, had tried to reduce their costs. Both faced a situation where the habitual Western inadequacy in conventional forces was no longer thought to be compensated by a clear superiority in strategic forces. Both sought to build up conventional strength and to restore strategic superiority. Reagan's task was, if anything, more difficult. Soviet military technology had greatly improved since the 1960s, while the end of U.S. conscription in the 1970s meant greatly increased manpower costs for any conventional buildup.

From this perspective, Reagan's huge deficits should be blamed not on the restored military budget, but on the country's unwillingness either to tax itself adequately or to adjust its civilian expenditures correspondingly. Even those who have found Reagan's supply-side fiscal formula dangerous nonsense ought not to fault his military budget, but rather his failure to finance it in a straightforward fashion. The logic of such arguments seems self-evident, once the need for Reagan's level of military spending is accepted. But is the premise correct? Were the Reagan increases actually justified in military terms?

Here economic analysis reaches its limits. The economic imperative is to bring fiscal resources and military requirements into balance. How much this ought to require changes in fiscal priorities as opposed to military requirements depends on whether the American defense establishment under Reagan meets the country's perceived security needs adequately and efficiently. More fundamentally, however, it requires evaluating the appropriateness of the current definition of America's security requirements. Does this definition, and the commitments that flow from it, reflect a realistic view of America's geopolitical interests and capabilities? Beyond management efficiency, in other words, lies geopolitical efficiency.

Management efficiency requires the military establishment to employ its resources well, at least by the technical and managerial standards normal elsewhere in the national economy. It also requires military organization, tactics, and weapons appropriate to achieving whatever strategy the country has chosen to preserve its security. Regularly building forces or weapons irrelevant to that strategy is obviously inefficient. So is a military organization that makes the strategy difficult to accomplish. Measuring management efficiency may also be approached comparatively. How much do Soviets or Europeans get for their spending as opposed to what Americans get for theirs?

Geopolitical efficiency requires assessing a country's strategy and forces in terms of its position in the world. What are the country's international interests? Are its military strategy and forces rational in terms of those interests? More even than management efficiency, geopolitical efficiency needs to be assessed comparatively— in relation to the capabilities and situations of other powers.

How does Reagan's military buildup stand in relation to these two criteria? The Reagan Pentagon has been widely and severely criticized on grounds of management inefficiency. Similar criticism has been heard often since World War II. Starting with the first postwar secretary of defense, James Forrestal, many of those most intimately involved with directing the military establishment have found its performance and structure manifestly deficient.[18] All vast organizations have inefficiencies of scale. With the Pentagon, these are exacerbated by the detailed and unsystematic congressional interference characteristic of the American federal administration. But these failings are compounded by the military's own fragmented organizational structure. The jealous independence of the separate military services commonly gets much of the blame. While the changing nature of warfare is said to have made the traditional service boundaries obsolete, the Joint Chiefs of Staff are widely seen as mere advocates for their services, rather than as genuine coordinators of a united military.[19]

The civilian side of the Defense Department, while often faulted for failing to impose more coherence on the military, is also blamed for undermining its professional competence and morale. With an immense civilian bureaucracy invading much of the professional military sphere, critics complain that inappropriate civilian criteria often shape military operations and structures. Military values—in their intellectual, historical, moral, or psychological dimensions—are found curiously lacking in the Pentagon. Technology and accounting often appear to have displaced strategy and command, with results unfavorable even to economic efficiency. Exasperated critics call the American officer corps a profession not of commanders but of bureaucrats, lobbyists, and bookkeepers. Military officers and their industrial suppliers often seem intimate to an improper and demoralizing degree.

The Pentagon's shortcomings have inspired innumerable studies, many from the inside. In 1983, for example, General David C. Jones, retiring chairman of the Joint Chiefs of Staff, delivered a trenchant indictment of the military structure and suggested radical changes. Congress and most postwar administrations have tried to reform the military establishment but have seldom made fundamental progress.[20]

Seen in historical perspective, America's military shortcomings are not altogether surprising. The country's shift from isolation to world leadership was remarkably abrupt. Before 1945, neither the American political system nor its military establishment had had much peacetime experience with an active global policy or the large and permanent defense establishment required for it. As a relatively isolated great power, the United States had, throughout its history, oscillated abruptly from relative unconcern with military strength to all-out war. For America, the world wars were brief, convulsive, all-consuming efforts, where allies bore the brunt of the early fighting and provided the grace period to arm in safety. Once armed, America's resources were overwhelmingly greater than those of its already overstretched opponents. In short, the United States never had to reconcile the costs of an active and sustained global policy with society's other goals and limited resources.

Such a military tradition hardly suits America's present role of world manager, a task that calls for a consistent, long-range, and closely measured foreign policy, along with a military establishment that carefully husbands its means. With a tradition unsuited to its role, the United States has shaped and financed its postwar military establishment as if engaged in a short, climactic war rather than managing a long-term burden. Financing defense by debt may be the natural recourse in wartime. In times of peace, it reveals a political system unable to bring its military needs and economic means into some rational relationship.[21]

If current American military practice seems to offer ample room for improved management efficiency, the nation's basic character indicates certain limits. A country's vices are often closely related to its virtues. The United States cannot easily shed its past or its basic character. It remains a continent-sized, pluralist democracy whose scale, diversity, history, constitution, and political culture all conspire to limit its efficiency. The Pentagon is a giant mirror for the system as a whole. The image it reflects may be exaggerated, but it is entirely identifiable.

Are military establishments more efficient in other political systems? Do the Europeans, who spend much less proportionately as well as absolutely, get more military value for their economic resources? Do the Soviets really have more resources for military purposes, or do they merely use them better? Systematic and comprehensive answers require elaborate and contentious studies. Many of the factors to be compared are elusive, like the quality of troops or the advantages of different weapons. Monetary comparisons are often misleading, even between countries with a similar standard of living and scale of costs.

In any event, as has already been argued at length, simple comparisons of military forces and spending, besides being objectively difficult, may also be highly misleading. A country's military efficiency depends not only on what it gets for what it spends, but also on whether its military forces and organization are compatible with its national strategy. And that strategy, with its consequent goals and commitments, needs to be judged by its geopolitical efficiency—its relationship to the nation's relative situation in the world.

No Western European state, for example, has the same geopolitical horizon as the United States. France is probably the Western European power that comes closest. France has strategic and tactical nuclear forces, along with sizable land, naval, and air forces geared to uphold French interests in Europe, Africa, and occasionally the Middle East and elsewhere. France also has a flourishing defense industry and is, after the two superpowers, the world's largest exporter of arms.

Since any more indigenous European defense would almost certainly have to be built around a Franco-German core, it is interesting to consider French and West German forces combined. The German Federal Republic has specialized in ground forces, which seems proper for a front-line continental power committed only to defending its own territory. Much of its large land army consists of mobile, heavily armored forces. There are also numerous well-trained reserve forces, capable of being mobilized quickly. A sizable land-based air force complements the ground forces. Naval forces are relatively negligible. France's professional army is well-trained but smaller, lighter, and more mobile—designed primarily for intervention outside Europe. Like Germany, France has a sizable land-based air force.

Given France's importance, its land army for Europe seems relatively small and underdeveloped; its reserves, while large, are not particularly well-trained or easy to mobilize. In effect, France's mixture of forces reflects a deliberate policy to make the most of the country's unique geographical and political situation in order to extend its military reach. Unlike Germany, France has a powerful strategic nuclear deterrent—with its own triad of bombers and sea and land missiles—all built independently from the Americans. Whereas the Germans only share in a NATO tactical nuclear arsenal that remains under American command, the French

TABLE 7.4

Comparison of Franco-German and U.S. Forces and Budgets (1984)

	U.S.	France	W. Germany	France and W. Germany total	as % of U.S.
Total Military Budget[a]	258.2	20.1	20.4	40.5	15.7
Personnel					
Total Armed Forces	2,151,568	476,560	478,000	954,560	44.4
Army (plus U.S. Marine					
Corps)	898,889	300,000	335,600	635,600	70.7
Navy	568,781	67,710	36,200	103,910	18.3
Air Force	603,898	96,550	106,000	202,550	33.5
Equipment					
Main Battle Tanks	13,423	1,260	4,662	5,992	44.1
Major Naval Surface					
Combatants	200	46	16	62	31.0
Attack Submarines	95	18	24	42	44.2
Aircraft Carriers	14	2	0	2	15.4
Naval Aircraft	1,350	78	0	78	5.0
Combat Aircraft	3,700	475	586	1,061	28.7
Nuclear Warheads					
Strategic	10,174	200	0	200	2.0

[a] Figures reflect NATO budget definitions (for France and Germany, 1984) and are measured in billions of U.S. dollars, using 1984 exchange rates.
SOURCES: I.I.S.S., *The Military Balance 1985–1986*; German Defense Ministry, *White Paper 1983*; U.S. Secretary of Defense, *Report to the Congress, Fiscal Year 1985*.

army has its own tactical nuclear forces for battlefield use. France also has a good-sized navy, with two aircraft carriers and five ballistic missile submarines capable of striking the Soviet Union.

Taken in combination, the French and German military establishments have a certain complementarity and make up a rather formidable force at a cost proportionally much lower than that of the American forces (see table 7.4).[22]

America's usual reference point for military prowess and efficiency, however, is not Western Europe but the Soviet Union. America's huge defense budget is regularly justified by the need to match the Soviets. There has always been a great deal of controversy over whether, despite its huge outlays for defense, the United States succeeds. Here the normal difficulties of military comparisons are compounded, and not only by secrecy and deception. Technological and manpower costs are radically different, while monetary comparisons are notoriously arbitrary. The U.S. Defense Department estimated in 1982 that Soviet defense expenditures were 12 to 14 percent of the Soviet GNP, whereas U.S. spending was 6.5 percent of its GNP. Measuring the comparative GNPs is, in itself, a highly uncertain exercise. All these difficulties give rise to interminable debates among experts.[23] Table 7.5 provides a crude summary of outlays and capabilities.

TABLE 7.5

Rough U.S.-Soviet Force Comparisons

	United States	Soviet Union
Total Armed Forces[a]	2,151,568	5,300,000
Ground Forces[b]	978,889	2,011,000
Main Battle Tanks	14,139	52,755
Helicopters[c]	8,800	6,950
Naval Forces	568,781	480,000
Aircraft Carriers[d]	13	4
Combat Aircraft	1,350	931
Major Surface Combatants	200	285
Minor Surface Combatants	89	700
Attack Submarines	95	203
Nuclear-powered	91	72
Cruise Missile Submarines	4	66
Nuclear-powered	4	49
Air Forces	603,898	570,000
Combat Aircraft[e]	3,700	5,900

[a] Soviet figures include roughly 1.3 million whose function would be civilian in the United States (see chapter 9).
[b] These figures combine army and marine corps for both countries.
[c] This figure includes the 2,650 attack helicopters assigned to the Soviet Air Force.
[d] Soviet aircraft carriers are small by U.S. standards, each carrying only fourteen VSTOL aircraft. In addition, the Soviets deploy two helicopter carriers. The bulk of Soviet naval aviation (875 aircraft) is land-deployed.
[e] The Soviets also deploy a significant air defense force, the APVO, separate from the air force. The APVO has some 635,000 men, 1,200 interceptor aircraft, and 9,600 SAM launchers.
SOURCE: *The Military Balance 1985–1986* (London: International Institute of Strategic Studies, 1985), 3–30.

A general study of this kind cannot enter deeply into the technical debate about comparative outlays and forces, but it can raise a fundamental and significant question—one that puts the technical debate into its proper geopolitical framework: to what extent is it necessary or appropriate for the United States to match, surpass, or even imitate the military forces of the Soviet Union? Does it make sense for us to do so according to the criterion of geopolitical efficiency? Answering the question requires a considerable digression into geopolitical and strategic considerations. But for reasons that have, by now, been argued several times, geopolitical efficiency is critical in determining what budgetary policy should be.

Although both America and Russia are called global superpowers, they are not equally endowed players opening from opposing but otherwise identical positions on the same chessboard. On the contrary, each is in a radically different geopolitical situation, giving it distinctive assets and vulnerabilities. Comparative assessments cannot, therefore, simply use the military forces of one as the standard of adequacy for the other. Their differing geopolitical situations mean that forces needed by one may be quite inappropriate for the other.

Geography puts the Soviet Union in the middle of the Eurasian land mass. Eurasia has almost three-quarters of the world's population and more than half its productive capacity. If the Soviets could control it, they would be the world's leading power. For the purpose of exerting military power over Eurasia, geography obviously favors the Soviet Union over the United States. Maintaining a standing U.S. military presence in Eurasia requires stationing forces far from home and maintaining a giant naval capacity to supply them. American reserve forces are not easily brought to bear in a crisis.

The Soviets' geographical advantage is also their greatest liability. Whereas the United States is surrounded by unarmed, dependent, and friendly neighbors, the Soviet Union is ringed by powerful antagonists. History gives ample encouragement to Russian apprehensions about those neighbors. The Russians may also be excused for feeling vulnerable about their future. The Soviet Union, together with its Eastern European protectorates, forms the world's last great multinational empire. Most neighboring states have at least latent irredentist claims on it. Some of these claims might, under the right circumstances, prove to have resonance within the Soviet Union itself, where the relative numerical decline of Russian Slavs is sometimes thought to undermine the empire's unity.[24] In short, the Soviet Union is one of those states condemned to be either very strong or very weak. Given its encirclement in Eurasia, Soviet enthusiasm for a bipolar world becomes easier to understand.

Since World War II, nuclear weapons have greatly affected these traditional geopolitical calculations. In the beginning of the postwar era, nuclear weapons devalued Soviet advantages and increased Soviet vulnerabilities, to the corresponding benefit of the Americans and their allies. The retaliatory power of nuclear weapons was so destructive and certain that an aggressive attack against a nuclear power or its protectorates was patently irrational. So long as geography made the United States practically invulnerable to a direct Soviet nuclear attack, and nuclear weapons were a cheap and mobile counterweight to conventional forces, America's extended nuclear deterrence was able to devalue and contain Soviet conventional superiority in Eurasia.

In due course, the progress of nuclear weaponry also proceeded to undermine America's traditional geopolitical advantage. As the Soviets acquired an intercontinental nuclear strike force, the United States lost its historic security against foreign attack. Although this new "balance of terror" was still sufficient to counter Soviet conventional superiority in Eurasia, it exposed the United States to a level of risk highly unusual in its history. For the past generation, America's dilemma has been how to limit vulnerability at home while reassuring allies in Eurasia. American strategic debates have revolved around this dilemma.

While we have been preoccupied with how to stabilize nuclear duopoly, the strategic situation has changed radically. At least four of Russia's Eurasian neighbors have built nuclear forces of their own. Two of them, Britain and France, could gravely wound and possibly disable the Soviet state without any American help. Both British and French nuclear forces, moreover, are scheduled for major upgrading in the 1990s.[25] Even if Europe's own vulnerability makes any unprovoked European nuclear first strike on the Soviets extremely improbable, a deadly European second strike in response to a Soviet nuclear attack would be highly likely. What is more, a European nuclear response to a major conventional attack is not at all inconceivable.

On the East Asian side of the Soviet Empire, China also has nuclear weapons and presumably will eventually acquire a capacity to deliver them comparable to that of Britain and France. China would be less vulnerable in a nuclear exchange than either of the Western European nuclear powers. Possibly the Chinese state would prove less vulnerable than the Soviet state. China is unlikely to be Asia's only other nuclear power. India, another giant and rapidly industrializing regional power, has already demonstrated a capability for producing nuclear weapons. India's neighbor, Pakistan, harbors active nuclear ambitions. So, possibly, does volatile Iran. Meanwhile, Japan and Germany, the two major states without nuclear weapons, but with an undeniable capacity to develop them and their delivery systems quickly, also border the Soviet empire. Both harbor deep historical grievances against the Russians. Even Russia's old enemy Sweden seems poised to enter the nuclear circle with little notice.[26] Eurasian nuclear powers, the Soviets included, are intrinsically more vulnerable to each other than intercontinental rivals. The shorter distances make attack much easier and defense far more difficult than for intercontinental exchanges. Given this geographical proximity, even relatively primitive nuclear forces have substantial deterrent power. In short, from Moscow's perspective, nuclear proliferation has compounded Russia's traditional Eurasian vulnerability.

Soviet military policy in the 1970s was apparently dedicated to achieving massive regional superiority. The widespread deployment of SS-20 missiles in Eastern Europe and Asia, on top of their other capabilities, suggested that the Soviets were aiming for a first-strike capacity against all their Eurasian neighbors combined.[27] But as these neighbors have been developing increasingly formidable forces, the aim of denying them a second-strike capability has seemed increasingly unattainable—without some major technological breakthrough withheld from the neighbors. At present, even without taking the American reaction into consideration, a successful Soviet first strike against Western Europe, let alone against Europe and China simultaneously, already runs a high risk of devastating failure.

At the same time, the Soviets cannot feel overly complacent about the conventional military sphere. While Western analyses often concede the Soviets an edge over NATO's conventional forces, the edge is by no means indisputable, and certainly not irremediable, as later chapters will discuss. And a Soviet victory could not be taken for granted in a prolonged conventional war with China. All-out conventional war against China and Europe simultaneously would certainly place the Soviets in great difficulty.[28] The gradual rearmament of Japan suggests still less assurance in the future.

What are the geopolitical consequences of these strategic trends? Broadly speaking, the progress of nuclear arms, which initially reinforced American world preeminence, and then replaced it with Soviet-American duopoly, now seems to be undermining duopoly as well. All in all, the disposition of military power around the world seems to be moving toward a more plural pattern. This trend seems most clearly established in Eurasia itself, where, as America's extended deterrence has weakened, an indigenous nuclear balance has been forming.

New escalations in the arms race, most notably Reagan's Strategic Defense Initiative, may call these trends into question. Depending on the relative pace of technological progress, anti-missile defense may eventually bring a restoration of American world hegemony, a reaffirmation of bipolarity, a consolidation of strategic pluralism, or—as many of Reagan's critics fear—a chaotic destabilization of the strategic balance. Today, in the mid-1980s, the technological uncertainties for strategic defense seem incalculable, and significant results very long-term at best. But whatever happens, strategic defense is unlikely to eliminate fundamental geographical differences. Eurasian nuclear powers, the Soviet Union included, will remain highly vulnerable to each other. Nuclear attacks launched from within the same continent will always be more difficult to guard against than attacks from another continent. Conceivably, the Soviets might build some combination of defensive and offensive superiority sufficient to rob other Eurasian powers of any credible second-strike capability. More probably, European or combined transatlantic technology will prevent or reverse such a Soviet advantage. In any event, the already existing trend toward a more plural nuclear balance seems likely to prevail well into the 1990s. Beyond that is anyone's guess.

Strategic pluralism, it should be noted, is not only the prevailing military trend, but it also seems in harmony with the world's general politico-economic evolution since the 1960s. The reconstruction of Western Europe and Japan, and the uneven but often striking rise of major Third World states, have all been changing the world's broad political and economic balance in this same plural direction. In the face of these politico-economic trends, the lingering bipolarity in the strategic sphere seems increasingly anomalous.

What does this evolution toward strategic pluralism have to do with the geopolitical efficiency of America's military strategy and forces, or with the appropriateness of comparing its forces with those of the Soviet Union? While the trend toward pluralism disturbs both superpowers, on balance it would seem far more favorable to American than to Soviet strategic interests. Moving from a bipolar to a plural strategic order may pose problems of adjustment for a United States habituated to hegemonic leadership, or for a Europe habituated to cheap defense. But it carries dangers of an entirely different magnitude for the Soviet empire. A plural diffusion of strategic power means, in actual substance, the rise of those very Eurasian neighbors who are historically the principal threats to Russian security and ambition. Stifling independent nuclear capacities among other Eurasian nations must seem to the Soviets very much in their interest, and enlisting American aid in the name of duopoly must seem to them a particularly satisfactory course.

While preserving the original nuclear predominance was clearly in the interest of the United States, the rationale for preserving nuclear duopoly seems problematical. Without nuclear superiority over the Soviets, America's Eurasian commitments have grown less plausible and thereby increasingly risky. But if nuclear duopoly increased America's geopolitical vulnerability, the trend toward strategic pluralism reduces it and increases that of the Soviet Union. Strategic pluralism means, in effect, independent nuclear forces for Russia's major European and Asian neighbors. They will no longer need to rely exclusively on America's extended deterrence to contain Soviet power. Under such circumstances, selective proliferation and devolution might seem the natural American strategy.

As duopoly has faded, however, the United States has still gone on trying to preserve it. Thus, the United States has traditionally continued to apply nuclear nonproliferation policies even to its closest allies, with Britain the exclusive and grudging exception. The basic thrust of American nuclear policy stands most clearly revealed in those countries where it has had its way most easily—Japan and Germany. American policy has not, of course, tried to inhibit the growth of conventional military capabilities among its protectorates: quite the contrary, since stronger conventional forces are thought to raise the nuclear threshold and thus lower the American risk. But American policy has sought to tie those allied conventional forces to American command. So long as the United States has been primarily responsible for the nuclear defense of Russia's Eurasian neighbors, American policy has instinctively tried to limit independent military capabilities among its dependencies: hence the integrated command structure of NATO. Less dependent allies, it has been feared, could draw the United States into a nuclear war by their own autonomous action—particularly allies able to initiate nuclear war themselves.

Such a geopolitical policy inevitably places very heavy burdens on American military strategy and on American military forces. In the nuclear sphere, extended deterrence under conditions of parity carries catastrophic risks for American home territory—all for the sake of foreign commitments. Such a posture leads naturally toward a counterforce strategy that aims to insulate, attenuate, and otherwise limit nuclear confrontations. Counterforce strategy implies nuclear arsenals many times greater than what might seem adequate for a second-strike capability designed to deter a direct attack on the United States itself. And in the conventional sphere, if the United States is to command Europe's territorial defense, it must possess and commit ground forces of sufficient size to make such a leading role plausible. These extended ground forces require, in turn, appropriate naval supply and air support capabilities.

Today's emerging strategic pluralism ought to provoke a general reassessment of this traditional view of postwar America's geopolitical position and interest, as well as a reassessment of the military forces sufficient to serve that interest. Since the Soviet Union is closely ringed by major regional powers, and since, given nuclear parity and proliferation, these neighbors are increasingly better protected by their own forces than by those of the Americans, the United States should take a less direct role in maintaining Eurasia's regional balances. This means encouraging its major allies to develop adequate nuclear deterrents of their own. It also means devolving to them the primary responsibility for sustaining Eurasia's conventional as well as nuclear balance. It means concentrating America's own military effort on intercontinental deterrence and global balance, while gradually renouncing primary responsibility for directly maintaining the Eurasian territorial balance, above all in Western Europe and East Asia, where the potential for adequate indigenous forces clearly exists. Direct American efforts should presumably concentrate on those regions where an indigenous balance still seems unattainable, as is perhaps the situation around the Persian Gulf.[29]

Such a geopolitical analysis carries telling implications for the military budget. United States conventional force requirements are currently dictated by the manifestly unrealistic pretension that it can take the immediate lead in two major continental land wars simultaneously.[30] In reality, the United States cannot take the European conventional lead effectively, as NATO's perpetual wrangling over the conventional balance suggests. Once the pretension to run European defense is abandoned, America's standing contribution to Europe's territorial defense can be limited to the equivalent of two or three heavy divisions, with perhaps another division or two in the continental United States earmarked for Europe. With its European commitment thus reshaped, the U.S. army could have more ample manpower for mobile rapid intervention forces to discourage Soviet global adventures. Five divisions would probably be adequate for such a global force. Such global forces have very different requirements from those needed to replay World War II on the North German plain. Altogether, a refashioned American army might total around ten divisions, a drastic cut from the traditional sixteen.[31] As a hedge against a longer war, nothing, of course, would prevent a systematic strengthening of American reserves.

Such a transformation would make sense by the standards of geopolitical efficiency; it also ought to permit very large long-term fiscal savings, assuming some reasonable control over the scope and cost of global missions and forces. What portion of the U.S. defense budget goes toward NATO is obviously a complex and contentious calculation. Experts differ, with the Pentagon setting the proportion at 58 percent of its requested defense budget in 1985. Brief reflection can suggest why the magnitude is so great. Roughly 40 percent of the defense budget is manpower cost. Roughly one-third of the army's standing divisions are in Europe; another third have European defense as their primary mission. These heavily armored divisions have enormous associated capital expenditures, including major equipment and ammunition. Since the mid-1970s, these capital costs have been growing in relation to manpower costs.[32] Savings from European devolution, of course, would be distributed somewhat across the other services. Devolution of European ground defense would imply considerable reductions in the Reagan plans for a six-hundred-ship navy, a goal that apparently envisages World War II's leisurely American liberation of Europe, with a massive American naval supply train overcoming a Soviet blockade. The air force would presumably be least affected, since it is the one branch that is highly mobile and whose reserve forces could be quickly mobilized for a European emergency.[33]

None of the economic advantages from a more modest geopolitical role would follow automatically. Exchanging commitments in Europe for massive or widespread interventions in the Third World would hardly improve America's fiscal or geopolitical posture. To reap the budgetary advantages of European devolution, or to carry out any geopolitical strategy with tolerable efficiency, would still require a serious overhaul of the American military machine and the process of congressional oversight that has so long been postponed. The United States would still need to endow itself with the military and civilian structure to reconcile geopolitical pretensions with fiscal discipline over a long period of time.

Controlling the military budget, moreover, can never be, in itself, a panacea for chronic fiscal disorder. As the post-Vietnam era demonstrated, if other federal expenditures explode with no corresponding increase in revenues, fiscal balance remains as elusive as ever. But controlling military expenditures would greatly improve the prospects for fiscal balance. Again, fiscal balance would not guarantee a prudent and steady monetary policy. It would, however, make such a policy possible. With monetary stability in the United States, the way would lie open for the relatively steady exchange rates of the Bretton Woods era. Ending the monetary casino of recent decades would make possible, in turn, more rational and more productive patterns of saving, investment, and trade throughout the international system. And such a transformation would greatly improve the prospects for coping with the world economy's current structural problems and entering a new era of stable, long-term growth.

In short, even though restoring American fiscal equilibrium through military savings would hardly solve all the world's economic problems automatically, the chances for being able to treat those problems within the framework of a liberal world economy would greatly improve. By contrast, the probable long-range cost of not controlling America's disequilibrium, and thereby perpetuating the monetary instability of the past two decades, seems difficult to exaggerate.

To remain a viable world system in a pluralist age, liberal capitalism needs discipline and self-restraint from its leading power as well as from its lesser adherents. A reasonable case can be made that America's endemic economic disorder is today a more serious threat to the postwar international liberal order than is any plausible Soviet aggression. For whereas Soviet expansionism is reasonably contained, American fiscal and monetary disorder is not. So long as America continues its present geopolitical role, containing Soviet military power and maintaining a viable world economy seem increasingly incompatible. A strategy of devolution, designed to promote and profit from strategic pluralism, seems the logical way out.

Other options can certainly be imagined. The United States could, in theory, find some novel formula for military efficiency and fiscal discipline sufficient to reconcile the hegemonic military role with national economic equilibrium. Americans could, for example, accept conscription and sharply raise their taxes.[34] Reform of the military might succeed in radically improving America's poor ratio of power for spending.[35] Some of these policies, military reform in particular, would have to be pursued even under a strategy of geopolitical devolution. But it seems improbable that any such reforming innovations could succeed to the degree necessary to reconcile hegemony in Eurasia with solvency at home. The United States is what it is—a great sprawling and diverse democracy, full of contentious and extravagant vitality. It is not a continental Prussia—a tight, disciplined state designed for the protracted strain of an overstretched imperial role. Solutions that call for heroic changes in American character and practice seem less promising than solutions proposing that America adapt itself to the real world.

PART III

Prospects for Devolution

8

The *Pax Americana* and the *Pax Britannica*

THE NOTION of an American geopolitical devolution in Europe may sound radical, but it is certainly not novel. As a theoretical solution for American over-extension, devolution is overwhelmingly obvious. Why has it not been adopted, particularly as the instabilities of the present situation have grown more and more blatant? Two serious objections are raised against devolution. The first is that modern history is said to demonstrate that any plural system—that is, any system without a hegemonic power—is inherently unstable. The second is that to succeed, a policy of American devolution requires that Europe rise to the occasion, and it is unlikely to do so. Both are powerful arguments.

Like the two arguments against devolution, the case for it must inevitably be laced with hypothesis and speculation. Arguing that a different international arrangement would ultimately be more stable than what exists now inevitably involves a high degree of intuitive judgment and conjecture. The most that can be expected is a reasonable case for the viability of these hypothetical new arrangements—a case that has to be measured, after all, against the predictable deterioration of the status quo. The present transatlantic relationship will assuredly be forced to change. The real question is whether the change must end in a catastrophe.

This chapter examines the general historical case against pluralist systems. Using history to judge prescriptions for the future is obviously a tricky business. For those who crave precision and certainty, history is an exasperating discipline—a volatile mixture of art, science, philosophy, and literature. History does have its own "scientific method"—if science is taken in its broader philosophical meaning—but that method is one that must accommodate the high degree of uncertainty and ambiguity that inevitably accompanies the analysis of human affairs. Even where the facts seem relatively clear, few questions in history are ever settled. The human past is so copious a reality that no particular version ever captures more than a selective fragment. New interpretations are always suggesting themselves. To have history, moreover, requires not only a past but also a present that contemplates it. Each succeeding age, with its own needs and experiences, inevitably sees what went before through different eyes. New problems in the present continually engender new views of the past, and almost every age feels compelled to write its own account of what has gone before. Thus, however elusive the search for wisdom from the past, the quest is inevitable. Historians cannot easily escape from responsibility to their own time.

To add to the difficulty, the writing of history can seldom separate itself from contemporary struggles for power. Serious contemporary political participants and movements feel the need to orient themselves through some coherent view of their own roots. Generally, nations and elites that aspire to a grand role search for a historical vision, a "usable past," to justify and guide themselves. The discipline of history becomes not so much a refuge from contemporary struggles for power as one of the arenas in which the struggles take place.

The early years of the postwar *Pax Americana* illustrate this phenomenon particularly well. The leaders who laid its foundations were often rather self-conscious about their role in history. They believed that their generation had lived through the death of an old order and that it was their particular responsibility to endow the world with a new one. Their general outlook was frequently informed by what may be described as a hegemonic approach to world order, an approach that pervades many historical accounts of modern times.

As its fundamental tenet, the hegemonic approach assumes that stable peace and prosperity in the world require a benevolent hegemonic power—a predominant state managing the world system in the general cosmopolitan interest. The thesis can apply to every sphere, from keeping the peace to stemming financial panic. It provides, moreover, a broad and plausible interpretation of international history in the nineteenth and twentieth centuries, one that many postwar American leaders found particularly convincing. Britain, they believed, had played this benevolent hegemonic role throughout much of the nineteenth century. The world had enjoyed a long peace and prospered accordingly. But as other nations, most notably Germany, rose to challenge Britain's position, the orderly world of the *Pax Britannica* broke up in chaos. Benevolent liberal cosmopolitanism gave way to nationalism. Protectionism and neo-mercantilism blighted prosperity; imperial and military competition brought war. After World War I, Britain, although victorious, was too exhausted to resume its world role. Only the United States was strong enough to have assumed it. But gripped by provincial isolationism, America refused its natural destiny. As a result, the attempt to restore the liberal world failed. The global system degenerated and, by the 1930s, appeasement and economic blocs had become the order of the day. Economic misery and political revolution pointed to a second world war. As they thought of the future, America's wartime leaders and elites, nerved by this view of the past, resolved not to fail history a second time. The postwar *Pax Americana* is their creation and their monument.[1]

To say that every age seeks a view of history suitable for its needs is not to say that it will find one. Instead, political elites may cling to a view of the past quite unfitted to their present situation. Historical interpretations, like all ideas, take on a life of their own. They may easily outlive the circumstances that made them appropriate. An idea, adopted by one generation for its convenience, may come to possess the next generation and drive it to ruin. If, for example, the hegemonic view of world history suited America's position very well in 1945, and justified the role the United States was about to assume, it may equally well prove inappropriate to the American position at the end of the twentieth century. Clearly, a view of the past that sees no options between the hegemony of a single power and systemic chaos is unlikely to prove constructive in any period when the world balance of forces makes hegemony increasingly unsustainable. Policy under the influence of such a view may well have a strong tendency to alternate between despair and heroic expedients doomed to fail.

In any event, the more time that elapses, the more uncomfortable a guide the hegemonic theory becomes. The same broad reading of the past two centuries that supports a hegemonic theory of world order can also easily suggest a self-destructive evolution for all hegemonic systems. Many historians believe hegemony weakened Britain.[2] If the future follows their view of history, hegemony can be expected to weaken the United States, and the *Pax Americana*, like the *Pax Britannica*, can be expected to disintegrate. In this perspective, the gathering problems of the postwar order, exemplified in NATO, become merely a stage in this hegemonic disintegration, a rerun of the crisis of the old order. In short, the same historical view that justifies creating a hegemonic system becomes increasingly inconvenient as the hegemony matures. For, as hegemony matures, it also declines.

Unwelcome implications do not make a historical view invalid. The decline and fall of imperial systems is a recurring pattern throughout history. It seems improbable that it will never again be repeated. But does hegemonic theory give a sound view of Britain's imperial role or of general world politics in the century before World War II? Are there better explanations for how and why the old global order collapsed and the *Pax Americana* emerged from the wreckage? Do these alternate explanations give greater hope for a system without hegemony? Obviously, these are vast questions with many dimensions. Among historians, there is no definitive interpretation of them. My purpose here is to sketch two broad views about the decline of the old order, essentially to show the shortcomings of the hegemonic interpretation and the hazards of applying facile lessons from the past.

The first historical issue is the actual nature of the "old order" that gave way to the *Pax Americana*. To what extent was it, in fact, a hegemonic *Pax Britannica*? The global system before World War II, it is often said, was Europe-centered. The *Pax Americana* is supposed to mark Europe's geopolitical demotion. In some respects, this view is misleading. In reality, Europe's demotion had begun several decades before World War II and was one of the principal causes of both world wars. Part of the confusion springs from the dual nature of the international system in the last century. When people speak of the old order, they often mean two quite distinct phenomena: the European continental balance of 1815, struck at the Congress of Vienna and confirmed at Waterloo, and the global *Pax Britannica* of the mid-nineteenth century. The first was a continental balance of power; the second was a British hegemony over much of the world beyond Europe. The two, though linked to one another, were distinct.[3] Both, however, were fatally undermined well before the end of the nineteenth century.

The settlement reached at Vienna in 1815 had left the continent's major powers finely enough balanced to prevent any one of them from approaching regional predominance. With the great continental powers thus encumbered with each other, Britain had a relatively free hand to consolidate an imperial economic and military sway over vast parts of the globe. It was a moment in history when superior technology gave Western states easy access to and military advantage against not only relatively primitive peoples, but also such ancient, civilized, and formerly powerful empires as China and Turkey. Britain, already ahead of other European states in industrialization, was the principal beneficiary. Much of the rest of the globe had fallen under British hegemony, and the British Empire grew into a politico-economic entity well beyond the scale of Europe's traditional continental states. For more than half a century after 1815, Britain was the world's greatest industrial and commercial power, with the British fleet considered invincible and London the center of the world's major financial network.

Over time, Britain's global preeminence grew increasingly precarious. Militarily, it depended not only on a continental European balance, which Britain's own rise was likely to disturb, but also on an absence of other large powers outside the European balance. It further depended on an enduring Western military and political superiority that kept non-Western regions relatively easy to govern.[4]

By the mid-nineteenth century, Britain's global position already faced two obvious threats. The world had two other outsized states—Russia and the United States. Both were still preoccupied with filling out their respective continental hinterlands.

Russia's continental drive pressed the British position in India and along the whole rim of Asia. But the Russian threat proved relatively easy to contain. Russia was embraced in the European system, with ambitions toward the Ottoman Empire that directly threatened the European balance. Britain was thus able to mobilize European support against Russia, most notably in the mid-century Crimean War. Later, as Russia pressed into China, Britain struck an alliance with Japan, the first of the modern Asian states.

The American threat began to develop after President Lincoln rescued the disintegrating national government. Within a few decades, the United States had emerged as a world power, acknowledged by the 1880s to be the world's largest economy. By the 1890s, it was building a fleet, bullying the British in North America and the Caribbean, and demanding imperial status in Asia. In many areas, the British gradually decided to conciliate and co-opt rather than resist the Americans. Their American strategy grew into a sort of tactical appeasement. By 1900, British policy had started to lay the foundations for the special relationship built in World War II.[5]

Before the Russian or American threats had matured, the *Pax Britannica* faced a more immediate threat from Europe itself. As Lincoln was reaffirming federal authority in the United States, Bismarck was expanding Prussian hegemony into a powerful new German empire. As in America, political centralization in Germany accompanied a dramatic spread of industrialization. The Germans also proved excellent traders. Commercially, the British had already been driven from Europe and were increasingly menaced in their traditional world markets.[6] Unlike America, Germany was not a huge continental autarchy with vast room to expand on the other side of the Atlantic, but a limited state in Europe. To acquire a more ample territory, Germany either had to move out into the world and thus challenge Britain's global position, or else expand in Europe itself and thus break the continental balance of 1815. When Germany began adding a fleet to its already superb army, it seemed to be pursuing both goals simultaneously. Britain looked to its traditional remedy, a continental coalition to maintain the European balance. With the Franco-Russian Alliance of 1894, an anti-German combination was already in place. When Britain joined it in 1904, the lines began to form for a global showdown.[7]

The First World War proved a more severe crisis for the international system than nearly anyone had envisaged. At the heart of the conflict was a quarrel over the actual nature of the global system and its balances. From a British perspective, Germany was the aggressor, a view shared by Germany's continental neighbors, France and Russia. Germany seemed to be attempting, in its turn, the continental hegemony once pursued by Hapsburg Spain and later by both Bourbon and Napoleonic France. From the German perspective, however, the old notion of a continental balance had lost its meaning. Modern industrialization in a world political economy had already changed the entire framework of geopolitics. Not only had Britain become a world power well beyond the old European frame, but Russia and the United States—two global powers potentially greater than Britain—were already waiting in the wings.

Under these circumstances, the Germans believed the old European balance had become obsolete. A new "world balance" was needed. The notion of a European balance had become merely a British ideological weapon to prevent Germany from becoming a world power like Britain.[8] As the Germans saw it, only by breaking the obsolescent continental frame could Germany liberate its immense vitality to become a world power on the scale of Britain, America, or Russia. Like many up-and-coming aggressors, the Germans felt increasingly threatened, as indeed they were. The French refused to accept German hegemony and their own geopolitical demotion.[9] By 1914, both Russia and Britain were aroused and proved ready to join France in a war to contain the upstart.

For all its slaughter, the war provided little respite for the old order. Although the status-quo powers, Britain and France, had defeated Germany, they were unable to reconstitute either a European balance or a stable global system. Instead, the interwar years proved an interregnum during which the empty forms of the old order provided a sort of phantom system without stability or conviction. An indigenous European balance against Germany was even less attainable than before 1914. In the end, Britain, France, and Russia together had been able to defeat Germany only by bringing in the Americans. France emerged greatly weakened physically, demographically and diplomatically. Revolutionary convulsions had left Russia in hostile isolation. Without a Russian alliance, France was far less a match for Germany. With France enfeebled and Russia isolated, the continental balance could no longer liberate British power for a world role. Instead, any balance depended more than ever on Britain's active participation.

Britain was also greatly weakened. It, too, had contributed a generation to the slaughter, and its economic base was further eroded. Its long decline in trade competitiveness accelerated, while its balance of payments grew ever more dependent on "invisible earnings" from the City. The British, nevertheless, did their best to reestablish the old liberal order. Britain went back to free trade and an open capital market, with the prewar exchange rate restored by 1925. The British Empire formally annexed a large part of the Ottoman Middle East and German Africa and was therefore larger than ever. But Britain was desperately overextended, militarily and financially. With no indigenous continental balance to hold Germany, a Britain embroiled in Europe lacked the military power to sustain its position elsewhere. The City went on lending to the rest of the world, but its deposit base increasingly depended on luring foreign short-term deposits to London. In effect, the City's global empire was in hock to foreign lenders. Meanwhile, the national economy, unable to make its industries competitive at home or abroad, was plagued with record unemployment, even in the years when Europe and America enjoyed a general prosperity.[10]

The Americans emerged as the war's real winners. They, and not the British, were henceforth the world's ultimate creditors. As the Europeans spent their treasure to finance the war, the United States acquired the better part of the world's gold.[11] American monetary and trade policies, the war debts–reparations tangle, and the fiscal profligacy of several shaky postwar European governments together impeded the restoration of a more normal monetary balance. As a result, monetary conditions in much of Europe continued to depend on American capital flows. Weimar Germany was in a particularly abject dependency. After the terrible inflation of the early 1920s, Germany's money supply was essentially based on short-term American deposits, while government budgets depended on regular American loans.[12] These vital American capital flows responded mainly to domestic American policies and market conditions. American economic policies continued to be framed with little thought for the international consequences, and often reflected rather eccentric economic theories and fitful coalitions of domestic interests. America had achieved world economic predominance, but without assuming conscious responsibility for running the system.[13]

America's interwar financial position was only one aspect of its new geopolitical primacy. In many respects, the United States was the world's preeminent power. Nevertheless the *Pax Americana* was refusing to be born. Having intervened decisively to thwart Germany from creating a new "global balance," the United States proved unready to guarantee or manage the system its intervention had created. Thus the phantom system of the 1920s, with America preeminent but irresponsible. Such an order could not long survive.

By 1931, the whole jerry-built structure of world credit had collapsed into a depression. The unreal liberal restoration gave way to increasingly unbridled protectionism and imperialism. The world economy broke up into blocs. Japan and Italy were building their empires. Britain itself went off the gold standard and began organizing an imperial trading bloc. Roosevelt, who had set the United States on a firmly nationalist economic policy, torpedoed the last attempt to save the liberal order, the London Economic Conference of 1933. At the same time, Germany abandoned the liberal system, such as it was, and American financial tutelage along with it. The new Germany was once more actively revisionist, in the hands of a ruthless dictatorship whose watchwords were autarchy and revenge.[14]

In many respects, the Second World War was a repetition of the First. Hitler's world vision, for all its lunatic idiosyncrasies, based itself on the familiar German geopolitical theme: the old European balance was obsolete; the world needed a new global balance, achievable only if Europe were united around German power. Otherwise, all the European powers, Britain included, would soon be overwhelmed by the rising superpowers on the periphery. If Europe did not have a leader from within, it would be ruled by a non-European giant from without. Britain could hold its world position only through a geopolitical deal with Germany. Partnership with England would permit Germany to crush France and Russia; together Germany and Britain would keep America in check. To build this new world balance, Hitler argued, Britain should begin by abandoning the whole notion of a European balance, which, as nothing more than an anti-German ideology, no longer served Britain's interest.

As Hitler went down to defeat, he blamed his failure on British stupidity. British imaginations, according to Hitler, had never advanced beyond the obsolete formulas of the early nineteenth century. They were still fighting Napoleon. In their stupidity, Hitler declared, they were easily manipulated by sinister forces, mostly Jewish, reflecting the interests of a rootless international capitalism opposed to any global system based on strong states.[15]

The idea of Europe's uniting to preserve its global importance was hardly new with Hitler, and has always had wide appeal—to some Americans as well as to many Europeans. Nazi Germany, however, was scarcely an appealing standard-bearer for European civilization. Hitler could hardly complain if those who believed in cosmopolitan tolerance, human dignity, and liberal political forms found his regime too alien and distasteful for any collaboration, let alone partnership. Even if Britain had been willing to discount the cultural, moral, and legal costs, Hitler's geopolitical arguments were still less than compelling. Even if Hitler had ever actually offered some plausible deal, no British leader could assume that once Russia and France were crushed, and the continent's industrial strength appropriated, Germany would be content to remain merely Britain's continental partner. Britain's empire would be too tempting and vulnerable a prize for a victorious Hitler or his successors. Britain's position as a German partner estranged from America would have been not only dishonorable but bleak.[16]

Whether Britain could have reached a more satisfactory accommodation with Imperial Germany is a more complex question. Before the terrible waste of 1914–18, Britain might have expected to hold its own in an alliance with Germany. The moral and cultural costs, moreover, would certainly not have been the same as with Hitler. Hegemony after all, has many fashions. Imperial Germany's predominance on the continent could have been very different from the terrible tyranny imposed by Hitler. While the Wilhelmian monarchy had its authoritarian and unstable aspects, it was a functioning constitutional order, whose differences from the political and social systems of Britain and France may easily be exaggerated.

Whatever the hypothetical possibilities, the rest of Europe was clearly not ready for German hegemony in 1914. With France crushed in 1940, Germany finally seemed to have achieved continental hegemony but, like Napoleonic France, could not consolidate it: not only because the war continued from without, but also because the Germans could not effectively unify the continent. Here, Hitler proved

Germany's worst enemy.[17] His new European order meant psychopathic racism, an obscene political culture, and relentless economic exploitation—all reinforced by pitiless terror. European unity or world balance was hardly worth such a cost to anyone in Europe, even the Germans. Any imaginable inconveniences of American hegemony seemed a small price to be rid of Hitler. Most Western Europeans thus welcomed the *Pax Americana* as an incomparably better resolution of their geopolitical dilemma than unity under the Nazis, even if it meant the loss of empire and the partition of Europe itself.[18] In summary, Germany's effort to build a plural world balance failed twice, not only because the world powers—Britain, America, and Russia—opposed it, but because German hegemony was unacceptable to the rest of Europe.

It is easy to see why the hegemonic theory of world order has been so popular a guide to these complicated events. It provides an explanation that appears to give the history of the past century a certain schematic inevitability. The creation of a world political economy depended on the rise of Britain as world arbiter. That rise depended on particular conditions. As those conditions changed, Britain's position, and the global system built around it, grew more and more uncertain. Heroic exertions could not restore Britain's unchallenged ascendance and only further depleted its national strength. The international system began to disintegrate into contentious territorial blocs. Until conditions were ripe for a new leader, the world suffered decades of political and economic conflict, culminating in two massively destructive wars. The lesson seems clear: without an effective hegemony, the world system breaks down into chaos. The lesson of the postwar era seems equally clear: when the Americans finally took up the British role, helped into it by the British themselves, the *Pax Americana* followed with four decades of stability.

Geopolitical theory does, however, provide a major alternative, a pluralist, or balance-of-power, model of international order that comes complete with a different set of historical interpretations. The basic idea of this model is simple: unchecked power corrupts its holder and leads to overextension, unnatural dependence, exploitation, instability, and desperate resistance. By contrast, a system of several closely integrated states remains orderly and peaceful so long as power is distributed evenly enough so that no single state or coalition is tempted to strike for domination or can succeed when it tries. Under such circumstances, enlightened self-interest bids all to accept the restraints of common rules, backed by sanctions inherent in the system.[19] In effect, the internal checks and balances of constitutionalism within the nation state are extended into the international system. This is, of course, the model that the Imperial Germans tried to invoke with their notion of a global balance. Were they entirely wrong? Should the breakdown of the old order be blamed exclusively on them? Do their misbegotten attempts forever discredit the notion of a global balance or a plural world order?

From the perspective of a balance-of-power view of world order, the blame for the conflict that led to World War I can just as logically be placed on the British. Britain's immense world empire can be seen not as a precondition for the nineteenth-century peace, but as a principal cause of its breakdown. By creating a world power out of scale with traditional European states, Britain inevitably provoked imitation. Once German industry had begun to catch up with British, nothing ordained that Germany should not try to emulate Britain's global power, particularly as the Germans considered their worldwide commerce a hostage to Britain's superior navy. By what historic right were the Germans to be kept tied up within their continental straitjacket? In this pluralist perspective, Britain destabilized the global system not only by the rise of its outsized power but also by the manner of its decline. Once Britain had become a hegemon in decay, its refusal to accommodate a rising Germany provoked a war that ruined Europe and prevented the new global balance that was in Europe's best interest. That was, of course, the Imperial German charge against the British in World War I.

Britain, to be sure, was hardly the only destabilizing giant before World War I. Even more than Britain, the United States, and potentially Russia, represented agglomerations of organized economic and military power that inevitably broke the frame of the nineteenth century's plural European order. For Germany, the Russian Empire was a challenge much nearer to home. Were the Imperial Germans altogether wrong to believe they either had to expand or be dominated in turn? Were they wrong to fear the consequences of the Russian Empire's patient but inexorable accretion of power and territory?

Balance-of-power theory can also offer a different assessment of the breakdown of the interwar system. Instead of blaming the failure to recreate a viable order on the absence of hegemonic power, it may just as well be blamed on the unbridled behavior of the two powers who aspired to hegemony—Britain, the hegemon in decline, and the United States, the hegemon on the rise. Both can be said to have behaved irresponsibly, nowhere more so than in their manipulations of the international financial system after World War I, where they may be said to have wrecked any chance of reestablishing the prewar gold standard. The bastard monetary system that they did establish, the gold-exchange standard, collapsed, as its critics had predicted, and with profound consequences for the domestic and international politics of the 1930s. This interpretation of interwar financial history is interesting both for its broad view of how the prewar geopolitical system broke down and because it anticipates the quarrels over monetary rules and practices prevalent during the later decades of the *Pax Americana*.[20]

Gold-standard theory is really balance-of-power theory. Indeed, the classic model of the gold standard is among the purest models of a balance-of-power system to be found. For the theoretical model to exist in practice, national money supplies must be strictly tied to national gold reserves, and a deficit in the balance of payments must necessarily result in a loss of gold. Under such arrangements, loss of gold perforce means a domestic monetary contraction while a balance-of-payments surplus means a corresponding gold inflow and domestic monetary expansion. In an open world with free trade and free capital movements, these automatic reactions in the domestic monetary climate are supposed to bring about the compensating adjustments in trade and capital flows needed to correct the external imbalances. Everyone is thus automatically constrained to avoid monetary inflation and protracted balance-of-payments disequilibria.

For well over half a century, historians have been unable to agree on how the historic gold standard actually worked. Many British and American financial historians deny that the theoretical or classic gold standard ever existed, even in its supposed heyday from 1870 to 1914.[21] The actual system, they argue, was really a sterling standard. Before 1914, it is said, the great majority of countries now in the International Monetary Fund used the pound sterling rather than gold as their monetary base and kept their sterling reserves on deposit in London banks. For these countries, monetary conditions were regulated not primarily by gold flows but by the Bank of England's discount rate. The City of London created or contracted money and credit as it believed necessary. Because of London's great attraction as a banking center, the pounds that flowed out for investment and trade returned as the deposits of nonresidents. Whenever a net outflow of capital threatened a loss of gold, the Bank of England could raise its discount rate and liquid capital would immediately flow in from the rest of the world. The Bank is thus said to have controlled the world's money supply by a mechanism at least superficially analogous to that which has given the U.S. Federal Reserve so much control over world liquidity in the *Pax Americana*. Britain's financial power, in other words, meant that it could export capital and run a basic balance-of-payments deficit without fearing a loss of gold. To hold such a view is not to say that Britain was unconcerned with monetary stability, but rather that monetary conditions were set by London for the rest of the world, and that actual British policy was not bound by the formal rules of the classic gold standard.

From this same view, the breakdown of the gold standard can be explained essentially as the breakdown of British hegemony. After World War I undermined Britain's political prestige, industrial vitality, and military power, London gradually proved unable to sustain its financial predominance. With investors losing confidence, the City could no longer attract credit at will. The pound was no longer believed as good as gold, and both it and the London-based world financial system tottered to collapse together. In effect, these historians offer a hegemonic rather than pluralist view of the historic gold standard.

Since the 1920s, a French monetarist school has been the most ardent defender of the classic gold-standard theory, as well as of a pluralist interpretation of how the system actually worked.[22] The best known of these economists after World War II was Jacques Rueff, a frequent adviser to General de Gaulle. Rueff denied that the pre-1914 gold standard was a sterling or a sterling-exchange standard. Even if the gold standard did not apply to relations between Britain and its dependencies, it did govern relations between London and the world's other major financial capitals: Paris, Berlin, Vienna, St. Petersburg, and later, New York. Among the major independent powers, financial equilibrium did exist. As *primus inter pares*, London may have played a special role in managing temporary disturbances but was not thereby exempted from the system's fundamental rules. Until World War I, London's accounts with the other financial powers were basically in balance.[23]

The gold-standard system broke down after World War I, according to Rueff, because the rules were changed in such a fashion that the system ceased being plural, in the sense of requiring all states to follow the same rules. Instead it endowed certain states with the exorbitant privilege of creating their own international currency by fiat. According to Rueff, the transformation could be traced to the Genoa Conference of 1922, convened to consider international monetary questions, Czarist Russian debts in particular, and overshadowed in most histories by the Russo-German Treaty at nearby Rapallo. The conference recommended "economizing the use of gold by maintaining reserves in the form of foreign balances." The recommendation guided the League of Nations' Financial Committee; using the dollar and pound sterling in place of gold became accepted practice. Thus the gold standard became the gold-exchange standard. Before Genoa, an independent country's monetary reserves were held in gold; only gold was acceptable for settling net official obligations among countries. After Genoa, pounds and dollars could also be used for reserves and settlements. American and British money could thus become the basis for the national money supplies of other countries. Unlike the gold standard, where everyone followed the same rules, the gold-exchange standard created a sort of monetary hegemony—shared by Britain and the United States. Money created by fiat in Britain or America became legal tender for the rest of the world. According to its French critics, such a system was also inevitably inflationary; it gave Britain and America a license to print paper gold. It would lead, sooner or later, to a breakdown of any integrated world monetary system, with a consequent collapse of international trade and prosperity. Rueff made the same prediction for the gold-exchange standard set up in 1944 at Bretton Woods, and with the same baleful accuracy.[24]

Ironically, Britain was constrained to behave in so high-handed a fashion in the 1920s not out of strength but out of weakness. Postwar Britain could continue its traditional role of overseas lending and investing only by itself borrowing heavily abroad. Running a reserve currency, with high interest rates to keep reserves in London, was naturally a major mechanism for borrowing. By these practices, the City's global role was perpetuated, although it was being surpassed by New York. But whereas Britain's role as global creditor was formerly based on domestic savings from centuries of profits, it was now based on debts to foreign depositors. Moreover, according to Rueff, the particular mechanism that facilitated the borrowing, the gold-exchange standard, was unstable because it was inherently inflationary. Thanks to the reserve currency system, the money Britain or America was exporting abroad was not automatically being diminished correspondingly at home, as it would have been under the gold standard. In effect, Britain used its banking preeminence to create an unsound world credit structure based on inflated pounds without any real backing. When the inevitable crisis came, and depositors began demanding gold, Britain went off the gold standard it had already debased.[25] Translating Rueff's analysis of British monetary policy into geopolitical language, what broke down the world financial order after World War I was not the absence of a hegemonic power but the presence of a decaying hegemon, using its international predominance to compensate for its national weakness.

Sharing responsibility for the monetary debacle was the hegemon on the rise, the United States. The analogue to Britain's monetary weakness after World War I was the phenomenally swollen gold stock of the United States. Like the British, the Americans refused to play by the classic rules; international monetary relations could therefore never right themselves by the traditional mechanisms. The gold-exchange standard uncoupled U.S. monetary policy from the gold flows that were supposed to correct imbalances. Credits were extended to Europe without, in themselves, diminishing the American money supply. U.S. monetary policy swung sharply between expansion and contraction. Behind lofty rhetoric about holding the gold "in trust" for European nations, Europeans suspected a policy of hoarding. To compound its antisocial behavior, the United States erected a new series of trade barriers.[26]

As was only natural with the Americans monopolizing gold, the dollar became the principal source of international money. Instead of buying European goods, and thereby redistributing its gold, a protectionist America sent a flood of capital to finance the deficits of others. Under these conditions, few countries tried seriously to reestablish their finances on a sound basis. Weimar Germany, for example, refused to adjust its real economy to the country's actual postwar position. Instead, after a bout of hysterical inflation in the early 1920s, Germany depended on short-term American loans to finance an unreal prosperity.[27] France, trying to follow the classic rules, or at least to live within its means, soon found itself accumulating gold, but also having to hold sterling balances, lest the entire house of cards collapse. When the American capital hoard flowed back to New York in the stock market boom of 1928, and much of it was subsequently annihilated in the stock market crash of 1929, the system began to unravel. Britain and Germany's defection from the gold-exchange standard became inevitable. Both, in due course, turned to monetary controls and protected trade. Thanks in good part to its economic instability, Germany went over the brink into a criminal dictatorship.

It is tempting to make Rueff's view of monetary history a metaphor for the geopolitical history of the period. The fate of the gold-exchange standard becomes a pluralist cautionary tale: Britain, the hegemon in decline, hangs on by debasing the international order that it pretends to guard. Rising America takes shortsighted advantage to slide into a hegemonic role that must inevitably end in a monetary breakdown. The old and the aspiring hegemonic powers thus connive to corrupt the old liberal order. Britain, to prolong a tottering empire, betrays Europe, the world, and itself. America, to follow in Britain's footsteps, sets out on a path that leads to economic chaos, followed by its own world hegemony and eventual decline. Together, Britain and America make a genuine liberal system impossible after World War I. The consequent collapse of the 1930s brings misery and deep unrest to all countries and military dictatorships to several, Germany included. And by reestablishing the same misbegotten gold-exchange standard after World War II, Britain and America set out to make history repeat itself.

In effect, this pluralist interpretation of the past turns the hegemonic thesis on its head. It is not pluralistic systems that are unstable, but hegemonic systems. The international system breaks down not only because unbalanced and aggressive new powers seek to dominate their neighbors, but also because declining old powers, rather than adjusting and accommodating, try to convert their slipping preeminence into an exploitative hegemony.

The concept of the hegemon in decay gathers considerable reinforcement from within the hegemonic school itself. A substantial body of historical analysis teaches, for example, that Britain's long-term decline was tied to the perpetual outward looking of its political and economic elites, and the consequent neglect of the country's domestic economic and social development. Some of the most eloquent and convincing analysis along these lines comes from those historians of broad hegemonic persuasion who see a logical tendency for hegemonic systems, particularly liberal hegemonic systems, to disintegrate.[28] To function properly, a hegemonic system is said to require a substantial margin of disposable strength for the leading power. Britain's hegemony began slipping when other powers began catching up with its industrial development. Historians note Britain's failure to keep pace in the newer industries and speculate broadly on the economic, political, social, and cultural explanations.

Whatever course Britain followed, however, the rest of Europe or North America could not have been expected to remain as relatively backward industrially as in the earlier nineteenth century. Catching up was greatly stimulated by Britain's own liberal trade, investment, and peacekeeping in the rest of the world. Perhaps Britain could have been more ruthless in thwarting the industrial development of its rivals, but Britain's political traditions, economic necessities, and limited margin of military and financial superiority made such a policy unlikely to succeed for long. It is more probable that any such British policy would only have hastened the breakup of the *Pax Britannica* by eliminating its principal benefit to others.

The *Pax Americana* has, of course, evolved in the same direction. The great margin of American superiority in 1945 has predictably diminished with the rest of the world's recovery and development. In short, the decline of hegemonic powers appears to have a certain inevitability. This is not merely because exercising hegemony weakens the leader absolutely, though it may well do so, but because the success of a liberal hegemonic system tends to strengthen the other members relative to the leader. In this assessment, hegemonic and balance-of-power theorists tend to agree. The difference lies in the prescriptions that follow.

In the hegemonic vision, even if the process of decline makes collapse almost inevitable, the hegemon should hang on from a sense of duty and pride—perhaps to eke out a few more generations of advantage, perhaps to prepare the way for a successor. In the logic of the pluralist vision, the hegemonic power faces a crucial choice. It can defy the trend to a more pluralist world, or else adjust to it. If it adjusts, with the right mixture of appeasement and resistance, and others behave with reasonable prudence and responsibility, a stable plural balance may ensue. If the hegemon defies the pluralist trend, it can try to use its lingering hegemonic role as a means for bolstering its own faltering strength. Hegemony then deteriorates into the means for exploiting the international system for national ends rather than managing it in the general interest. Whereas national strength formerly upheld hegemony, national strength now increasingly depends on hegemony. Such a course predictably leads to increasing conflict and to the general breakdown of the world political economy.[29] Hence, for the pluralist view, the significance of the demise of the gold-exchange standard. It is a detailed case study of the mechanisms by which a hegemonic system progresses to its own disintegration.

As the preceding discussion illustrates, both hegemonic and balance-of-power theories of world order easily take on moral as well as descriptive dimensions. Hegemonic theory reminds the hegemon of its inescapable responsibilities for world order. Pluralist precepts demand a more universal sense of responsibility. All countries are supposed to internalize the system's restraints, since enlightened self-interest dictates that no state should permit itself to break the rules of international order. Aggression, exploitation, and imperialism, even when temporarily successful, are held ultimately to be self-destructive. To use a fortuitous superiority over neighbors in order to grow excessively large or otherwise overextended is, in the pluralist perspective, a formula for national disaster. So is the complacent weakness of lesser states whose inattention to their own independence and legitimate interests permits others to grow too powerful or ambitious.[30] Among the moral dangers of benevolent hegemony is the psychological and political decay of those lesser states that grow comfortable in their irresponsible dependency.

Broad geopolitical theories and their historical applications enrich our understanding of history while inevitably distorting it. Such theories can never be proved to everyone's satisfaction. For interpreting the last century and a half, the pluralist approach offers, at the very least, a vigorous theoretical alternative to the hegemonic view. The internal weakness of the hegemonic model—the self-destructive character of hegemony itself—seems obvious enough. As the histories of both the *Pax Britannica* and the *Pax Americana* appear to illustrate, the problem is more than theoretical.

The same histories suggest, however, that the practical problems of a pluralist system are scarcely less formidable. Clearly, a balance-of-power system, no less than a hegemonic system, can be stable only under favorable circumstances. Pluralist maxims about self-interest in self-restraint are likely to seem compelling only when world conditions provide few easy opportunities to evade them. Power vacuums tempt even the most virtuous or phlegmatic states into extending themselves, if only to preempt a competitor.

To reach the obvious conclusion: the relevance of theories of world order, like the relevance of most other political theories, is highly contingent on prevailing conditions. Chapter 3 discusses, for example, the impracticality of Kennan's pluralist vision in the years following World War II or, indeed, during the interwar years. The same impracticality may be seen to extend backward to the last century. Whatever the intrinsic weaknesses of hegemonic order, it must be confessed that neither the late nineteenth century nor the interwar period was well-suited to sustain a stable, pluralist system. If the hegemony of the *Pax Britannica* was doomed, so was the European balance of 1815.

Before World War II, two particular historical conditions appear to have made a pluralist world system inherently unstable. The first was the ease and vigor of Western political and military domination over the rest of the world. The second was the powerful impetus to territorial imperialism that arose from the nature of western industrial development.

The first condition seems relatively straightforward. The West's military technology and capacity for political mobilization were so superior that all the rest of the globe lay open to Western domination. Under such circumstances, it would have been unlikely for Britain, as the greatest seapower, to spurn the historic opportunity for world empire, any more than either the United States or Russia was likely to refuse its manifest destiny to reach the Pacific. With all the world a feast for Western imperialism, some sort of showdown between those Western powers who came to it early and those who came later seems to have been inevitable. Germany was arguably not more aggressive than the others, only less lucky in its historical timing and geographical location. Under the prevailing international circumstances, all Western states grew aggressive. Expansion was too easy and too rewarding. In short, the old order grew unstable because it could not cope with the scale of temptation created by the West's technological superiority over the rest of the world.

This geopolitical hypothesis grows more complex and fruitful when linked with theories about the ties between the West's internal economic development and its external aggression. Leninist historians insist, for example, that Western industrial growth created not only the external opportunity for aggression but also the inner compulsion. Whereas most geopolitical theories, following Hobbes, attribute external aggressiveness to more or less universal moral and psychological causes that operate whenever the opportunity presents itself, the Marxist-Leninst school links modern imperialism to specific forms of internal economic and social development. Lenin's *Imperialism: The Highest Stage of Capitalism*, written during World War I, is the classic statement of this view.[31] For Lenin, the West's industrialization created not only the power to pursue imperialism, but also the need.

In effect, the Leninist thesis about imperialism constitutes a third broad view of international order and interpretation of modern international history. Both the theory and the interpretation greatly reinforce the hegemonic view. Lenin's analysis of imperialism started with the Marxist analysis of capitalism. Because of its class system, capitalism's growth concentrated its rapidly increasing wealth in the elites instead of dispersing it democratically. The result, Marx taught, was an excess of capital for investment, which meant both rapid growth and an eventual shortage of demand for industry's products—in other words, underconsumption and a surplus of capital. Along with this familiar Marxist precept, Lenin incorporated a political and economic analysis of imperialism developed by several English liberal writers, notably John Stuart Mill and John Hobson.[32] Both saw imperial expansion to underdeveloped regions as the means to assuage the capitalist problems of surplus capital and overproduction. Empires could also provide a much-needed outlet for surplus population and redundant elites.

Mill wrote at mid-century, when Britain's global supremacy still seemed relatively unchallenged. On the whole, imperialism seemed to him a benevolent phenomenon, a means not only of spreading growth and enlightenment throughout the globe, but also of relieving stagnation and social tension in the capitalist homeland. Understandably, Lenin took a less complacent view in 1916. Now that there were several advanced capitalist states, Lenin argued, the problem of overproduction had come to encompass the entire world. There were now several industrial nations needing empires. Old imperial capitalist states, like Britain and France, naturally refused to make room for such newer arrivals as Germany. But with Germany united and industrialized, Britain and its allies were not strong enough to suppress Germany's challenge. The capitalist international system had broken down into an all-out war that would recur again and again so long as capitalism was the predominant politico-economic system among the great powers. In effect, Lenin's analysis merged Marxist and liberal insights with the views of the hegemonic school. Marxism explained why capitalism had an insatiable need for growth. Hobson and Mill showed how growth had transformed itself into imperialism. Hegemonic theory explained why, in the absence of a securely dominant power, capitalist international relations led inevitably to global war.

This is not the place to argue the multitudinous issues raised in Lenin's broad thesis. Despite the shortcomings many historians find in Lenin's theory, the conditions leading to World War I lent considerable plausibility to any thesis that linked capitalist industrialization with imperialism and war. Capitalism had liberated the exponential creativity of modern technology. Within the industrializing Western states, profound economic, social, and political transformations were inevitable. The West's overwhelming military and political superiority made imperialism seem an easy way to adjust. With Western countries reaching their capitalist maturity at different times, conflict between those who acquired empires early and those who sought them later was more or less inevitable. Economic rivalry thus turned eventually into territorial conflict.

Particular territorial quarrels over particular colonies seemed less significant than the general clash of expansive power and ambition. Thus Imperial Germany, which had, on the whole, scant interest in particular colonies, nevertheless felt compelled to build a fleet and become a "world power." To do otherwise and remain confined to Europe was widely thought to mean economic as well as strategic strangulation.

As a Marxist, Lenin could claim that replacing capitalist with communist politico-economic systems would eventually end the global territorial conflict. Lenin's claim reflected an idea as old as Plato: a nation in internal equilibrium—at peace with itself—would be at peace with its neighbors.[33] For those skeptical that communist regimes would eliminate international conflict, or opposed to communism in any case, Lenin's solution was unconvincing and unwelcome. But under the circumstances of the time, the link between capitalist industrialization and geopolitical conflict was difficult to brush aside. The question is whether a similar analysis seems valid now. In other words, in our own time, as the *Pax Americana* fades, do the same broad conditions that formerly made plural systems unstable still prevail?

There is some cause for relative optimism. Two mutations seem to have made the postwar world political economy radically different from those of the late nineteenth or early twentieth centuries. One change, essentially political and military, has been the rise of independent Third World states; the other, essentially economic and social, has been the apparent capability of Western governments to sustain prosperity without empires. The two changes have been complementary. At the same time as the political and military changes have made imperialism more costly and hazardous, the economic changes have made it less necessary.

The first change has already been discussed at length. Even if decolonization after World War II left many of the Third World countries still economically dependent on the West, the political relationships nevertheless altered radically. Most of the globe ceased being a vacuum waiting to be filled by a handful of active geopolitical powers. For all their weaknesses, Third World countries were no longer merely passive objects of imperialist competition. Thus, while industrial states have continued to struggle for influence and markets, their competition has been limited by the independence of the Third World countries themselves. Even the super-powers have had great difficulty intervening successfully with military force.[34] In short, a vacuum no longer beckons. In this fundamental respect, not only is the present structurally more plural than the nineteenth century, but it also ought to be more favorable to peace among the advanced powers.

If this pluralist evolution removes a major source of conflict among states at the center of the global system, it obviously creates a great variety of new problems on the periphery. In the absence of Western domination, new national states have to define themselves, and regional sub-systems, hegemonic or plural, need to evolve. Breakdowns in these processes invite outside interventions, which renew the danger of conflicts among major world powers, particularly the superpowers, as postwar history amply demonstrates. Still, the high costs and hazards of intervention induce prudence. Thus, while regional wars among Third World states may become an increasing problem, particularly as some approach the status of important military powers, direct clashes between outside powers seem less and less probable.[35]

What about the second mutation? In our current stage of industrial development, do advanced economies no longer need empires in order to prosper?

For several postwar decades, Western capitalism has resolved the old problem of overproduction, thus removing what Lenin believed was the major incentive for imperialism and war. Postwar capitalism's success in this respect can be laid to many causes. Accumulating wealth has given governments the means to raise social welfare and thus buy domestic political peace without foreign diversions. The arms race and proxy wars have perhaps become an economic and political substitute for imperialist expansion. Most of all, Western industry has oriented itself around mass consumption—a trend long in the making with the rise of such industries as house-hold and electrical goods, food processing, mass entertainment, and, above all, automobiles. With the predominance of these industries came the postwar consumer society, an economy in which the mass public of the producing country could absorb the product of its own industry. Mass consumption and Keynesian demand management were obvious twins. The Keynesian welfare state could sustain demand by domestic redistribution of incomes and purchasing power.[36] All these factors together produced a major change in the structural problems of the capitalist system after World War II. As the *Pax Americana* came into being, the principal difficulties of Western economies were no longer Leninist underconsumption and excessive saving; instead, inflation—produced by overconsumption and undersaving— became the new Western ailment.

The change also appeared to affect greatly the economic position of Third World states. In the prewar era, Western industrial prosperity depended on favorable terms of trade for agricultural products and other raw materials. Since the critical markets were outside the industrial countries themselves, an industrial depression was likely to follow whenever the price of food and raw materials turned down in relation to the price of industrial goods. By contrast, for much of the period after World War II, the industrial countries sustained record growth and prosperity in the face of declining raw materials and food prices. In effect, the demand that once depended on prosperity in the nonindustrial world was being stimulated at home. When the terms of trade did reverse themselves to favor raw materials over manufactures, in the sharp secular rise in prices for oil, food, and some other commodities in the early 1970s, the result was a sharp check to Western prosperity. Industrial nations had great difficulty limiting domestic consumption and reorienting production to exports.[37]

Prolonged unfavorable terms of trade for raw materials throughout the 1950s and 1960s naturally had discouraging effects in many Third World countries.[38] The price revolutions of the 1970s benefited some while gravely hurting others. The rapid fall of oil prices in the mid-1980s brought a new round of economic dislocations to the Third World.

But as chapter 2 observes, political considerations have regularly mitigated the Third World's economic disadvantages. Third World governments have demanded development aid to modernize and diversify their economies. American and European support has been sharpened by the fear of spreading Soviet influence, as well as by the lure of high profits for multinational firms. Often with abundant Western help, some Third World states have themselves developed into important industrial producers. In effect, global industrial pluralism has gradually followed political pluralism.

By the 1970s, Third World industrialization was creating new relationships and acute new problems within the world political economy.[39] In due course, the problems within and between the First and Third Worlds may themselves generate a capitalist crisis, as the growing politicization of trade disputes in the 1980s began to suggest. But this new crisis, if it comes, is not likely to be an old-fashioned imperialist falling-out over the spoils. Rather it will arise from the failure to adjust to the shifting strength of America, Europe, Japan, and the Third World, or to maintain a global financial framework conducive to rational adjustments within real economies. It will be a failure to accommodate the new industrial pluralism. As the rise of American protectionism began to make clear in the 1980s, the burden of accommodation cannot be borne by the Americans alone, nor can the global system expect to make much progress until the United States puts its own house in order. That, of course, brings us back to America's fiscal crisis, its geopolitical causes, and the prospects for helping to resolve it through European devolution.

Before going on, we need to take a final look at this grand argument about plural and hegemonic systems in history. What, finally, are the lessons to be drawn from the demise of the old order for the future of the *Pax Americana*?

Since World War II, the international system has enjoyed a stability and prosperity that calls to mind the Victorian *Pax Britannica*. The hegemonic view naturally attributes these conditions to the predominance of the United States. This chapter began by noting how important hegemonic geopolitical theory and historical interpretation based on it have been for postwar American policy. But while the hegemonic view served well enough to inspire the creation of the *Pax Americana*, it also carried troubling implications for its future, the future that now seems fast upon us. Hegemony has a tendency to break down because of the absolute or relative weakening of the hegemonic power itself. A hegemon in decay begins to exploit the system in order to compensate for its progressing debility.

Present events appear to fit this pattern all too well. Under the mantle of *Pax Americana*, the rise of Europe, Japan, China, and other developing states has made American predominance increasingly strained. As a result, today's historic challenge lies in adapting the postwar system to the decline of American predominance and to the rise of middle-range powers—old and new—not only in the First World but also in the Third World. The danger is not merely that America's lingering hegemony will collapse, but that the attempt to hang on to it will ruin the chances for stability in a more plural system.

The same past that gives ample warning about the danger of outmoded hegemony does not, of course, guarantee success for any succeeding pluralist regime. As Leninist, as well as hegemonic, analysis proclaims, plural systems are themselves inherently unstable, in Lenin's view because of the compulsive imperialism of industrial capitalism. During the years of the *Pax Americana*, however, basic changes in the fundamental character both of the global system and of capitalist competition have gradually improved the prospects for pluralist stability. The political and military rise of the Third World appears to doom colonialism while changes in the nature of Western economies appear to make it unnecessary. Under these circumstances, many of the lessons of the past, as seen through hegemonic or Leninist perspectives, seem of questionable relevance.

In summary, whether the *Pax Americana* can be successfully transformed into a more plural structure depends less on any iron laws of history than on whether, for a start, the United States and Europe can rise to the occasion of a more plural sharing of responsibilities. If they cannot, or will not, history is full of dismal lessons about what to expect. Under the circumstances, American and European elites need, at the very least, a more useful and ample view of the past than the hegemonic interpretation provides.

9

Military Arrangements

NO ONE can prove that Europe would rise to the occasion of an American devolution. But since the major European states are advanced, populous, rich, and powerful militarily, and since they have long historical experience with defending themselves, it seems reasonable to wonder why they shouldn't be able to manage their own defense. From any historical perspective, the notion that France and Germany together should not be able to balance Russia in Europe strains credulity. What then are we to think of France and Germany allied with Britain, Italy, and all the rest of NATO? Nevertheless, throughout the postwar period conventional wisdom has counted the Europeans unable to manage their own defense unless America takes the leading role. Three broad reasons are usually given: (1) without a hegemonic American protectorate, Western European states lack the military capacity to balance the Soviets in Europe; (2) without American hegemony in NATO, Western European states lack the political cohesion among themselves to sustain a military coalition; and (3) without American hegemony in NATO, the Soviet Union's attraction would prove too powerful for Western Europe to sustain a cohesive coalition against it.

This chapter discusses Western Europe's military capacities. Chapter 10 examines its political cohesion, and chapter 11, the Soviet threat and its limits.

For American devolution to succeed militarily, a Europeanized NATO would not have to constitute a military improvement; it would need only to be adequate

TABLE 9.1

NATO and Warsaw Pact Manpower and Divisions

	NATO	Warsaw Pact
Total Ground Forces*	2,979	2,809
Total Ground Force Reserves*	4,681	5,280
Total Ground Forces Deployed in Europe*	2,088	2,685
Divisions deployed in Europe manned in peacetime	33	78⅓
Divisions manned and available for immediate frontal reinforcement	100	98
Total war-mobilized divisions	133	176⅓

* Troop figures given in thousands.
SOURCE: I.I.S.S., *The Military Balance 1985–1986* (London: International Institute for Strategic Studies, 1985), 186.

or, in any event, no worse militarily than what is now in place. As it happens, however, Europeanization is probably the only way the alliance can resolve its long-range military difficulties.

Judging the current military situation is easier said than done. Critics and apologists alike frequently assert that NATO suffers from a severe shortage of military means. By any reasonable reckoning, however, NATO spends a great deal more money on defense than does the Warsaw Pact. And, for whatever it is worth, NATO has roughly the same number of men under arms. Even the most pessimistic calculations give NATO five million versus six million for the Warsaw Pact. Total reserves also show a rough balance, a ratio of only 1.13 to 1 in favor of the Warsaw Pact. Within Europe itself, a rough balance exists in ground forces, a ratio of 1.29 to 1 in favor of the Warsaw Pact. Even without American forces in Europe, Warsaw Pact manpower achieves only a 1.44 to 1 advantage.[1]

Broad comparisons of manpower are useful to dispel persistent illusions about Eastern hordes. But raw numbers may easily prove misleading. The organization and general quality of manpower and equipment are critical for determining real combat power. Such criteria are often difficult to measure or even to define in comparative terms. The Soviets, for instance, are markedly superior in the number of divisions, disproportionately so compared to the overall manpower totals (see table 9.1).

Not only are Soviet divisions smaller, and thus more numerous in proportion to manpower, but internally they have a relatively high ratio of combat to support troops. Superiority in the number of divisions, or in the ratio of combat to support troops, does not automatically mean superior combat power. Defenders of NATO's practice believe Western divisions are more flexible and better able to carry on sustained operations. Soviet divisions, lacking support troops, have been said to be incapable of anything other than a quick blitzkrieg. But many other Western experts have disagreed.[2]

Comparing the quality of manpower also involves reckoning elusive variables like training, morale, and loyalty. Warsaw Pact totals, for example, include a substantial number of Eastern European satellite armies whose training and equipment vary and whose political reliability must seem doubtful to Moscow. How should these forces be weighed in a military balance? Judging differences in weapons and equipment is no less complex. American high performance and multipurpose fighter aircraft are difficult to compare with more numerous but less sophisticated Soviet fighters. The Warsaw Pact's superiority in main battle tanks represents, among other things, an early NATO decision to downplay tanks because of highly sophisticated guided antitank weapons. How, then, should the differences in aircraft or tanks be assessed?[3]

Military experts argue endlessly over these matters. Much of what they say publicly is with an eye to budgetary debates. Before Congress or the press, the same army that favors large divisions as more efficient is not above counting the smaller enemy divisions as equivalent to its own. The same air force that builds much more complex and expensive airplanes than its adversary is not above pointing with alarm at the enemy's consequent numerical superiority in aircraft.[4]

Any comparison of forces must weigh the relative efficiency of their deployment and mobilization. Even when an overall balance of conventional forces exists, significant imbalances on certain fronts, or critical differences in the speed of mobilization and reinforcement on those fronts, may prove vital in an actual attack. Thus, in theory, the balance needs to be reckoned for each of NATO's major sectors—its Northern and Mediterranean flanks as well as its Central Front.[5]

The Central Front, however, is obviously the critical sector for any East-West military confrontation in Europe. Along that Central Front (Denmark, the Low Countries, West Germany and Berlin, East Germany, Poland, and Czechoslovakia), NATO and the Warsaw Pact seem to have approximately the same number of active ground troops. The Warsaw Pact has around 975,000 troops compared to NATO's 814,300—a ratio of 1.2 to 1. NATO totals include French forces in Germany but not those in France itself (see table 9.2).

Attempts to translate these figures into combat strength suffer from the ambiguities just mentioned—the different divisional sizes and structures as well as the different types and qualities of weapons, or political reliability and morale. An unusually judicious and comprehensive study was made public in 1976 by Robert Lucas Fischer, an arms control expert in the Arms Control and Disarmament Agency (ACDA) with access to classified sources. Allowing for the multiplicity of organizational variables, the Fischer study estimated NATO and Warsaw Pact combat manpower at a ratio of 1 to 1.36—an imbalance not unfavorable enough to be, in

TABLE 9.2

Ground Force Manpower: Central Front (in thousands)

NATO		Warsaw Pact	
Belgium	67.2	Czechoslovakia	145
Britain (BAOR)	55.2	East Germany	120
Canada	6.3	Poland	210
Denmark	17.0	Soviet Union	500
France	48.5		
Luxembourg	0.7		
Netherlands	67.0		
United States	206.8		
West Germany	335.6		
In Berlin:			
Britain	3.0		
France	2.7		
United States	4.3		
Total	814.3		975

SOURCE: I.I.S.S. *The Military Balance 1985–1986*, 3–36.

itself, a great cause for alarm. Taking into account differences in weapons, Fischer concluded that in peacetime there exists a rough balance of conventional forces on the Central Front.[6]

The study found, however, that because relative capacities for mobilization differed significantly, *when* NATO began to mobilize in response to a full-scale Soviet buildup would be critical. Most experts foresee serious difficulties for NATO if its mobilization were to begin seven days or more after that of the Warsaw Pact. Since a Warsaw Pact mobilization will probably seem ambiguous in its early stages, many analysts fear democratic Western governments will hesitate too long (see table 9.3).[7]

The most dangerous period, according to Fischer, thus falls between M+7 (seven days after the Warsaw Pact mobilizes) and M+14. During this time, the numbers favor the Warsaw Pact by between 1.6 and 1.95 to 1. Since a 3:1 ratio is commonly thought necessary for a successful offensive breakthrough, NATO's situation— even in this worst period—seems far from desperate.[8]

How significant are such elaborate calculations? With so many variables, and so little agreement on how to measure them, any reckoning of the actual or potential conventional military balance inevitably remains highly problematical. The notion that military confrontations can be reduced to precise rules, mathematical equations, or economic bookkeeping has long beguiled military practitioners as well as their civilian colleagues. But the realities of military strength have nevertheless remained invincibly elusive until the moment of testing. Throughout most of history, winning and losing battles has been only loosely correlated to the size of armies or the

TABLE 9.3

Mobilization and Reinforcement (divisional manpower in 10,000s)

	M	+7	+14	+21	+28	+35
NATO						
Belgium	2.5	2.5	3.3	3.3	3.3	3.3
Britain	4.1	4.5	5.9	6.6	6.6	6.6
Canada	0.3	0.3	0.3	0.3	0.3	0.3
Denmark	1.7	2.0	2.0	2.0	2.0	2.0
France	3.4	8.2	9.2	9.2	9.2	9.2
Luxembourg	—	—	—	—	—	—
Netherlands	3.0	3.0	5.0	5.0	5.0	5.0
United States	8.4	9.0	12.2	14.9	15.8	18.6
West Germany	18.0	18.5	21.0	21.0	21.0	21.0
Total	41.4	48.0	58.9	62.3	63.2	66.0
Warsaw Pact						
Czechoslovakia	8.3	8.3	10.3	10.3	10.3	10.3
East Germany	6.0	6.0	6.0	6.0	6.0	6.0
Poland	12.4	12.4	14.4	14.4	14.4	14.4
Soviet Union	29.7	39.6	62.7	62.7	62.7	62.7
Total	56.4	66.3	93.4	93.4	93.4	93.4

SOURCE: Robert Lucas Fischer, *Defending the Central Front: The Balance of Forces*, Adelphi Paper, no. 127 (London: I.I.S.S., 1977), 23.

weight of their arms. Training and morale, quality and readiness of equipment, superior tactics and strategy, surprise, unpredictable allies, and plain luck have all played critical roles. War has always been and remains a highly inexact science.

In today's world, weighing the significance of any balance of conventional forces is profoundly complicated by the presence of nuclear arms. No conventional attack can succeed in the face of an extensive nuclear counterattack directed against either the attacking forces, their rearward reinforcements, or even their command, communications, or supply centers. Military planners sometimes envisage future conflicts as an intimate mixture of nuclear and conventional arms—with troops maneuvering through repeated nuclear exchanges. But so long as both sides are well endowed with, and use, their nuclear weapons, decisive victory for one side or the other seems improbable. Clearly, trading nuclear exchanges cannot go on for very long in any territory without making any form of organized ground warfare impossible. In other words, if both sides possess and use nuclear weapons, one cannot defeat the other with conventional forces.

A limited nuclear first strike to prepare the ground for a successful conventional attack is another scenario that seems unconvincing. Theoretically, a nuclear first strike by the attacking forces could destroy the opponent's capacity for nuclear retaliation on the battlefield, as well as greatly reduce his capacity for conventional defense. Some military experts, among the French in particular, fear that the massive installation of Soviet SS-20s aimed at Europe had precisely this purpose. Soviet missiles, if accurate enough, could even be armed with conventional warheads. But even if the Soviets could preempt the entire American arsenal of nuclear-armed missiles and airplanes based in Europe, the United States could still strike the European battlefield from the sea or from the U.S. itself. A Soviet first strike against American home territory, even if intentionally limited to strategic targets, would be less likely to eliminate the American capacity to wage nuclear war in Europe than to ensure a massive retaliation on the Soviet Union. Such an exchange would soon make the European conventional battle irrelevant.[9] As for France, even its relatively limited tactical and theater nuclear forces could be preempted only by a multiple strike against France itself. Such a Soviet attack would be massive and devastating enough to run a high risk of triggering a direct retaliation on the major cities of the Soviet Union from France's sea-based strategic missiles. Again, such an exchange would soon make the outcome of a European territorial battle irrelevant to both France and the Soviet Union.

If a nuclear counterattack can stop any conventional thrust, what then is the purpose of conventional forces in European defense? In the days of overwhelming American nuclear superiority, conventional defense was counted merely as a "trip wire" for the nuclear forces, or a "plate-glass window" to guard against limited grabs for specific territories.[10] Risking America's nuclear wrath was thought to be so preposterous that a brief pause seemed adequate to permit the Soviets to back down. In the age of strategic parity and multiple European deterrents, however, the roles assigned to conventional forces have grown more complex. Conventional defense constitutes several vital links in a chain of graduated responses on the way to full-scale nuclear war. In its armory of responses, the relative emphasis a country assigns to conventional defense depends, presumably, on how it assesses its own relative strengths and vulnerabilities in conventional versus nuclear warfare. Logically, the balance depends on what might be called asymmetries of vulnerability and asymmetries of commitment.

Nuclear vulnerability varies significantly among the major European powers. Germans, East and West, are the most vulnerable. Germany is a small country compared to the superpowers. Its territory is the most likely site for a conventional battle. If the battle escalates to tactical nuclear weapons, they will most likely be used on German soil. What seems merely tactical use to the Soviets or to Germany's own allies will quickly seem strategic to the Germans. So-called limited nuclear war would rapidly destroy the whole country. Since the German Federal Republic has no nuclear weapons of its own, it cannot threaten to retaliate in kind on the territory of its attackers. For that, Germany must rely on its American ally.

Somewhat less vulnerable are the British and French. Either one is too small to have much hope of surviving extensive nuclear attack. But because they possess their own strategic deterrents, they may hope to escape direct attack on their home territories. Both could probably devastate the Soviet Union even if they were themselves destroyed in the exchange. For Britain, which is an island, the prospects are doubtless better than for France, whose own territory forms the immediate rear of any West German defense and could be the staging area for launching nuclear missiles on the battlefield.

Less vulnerable still is the Soviet Union, which is far enough away from the battlefield to escape having its own territory involved in conventional or limited nuclear fighting. The Soviets must expect, moreover, that their overwhelming nuclear arsenal makes it improbable that the Europeans would strike first against Russian home territory—particularly since Soviet missiles used in a German battle could be fired from Eastern Europe rather than from the Soviet Union itself.

Least vulnerable, of course, is the United States. Its territory is far away from the European battlefield and its supply of missiles and delivery systems guarantees that it can never be deprived of the capacity either to devastate the Soviet Union or to intervene with nuclear weapons in any European battle. In that event, the United States would do its best to limit nuclear exchanges to Europe itself. Logically, it should be loath to attack the Soviet Union—even in the most limited fashion—because that would invite a retaliatory nuclear attack on the United States.

Despite their giant nuclear arsenals and relative invulnerability, the superpowers have nevertheless been the most interested in the conventional military balance. Western European governments, by contrast, have generally seemed more content to rest Europe's security on the threat of nuclear escalation. Traditionally, the NATO allies have resisted American efforts to strengthen conventional defense to where it might be considered safely adequate to prevent a Soviet conventional attack. Their resistance persists today, even in the face of a strong peace movement that reflects increased popular consciousness of the futility and horror of nuclear war and often urges stronger conventional defense as an alternative.[11]

Beyond questions of cost, European governments believe nuclear deterrence to be safer than conventional deterrence. The possibility of a war in Europe is far less with nuclear deterrence, they assume, than without it. Historically, they are probably correct. Had it not been for nuclear weapons, it is difficult to believe that Europe could have avoided a war from 1945 to the present—given the division of Germany and the restiveness of Eastern Europe. Thanks to nuclear deterrence, Europe has had a degree of security against military attack unknown in its modern history—despite the lack of an otherwise viable political settlement. European governments have no desire to weaken the effect of nuclear deterrence by suggesting, through a larger conventional buildup, any diminishing of NATO's will to use its nuclear forces. As European strategists see it, their differences with the Americans, in this respect, merely indicate an asymmetry of commitment. European governments are willing to risk a strategic nuclear war to save Europe from invasion; the United States would prefer a form of deterrence less threatening to itself.

Throughout the history of the alliance, the Europeans have essentially had their way. The reason is quite simple: NATO cannot have a conventional deterrent unless the Europeans themselves provide the forces. The United States is incapable of supporting the land forces needed for a European conventional deterrent over a long period. Even the present U.S. conventional commitment severely strains American resources. In short, America's role as Europe's protector is possible only so long as it is based on nuclear rather than conventional forces. Hence, the weakening credibility of American nuclear protection, thanks to parity, is NATO's fundamental military problem. But the solution American administrations have preferred since Kennedy—a conventional deterrent in Europe—has always been beyond America's means.

The Europeans themselves, however, have been highly selective in pursuing the logic of their own preferences. Compensating for superpower parity without a European conventional buildup presumably requires increased European nuclear capabilities. But while Britain and France have built their own national nuclear forces, there is no European nuclear force for Germany, the country most immediately threatened. Creating such a European or German force would raise acute political problems among the Europeans themselves, as well as with the Russians and Americans. Rather than facing those problems, Europeans—Germans included—have preferred to leave the defense of Germany to the Americans. Hence, as American deterrence has grown more uncertain, Europe's German problem has begun to stir. The problem of deterrence for Europe thus seems to have caught both Americans and Europeans in a basic dilemma: the solution the Americans would logically prefer—conventional deterrence—the Americans cannot provide. The solution the Europeans should logically prefer—an indigenous nuclear deterrent—they cannot or will not provide, at least not for Germany, where it is most needed.

Fortunately, both sides have been able to compromise enough to keep the alliance afloat. To satisfy the Europeans, the Americans have put nuclear weapons in Europe and have appeared to engage themselves in a greater degree of nuclear coupling than they would like. To satisfy the Americans, the Europeans have contributed a more serious conventional force than their basic strategy probably requires. The result is a large and expensive NATO conventional force that nevertheless falls short of constituting an adequate conventional deterrent. Both sides have collaborated to develop a plausible theory to explain such a result: NATO's high but inadequate level of conventional forces is needed to deny the Warsaw Pact the prospect of any quick and easy conventional victory. If Soviet troops could count on being able to smash their way across West Germany with little serious opposition, they might be tempted to present NATO with a *fait accompli* before the alliance could make up its mind to react with nuclear weapons. Once the

Soviets were installed in Germany, neither Americans nor West Europeans might be inclined to risk a nuclear riposte—on Germany or the Soviet Union. More realistically, to leave the Soviets the option of a quick and certain conventional victory would make them more aggressive politically. Miscalculation leading to war would grow more likely. Neutralism and appeasement would appeal more strongly to Europeans and disengagement to Americans. A more divided NATO would reinforce Soviet boldness and overreaching.

Does NATO in the 1980s have the conventional capacity to fulfill even the relatively modest aim of blocking a quick and certain Soviet conventional victory? The broad answer is certainly that it does. While it seems widely assumed that the Soviets would win a prolonged conventional war in Europe, most analysts consider NATO capable of waging a major battle against a Soviet conventional attack—the least that might be expected, given NATO's large forces and huge expenditures. Beyond a short war, however, NATO would have to use nuclear weapons. This is the conventional wisdom about the military balance. As things now stand, it is probably correct.

Many analysts believe NATO's forces could easily be greatly strengthened, often by only marginal increases in spending or manpower, or by removing political impediments to a more coherent strategy and deployment. Some believe NATO ought to be able to handle almost any conventional attack without needing to resort to nuclear weapons.[12] The obviousness of some of the measures proposed suggests that NATO either has never taken the possibility of a conventional war very seriously or else has deliberately avoided reaching a conventional balance with the Soviets. Examining the major proposals for strengthening NATO's conventional deterrence perhaps reveals better than anything else its actual military condition.

The oldest proposal is that NATO bring its force structure and deployment into greater harmony with its strategy. That strategy commits the alliance to a forward defense. A Soviet attack is to be met on the West German frontier, not "in depth" between the frontier and the Rhine. The Germans, understandably, are resolutely opposed to a strategy that calls for yielding large amounts of territory to fight an extended war of maneuver. While experts quarrel over whether NATO should commit itself to a static and rigid defense, no one denies that fortifying the border would substantially increase the effectiveness of forward defense—or defense of any other kind. Despite the appeal of forward defense, however, West German sensibilities prohibit NATO from fortifying the border because it would suggest a permanent separation of the Federal Republic from the German Democratic Republic.[13] Indulging these German sensibilities was relatively harmless under a strategy of massive retaliation, where conventional defense was merely a trip wire, but obviously grows more inappropriate under flexible response, where conventional defense is supposed to be taken seriously.

The same lack of concern for conventional defense is mirrored in the composition and deployment of the NATO forces actually stationed along the Central Front. On the one hand, the uneven quality of forces on the line exposes NATO to a quick breakthrough—the principal danger in any rigid forward strategy. On the other hand, NATO's lack of armored operational reserves not committed to the front line almost guarantees that any breakthrough would prove fatal. Whatever its merits, forward defense is unlikely to succeed if obvious holes are left in the line. As the Central Front is now constituted, the British, Belgians, Dutch, and Germans cover the North; Germans hold the Center; and Americans and Germans cover the South. NATO forces in the North are easily the weakest. Not only are the Belgian forces generally inadequate but two-thirds of the Dutch forces theoretically at the front are actually back in Holland. Under the best of circumstances, it would take them at least five hours and perhaps up to two days to reach the forward position they are meant to be holding. Again, such arrangements may have been understandable with a strategy of massive retaliation, when the appearance of West European solidarity was more important than the actual military effectiveness of conventional forces. But under flexible response, such arrangements can only be described as frivolous.[14]

The lack of operational reserves—heavily armed mobile troops standing ready to defeat any breakthrough of the forward defense—is probably NATO's greatest single military deficiency. The lack of such reserves is closely linked to the critical issue of French participation. France currently keeps three small divisions in Germany, well behind the front lines. The French First Army, stationed in France, also supposedly has the defense of Germany as its mission. A highly mobile Rapid Action Force is newly developed for this First Army, with rapid reinforcement of NATO's forward defense said to be among its possible missions. In theory, French forces could be NATO's missing operational reserves. The present French forces, however, are not large enough for this function. Some question exists about whether they are heavily enough armored. Most importantly, their availability is conjectural, since they are not under the command of the SACEUR and their participation in Germany's defense depends on the French government of the time.[15]

The same conditionality characterizes NATO's use of French territory. Without the use of French space, however, a NATO conventional defense of Germany is difficult to take seriously. At its widest point, West Germany's western border is only 275 miles from its eastern border. Without French participation, the German front would have to be provisioned exclusively through Bremerhaven, Hamburg, or, at best, the crowded ports of the Low Countries and then down the narrow Rhineland corridor, altogether one of the world's most heavily populated regions and highly vulnerable to attack. Hamburg is only 25 miles from the East German border, and Holland itself only 145 miles. In short, even if a conventional defense of Germany could do without French military forces, which it cannot, it would still need French space and logistical resources. Without France, NATO's defense must soon collapse or else turn to nuclear weapons.

Aside from remedying these obvious but critical deficiencies in NATO's forces, deployment, and logistical base, some analysts have also argued for different tactics. In the late 1970s, the NATO SACEUR, General Bernard Rogers, proposed that NATO consider adopting the new U.S. doctrine of Airland Battle 2000. As Rogers saw it, NATO defense could strike behind the front lines to break up Soviet second-echelon forces and supply columns—and thus make any protracted conventional attack impossible. The result was a proposal from NATO's military headquarters (SHAPE—Supreme Headquarters, Allied Powers, Europe) for a Follow on Forces Attack (FOFA) doctrine. The proposal relied heavily on the accuracy and selectivity of new electronically guided conventional weapons, in some cases to substitute for what had hitherto been the role of nuclear weapons. Initial European responses were lukewarm.[16] The proposals implied huge purchases of expensive and untried American equipment, as well as yet another major revision of NATO doctrine at the behest of the Americans. Resistance sprang from the budgetary implications, impatience with American military leadership, and anger over pressure for arms sales.

Aside from General Rogers, several groups of reformers have long urged major changes of NATO tactics, often involving a general reshaping of NATO force structures as well. One major school of thought has argued for abandoning forward defense for a mobile defense in depth.[17] To its advocates, a war of maneuver seems more rational for NATO, since the Soviet preponderance in heavily armed forces gives them the advantage of superior firepower in a static war of attrition. Partisans of the traditional forward defense, on the other hand, consider a war of maneuver totally unsuited to NATO's current situation.[18] Given the shortness of the front, the highly defensible terrain of much of it, and the absence of a secure rear area in France, a well-fortified forward defense seems to them an ideal strategy, provided adequate operational reserves exist in the rear to plug any breakthrough. Redesigning NATO strategy and forces to fight a war of maneuver in the crowded urban territory of West Germany would risk devastating breakthroughs and throw away the natural advantage of the defense. Forward defense would be more convincing, to be sure, if adequate operational reserves did, in fact, exist and if the front were adequately fortified. All analysts agree, it seems, on the need for more operational reserves. Recent changes in standard U.S. Army tactics also point to a greater use of maneuver and blur somewhat the old distinctions between forward defense and defense in depth.[19]

Advocates of a mobile defense in depth have also frequently recommended a major restructuring of NATO's standing forces to provide a larger number of heavily armed fighting divisions—in effect, shedding support troops and remaking

NATO divisions closer to the Soviet model.[20] According to these analysts the stupefying firepower of modern weapons makes any European war likely to end quickly. But NATO forces—particularly American NATO forces—are still mistakenly anticipating the long drawn-out battles of World War II. As a result, they are grossly overstaffed with command, support, and administrative personnel, and consequently have a low ratio of combat strength to manpower and are unable to maneuver at a rapid tempo. Bloated headquarters staffs result in an unprecedented proportion of officers to men and a remarkable number of American generals stationed in Europe, while NATO's own headquarters replicate, in caricature, the Pentagon.[21]

Proposals for restructuring existing heavy forces have often been accompanied by proposals for creating more lightly armed but well-trained reserve divisions. These might cover parts of the front line that are heavily forested or otherwise well-endowed with natural cover.[22] Heavy divisions would be freed to augment the now slender operational reserves. These lightly armed reserve divisions could also provide a defense in depth against Soviet airdrops in rear areas, or even against advancing Soviet heavy armor. More radical proposals call for replacing allegedly outmoded concepts of tank warfare with a new doctrine based largely on lightly armed reserves. In recent years, the growing emphasis on global rapid deployment missions has, in itself, encouraged the U.S. Army toward more lightly armed and more maneuverable forces than those traditionally thought appropriate for NATO.[23]

Too radical an improvement in NATO's conventional capabilities is difficult to manage without appearing to be an offensive threat against the Soviets. Proposals for restructuring to provide more armored divisions, for example, imply a NATO capability for offense as well as defense. A war of maneuver can obviously go forward as well as rearward. More armored forces, held away from the front and complemented by already powerful tactical air forces, or the weapons needed for SHAPE's FOFA strategy, would make NATO much more capable of an offensive counterattack into East Germany and Czechoslovakia.[24] The probable Soviet countermeasures to such improvements might well deteriorate Europe's political climate and, in the end, reduce security all around—a further reason for European governments to prefer nuclear deterrence and to remain diffident toward radical strengthening of conventional forces. This scenario also helps to explain the attraction for many Europeans opposed to nuclear weapons of proposals for defense based on reserves and civilian militia rather than on heavily armored standing forces.[25]

Until the FOFA initiative in 1979, radical suggestions for improving conventional defense seemed to have had little influence on America's NATO policy, and official U.S. proposals remained along highly traditional lines. Typical was the Carter administration's Long Term Defense Program, asking NATO countries to pledge annual 3 percent real increases in national military budgets over a five-year period.

The 3 percent initiative reflected the Pentagon's familiar quantitative emphasis and, in effect, implied satisfaction with NATO's existing force structure, general strategy, armament, and division of labor.[26] The Carter administration also pressed strongly for a greater standardization of NATO's arms on grounds of both operational efficiency and economies of scale. Again, European responses were unenthusiastic. Standardization was widely greeted as an American design to parlay military into industrial hegemony. To assuage European fears, the Carter administration subscribed to a "two-way street" policy for weapons procurement. By the early eighties, however, European industrialists and politicians had grown generally disillusioned with the results. The Americans, with virtually unlimited quantities of arms for sale, were selling five times as many weapons to the NATO allies as they were buying from them. Europeans thus suspected the motives behind the impassioned American enthusiasm for standardization, "smart" weapons, and, later, Reagan's Strategic Defense Initiative. European resentment led to a mushrooming of cooperative European arms projects.[27] The prolonged quarrel over the dangers of technology transfer only heightened European cynicism.

By the early 1980s, the continuing European resistance to American proposals for improving conventional forces, combined with growing American concern over the liabilities of its European nuclear position, prompted former Secretary of State Henry Kissinger to propose a European SACEUR.[28] The idea was hardly new, but the logic behind it seemed more compelling from an American perspective. Reflecting on the reform proposals of the 1970s suggests the reason. The very nature of such proposals, and the situations they sought to remedy, made it clear that NATO had never seriously hoped to rely on conventional defense. The military deficiencies were too obvious and too severe. But if conventional deterrence were ever taken seriously, American hegemony would cease to be appropriate.

America's incapacity for European conventional defense seems in the very nature of things. With no conscription in America and many commitments elsewhere, American regular forces are expensive and in short supply. American forces in Europe are an expeditionary force far from home: hence, their heavy logistical requirements, high cost, and poor ratio of fighting strength to manpower. Geography disables the United States from providing an effective reserve army for Europe— except in the event of a very long war, much longer than nearly anyone now imagines. A large-scale American mobilization—with troops mustered, equipped, retrained, and transported with their matériel in time for the decisive battles— seems a patently unconvincing scenario. Even the present arrangements, which call for bringing over five standing divisions and one reserve division from the continental United States to "marry up" with their prepositioned weapons in Germany, seems a dubious plan militarily; its logistical requirements are preposterously expensive, particularly when compared to the cost of equivalent European forces. It would doubtless prove far more cost-effective to subsidize Europeans than to send over Americans. Even the cost of storing, maintaining, and guarding the weapons in Germany is inordinate.[29] Meanwhile, the implications for American naval requirements are substantial. In short, if European conventional defense is to be made stronger, the Europeans must provide the forces. They are unlikely to do so, however, so long as European defense is under American direction. Politically and psychologically, a Europeanized NATO implies a shift in the American role from managing protector to supporting ally.

A European SACEUR would naturally raise an acute problem of precedence among the Europeans. A strong case can be made for either a German or a Frenchman. The Germans would be providing the bulk of the forces, as well as the territory to be defended. The full adhesion of the French, on the other hand, could give NATO the space and manpower resources needed to make Germany's conventional defense plausible. In the early days of NATO, the French clearly wanted the position. Today, they could bring more to it than previously. A French SACEUR would efficiently link NATO defense and the French nuclear deterrent. For all the reasons suggested earlier, conventional and nuclear defense cannot realistically be separated, above all in Europe.[30]

The inseparability of nuclear and conventional deterrence explains, of course, why Europeans, Germans above all, have always preferred an American SACEUR and were uninterested in the Kissinger proposal. A European SACEUR could not function effectively without some independent and reasonably credible nuclear deterrent. Kissinger assumed the Americans would continue to provide and, therefore, to control NATO's nuclear defense. His proposals thus seemed to represent yet another attempt to give the appearance of devolution without its substance. Worse, a Europeanized conventional defense would attenuate Europe's link with the American deterrent. A European SACEUR, lacking an indigenous European deterrent, would, in fact, represent a form of decoupling without compensation.

This long discourse on NATO's forces and stymied reforms leads back to the fundamental point with which the chapter began. NATO's worsening military dilemma cannot be resolved by the United States. The essence of the American military protectorate is America's extended nuclear deterrent. Inevitably, that deterrent has become less reliable and therefore more dangerous as the Soviets have reached strategic parity. Accordingly, the traditional NATO strategy under the American protectorate—American nuclear deterrence bolstered by limited conventional defense—has been steadily undermined.

As previous chapters discuss in some detail, European doubts and American apprehensions have risen together. Many of the policies taken to reassure U.S. or European sensibilities have, in fact, ended up weakening the alliance. American attempts at a tight control of European forces are seen by the Europeans as incompatible with Europe's political independence and diplomatic goals, as de Gaulle's partial defection made eminently clear in the 1960s. Stationing American-controlled missiles on European soil does not resolve the problem of American credibility, but it does disturb public opinion on both sides of the Atlantic. Meanwhile, America's European commitment is a major contributor to America's increasingly desperate fiscal crisis. Remedies have grown more and more radical. By the mid-1980s, parts of the American and European center and left were emphasizing conventional over nuclear deterrence to the point of advocating a No-First-Use policy for NATO; the Reagan administration, meanwhile, was enamored of a Strategic Defense Initiative to reestablish American strategic invulnerability. Technically, neither No First Use nor SDI was a feasible substitute for classic nuclear deterrence. Either, however, would undermine that deterrence by decoupling American and European defense, but without endowing Europe with any indigenous substitute for its American protectorate. More logically, and ominously, significant elements of the neoconservative right began advocating U.S. withdrawal from the alliance.[31]

The most logical solution to the growing problems of extended deterrence remains a more indigenous European defense. If the use of nuclear weapons can only be imagined as a desperate act of self-defense, then Europe should control its own nuclear weapons. If mutual vulnerabilities make nuclear weapons nearly or entirely unusable in any case, and a serious conventional defense is required, only Europe can provide the forces needed. To expect the United States to sustain a massive land army for Europe is politically and economically unrealistic. Thus, a more indigenous European defense is not only the most logical resolution of the problems of extended deterrence under conditions of parity; increasingly, it seems the only solution.

Logic is not always a reliable guide to the future. A Europeanization of NATO may be highly desirable in theory, but could it be feasible in practice?

The answer depends to a considerable extent on what the Europeanization of NATO would entail. Europeans suspect that American hegemony is inseparable from American participation. Europeanization, they fear, simply means the departure of the United States. But, as contemplated here, Europeanization means an end to American hegemony but not an end to American participation in Europe's defense. It would certainly not require denouncing or even amending the NATO treaty. Its present language seems adaptable enough for almost any arrangement, while negotiating a new formal alliance with the Americans, let alone among the Western Europeans themselves, seems a gratuitous complication. The practical changes would not have to appear unduly radical nor be faced all at once. If the Europeans preferred, they could rearrange NATO's internal structures or build parallel arrangements alongside.[32]

It seems in everyone's interest, however, that the Americans continue to station a substantial contingent of conventional forces on the Central Front, as well as significant air and naval forces throughout the region. What then would be the change? What is the practical difference between American hegemony and American participation?

For the United States, it would mean abandoning plans for fielding ten divisions in Europe—five of which are in place and five more committed to a NATO mobilization. Instead of ten standing divisions for Europe, the United States might keep five and disband the other five—a direct reduction of one-third of the U.S. Army's standing divisions. This alone would bring enormous savings to the military budget.[33] Two or three of the five remaining European-oriented divisions could continue to be stationed in Europe and would still constitute a formidable American presence on the front line. The remaining divisions could remain in the United States as part of a mobile intervention force with a European mission. This would still leave an additional five to seven army or marine divisions for a global intervention force—lightly armed units with radically different requirements from those needed in Europe.

Would five European-oriented U.S. divisions be enough? As European leaders have sometimes said in moments of high candor, the number of American divisions in or for Europe is less important than the stability of their commitment.[34] Five divisions within a sustainable military budget are greatly superior to ten that are the product of a fiscal nightmare. A concomitant strengthening of U.S. ready reserves, moreover, could provide insurance against a long European war, however improbable it may seem at present.

For Europe, American devolution would mean adapting command structures to a more plural arrangement. It would also mean having to decide whether the present uneasy mix of nuclear and conventional deterrence should be continued and, in any case, what forces would be needed for the future. What sort of conventional balance, for example, could a European coalition maintain with a reduced American contingent? The answer would depend, as now, on how seriously NATO wishes to take its conventional deterrence. Europeanization would not, in itself, resolve the issue one way or another. Europeans might well decide to continue relying heavily on nuclear deterrence to halt a conventional attack. If so, they would have to build up nuclear forces and thrash out arrangements for their use. But Europeans would also have, if they wished it, the potential for a more serious conventional deterrent. Substantial manpower resources are already in hand even without the Americans (see table 9.4).

As argued at length in the previous section, many of NATO's deficiencies in conventional forces are less a matter of resources than of poor or inconsistent organization, deployment, and doctrine. The Europeanization of NATO could conceivably make it easier to remedy some of these problems. A German or French SACEUR might be in a better position to demand, for example, the fortifications and deployments needed to make forward defense effective. More direct respon-

TABLE 9.4

Military Resources: France, Germany, and Britain

	France	Germany	Britain
Total armed forces*	557.5	485.8	323.8
Ground forces*	296.4	340.8	169.7
Main battle tanks	1,300	4,895	1,150
Combat aircraft	677	630	661

* Troop figures given in thousands.
SOURCE: I.I.S.S., *The Military Balance 1986–1987*, pp. 57–60, 63–69.

sibility for organizing their own defense should have a tonic effect on Europe's professional soldiers. The intellectual traditions of the British, French, or German military hardly leave them less well-endowed for organizing European defense than their American counterparts. The reforming remedies for NATO's conventional weakness are at least as likely to emerge from the European military as from the American. Indeed, many of the ideas of American military reformers in the 1970s came from studying actual practices in the European armies.[35]

A Europeanized NATO might also contribute to rejuvenating a broad military patriotism among European publics, whose feeling of responsibility for national self-defense has been undermined by the comfortable American protectorate. It is not merely an accident of national character that public opinion in France, the most independent of the NATO allies, is less susceptible to the wiles of pacifism than elsewhere. It would, moreover, be a very superficial reading to see the current diffuse antinuclear discontent among Europe's young as precluding a revival of martial patriotism among them.

Success in building a stronger conventional deterrent would require, above all, that France take a leading part alongside the German Federal Republic. If Europe is ever to have the operational reserves it requires, France is the logical country to provide them. To do so, the French would have to continue to reshape their army toward a serious European role. Traditionally, the elite French forces have been designed mostly for intervention in the Third World. Reorientation toward Europe began hesitantly in the 1970s and seemed more resolute, theoretically at least, by the mid-1980s.[36] A reorganization of France's conscript army and reserves could also make a massive contribution to NATO's mobilization capacities. A large French conscript army already exists, although it is poorly trained and, in many respects, has no real military purpose. With French youth unemployment running at around 25 percent in the mid-1980s, some more serious reserve program hardly seems unimaginable. The potential, of course, is enormous. In 1914, a much less populous France fielded an army of seven million![37]

It obviously makes more sense for the French to provide the critical forces for

European conventional defense than it does for the Americans. How could they be persuaded to do so? The French would clearly be reluctant to attenuate their nuclear or global capacities for the sake of German defense. But augmented conventional forces would have serious financial implications for the French budget, difficult to resolve in a time of general fiscal austerity. Since a more serious French European army would benefit the Germans more than anyone else, and since Germany's relative military expenditures are substantially lower than France's, burden sharing to augment French conventional forces would be an excellent investment for the German Federal Republic.[38]

If the French provided the operational reserves and the reserve army for a full mobilization, the Germans would continue to provide the main standing forces on the Central Front. For this they already have a substantial army and a large and relatively efficient reserve. Should the Europeans decide to build a real conventional defense, Germany's much lamented manpower shortage could be countered by increasing the length of conscript service from eighteen months to two years. With German youth unemployment at around 13 percent, a severe labor shortage would be unlikely. There also exists in Germany a large pool of recently released reservists whose military training is still current. Changing reserve requirements, perhaps by creating a standby reserve, could, according to some experts, add as many as three million men to the German Federal Republic's mobilization capabilities.[39]

Germany's well-organized reserve forces could easily be the appropriate pattern elsewhere, not only in France or Britain but also in the smaller countries. Holland, of course, has already developed a highly imaginative mobilization plan. As the Dutch situation suggests, sustaining reserve forces for home defense is a more plausible and congenial task for the smaller European countries than trying to maintain standing, heavily-armed, professional forces for the front line.

Along with France and Germany, Britain is Western Europe's other major military power. If so inclined, Britain could become another major source of conventional strength. The British already provide a sizable contingent of heavy troops for the front line. Reactivation of a territorial reserve army for Europe could be a substantial addition to NATO's conventional strength. Like the French, the British are also a global and nuclear power. Their military budget is stretched by European standards and they would be unlikely to undertake any new commitment to conventional defense without some kind of financial compensation. Again, Germany—whose military budget is proportionately far below Britain's—would seem well-served by some form of financial burden-sharing (see table 9.5). In any event, if a Europeanized NATO wanted a stronger conventional defense, the problem would not be any lack of military potential.

Longer active and reserve service obligations or higher budgetary outlays would doubtless arouse substantial popular opposition. Still, most continental countries already have universal conscription. The burdens ought to be more acceptable,

TABLE 9.5
Comparative Western Defense Expenditures, 1984

	Germany	France	Britain	U.S.
Defense expenditure as percentage of GDP	3.3%	4.1%	5.5%	6.4%
Total defense expenditure (millions of U.S. dollars)	20,125	20,212	23,294	237,052
Per Capita Defense Expenditure (U.S. dollars)	328	370	416	1,001

SOURCE: I.I.S.S., *The Military Balance 1986–87* (London: International Institute for Strategic Studies, 1986), 212.

moreover, with Europeans clearly in charge of NATO and no longer inclined to see themselves merely as auxiliaries for their American protectors.

Whatever conventional defense a Europeanized NATO might develop, nuclear weapons would inevitably remain an indispensable element in the panoply of deterrence. While American nuclear weapons, along with American forces, would presumably remain deployed or otherwise earmarked for Europe, Europeanization implies the development of parallel European nuclear forces. To have Europeans in command, but relying exclusively on American nuclear weapons, could never be a satisfactory or stable arrangement. Europeans, in fact, already possess the essential means for their own nuclear force. At the tactical level, French nuclear missiles and bombers could probably stop a conventional attack through Germany. The physical means for a European strategic deterrent also seem in hand. By 1985, the British and French possessed some 258 strategic warheads—along with a fleet of 10 nuclear submarines. Within a decade, those nuclear forces are scheduled to total 1,218 warheads and 11 nuclear submarines—forces collectively or separately more than adequate for a European second strike.[40]

The effectiveness of European forces as a collective deterrent seems more a political than a military question. The essential difficulty lies, as it always has, in whether any national force seems plausible when extended to cover the defense of others. NATO's most significant "other" is, of course, the non-nuclear German Federal Republic, whose territory constitutes the Central Front. Exchanging the American deterrent for the French or British has always seemed a poor deal for the Germans. But as the European forces grow more formidable, and with American deterrence subject to increasing difficulties, Germans ought to welcome at least a multiple deterrent rather than an exclusively American one. It is not necessarily true, moreover, that American nuclear forces are manifestly more effective deterrents than French or British. Britain and France are both more vulnerable than the United States, but they could arguably also be said to be more inherently committed to European defense. America's technical superiority consists essentially of elaborate counterforce capabilities—made necessary, in good part, by America's diffidence over risking its home territory for its NATO commitment. Britain's, and especially France's, geographic proximity could be seen to deny them the luxury of America's standoff commitment.

Whether such theoretical arguments would have any practical weight with the Germans would depend on the quality of the military and political arrangements that actually developed around an indigenous European deterrent. Declaratory guarantees would have to be confirmed by close military planning. It would be in everyone's interest in the West to find a successful formula. A wide variety of forms is easily imagined—a European federal or multilateral nuclear force, various two-key arrangements, or simple Franco-British guarantees.

The imagination should not be limited to the traditional formulations of postwar European federalists. A collective deterrent does not require a supranational state. The European institutions that have actually developed provide a better indication of the possibilities for European cooperation than the old supranational models that were once so ardently expected. Despite the disappointment of federalist hopes, Europe has, in fact, developed a confederal politico-economic structure of great sophistication and considerable effectiveness. There is no good reason to suppose that a European nuclear force cannot also emerge in some confederal form. A collective deterrent for Germany may well take shape in a quiet Franco-German deal, perhaps expanded to include the British, with a benevolent but not insistent American blessing. What matters is that the Europeans work out an arrangement that satisfies them and impresses the Soviets.

The military effectiveness of any European strategic nuclear force depends on whether it seems adequate for a second-strike deterrent. Technically, it need not require any improbable new European armament. It would be enough for the French to go ahead with the nuclear forces already planned and for the British to buy the Trident II missiles for which they have already contracted. The 1,218 strategic warheads projected are certainly adequate to cripple the Soviet Union. Since Europe's deterrent will not be extended in the same sense as the American, it will presumably never need the elaborate counterforce strategy or arsenal of the superpowers. Given their resources, Europeans could, if they wished, develop such an arsenal. But since the redundance of the superpower arms race already seems near lunacy, common sense would probably reinforce Europe's habitual parsimony to limit the European nuclear arsenal. As chapter 11 will discuss, an independent European deterrent should encourage the superpowers to drastic reductions in their own bilateral balance.

In theory, a greatly enhanced Soviet antimissile defense could radically diminish the effectiveness of European nuclear forces. Some analysts also fear that new and extremely precise non-nuclear missiles may someday be able to devastate Europe's nuclear and conventional capabilities without constituting a reasonable pretext for a nuclear riposte.[41] While the current vogue for science fiction has greatly expanded the range of weapons that can be imagined, the essential robustness of nuclear deterrence should not be forgotten. It seems improbable that Soviet technology can render Europe's forces obsolete. In a three-cornered race for technological innovations, it is by no means assumed that Europe would run last. America's national interest lies in ensuring Europe the technology to sustain its independence. Certainly it would never be in the American interest to curry favor with the Soviets by denying Western Europe the means to defend itself.

There are, of course, logical alternatives to a NATO or bilateral European deterrent that covers Germany. One is presumably a neutral Germany without nuclear weapons. Another is a Germany with its own nuclear forces—in or out of NATO. A neutral Germany, armed or not, would be a severe and probably fatal blow for any Western European coalition as a major force in the world. The European conventional balance would shift sharply against the West. A national Germany floating between East and West would make the intimacy of the Common Market difficult to sustain. Europeans, in particular the French and West German heirs of Monnet, de Gaulle, and Adenauer, should go a long way to avoid such an outcome. From a European perspective, an independent German nuclear force within a Europeanized NATO might well come to seem, by comparison, a less disastrous option.

At the present time no one, including the Germans, wants an independent German nuclear force. It should not be imagined, however, that this self-prohibition must last forever. If the American deterrent continues to lose its credibility while increasing its political and economic price, and if France and Britain cannot bring themselves to construe their national security interests to include their German neighbor, no one should be surprised if the Germans ultimately turn to political neutralism or their own military resources. A German nuclear force would, of course, allow the French to retain their sanctuary, while contributing as much or as little "uncertainty" to Germany's nuclear defense as suited both parties. Germany would certainly be the most vulnerable of nuclear powers, with its total destruction the seemingly inevitable outcome of any European nuclear war. Under the circumstances, a nuclear Federal Republic could hardly be considered a plausible aggressor against the Soviet Union.

For all sorts of obvious reasons, however, a German nuclear force would be very much a second-best solution to the problems of extended deterrence. Germany's inherent weakness as a nuclear power makes some more collective Western European deterrent preferable militarily. The opportunity to institutionalize European solidarity in a nuclear force certainly makes a collective deterrent vastly preferable politically. But if such an imaginative act proves impossible for the Europeans, a German national deterrent might seem more stable in the long run than America's increasingly unmanageable protectorate, an inadequate French partnership, or a neutral Germany detached from the West. It is up to Western governments not to let themselves be trapped among such options.

In conclusion, the possible outlines and rationale for a more European version of NATO are not difficult to sketch. Adequate military arrangements are within a reasonable stretch of the imagination. In most respects, they merely rearrange existing or planned capacities. Admittedly, no one can prove that Europe would build a viable military coalition in response to an American devolution within NATO. But if Europe failed to do so, the cause should not be a lack of military means. The military potential certainly is there. In many instances, the military forces already exist, but have been robbed of their effectiveness by poor organization and incoherent strategies.

The military case can be put more strongly. A rapid survey of the principal criticisms of NATO's conventional military posture, and the proffered reforms, suggests that Europeanization is probably the only way to reach a convincing conventional balance, should one eventually be desired. And given the intractable problems of extended nuclear protection, Europeanization may prove the only way to sustain nuclear deterrence as well. Should Europe have the political will, the military way could certainly be found.

10

Managing the
European Coalition:
The Franco-German Minuet

AS EUROPEANS never tire of telling Americans, Europe is not one country but several. Even if ample military capacity for a balance exists collectively, Europe's states might still lack the political capacity to combine and organize their forces. Measuring political potential is even more elusive than measuring military potential. No one can prove how Europeans would react to an American devolution in NATO. What to expect if the alliance does not reform its internal balance is, however, much more certain. As this book's first seven chapters conclude, the transatlantic relationship in its present form is undergoing a gradual but palpable, predictable, and potentially disastrous deterioration. If the alliance is to be preserved at all, a substantial change in the European-American relationship within NATO seems essential. That change requires, in turn, a major step in the evolution of relationships among the Europeans themselves.

This is not the first time postwar Europe and America have faced such a dual challenge. In the 1950s, the Europeans needed an economic bloc of their own before they could fit comfortably into the emerging transatlantic economy. With

American encouragement, they did rise to that occasion and, in due course, formed the EEC. By the 1960s, their distinctive needs in the diplomatic sphere led to a variety of intra-European political arrangements, including the Franco-German Treaty of 1963 and the European Political Cooperation that followed in the 1970s.[1] Today, given the accumulating strategic and financial difficulties of America's extended deterrence, a distinctive European military coalition within NATO seems the next logical step.

European cooperation in the economic and political spheres has never implied a break with the United States. Quite the contrary, intra-European development seemed essential for the transatlantic relationship to function smoothly enough to continue. Forming the European Economic Community did not mean opting out of the global economy of the *Pax Americana*. Instead, it has become a precondition for Europe's operating effectively within it. By the same logic, extending European cooperation to the military sphere should mean a more balanced and therefore more successful transatlantic alliance.

A study of this sort is not the place for detailed blueprints on how Europe should organize its military coalition, a task probably best left to the diplomats. Our question is whether the underlying political conditions exist for such a coalition. Current tendencies toward military cooperation, although interesting, hardly indicate what could develop in response to an American devolution. Our interest is in what the Europeans would actually do then. Their real potential can be inferred primarily in two ways: by assessing how much the underlying geopolitical interests of Europe's leading states converge, and by examining the actual European record in those spheres where the need for close cooperation has already been accepted.

To start with the record: the principal institutional monument to Europe's postwar cooperation is the European Community. While military arrangements hardly need a similar structure, the EC does give a picture of how well European cooperation works in one broad sphere. Without going into a lengthy historical review, certain practical and theoretical characteristics of that cooperation should be emphasized.

The EC is a confederal as opposed to a federal or supranational regime. As such, it is far more complex than the early and simpleminded theories of political integration led their devotees to expect.[2] It is ironic that those who look for evidence of the intractable disunity among European states often point to the experience of the Common Market. After years of expecting a federal state to emerge momentarily, the new fashion is to denigrate the multilateral structures Europeans have actually developed. Both old and new fashions are highly superficial views of what is, after all, probably the most impressive experiment in intergovernmental cooperation in modern times. More remarkable than Europe's dissension is the practical integration that has been achieved.

Political scientists have never forgiven Europe for not living up to integration theory. Their disillusionment has unfortunately spilled over into the general public.

In reality, the record of the EC hardly proves European states incapable of organizing their collective affairs. Instead, their cohabitation in the Community has forced them to reconcile some of the most minute and difficult details of their domestic political economies. Certainly the Common Market, its membership greatly expanded in recent years, harbors serious disagreements and tortuous disputes. But intractable problems are to be expected in any politico-economic structure that tries to manage a huge and diverse continental economy, particularly during a period of rapid economic change and dislocation. Similarly intractable problems plague the continental-scale governments of the Soviet Union or the United States. It could be argued that Europe's structural and social problems are worse than those of either superpower, and that the fault may be laid to Europe's inadequate political structures. But the case would be far from self-evident. Certainly over the past twenty-five years the European economic record has not been unimpressive compared with that of either the United States or the Soviet Union.[3] In short, in the economic field, where it has made sense for Europeans to cooperate closely, they have done so—and successfully.

The fact that economic integration in the EC has not followed a federalist model tells something critical about the workings of postwar European cooperation. The EC has not made the traditional nation states fade away. On the contrary, they have grown more viable. Grouped together in their confederal structures, they have had more real control over their respective national economic environments than they would have had without such organization. Cooperation has increased rather than diminished national sovereignty.

Obviously, the member states of the EC have renounced some formal sovereignty. By taking on obligations toward each other they have restricted their abstract right to do anything they please. Thanks to those obligations, they are bound to a high degree of mutual interdependence and a considerable degree of mutual policy-making. While these obligations represent formal and legal restrictions on sovereignty, in political terms they are enhancements of sovereignty. Given the realities of modern economic life, European countries that try to opt out of their economic interdependence will predictably suffer a serious drop in living standards. Since no state wishes to choose such a policy, practical self-determination of sovereignty means the ability to have as much say as possible in regulating the terms of interdependence. Since the Common Market has greatly increased the say of European states over European economic conditions, and to some considerable extent over transatlantic conditions as well, European integration has increased national self-determination, not reduced it. Conversely, this rejuvenation of the nation-state has not undermined European cooperation. On the contrary, it has been its principal incentive. The proper index of success in European cooperation is not the degree to which the participating states are enfeebled by it, but the extent to which their practical self-determination is enhanced.

The point should not be lost in considering the likely character and prospects of a confederal military coalition. By joining such a coalition, Europe's states would hope to increase their independence in real terms. Their calculation of interest would depend on how they perceived the military situation. European states have made themselves very comfortable within their American protectorate; a European military coalition might well prove more binding and onerous than free riding on American hegemony in NATO. So long as the American protectorate seems viable, European interest in exploring other arrangements can be expected to remain limited. Faced with a withdrawing American protectorate, however, no European state is likely to regard a European coalition more damaging to independence than Soviet military preponderance.

Perceptions and reactions will naturally vary from small powers to large powers. Small or peripheral countries can always hope to be ignored or merely Finlandized. Big, rich, and central powers, on the other hand, cannot be so sanguine about their prospects in the absence of an adequate military balance. In any event, big powers have more means and therefore more options. Most notably, they can try to build military forces, alone or in concert, adequate to prevent compromising their political independence. Countries that have traditionally been great powers are more likely to choose such an option, since it accords best with their own historical experience and image of themselves.

This difference between great and lesser powers means that military coalitions often exhibit a markedly differentiated pattern of participation. Even when there is no single hegemonic power, there must be some leading powers who take a greater role. That would most certainly be the case in a Europeanized NATO. No single European power could, by itself, provide a military protectorate for the others. No single power, therefore, could fill the hegemonic American role. In this respect, a Europeanized NATO would probably evolve a leadership structure more like the actual pattern of the EC; that is, there would be two or three leading nations, with policy stabilized by a special relationship between at least two of them. The formal structure of the EC, on the other hand, seems largely irrelevant. A military coalition should almost certainly not try to replicate the EC's supranational pretensions—in the manner, for example, of the stillborn European Defense Community of the 1950s.[4] Unlike the EC, a European defense coalition is unlikely to have a large role for a supranational bureaucracy. Nor is it likely to permit smaller members to block action by the largest.

The EC itself—and certainly the diplomatic or political cooperation that has grown up alongside it—has already been moving toward what is sometimes dubbed *l'Europe à deux vitesses*.[5] The leading powers proceed at their own speed while others follow or lag according to their own requirements and perspectives. Such a pattern of leadership can certainly be imagined for a military coalition, where special and sometimes informal understandings between major powers would easily be more significant than ritual unanimity among all the members. Such diverse compliance with leadership would not be very different from the actual situation in NATO under the American protectorate. The tendency among smaller states to wander into private accommodations suggests, moreover, the wisdom of keeping NATO's existing formal structure, while Europeanizing its direction, rather than ostentatiously negotiating some completely new treaty.

Whatever the formal structure, certain big states would have to take the initiative and put up the major forces. Of Western Europe's four major powers, France and Germany seem the most obviously suited for such a role. As the history of the EC amply demonstrates, Western Europe's other major powers have been unable or disinclined to take a leading position. Italy, while possessing a large and rapidly growing economy, has lacked and perhaps not wanted the national political structure needed to sustain a leading role in European affairs. Britain has been odd-man-out throughout the EC's history. For complex reasons, Britain's economy has been in a melancholy, relative decline throughout most of the postwar period. The country has been a long time reconciling itself to being primarily a European rather than a global power. On several occasions, it has tried to play a spoiler's role in European cooperation. A European defense coalition might offer Britain a golden opportunity to change its role. Thanks to its nuclear deterrent, Britain's military weight is substantially greater than its economic weight. Britain also has a disproportionate interest in the technological aspects of military cooperation. But Britain's past record belies any exuberant hopes for constructive British leadership in the early stages of a military coalition. Even more than the others, Britain would be unlikely to commit itself firmly until convinced the American protectorate was really no longer available. The usual patience, bribery, and strong boost from the Americans would doubtless be required.

Having France and Germany take the lead in a military coalition would merely repeat the pattern already set in Europe's existing economic and diplomatic collaboration. Assessing their prospects for military collaboration requires explaining more fully their already successful convergence of interests in the economic sphere, while examining the reasons why such convergence might succeed or fail in the military sphere.

That France and Germany have taken the lead in postwar Europe is hardly surprising. They are, by a considerable margin, Western Europe's greatest political and economic powers. Both are major states in global terms, and both have long been among the world's half-dozen greatest military powers. Today, however, each is paying less for its defense, proportionate to its wealth, than in most years of this century.[6] Their ardent mutual antagonism was, of course, a principal reason for the relatively heavy military spending in the past. Their enmity shaped much of continental politics from 1870 until the end of World War II, just as their cooperation has shaped much of Europe's development since. Their continued cooperation would obviously be vital for any indigenous European military coalition. The two are not only Western Europe's leading military powers, along with Great Britain, but both are geographically essential to any serious conventional defense of European territory. The Federal Republic actually constitutes Western Europe's Central Front, while France provides the space and logistics needed for the defense of that front.

Doubts about Franco-German military cooperation are only natural. Given their historic antagonism, their long and efficacious postwar economic cooperation could not have been easily anticipated. Historic enmity aside, their enduring geopolitical differences seemed a formidable obstacle to so lasting and intimate an alliance. The two countries proved, however, to have more in common than was at first supposed. While France was technically among the victors and Germany among the vanquished, both emerged from World War II with a heavy load of shame. The French army had collapsed ignominiously in 1940; the country had then endured four years of occupation, during which a substantial proportion of the population had collaborated with the enemy.[7] Thanks to the efforts of de Gaulle, Churchill, and the French Resistance, "Free France" did emerge as an independent great power by the end of the war, but not even de Gaulle's mythic sorcery could conjure away the wounds to French morale and cohesion. As for the Germans, the war's end saw them defeated, devastated, and divided. Alongside the physical ruin was the moral desolation of a country that had invested its idealism in a gangster regime of stupefying barbarism. For so civilized a country, once proud of its vigorous and humane culture, the task of restoring its own self-esteem and unity, let alone its standing in the world, was an excruciating burden.

Both countries were fortunate in their postwar leadership. De Gaulle and Adenauer must certainly rank among the greatest statesmen of the century. In due course, each country managed to endow itself with stable political institutions able to reconcile strong government with democracy and efficiency. In both countries, the task of national restoration was helped immeasurably by a remarkable record of postwar economic growth. Both had their economic "miracles" where production quickly surpassed its anemic prewar level. Both countries, along with much of the rest of Europe, boldly set out not merely to recover but also to achieve an entirely new level of growth and prosperity.[8] Both saw growth as capitalism's salvation from its traditional problems of recurring overproduction and persistent unemployment— the social and political consequences of which had done much to lead both countries to catastrophe.

As each country emerged from its respective "abyss," strong common interests began to develop between them.[9] Both had begun to profit greatly from their American connection and from the *Pax Americana* in general. Germany enjoyed a worldwide economic access denied it in the prewar international system. France was opening its national economy to an unprecedented degree, which had more than a little to do with its remarkable postwar growth. Like other Western European powers, France and Germany framed national policies to enjoy the benefits of American hegemony while escaping as many of its constraints as possible. They gradually discovered the great advantages of pursuing such policies together rather than separately.

The European Economic Community, negotiated in the 1950s, is the classic example of bilateral Franco-German collaboration within an Atlantic context. America's military protectorate made Europe's economic interdependence with America almost inevitable. As the Europeans recovered, the Americans were demanding liberal trade and monetary convertibility. There were many obvious advantages for France and Germany, provided each was strong enough to meet American competition while preserving an acceptable degree of economic security and self-determination. Their inspired response was to build a European economic bloc together with Italy and the Low Countries.[10] Faced with the American giant, a European Economic Community compounded the national economic strength of each partner. Given economic interdependence, each partner had more economic prosperity, security, and genuine self-determination within the community than any would have had outside it.

For Germany, the EEC was the means to secure its most important market. For France, it was the way to combine the liberalism needed for growth with the protection needed for stability. France used its weight in the EEC to define Europe's economic interests in a fashion favorable to itself. Thus leveraged, French interests could more easily be defended against the Americans, as well as against other European interests unfavorable to France: hence, the Common Agricultural Policy, the veto of British entry, and the protracted bargaining over transatlantic trade arrangements during the Kennedy Round. Inevitably, French policy exacerbated the inherent tensions between American and European interests and created particular problems for West Germany. But the EEC was essentially a good deal for Germany as well. It was France's price for open trade with the rest of Europe. No German government could risk breaking up its most promising market or alienating its most powerful Western European neighbor. The EEC also seemed a good deal for the United States. In practice it permitted a more open transatlantic economy than would otherwise have been likely.

In the early years of their collaboration in the EEC, France and Germany were often in serious disagreement. As chapter 4 recounts, Adenauer and de Gaulle's Franco-German Treaty of 1963 met a stormy reception in the Bundestag. In 1965, the Common Market almost broke up as a result of a complex quarrel over the Common Agricultural Policy, British membership, the Kennedy Round, and the EEC's own rules of procedure. France and Germany opposed each other on these issues—with Germany's position generally much closer to that of the United States. Nevertheless, the two countries regularly managed to compromise sufficiently to keep their European bloc together and to negotiate successfully with the Americans.[11]

Despite their ups and downs since the 1960s, both France and Germany have gradually accepted that their mutual relations are privileged and constitute a broad partnership deeply anchored in joint self-interest. In due course, even their differences began to have a certain collaborative character. Under de Gaulle, the French assumed that they were the only power able to assert Europe's true interests frankly against the Americans. The French disposition toward intransigence often made it easier for Germany to negotiate a reasonable compromise, to the benefit of the French as well as themselves. And as the world economy has proceeded along the path outlined in chapter 6, Franco-German irritation at erratic and imperious American policy has grown more and more into a common bond. In the early 1970s, the collapse of monetary stability, followed by the oil shocks, prompted a renewed Franco-German concern for consolidating and preserving the accomplishments of the European Community. The later 1970s saw a notable blossoming of close economic cooperation, often sparked by a mutual abhorrence for the economic policy of the Carter administration. By 1979, Germany and France seemed to have reached a broad consensus on economic policy. Together, Helmut Schmidt and Valéry Giscard d'Estaing imposed a European Monetary System on their own countries, with most of the rest of the EC in train.[12]

France and Germany have also slowly elaborated a collaborative policy in their pan-European diplomacy. Here again the early stage saw considerable friction. Chapter 4 outlined the tensions that resulted when de Gaulle attempted to use the détente issue to wean the Federal Republic from American diplomatic tutelage. That chapter also discussed how the conflicts grew as Germany's own pan-European policy evolved from the Erhard through the Brandt chancellorships. Paris, the original promoter of an opening to the East, began to find actual *Ostpolitik* more German than European. It was one thing for France to promote a Western European bloc between the superpowers; it was quite another for a neutral Germany to float, by itself, between the Soviets and an Atlanticized Europe. French anxieties in the early 1970s contributed greatly to the thaw in Anglo-French relations that finally permitted Britain to enter the Common Market.[13]

Schmidt's arrival as chancellor in 1974 signaled a certain relative cooling of German ardor for *Ostpolitik*. The process of Germany's coming to terms with the consequences of World War II in the East had more or less run its course. Under Brandt, the Federal Republic had formally accepted the loss of German prewar territories to Poland and Czechoslovakia. It had signed a nonaggression pact with the Soviets. It had recognized the German Democractic Republic as a separate sovereign state "within one nation." In turn, the four occupying powers had formally confirmed the independent status of West Berlin.[14]

At the completion of this great diplomatic labor, a certain melancholy reaction was doubtless inevitable. Germany had made great concessions of principle—for ambiguous benefits that could emerge only gradually and would probably prove rather expensive economically. Meanwhile, the dreary realities of Russia's stultifying hegemony over Eastern Europe remained. High expectations for *Ostpolitik* gradually evaporated. By the late 1970s the breakup of superpower détente and the economic and political problems of Poland were indicating its external and indigenous limits. No German chancellor of any party was prepared to abandon *Ostpolitik*, but a more sober view of its prospects did encourage a more solicitous care for Germany's other options. In the mid-1970s, under Schmidt and Giscard d'Estaing, Germany's *Ostpolitik* and France's own long-range preoccupation with pan-European relations had reached a certain harmonious cooperation. Long collaboration seemed to have brought French and German diplomatic policies and perspectives into rather deep consensus. Thus, when Soviet-American détente deteriorated in the late 1970s, the French firmly supported the Germans in pressing forward with closer Soviet-European economic ties, despite strong American pressure to the contrary.[15]

In the early 1980s, both countries had major changes of government. The French elected a Socialist president in 1981; the Germans chose a Christian Democratic chancellor in 1983. A period of severe testing seemed to be in the offing. Before coming to power, the French Socialists were not only strongly anti-Soviet, but in some quarters strongly anti-German as well. Nevertheless the Mitterrand government quickly reaffirmed French ties with Bonn.[16] The Socialists' economic policies, however, made friction inevitable.

François Mitterrand's presidency began with an exuberant macroeconomic expansion combined with widespread nationalizations and extended social benefits—all egregiously unsuited to the international economic conditions of the early 1980s. As the franc tottered, it was the German mark against which it had to be devalued within the European Monetary System. To stop the franc's fall, Socialist economic policy finally had to be abandoned. This painful adaptation was accomplished, all things considered, with remarkable swiftness and without lasting rancor toward the Germans. Indeed, the Mitterrand government is said to have manipulated German pressure rather skillfully to prevail in its own internal debate.[17]

The limits to France's economic autonomy proved a harsh lesson for the Socialists, hoping at long last to progress rapidly toward the society of their ideals. The lesson was nevertheless taken. The macroeconomic restraint that Mitterrand ultimately espoused meant worse unemployment but achieved not unimpressive results for the country's balance of payments.[18]

Its original policy thus abandoned, the leftist regime shifted its rhetoric from social progress to economic competitiveness and European cooperation. In effect, the Socialist regime made a fundamental strategic decision: it rejected recourse to France's traditional protectionism, even to save its social program, opting instead for a rigorous defense of France's position within the international liberal economy. When faced with the need for decisive action, the left unequivocably chose modernization and Europe over socialism and nationalist isolation. In the end, Mitterrand's Socialists followed the same broad national strategy as their Gaullist predecessors and carried it through with impressive tough-mindedness and competence. In so doing, Mitterrand naturally reaffirmed the close economic collaboration with Germany that has always been indispensable to such a policy.

Mitterrand's determination to put the economy in order went hand in hand with a vigorous European policy. France proceeded to take a leading role both in the European missiles crisis and in resolving many of the accumulated problems of the Common Market. France's renewed European activism brought the first stirrings of serious Franco-German military cooperation.

Such cooperation had remained relatively underdeveloped throughout the sixties and seventies. The Germans never ceased to insist that their close economic and political relationship with the French must not, in any way, undermine their military allegiance to NATO. Nevertheless, when France withdrew from the NATO command in 1966, the Federal Republic agreed that two French divisions should continue to remain on West German soil, an arrangement not opposed by the Americans.[19]

In the seventies, French plans for using nuclear-armed tactical rockets led almost inevitably to some Franco-German military consultation. As France under Giscard d'Estaing grew more relaxed about cooperating with NATO, constraints that formerly bedeviled Franco-German military cooperation began to ease.[20] Proposals for industrial cooperation to produce armaments began to form another regular topic of Franco-German consultation, with appreciable though limited results.

Under President Mitterrand and Chancellor Kohl, the trend toward Franco-German military cooperation seemed to accelerate. Their first regular bilateral meeting brought forth a joint declaration promising to begin giving substance to the military dimension of the original Franco-German Treaty.[21] Shortly thereafter came Mitterrand's dramatic intervention in the German Euromissiles debate. Kohl's government was firmly resolved to deploy the new American missiles in Europe that the Schmidt government had initially requested, notwithstanding the popular tumult in Germany against them. The Mitterrand government went to extraordinary lengths to support Kohl's resolution. Appearing before the Bundestag, Mitterrand warned the Germans against the delusions of neutralism and stressed the urgent need to deploy the American missiles.[22] The French could hardly have done more to give a European blessing to what was, on its face, an Atlantic solution. Under the circumstances, the Kohl government's success in having the missiles deployed appeared as much a reaffirmation of Germany's European and specifically French orientation as of its Atlantic dependence. Mitterrand's stance on the missiles, moreover, reduced American suspicions about Franco-German military cooperation and undermined Atlanticist opposition to the French connection within Germany.

The fact remained, however, that the French would never have accepted American missiles on their own soil, an anomaly not lost on critics in Germany at the time.[23] Mitterrand's position reflected a seeming inconsistency in French policy stretching back to de Gaulle's era. While France had sought to woo Germany into a distinctive European economic and diplomatic coalition, often in opposition to particular U.S. policies, the French had never offered the Germans any serious alternative to nuclear dependence on the Americans. To some extent, they did not because they could not. Exchanging the still relatively tiny French nuclear deterrent for the American could never seem a desirable military alternative for the Germans. The French might, however, have offered a nuclear guarantee to supplement the American, but they had always drawn back from any firm commitment. Long-standing French military doctrine saw Germany, under American protection, merely as a glacis for the French national sanctuary. Meanwhile, the French regularly professed to be horrified at any suggestion that the Germans might follow their example and build a nuclear deterrent of their own.[24]

Logically, France's refusal to give Germany a nuclear guarantee, or to contemplate the Federal Republic's having its own deterrent, left the Germans no military option between the extremes of American protection and neutralism. As Mitterrand's intervention in the missiles debate made clear, the French were no less opposed to German neutralism than were the Americans. In short, the logical and practical thrust of traditional French policy was to keep Germany firmly under America's hegemonic military protection. France, while rallying the Germans against the Americans in the economic and diplomatic spheres, pushed them to remain dependent in the military sphere.

Its inherent contradictions notwithstanding, France's bifurcated policy has generally served French interests very well; moreover, it has not even seriously disturbed the Germans. With the Americans as their protectors, France and Germany have no real need for each other in the military sphere. Instead, they need each other against the Americans in the economic sphere. America's economic threat to Europe arises not from ill will, but from the American economy's size, dynamism, competitive strength, and internal imbalances. It was to make cohabitation in an Atlantic Community bearable that the European states grouped together in the EC. But since both France and Germany have emphatically wanted the American military protectorate to continue, they have never cooperated to replace it. That Franco-German military cooperation has not developed under these circumstances in no way proves that it could not, merely that it has not been necessary.

What would happen if the American military protectorate were so substantially modified that the United States became merely an ally rather than a protector? Presumably, the change would involve the withdrawal of some American ground forces and a devolution of overall command. Given Europe's resources, the most logical and natural outcome would be for European states to make a greater military effort of their own to sustain a balance against Soviet power. France and Germany, under such circumstances, would therefore need each other as never before. Their present alliance would then expand to the military sphere. It would evolve from being primarily an economic and diplomatic counterpoise to American power within a transatlantic system to being also an anti-Soviet military coalition within a pan-European system. In this dual context, the European coalition built up around France and Germany in the EC would not so much lose its old purpose of balancing the Americans in the economic sphere as acquire the new purpose of balancing the Soviets in the military sphere. Europe would remain closely involved with America in the global economy, and thus a collective European counterbalance to the giant American economy would still be needed. Some form of transatlantic military alliance would also remain clearly in Europe's interest. Geography, not to mention culture and temperament, would continue to make Russia a military threat and the United States a natural ally. But with the Americans as allies rather than protectors, the needs of Europe's military security would require the Franco-German military cooperation that has hitherto been superfluous or unwelcome.

Would this obvious logic prevail in fact as well as in theory? Technically, as the last chapter indicates, the necessary military means could be found. Given the long-standing strength of the Franco-German relationship, why should it not extend itself into the military sphere? Two principal geopolitical obstacles suggest themselves: one is Germany's persistent tendency toward a nationalist Eastern policy; the other is France's traditionally nationalist military strategy. Both have developed in the shelter of the American protectorate, but both may have developed too far to be reversed, even if the protectorate were removed. Assessing the strength and significance of each is, therefore, critical to assessing the prospects for European military cooperation.

Fears of German *Ostpolitik* are closely linked to fears of German "neutralism." What makes these fears plausible is Germany's abiding interest in national reunification, a goal to which the Soviet Union holds the key. Throughout the postwar era prominent German political figures and groups have argued that a nonaligned Germany would be in a better position to deal with the Soviets on reunification. Unquestionably, this has been a major theme in German thinking about the future. The relative pull of this Eastern option has to be assessed in the general context of postwar German foreign policy as a whole. Like most powers, the Federal Republic has followed differing geopolitical orientations in some tension with one another. Broadly speaking, there have been three sets of relationships, which may be described as Atlantic, European, and Eastern. Each set corresponds to a traditional geopolitical option familiar to students of German history. Postwar policy has sought not only to cultivate each orientation but also to avoid any definitive choice of one that might foreclose the others.[25]

The Atlantic orientation encompasses Germany's political and military relations with the United States, together with its special interests as a global commercial power. Historically, this Atlantic option corresponds to the traditional "Little German" or *kleindeutsch* model for German foreign policy. It presupposes that Germany will remain a national state with territory so limited that it cannot hope to be self-sufficient economically. To prosper, *Kleindeutschland* needs an oversized manufacturing sector whose worldwide exports cover its imports. Bismarck's Imperial Reich in its initial "Liberal" phase can be said to have constituted such a model. After 1870, it was territorially satisfied. At home, it pursued a rather manic industrialization; abroad, it was highly aggressive commercially. Until the slumping world economy began to close against it, the Reich had no interest in incorporating Austria, or other Germanic territories in Europe, and was relatively diffident about a colonial empire.

The postwar Federal Republic replicates this early Bismarckian model in an extreme form. Shorn of its East German agriculture, the prosperity of the Federal Republic's unbalanced, industrial economy depends on secure access to external markets. The Atlantic connection provides both military security and an open door to American and global markets. In effect, the *Pax Americana* has guaranteed German trade the access to world markets that Imperial Germany was forever fearful of losing.

The Federal Republic's European option is also deeply rooted in German history. Historically, alongside the *kleindeutsch* policy, there was also a *grossdeutsch*, or "Big German," policy that dreamt of a much larger German-dominated *Mitteleuropa*—a bloc relatively balanced and self-sufficient economically. In later Imperial times, visions of *Mitteleuropa* flourished on both left and right ends of the political spectrum. Thereafter, Hitler made his own version critical to Nazi geopolitical strategy. This *grossdeutsch* model invariably gained popularity whenever the world economy turned protectionist. After World War II, the model reappeared in the benign form of German enthusiasm for the Common Market. Western European federation provided a peaceful and plural *Mitteleuropa*, which hoped to transform the traditional rivalry with France into a special partnership.

Postwar Germany's third option perhaps can best be described as an Eastern-oriented version of *grossdeutsch* policy. It encompasses not only national reunification but also the traditional German economic penetration of Eastern Europe, including the Russian economy itself. This Eastern orientation weighed heavily on the Social Democratic Party's ideas about foreign policy in the early postwar period and had strong attraction for other parties as well, including the Christian Democrats. Critics also found it predominant in Brandt's *Ostpolitik*, at the expense of the Atlantic and Western European orientations. This Eastern option's preoccupation with reunification through nonalignment makes it tempting to call it the "nationalist" option, which is not meant to label it illegitimate or sinister or to suggest that other options are less concerned with national interest. But the Atlantic and European options stress achieving German national goals through alignments with other major states. The nationalist option, by contrast, would achieve its aims by deliberately remaining aloof from any superpower or general European bloc.

Critics often link the nationalist option with Finlandization—trading American hegemony for Soviet hegemony. Its advocates, however, envision a Germany that is genuinely neutral—not aggressively armed or allied but an independent buffer between the Soviets and the West. Such a nonthreatening Germany, they hope, would permit the Soviet Union to relax its iron grip on the restive Eastern European satellite countries and gradually withdraw from its overextended military position. In the more relaxed political climate that would follow, a neutral and independent Germany could become the East's favored and much-needed commercial and industrial partner.

That the French find such a vision troubling is hardly surprising. De Gaulle's "Europe from the Atlantic to the Urals" was, in some respects, an attempt to Europeanize this nationalist German *Mitteleuropa*. His own overtures to the Soviets were, in part, to preempt it.

At one time or another, the Federal Republic has pursued versions of all three of these resurrected foreign policies. Adenauer used NATO to cement Germany's Atlantic connection and the Common Market to structure its European connection. NATO involved a special relationship with the United States; the EEC, with France. Brandt's *Ostpolitik* sought to give limited substance to the Eastern option as well. Since the 1960s, German foreign policy has tried to avoid pursuing any one of the three options to an extent that might seriously threaten the others: thus, Germany's rather bigamous relation with the United States and France, as well as its tenacious insistence on pan-European détente. Germany's internal prosperity and equilibrium have been seen to depend on sustaining this geopolitical balance.

Would an American devolution within NATO destabilize that German balance? In any abrupt collapse of the American protectorate, a traumatic German reaction could hardly be ruled out. A gentler devolution from protectorate to alliance would certainly require some major adjustments in German policy. The reaction consistent with the Federal Republic's independence, democracy, and prosperity would be to pursue a further development of the European option by extending the already strong French connection to the military sphere. Such a European option, moreover, would not necessarily have to be pursued at any real long-term cost to the other options. A more comprehensive European relationship with France should not rupture Germany's American ties or pan-European interest. In particular, a some-what more withdrawn United States should not appear a less attractive ally. German interest in remaining part of a liberal world economy would hardly diminish. If devolution made possible a long-overdue straightening out of American fiscal policy, the prospects for preserving an open global economy would probably be much brighter. The French, moreover, should be as eager as the Germans to continue American involvement in European defense or to preserve American-European partnership in a global economic system.

In theory, the greatest danger of devolution is that Germany might hope to compensate by pursuing the Eastern or nationalist option in isolated neutralism from both America and France, presumably through close accommodation with the Soviets. Logically, such an evolution can never be excluded. But quite apart from Soviet diffidence, little in the history of postwar German politics suggests the likelihood of such a choice from the Germans themselves. Since Adenauer's time, Germans have pursued their *Ostpolitik* only when firmly anchored in a transatlantic protectorate and a Western European coalition. A strong American military presence has, in fact, been the vital precondition. Limited accommodation with the Soviet Union has not been an alternative to the American military protectorate but a political counterpoise within it. Postwar German *Ostpolitik* has never sought a flirtatious realignment from West to East, but rather an imaginative exploration of the national possibilities within a Western alignment. With American devolution, for Germany to shift its balance somewhat from an Atlantic to a Western European orientation would seem a natural acknowledgment of evolving circumstances. But for Germany to give up Western alignment for *Ostpolitik* would be a radical change. It would represent a remarkable leap in the dark. So far, the great majority of West Germans—and their elites—have never been prepared to risk their Western liberty and prosperity for any such adventure.

Economically, the shift would be difficult to justify. Germany's entire trade with the East constitutes no more than 4 percent of its exports. By contrast, France—its largest trading partner—alone absorbs 13 percent; the EC altogether takes 48 percent; the United States, 10 percent.[26] From a longer historical perspective, neutralist reunification also seems a highly questionable goal. Politically, East Germany would by now prove highly indigestible. Seriously pursuing a reunified state would suggest that the Germans had learned nothing from the terrible tragedy of their own history. Once more they would be recreating an isolated Germany—too large to live comfortably with the rest of Europe—a Germany once more "born encircled." Europeans most conscious of the lessons of this bitter heritage believe Germany can only be united as a confederation, and only within the context of a more general European reunification. This emphasis on European as opposed to national German reunification is the thread running through the Eastern policies of the wisest postwar European statesmen—from Adenauer, who insisted on consolidating ties to the West before all else; to de Gaulle, who preached a Europe from the Atlantic to the Urals; to Brandt, who accepted two states within one nation; to Kohl, who again and again has renounced a purely nationalist form of reunification.[27]

A policy of self-denial that depends on the continuous wisdom of statesmen may be a precarious basis for optimism about the future. If history offered the Germans a new opportunity for a unified state, no one could be certain they would not seize it. But the opportunity is unlikely to present itself in any foreseeable future. Aside from the restraints imposed by Germany's Western allies, little suggests that the Russians would want or could handle a neutralist Germany.[28] As the next chapter will argue, the Soviets are in no position either to bid for hegemony over Western Europe or to expose their own political and economic system to a close German partnership. Under these circumstances, any German expectations about achieving reunification through a neutralist accommodation with the Soviets seem highly unrealistic. Ironically, wishful thinking about the Eastern option depends almost entirely on the general assumption that the American protectorate will last indefinitely. So long as the protectorate exists, it both fosters the illusion that accommodation with the Soviets would be easy except for American obstruction and also blocks development of a European defense option. In other words, the belief that the protectorate will never end feeds the fatal confidence that Germany can sustain a comfortable political relation with the Soviets without an adequate Western European military foundation. In this respect, as in so many others, the obsolescent arrangements of the Atlantic Alliance are a sort of incubator for illusions, misunderstandings, and resentments that slowly undermine Western solidarity and strength. Transforming NATO into a more balanced alliance should discourage these German illusions and promote a healthy interest in military cooperation with France.

Would the French be disposed to reciprocate the interest? No country, after all, has so jealously guarded its military independence. Even under the Fourth Republic, the French vetoed the European Defense Community, which their own statesmen had designed. Since de Gaulle's time, the gap between France's efforts to promote European solidarity and its nationalistic military posture has grown still more pronounced.

The seeming incongruity between military posture and diplomacy merely reflects the fundamental ambiguities of French diplomacy itself. French policy, like German, has almost instinctively struggled to keep open a series of geopolitical options— any one of which, if pursued to its logical conclusion, would be in great tension with the others. Not unlike the Federal Republic, France can be seen to have followed Atlantic, Eastern, and European policies. Accordingly, French governments have given different emphasis to special relations with the Americans, the Soviets, or the Germans. According to the circumstances of the moment, postwar Franco-German relations may be charted according to how the respective diplomatic blends of each country have meshed.

Rhetorically, French policy has always emphasized its independence. This emphasis is not merely eccentric nationalist egotism. A France that does not keep its options open risks being dominated by any one of its special relationships. Russia

and America are superpowers, and even the Federal Republic is superior in economic resources. To stay on tolerably equal terms, the French have had to rely on
their brains, agility, and panache. Typically, they use all the diplomatic leverage
available to them. Their considerable success can be measured in the respect and
sometimes the resentment of their partners.

Morale and élan are particular preoccupations for a weaker country playing a
great role. The French forever emphasize their grandeur, by which they mean not
so much power, which they lack in relation to the superpowers, but vision, intelligence, skill, taste, sympathy, and a certain moral authority that arises from these
qualities. Successive French governments have done their best to preserve a global
as well as European role for France. Their success, in Africa particularly, has been
considerable.

The central problem for France has been how to pursue the ambitious policy
that independence requires without sapping its own economic and political vitality
and thereby defeating its larger purpose. Nearly all of its postwar leaders, de Gaulle
not the least, have seen modernization of the domestic political economy and
society as the key to any long-range national success. Thus, however much France's
grandeur, safety, and vitality have been seen to require a vigorous foreign policy,
that policy has had to be designed to enhance rather than diminish France's domestic
rejuvenation. *Élan vital* has to be kept within the bounds of *mesure*.

French policy has always had to take care not to lose the balance needed to
preserve its independence. Pursuing French and European independence from
the Americans has had to be balanced against the risks of opening the door to
Russian hegemony or reviving German nationalism without achieving the pan-
European structure to contain it.

France's balancing act has naturally led it into ambiguous relations with the
Soviet Union. France has traditionally had certain special ties with Russia. Before
World War I, Imperial Russia was France's principal continental ally. In the interwar
years, losing Russia greatly weakened France's geopolitical position and made it
uncomfortably dependent on the British.[29] After World War II, de Gaulle saw
improved Franco-Soviet relations as a way to reduce the risk of European war and
dependence on the United States.[30] But Gaullist Soviet policy presumed the Atlantic
Alliance and always had one eye on Germany. De Gaulle's vision of a "Europe
from the Atlantic to the Urals" was designed not only to ease Russia out of its
overextended Eastern European hegemony, but also to suggest a Europeanized
context for some loose and nonthreatening form of German national reunification.

Like France, Russia has both opposed American pretensions to hegemony over
Western Europe and feared any revival of German hegemonic ambitions. These
shared interests might be seen to constitute a tacit Franco-Soviet reinsurance treaty,
a stabilizing link within any pan-European system—so long, that is, as France's
Soviet ties coincided with the American and German connections needed to contain

the Soviets. So far, France's Eastern policy, like Germany's hope for reunification, has been firmly disciplined by a clear priority for the Western link. Tactical flirtations notwithstanding, no French government has seriously considered trading its German or American alliance for Soviet favor. France, even while taking advantage of the American protectorate, seems never to have forgotten the need for a European military balance, as its own vigorous defense policy has always made clear.

Nowhere is the fundamental character of France's policy better displayed than in its military posture. Its long-standing strategy has made France militarily the most independent of Western Europe's powers. Geography has kept France safely under America's protection, even without integration in NATO. French policy has enhanced this natural advantage by building an independent nuclear deterrent. Initially, the French deterrent had its rationale almost exclusively as an extra trigger on the American deterrent. Once a nuclear exchange had begun, the Americans were thought unlikely to stay out. For a start, it was not easy to imagine the political or military circumstances in which the French strategic deterrent would be used but not the American.[31] In the shock and chaos following the French attack, the Soviets might imagine the Americans had already struck. In any event, the Russians, calculating that the Americans would attack them, would, it was supposed, launch a preemptive attack on the United States.

In due course, the *force de dissuasion* has acquired a major military significance of its own. Still relatively small in the mid-1980s, France's strategic deterrent would not permit the elaborate trading of targets foreseen in American "counterforce" nuclear doctrine. To maximize its deterrence, French nuclear forces have been targeted directly against Soviet cities. A massive attack on Soviet population centers would be tantamount to national suicide for the French, as the Russians would almost certainly retaliate in kind. But according to the French strategic doctrine of "proportional deterrence," the exchange, if fatal to France, would not be in any way advantageous to the Soviets. The French force is sufficiently large and secure that no Soviet first strike could count on destroying it. Thus even if France were largely destroyed, the Soviets would themselves sustain appalling losses, including presumably the destruction of their capital and a large part of their government. In theory, all this could take place without America's deterrent being involved in any way.

Whether the French would have the political will to use their strategic deterrent must naturally remain in doubt. But doubts of this kind are inseparable from the nature of all nuclear deterrence. There is no reason to take for granted, for example, that American deterrence for Europe is any more resolute than French deterrence for France. The most sensible view concludes that any nation's strategic nuclear deterrence is most credible as a retaliation for a strategic nuclear attack against that nation itself. In other words, if the Soviets launched a nuclear attack against France, they could expect a devastating French riposte, even from a France that was mortally wounded. The capacity for such deterrence greatly limits the Soviet capacity for nuclear blackmail. The technical credibility of French deterrence is, moreover, scheduled for a major upgrading over the next decade. By the mid-1990s, the French should have a much more formidable strategic force.[32]

Over the years, the French have also developed a tactical nuclear capability to complement their strategic deterrent. Airplanes or rockets permit small-scale French nuclear strikes in Germany or Eastern Europe. The French are developing newer, longer-range tactical rockets and are said to be developing a neutron bomb for such purposes as well.[33] There has always been considerable confusion and controversy over the function of these new weapons. Particularly as the range of French tactical rockets has stretched farther, French diplomacy has flirted with extending nuclear protection to West German territory. In traditional French doctrine, however, these small-scale nuclear weapons are to be used in the German battlefield for demonstrating French resolve and testing Soviet intentions, rather than for defending Germany. French tactical weapons are reserved for a distinctive "second battle" in Germany, should the initial battle between invading Warsaw Pact forces and NATO not stop the advance. French forces would engage in this second battle in order to determine Soviet intentions toward the French national *sanctuaire*. A continued Soviet advance would trigger the French strategic deterrent. The degree of French participation in NATO's initial defense would depend on the circumstances. Meanwhile, no automatic commitment would be given and no French forces would be stationed near the front line. In short, French military doctrine has clearly distinguished between the defense of France and the defense of the Federal Republic.

Since this doctrine of the two battles was spelled out in the French White Paper of 1972, it has been subject to a certain amount of rhetorical manipulation by successive governments and a great deal of argument and speculation among defense experts and within the various political parties. During Giscard d'Estaing's presidency, a number of delphic references were made to *"sanctuarisation élargie,"* implying a French national interest in defending Germany. The same combination of official ambiguity and unofficial debate continued to characterize the Mitterrand presidency. Flirtation, in other words, always stopped short of permanent engagement. French military doctrine has continued to conceive of nuclear deterrence for national rather than European defense, even if French weapons might actually be used in Germany.

The nationalist logic of French military doctrine is entirely clear. With an independent strategic deterrent able to cause massive damage to the Soviets regardless of American reactions, France has been able to see itself as a *sanctuaire* able, in theory, to stand aside from a general nuclear conflagration.[34]

French diplomacy has, of course, done its best to point out the advantages of France's nationalist deterrence for others. Leaders have occasionally described the national deterrent as being in reserve for Europe, which implies it might someday become the basis for a collective and independent European nuclear force.[35] The French have also always claimed their *force de dissuasion* to be a significant reinforcement of NATO's American deterrent and have developed an elaborate military doctrine to bolster the claim. French deterrent theory traditionally stresses the significance of uncertainty and the usefulness of multiple deterrence. Having two or three separate political authorities capable of starting a nuclear war is said to be a more formidable deterrent than having only one, particularly when that one, the United States, is not defending its own home territory.[36]

While the Americans initially scorned all such doctrines, with their scorn frequently echoed by the other Europeans, they have grown more appreciative in recent years.[37] At the very least, France's having its own nuclear force seems to have inoculated its public from the antinuclear pacifism influential in German public opinion. While the French have always jealously guarded their nuclear force from any hint of integration into NATO's command structure, consultations with the Germans and the NATO command grew more frequent by the mid-1970s, particularly as the development of French tactical nuclear weapons made their possible use in Germany a practical concern. Nevertheless, by the mid-1980s, the French were still unable to bring themselves to a formal public commitment to German nuclear defense. In effect, French military doctrine still left Germany's territorial defense to the Americans and Germans. So secure have the French felt behind their German-American glacis that most of their professional ground forces have been designed for use in the Third World.[38]

If irritating to its allies, France's military posture nevertheless represents a highly intelligent use of resources—above all, the geopolitical advantage of being automatically protected by the Americans. Probably never in its modern history has France seemed so secure militarily. A country invaded three times since 1870 may hardly be expected to underestimate its current advantages. At the same time, French military budgets have not exceeded 5 percent of GNP since the early 1960s—a level substantially below the American and British, although notably higher than the German.[39]

Could France ever bear to abandon its present comfortable disengagement, even if the transformation of the American protectorate radically changed the context? In the French case, it is important to note that comfort has not bred complacency. Even if a free rider from an American perspective, France cannot be accused of neglecting its own military prowess. On the contrary, France has gone to great efforts to develop its independent nuclear force. France also has a formidable navy, air force, and global intervention force, and the French defense establishment is certainly one of the most efficiently managed in the world.[40] In effect, France has used the leverage provided by the American protectorate to make itself a strategic and global power, but within a range of expenditure that does not threaten the country's economic welfare or put its civilian and military goals in serious conflict. Nor can the American military protectorate be said to have dulled France's political and diplomatic activism. As France's habitual position in the EC demonstrates, the French are quite capable of taking a leading role where their own interest appears to require it.

The explanation for France's passive role in NATO and active role in the EC lies in the difference between France's secure position in the military sphere and its relatively vulnerable position in the economic sphere. In postwar circumstances, France is more exposed economically than militarily. Paradoxically, France's economic vulnerability is inseparable from its great postwar economic progress. While the French GNP has remained lower than that even of a Germany reduced to the Federal Republic, French GNP growth has exceeded its West German counterpart throughout much of the postwar era. France has become, in some respects, Europe's leading technological power and is currently Europe's second- and the world's fourth-largest trading nation. In effect, the French economy has emerged from its traditional protectionist sanctuary into the world economy.[41]

The French have not found all the consequences to their liking. A France both more open and more successful economically is also more vulnerable to external shocks. And, as the events of May 1968 suggested, France may have a lingering prediliction to social and political instability. The 1970s saw the French economy severely buffeted by inflation and the oil shocks. Growth slowed and the French became deeply worried about their future competitiveness.[42] France's traditional industries, in common with those of the rest of Europe, have been slow to adapt to the growing prowess of newly industrializing countries. And despite heavy investment and impressive achievements in technology, France's advanced industries suffer competitively from a relatively small national market and limited resources. Many Frenchmen fear that their traditional economic culture, with its elitism, statism, and lack of commercial energy, is inappropriate to an era of chaotic change and intense international rivalry. The early experiences of the Socialist government's isolated economic experiment intensified the country's sense of economic vulnerability. Mitterrand's strong reaction, however, amounted to a vigorous reinforcement of France's European commitment. As Socialist policy was abandoned for European policy, France decided it needed Germany and Europe more than ever. Dissatisfaction with the Americans over a wide range of diplomatic and economic issues seemed to make German support all the more vital for French independence and prosperity.

While the commitment to Europe's economic coalition seems robust and long-standing, would France ever accept the military implications of that commitment? There seems no compelling reason to suppose not, should the need arise. Only the prospect of an end or transformation of the American protectorate would, however, be likely to make the need seem real. In the early 1980s America's growing dissatisfaction with the NATO commitment, Europe's wariness over American economic and diplomatic policies, and the Federal Republic's rising anti-American neutralism began to suggest the need for a more active European military policy. French political elites grew increasingly uneasy over the long-standing contradictions between France's nationalist military doctrine and its close political and economic alliance with Germany. Important factions within Gaullist, centrist, and Socialist parties began issuing pronouncements and studies warning of an upsurge of neutralism among the Germans and urging a more forthright French military commitment to the Federal Republic. The press was full of articles along the same lines, and a spate of important new books captured public attention.[43] The government's formal position, however, appeared unchanged. Mitterrand reaffirmed the traditional views about the advantages of "uncertainty," while pointedly observing the general unacceptability of any independent German nuclear force. Mitterrand's 1983 Bundestag speech supporting U.S. missiles in Germany was a blatant expression of the traditional French position: Atlantic military integration for the Germans but not for the French.[44]

Scattered but accumulating signs nevertheless suggested movement toward a more serious French commitment to German defense. After Mitterrand and Kohl had agreed to activate the Franco-German Treaty's hitherto moribund military provisions, the subsequent bilateral consultations were said to have made considerable operational progress. Among the topics, presumably, were the circumstances under which French medium-range nuclear rockets might be used in a European battle.[45] France's 1983 Five-Year Military Plan called for a mobile intervention force, the *Force d'Action Rapide*, justified officially by its possibly critical role in any European land battle.[46] The heavy cost made it a major item in France's military budget and, in a period of unprecedented fiscal austerity, appeared to represent a significant shift toward European defense. In 1984, the French and German governments also resurrected the old Western European Union (WEU) and apparently committed themselves to a series of significant bilateral and European agreements to develop new weapons systems.[47] France launched and Germany subscribed to the Eureka project—a broad cooperative venture in advanced technology meant to provide a European civilian counter to Reagan's Star Wars project.[48]

By the middle of the 1980s, however, a certain mutual disillusionment appeared on both sides. From a German perspective, the French were still not offering much except the right to help pay for French-dominated armaments projects. Despite random signs of a more forthcoming military policy, the French had clearly not abandoned their traditional ambivalent detachment toward German defense. If they were proceeding to lay the ground for possible changes, they were doing so with great circumspection. The French were themselves disappointed with the tepid German response and understandably diffident about pressing military offers that might not be accepted but would nevertheless arouse American fears and

European opposition. Moreover, seriously pursuing the military dimension of the Franco-German coalition would soon raise the delicate and thorny issues of German deterrence.

New factors complicated the prospects for Franco-German cooperation. Vigorous American salesmanship of the Strategic Defense Initiative distracted Europeans from their own industrial cooperation. Renewed Soviet-American arms talks in Geneva raised the issue of a nuclear-free Europe, prompting, among other things, a fresh interest in Anglo-French military cooperation. The tribulations of the Reagan administration in its later years promised new uncertainty and volatility in American policy. Meanwhile, between 1986 and 1988 political leadership in Britain, France, Germany, and Italy all faced national elections in which defense questions were, or threatened to be, major issues. All the same, the period was prolific with projects and manifestos for European cooperation—in France not least. Even in the uncertain political environment of *cohabitation* between a Socialist president and a Gaullist prime minister, France's long-term defense budgeting confirmed a gradual military tilt toward Europe.[49]

In summary, the situation in the late 1980s reveals not only an apparent drift toward European cooperation, but also the continuing factors that limit and condition that cooperation. Behind France's perennial diffidence about German military engagements lies its essential satisfaction with the military status quo. Given their apprehensions about Germany's greater economic strength, permanent Eastern interests, and recurring neutralist predelictions, the French are reluctant to yoke their own national security formally with Germany's—so long as they see nothing to gain from doing so. They naturally prefer the conditional link made possible by the American protectorate. French involvement in German defense thus seems the reciprocal of American protection. Whenever the American protectorate appears unusually shaky or onerous, the French intensify their fitful defense dialogue with the Germans. The same, of course, is true of the Germans. So long as they are convinced of American nuclear protection, they see little need to pay anything to acquire French engagement—particularly if it risks alienating the Americans. The Franco-German military relationship has thus become a sort of minuet. The partners go round and round, but they return to the same places.

Does this minuet really mean that Europeans lack the political will to assume the major responsibility for their own security? The arguments are often highly circular. European states will not unite to provide an adequate defense, it is said, because they have not done so since the Second World War—that is, during the long period of American protection. In this sort of argument, the effect becomes the cause. The opportunistic European nationalism that the American subsidy has made possible is used as the reason the subsidy cannot be withdrawn. Among other things, this pessimism flies in the face of postwar Europe's impressive cooperation in the economic sphere. Why should cooperation in the military sphere be thought less probable? The basic national interests of the Western European states do not make a military coalition more difficult politically than an economic coalition. The problems of military cooperation are, after all, rather simple in comparison with the contentious complexities of economic collaboration. If France and Germany have together been able to sustain an economic community, why should they not be able to sustain a military coalition? Granted, they would prefer their present comfortable protectorate. But if it is no longer sustainable, why should they shrink from the self-evident remedy?

The whole issue ought perhaps to be seen in a broader historical perspective. Today's Europe, it should be remembered, is far from the dispirited and unhinged Europe of the 1930s. Its present prosperity would have been considered an extravagant dream fifty years ago. Europeans have used that prosperity to create humane societies and civilized political systems whose independence seems eminently worth preserving. A good deal of Europe's achievement can be laid to its own cooperation. France and Germany have led that cooperation. Much of what they possess is bound up in their partnership and the Europe made possible by it. Why, when the time comes, should they not take the obvious military steps needed to safeguard their own proud creation?

11

The Russian Role

NO ALLIANCE exists without an adversary; every alliance relationship is at least a triangle. These triangular connections, in turn, exist in a political as well as military context, and are often polymorphous. While an adversarial relationship by definition implies some degree of hostility, opposition in one set of relations does not necessarily preclude cooperation in others. Each ally may have his own separate understandings with the adversary, or adversaries. These may include tacit or secret understandings to cooperate or shift allegiances under certain circumstances.

The postwar links within the Atlantic Alliance illustrate all these generalizations. American-European relationships have been not merely bilateral, but also triangular. The Soviet Union has been very much part of postwar Europe, and without a Soviet threat to contain, the United States would have been very much less. Without the Soviet threat, a North Atlantic Treaty would presumably never have come into being—certainly not the hegemonic military machinery of NATO. Even in the economic sphere, it took the Cold War to mobilize American domestic support for the massive aid Europe required to participate in a transatlantic liberal system. Had no Russian military power pressed them, Europeans would have resisted American economic penetration even more than they have.[1]

The triangular relationships also illustrate how alignments among the same powers may differ from one sphere to another. While France, the Federal Republic, and the United States are military allies, each has cultivated special diplomatic and economic relations with the Soviets, in some instances to gain leverage over one another. The Franco-German coalition and the EC have so far been primarily a European combination to counter the Americans within the global economic system. Should the Western Europeans take over managing their military balance, their military coalition would presumably be directed toward a different adversary—the Soviets.

The Russians are hardly unknown as adversaries. Europeans have lived with the Russian Empire for several centuries. America and Western Europe have been confronting the Soviets through NATO since 1949. How formidable an adversary would the Soviets be against a NATO run by the Western Europeans? The answer depends not merely on the Soviet Union's military capacities but also on its political and economic character, and how its corresponding interests and ambitions interact with the distinctive aims and ambitions of the various Western powers. Different NATO allies have naturally had different interests in their Soviet relationships. In common with the United States, the Western European states have been unwilling to accept Soviet domination over Western Europe—even if, to avoid a war, they tolerate it in Eastern Europe. Beyond this point, American and European interests begin to diverge, with corresponding differences in their Soviet policies and relationships.

⌈As previous chapters observe in detail, Americans take a more global view of their Soviet relationship, whereas the Europeans give greater priority to its European dimension.⌋ At the same time, the Europeans are also more ambitious about what can be achieved in Europe. Western European governments generally want a reduction of East-West military tensions that passes beyond a mere stabilization of the European status quo. Most would prefer to lower political and economic barriers sufficiently so that an interdependent pan-European system might develop—without, of course, accepting Soviet hegemony in the process. European motives are as much economic, cultural, and moral as they are strategic. Traditionally, Eastern and Western Europe have never been so divided economically and culturally as at present. The moral tensions of a continent half free and half in bondage continue to trouble European consciences on both sides of the Iron Curtain. The division is particularly painful for the Germans. Economically, Eastern European trade is at least of marginal interest to Western Europe, and the Soviet Union's vast untapped natural resources and underdeveloped markets form an intriguing long-range prospect.

Within these common Western European interests, strong national differences give distinctive overtones to policies. The previous chapter discusses French and German interests. Naturally, other European states also have distinctive Soviet relations. British diplomacy, if less involved with Eastern Europe than German or French diplomacy, has occasionally played a critical role.[2] Italy, with a large Communist Party that has long pursued a middle course between Moscow and the West, enjoys a wide range of interesting Eastern European ties.[3]

On the other side of the Iron Curtain, the Eastern bloc is hardly less diverse in its triangular interests, despite the heavy-handed Soviet protectorate. Up to a point, Eastern European regimes share the Western European desire for a looser pan-European order. Their own politico-economic development seems to require reducing the weight of Soviet hegemony, with its stultifying rigidity, while gaining greater access to Western trade and investment. The détente of the 1970s gave Eastern states greater access to credit and more freedom to maneuver. The institutionalized European Conference on Security and Cooperation (ECSC) has given them a forum through which to make their distinctive presence felt.[4] In all the Eastern-bloc countries, however, the desire for more national freedom and development is inhibited both by the limits of Soviet tolerance and by the fears of a resurgent Germany. In most of the same countries, moreover, unpopular elites and unstable regimes still depend on Soviet backing.[5]

Compared to the tortuous complexities of French, German, or Eastern European perspectives, America's European interests may seem relatively straightforward. The Americans must deny Soviet hegemony over Western Europe and preserve their own easy access, while avoiding a nuclear war that engulfs the American homeland. But America's policy has also frequently reflected more ambitious definitions of its European interest. While NATO is a defensive alliance to cover home territories, it also makes Western Europe a forward base of American military power. It puts formidable American ground, air, and naval forces—including strategic bombers and missiles—in close proximity to the Russian heartland. Before the introduction of intercontinental missiles, this forward base gave the United States an overwhelming strategic advantage. Europe can still provide a launching platform for projecting American power elsewhere—most notably during various Middle Eastern crises.[6]

American policy has often tried to extend the alliance's scope by enlisting Western Europe's economic, political, and even military power against Soviet policy in non-European regions—as in the Korean and Vietnam wars. Successive American administrations have sought to limit Western European–Soviet trade, investment, and technological exchange.[7] The United States has urged NATO sanctions over Afghanistan, Poland, and human rights in the Soviet Union.

There is nothing surprising about these regular American attempts to mobilize NATO for direct military or economic pressure against the Soviets, or for interventions beyond the treaty area. Given America's huge investment in NATO, it often does not seem enough merely to deny the Soviets European hegemony or to keep Western Europe itself within a congenial politico-economic world system. The United States hopes, in addition, to get some handle on Europe's military and economic resources for America's own purposes. Making a reality of that hope calls, in effect, for defining the American interest in Western Europe in a fashion not easily distinguishable from political as well as military hegemony.

Like other countries, America has found its larger ambitions limited by intractable circumstances. Using Europe to pressure the Soviets or as a platform for American interventions elsewhere requires European governments to cooperate. Given Europe's own distinctive Soviet and global interests, an easy convergence of transatlantic policies can hardly be taken for granted. And given the balance of forces between Western Europe and the United States, European states are not easily coerced. Since de Gaulle's partial defection in the mid-1960s, American administrations have been aware, or quickly learned, that pressing the Europeans for maximalist goals can destabilize the alliance itself. America's maximum goals thus risk its minimum goals. Trying to use Europe as a weapon risks losing it as an ally.

While the various Western perspectives and interests in the triangular relationship are diverse and ambivalent, so are those of the common Soviet adversary. What are the Soviet aims in Europe? Any attempt to define Russian goals and interests soon raises the problems of the Soviet Union's unique character as a state. Russian history and size are thought to make the Soviet state so distinctive that the usual techniques for estimating national interest and ambition when dealing with Western states are believed inadequate in treating the Soviets. Soviet character is thought to make Soviet policies significantly more aggressive than those of Western states. Some analysts note simply Soviet capabilities and assume they will be fully exploited.[8] Not everyone, of course, accepts such premises, let alone their logical conclusion— an intensive and perpetual arms race. Widely different views of the Soviet character have come in and out of fashion throughout the postwar period. All too often, American views of the Soviets are heavily laced with projections of internal Western fantasies. An effective foreign policy cannot keep changing its basic perspectives, oscillating fitfully from one extreme view of its adversary to another. Most of the contrasting traditional views of the Soviets have some validity, but each needs to be considered in a broader context that takes account of the others.[9]

Like any society, the Soviet Union is full of contradictory tendencies. Like the United States it is vast and multiracial. Like any other country, its perspectives are rooted in a broad historical and geopolitical context. Well before the beginning of the last century, the Russian czars had already subjugated dozens of neighboring European and Asian peoples into a huge land empire in the center of Eurasia. Russia's central position, as suggested earlier, is both an advantage and a curse. On the one hand, the Russians have all the benefits of interior supply lines in directing force against their neighbors. On the other hand, they are encircled by a ring of powerful states, many of whom have irredentist claims. The violent mix of Russian history—imperial expansionism alternating with repeated invasions from abroad— lends credence to the notion of force as both a necessity and a value in itself to be admired. Fear and ambition have thus regularly reinforced each other throughout Russian history. By now, the age of easy conquest appears over and the Russians cannot help but wonder if the age of retribution may be about to begin. From Moscow's perspective, its Eurasian neighbors must seem a formidable array, particularly since so many of them are linked together in a grand anti-Soviet coalition put together by the Americans.

Russian historical experience has differed greatly from American, which sometimes makes Americans poor interpreters of Soviet perspectives. The American passion for absolute security comes from being used to nothing else. Russians derive a similar passion from the opposite experience. If the Russians have been far more isolated culturally than the Americans, they have not been nearly so well protected. On the contrary, they have been devastated by three massive European invasions since the beginning of the nineteenth century—two of them in the first half of this century. And while their history of triumphant resistance is undoubtedly a source of great pride, it must equally be a source of great apprehension, for their history has given the Russians a well-deserved inferiority complex about their technological and managerial backwardness. The Russo-Japanese War, the First World War, and even the Second World War saw spectacular illustrations of astonishing Russian military incompetence, side by side with the extraordinary bravery and endurance of Russian soldiers. It is not entirely fortuitous that personal courage in the face of general incoherent disaster is such a pervasive theme in Russian literature.

Life under the Soviets, moreover, has not done as much as might have been hoped to infuse expectations of rationality, civility, and success among the populace. Despite undoubted technical prowess in the military field, Soviet standards of civilian consumption, public amenities, or rational and efficient public administration remain markedly inferior by normal Western standards. Under the circumstances, projecting an American confidence into Soviet behavior is likely to prove misleading.

To say that Russians feel more vulnerable and less confident than Americans is not to say, of course, that Soviet aggressiveness is thereby less formidable. It does suggest, however, that Soviet expectations and ambitions are less exalted than Americans might infer from Soviet behavior. Soviet nervousness about change in Eastern Europe will make European relations volatile and tense for the foreseeable future. But this same insecurity will continue to make the Soviets cautious in their behavior toward Western Europe. Given a reasonable military balance, the prospects for reaching some relatively stable *modus vivendi* are probably better than we think, at least in Europe.

The role of Marxist ideology is an additional complication in arriving at any stable view of Soviet behavior. The Soviets long ago gave priority to preserving socialism in one country rather than promoting world revolution. Russian national interests have been almost always paramount. Certainly Soviet leaders have routinely sacrificed the most vital interests of foreign communist parties whenever it has suited Russian purposes to do so. Yet it is undoubtedly a mistake to see Soviet policy as completely without Marxist scruples. Even if Western Marxists deny its legitimacy, the Soviet Union still sees itself the moral leader of a bloc, the best friend of revolutionary change around the world, and the most enduring opponent of counter-revolutionary repression.[10] But if history has taught the Russians anything, it is to maintain cynical prudence in the short term and visionary patience for the long term. These are traits that the West can learn to live with, so long as its own confidence has not been destroyed.

This being said, cooperative coexistence must also have rather strict limits. No matter how indulgently or sympathetically its behavior is analyzed, the Soviet Union is unlikely to shed its evil reputation. It is a power unlike any other. Even Westerners most sensitive to the shortcomings of their own societies are likely to find the Soviet Union a barbaric parody of a modern state. The politico-economic culture remains an invincibly distasteful blend of incompetence, privilege, and corruption. Ineptitude in meeting civilian goals breeds discontent, which, in turn, breeds repression—a dismal chain that the Soviets seem unable to break at home and do their best to impose on their neighbors. Soviet disregard for the dignity of the individual remains notorious, as the routine brutal treatment of dissidents makes clear. A vast apparatus of oppression is apparently as essential a part of Soviet economics as it is of Soviet politics.[11]

Disregard for human rights at home is matched by indifference to the national rights of others abroad—as Soviet relations within the Warsaw Pact repeatedly demonstrate. Not surprisingly, a regime whose political and economic priorities require so much coercion, both at home and abroad, grows so preoccupied with military power that it risks having the servant of the state become its master.[12] Like its czarist predecessor, the Soviet regime is also preoccupied with advancing its status as a world power. Its ideological pretension to be the bellwether of global revolutionary transformation apparently permits the Soviet regime to support a bleak assortment of oppressive states throughout the Third World, some with highly questionable Marxist credentials, along with a sanguinary army of terrorists.[13]

Unfortunately, these unlovable features of the Soviet regime are not merely accidents of an unlucky and bloodstained history but seem deep-rooted and self-perpetuating. By now, awareness of the intractable character of Soviet hostility and oppression is widely shared. Something of the old notion of "convergence" nevertheless also persists. While trying to avoid the cultural naïveté of the old convergence theory, many Western analysts point to objective considerations pressing the Soviet system toward far-reaching reform, at least in the economic sphere. As the Soviet Union has progressed into a modern economy, with more sophisticated industries and increasing demands for goods of higher quality, maintaining forward momentum has required a more efficient allocation of resources. The Soviets have had a wealth of discouraging experience, both at home and among their satellites, demonstrating the dangers inherent in partial economic reforms. But powerful political concerns block the kind of far-reaching reform that would not be so self-contradictory. Nevertheless, some degree of economic liberalization that increases the autonomy of various sectors, and permits a more efficient communication among them, is widely believed indispensable. Since foreign technology, trade, and investment also seem critical to the system's further progress, pressure for a greater opening to the West continues to build.[14]

If a new wave of disgust at Soviet oppression has chastened postwar revisionism, analysts still fault Western policy for its negative consequences on Soviet behavior. A hard line in the West is often believed to reinforce a hard line in the East. Western hostility and unwillingness to negotiate merely reinforce the already obdurate Soviet tendency to reject liberalization while clinging to traditional autarchy, domestic oppression, and foreign intimidation.[15]

Revisionism, thus watered down, blends into the conventional realist view. The Soviets, if aggressive and hostile, are nevertheless rational and prudent. Their geopolitical situation exposes them to dangers on many sides; it makes their external behavior understandable if not commendable. Dealing with them requires a steady mixture of strength and concession, with little room for sentimental hopes or disappointments.

Most European statesmen and foreign-policy analysts share this revised realism. Although disappointed at the slow and uncertain pace of change, most nevertheless regard the experiment with European détente an undoubted success. Conditions in Eastern Europe have certainly improved since the late 1960s, even if many shortcomings remain for the foreseeable future. Western blandishments have increasingly constrained the behavior of Eastern regimes, the Soviets included. There seems to be no alternative to pursuing such a realist détente, even if it will always require balancing political and economic accessibility with a high degree of military preparedness.[16]

By the mid-1980s, American governments, having oversold détente in the 1970s and then grown excessively skeptical of it, seemed slowly returning to a similarly balanced view.[17] Events in Russia hastened the shift. In retrospect at least, Yuri Andropov's brief ascendancy seems to have marked a new departure in Soviet policy. With a skillful and energetic young leader like Mikhail Gorbachev, the Soviet Union may prove more open to internal change and to external influence. It is still too early to say. While some signs point toward significant economic and administrative reforms, others point to even tighter political discipline. In any event, Russia under Gorbachev will prove probably a more formidable and certainly a less predictable adversary.[18]

In summary, while the four postwar decades amply demonstrate the fallacies of simpleminded interpretations of the Soviet Union, they also provide experience for a view of the Soviet character sufficiently comprehensive and balanced for a realistic diplomacy—a foreign policy based not only on deterrent force but also on the patient effort to reconcile divergent interests. If the Soviet Union is not a state like any other, neither is it invincibly impervious to the traditional diplomacy of national interest.

The preceding digression on Soviet character thus finally returns to the original question: What are the Soviet interests in Europe? Like the United States and the major Western European states, the Soviet Union has minimal and maximal goals. At a minimum, the Soviets, in common with everyone else in the triangular relationship, wish to prevent a war that threatens their homeland, or the territory of their close allies. The Soviet Union, not unlike others, believes the best way to prevent war is to prepare for it. Unfortunately, Soviet policies to prevent war are not easily distinguishable from Soviet policies to wage war.[19] Without negotiations to control the pace of armament, a reciprocal chain of fears and reactions threatens a general deterioration of political relations that makes the war no one wants more, rather than less, likely. And even if nuclear war remains highly unlikely, the economic deterioration on both sides should lend a powerful motive to serious negotiations to reduce armaments. On the Soviet side, the short-term savings would be minimal; there may even be extra costs associated with modernizing their deterrent in line with reduced numbers of warheads. But in the long run, the ever-escalating spending for new technology—a game, represented by Star Wars, in which the Soviets know they suffer from a comparative disadvantage—is almost completely at odds with modernizing the civilian economy. The new Soviet leaders are perhaps more sensitive on this point than their predecessors.

Next to preventing a European war, and especially one that devastates its own homeland, the Soviet Union presumably wishes to maintain its hegemonic Eastern European sphere—and at the same time to prevent Eastern European dissatisfaction and dissent from infecting Russia. Eastern Europe has considerable economic resources that have grown entwined with the Soviet economy. As with most empires, the balance of economic costs and benefits must be difficult to reckon. But the political cost of losing its ideological companions in the world would presumably be very high, more than any Soviet regime now imaginable may be expected to bear.[20] Even de Gaulle did not see the final stage of his pan-European order coming to pass until China had become a major threat and the Russian empire, menaced by internal disintegration, had profoundly changed its regime.[21] Ideological costs aside, no Russian state can be expected to tolerate losing military control of its Eastern European glacis to an American-dominated NATO, or to a revived Germany.

Containing Germany must be counted a third minimal Soviet interest. Postwar boundaries were established with this goal in mind. Germany was left divided into two states, with the Soviets the wardens of an eastern half closely integrated within the Eastern bloc. While the German Democratic Republic has gained greater autonomy in recent years, it nevertheless remains a Soviet diplomatic asset. With it, the Soviets can try to qualify West German adherence either to the Atlantic

Alliance or to any Western European coalition. But as the well-being of the GDR has grown more and more dependent on largesse from the Federal Republic, Soviet control of its asset has grown more and more complicated.[22]

A fourth minimal Soviet interest lies in preserving access to Western Europe—through trade, investment, and technology transfers. While it may be argued that the Soviet Union could return to Stalinist autarchy if necessary, the domestic economic and political cost would make such a policy an act of desperation.[23] This is not to say that the West can regularly trade specific economic deals for specific political concessions, in the manner of the Jackson-Vanik Amendment or the various attempts at sanctions. As the Soviets are well aware, the West's lack of consensus in such matters greatly limits its leverage. European governments will not adhere to a policy that seriously threatens the Soviets with economic isolation. A highly competitive capitalist world economy does not easily lend itself to mercantilist boycotts against a major buyer who is eminently solvent. Under the circumstances, it is not so much Western policy that limits access as the Eastern bloc's own economic and political rigidity.[24] Nevertheless, some access remains a major Soviet interest.

Alongside these minimal goals—preventing war and a German hegemonic revival, preserving their bloc in Eastern Europe, and having access to the West—the Russians doubtless have greater ambitions. A Western Europe without American military forces would be more to their liking. In the abstract, they might be expected to prefer a neutral, disunited, and disarmed Western Europe, alienated from America and too divided within itself to offer resistance to Soviet hegemony. The Europe that has historically been the major military and political threat to Russia would then be neutralized. America's principal base in Eurasia would be eliminated. Great resources would then be free for domestic growth or for dealing with the Americans or the actual or potential threats nearer to home—China, Japan, and the Moslem south. A Soviet Union that actually controlled Western Europe's resources would, of course, be immeasurably stronger.

Like the United States, however, the Soviet Union can easily live without achieving its maximal goals in Europe. Also like the Americans, the Soviets regularly rediscover how pursuing their greater European goals too energetically carries high risks. With the existence of two nuclear powers and a divided Germany, Russian policy should properly be diffident about any major change in the Western European order. Destabilizing Western Europe in some serious way may easily prove a success that brings more danger than benefit. In any event, building up military forces to intimidate the Americans or to divide the Europeans tends to be self-defeating. An actual military incursion into the West would almost certainly mean a major war that might easily risk the Soviet state's very survival. Even a United States weary of its protectorate would be unlikely to overlook its vital interest in Western Europe's independence from Soviet control. The more Russian military forces appear to menace Western Europe, the less inclined are the Americans to leave. And even if the Western Europeans grow sufficiently tired of American hegemony to demand a restructuring of the alliance, trading in NATO for Soviet hegemony is not likely to seem attractive. Nor, given their own military resources, let alone economic potential, would the Western European states need to be dominated by the Soviets, even without their American protectorate.

Beyond these nearly insuperable and supremely dangerous military obstacles to Soviet domination, the whole idea of a Western Europe led by the Soviet Union is a most improbable scenario. The Russians lack both the moral legitimacy and economic blandishments needed to sustain pan-European hegemony. With its widespread repression and exploitation, the Soviet system is no more attractive to Western Europeans than to Americans. As it is, the Soviet regime is already dangerously overextended trying to hang on to Eastern Europe, where it has great trouble maintaining moral face even among its own dependents. It has long since lost the sympathy of the left in the rest of Europe.[25] In short, the Soviet polity, beset by a broad range of intractable domestic problems and afflicted by advanced institutional sclerosis, lacks the imagination and agility to manage a system of powerful advanced states. The Soviet civilian economy is too backward and incompetent to engage in anything more than highly controlled relations with the modern economies of Western Europe. The principal reason more intense pan-European economic relations remain undeveloped is not because the Western Europeans refuse them but because the Soviet system cannot sustain them. Anything like a broad economic partnership is highly unlikely.

Under the circumstances, it seems hard to believe that domination of all Europe is a serious Soviet goal.[26] It may suit them to keep their powerful and arrogant Western neighbors off balance by encouraging trouble between Europe and America. But if the Western alliance falls apart, it is unlikely to be the fault of the Russians. In reality, their role is quite the reverse. They are the principal insurers of Western European solidarity and transatlantic friendship. Without the Russians, transatlantic relations would be far less intimate. And given the nature of their system and its problems, there seems little the Soviets can do to alter their vital Western role.

Reflecting on the European interests and goals of the two superpowers suggests an interesting conclusion. No serious and certainly no inevitable conflict of interest divides them. Both are prepared to live with the status quo: a bipolar Europe. Even if Americans genuinely deplore the oppression in Russia's Eastern European sphere, American policy does not seriously imagine risking a war to eject the Soviets from it. Moreover, a genuinely independent Eastern Europe might prove extremely unsettling for transatlantic military structures and political relationships.[27]

The Russian stake in the European status quo is far greater than the American— not only in the East but also in the West. While happy to see a modicum of disarray in the Atlantic Alliance, a neutral but nuclear-armed Western Europe would present Russia with all sorts of new challenges and dangers. In short, both superpowers traditionally find the status quo in Europe not only tolerable, but also probably the best arrangement that can reasonably be expected.

By contrast with the complacent superpowers, it is the Europeans themselves who are dissatisfied with Europe. It is European policy that is implicitly revisionist. This European dissatisfaction is only relative and varies greatly according to country and party. No European state is sufficiently dissatisfied even to contemplate a war to change the status quo. Nevertheless the thrust of European policy since the 1960s points toward a pan-European accommodation that would weaken Soviet influence in the East and American in the West. For the Russians especially, it poses an institutional and ideological challenge in Eastern Europe that the present Soviet system seems ill-suited to meet and one that could easily feed unrest within the Soviet Union itself.

The superpowers share another characteristic: both are overextended. Broadly speaking, the cause is the same. Neither has been able to adapt its own role to a world growing more plural. Here again, the Soviet difficulty seems more severe. If a more plural world presents the United States with new global problems, it presents the Soviet Union with resurgent traditional enemies on its borders.

The common problem seems to have given rise to similar reactions. Both superpowers have massively increased their military spending and forces, with a consequent militarization of diplomacy and retreat from the search for political compromise and accommodation. Each has nevertheless remained preoccupied with the other. Each tends to blame the other for the global changes over which neither has much real control. Confronted with a world that increasingly eludes their grasp, both have returned to the familiar intellectual terrain of the Cold War. The inevitable turmoil of a rapidly changing world is interpreted through a camera with a fixed bipolar focus. Both continue to see the rest of the world as a giant arena for playing out their own intimate struggle for mastery.

Their joint reaction has also had similar internal consequences, despite the radical differences between the two political economies. Greatly augmented military spending has created for both a serious problem of economic priority. In America, the habitual fiscal imbalance has achieved a new magnitude. In the Soviet Union, the tension between investment, consumption, and armaments has grown more and more difficult to manage. Under Leonid Brezhnev, the Soviet Union did strike an uneasy balance. Despite heavy outlays for military forces and investment, a substantial residue remained to improve living standards. If these standards seemed dismal by Western criteria, they were very acceptable by Soviet ones. After the devastating series of revolutions, wars, and purges in the first half of this century, it is not surprising that the Soviet population finds the second half a considerable improvement. Significant parts of Russian society, moreover, have done much better than the average. Membership in professional elites widened greatly in the Brezhnev years. The Communist Party apparatus was itself a major channel for ambitious young working-class members to enter the elites. Widening access has been particularly significant among the less privileged national minorities. Within the past generation, professional elites in the Asian republics have increasingly been drawn from the ethnic population itself, even if Russians remain in ultimate control. In general, the Soviet record in modernizing its central Asian republics is not unimpressive.[28]

But recent years have seen a notable slowing of Soviet growth. The causes are multiple and complex. Overall, the labor force has ceased growing rapidly, particularly in Russia proper. Although relatively high labor-force growth in the Central Asian republics creates opportunities for improving backward areas, diverting scarce investment from Russia itself poses divisive political problems. Soviet agriculture remains embarrassingly intractable, more than ever as the Soviet diet has greatly improved. Rising energy costs are another major impediment to growth. Vast reserves of oil, gas, and coal exist in Siberia, but their extraction requires huge investments. Capital is also urgently needed for improving the country's often backward infrastructure and transforming its industrial base to keep up with Western technological changes. The economic system needs to make itself a much more sensitive apparatus for sending and responding to information about supply and demand. Failure to do so has resulted in an increasingly irrational economy, characterized by a high degree of corruption, deception, covert trading, and waste.[29]

These accumulating problems present a formidable challenge to Soviet leadership, which has itself been in unprecedented flux. Ruling elites throughout the system were remarkably stable from the Stalinist purges to the 1980s. Brezhnev's death finally precipitated a sweeping generational change of the ruling class at all levels. Until Gorbachev's installation, leadership was unstable even at the top. With Gorbachev, economic transformation appears to be a major priority, possibly in tandem with a more serious concern over arms control. At best, Gorbachev will need time to consolidate his leadership, as well as a reasonably favorable environment to spell out and impose any new directions.[30]

American policy in the Reagan years has often seemed to draw questionable conclusions from the Soviet predicament. According to one line of thinking, Soviet vulnerability has grown so extreme that external pressure could force major policy changes or destabilize the regime. Blocking foreign credits and trade and greatly augmenting the arms race is half-expected to bring the Soviet system to collapse. Even threatening Russia to reinforce Soviet conservatism is sometimes counted a clever way to create even greater trouble for the system in the future.[31] Such a policy risks having quite contrary results. Its heavy strain on Western resources, and the consequent American fiscal disorder, suggests that it may not be the relatively primitive Soviet economy that breaks down first. Soviet history, moreover, does not suggest a low capacity to respond to external threats. A bellicose West provides the external excuse needed to justify the domestic discipline that resolving the present Soviet situation will very likely demand.

In any event, it cannot be taken for granted that America's national interest would be well served by an unviable Soviet regime. Certainly no one should contemplate with complacency any precipitate breakdown of a nuclear superpower able to destroy most of the world. Nuclear dangers aside, America's own geopolitical interest would not necessarily benefit from a sudden collapse of the Soviet Union as a world power. While having the Russians out of East Germany, Poland, Czechoslovakia, or Hungary would be deeply gratifying, without some modern-day version of the multinational Hapsburg Empire—or at least viable national regimes—the consequent power vacuum might also be deeply disturbing to intra-European and transatlantic relations. If the Soviets were to disappear as an international presence, as in the interwar years, what sort of alignments would follow? If something happier than the status quo can easily be imagined in Europe, so can something worse. The dislocations would also be greatly compounded in Asia.

If many American assumptions about the possibilities and advantages of breaking the Soviets seem misguided, habitual Soviet military policy seems even more counterproductive. The abiding Soviet preoccupation with military force is easily understood, given Russia's besieged geopolitical situation, not to mention its internal coercion. The arms race, moreover, can hardly be blamed entirely on the Soviets. Their buildup from the mid-1960s to the mid-1970s is often explained as a reaction to the bitter dispute with China, the American buildup of the Kennedy-Johnson era, the humiliation of the Cuban missile crisis, and the massive commitment of American power in Vietnam.[32] But while their buildup gave them strategic parity, improved their conventional strength on the Eurasian continent, and brought them a new global reach, it also greatly alarmed the West. Western Europeans substantially increased their own arms spending and, by requesting new U.S. missiles, rejuvenated the old American Forward Basing Systems. The Carter administration shifted its priority from arms control to rearmament. The Reagan administration's massive increases in military spending, including the Strategic Defense Initiative, challenged the Soviets to a major new round of strategic competition. The net result is difficult to count as anything other than a diminishing of Soviet security.[33] If the need to respond will not actually destabilize the Soviet regime, it will certainly make domestic economic troubles even more intractable.

The parallel between Soviet and American reactions and predicaments is disconcerting. In a world with many rising powers, both have relatively less weight in the international system as a whole. Each feels threatened, and each is inclined to interpret the threat in bipolar terms. Each has responded by building up its military forces and militarizing its diplomacy throughout the world. Each thus eggs the other on. Both superpowers have thereby not only reduced their actual military security, but also further accentuated their respective systemic crises over national priorities. With both superpowers overextended and reacting in the same way, convergence seems finally to have come into its own.

If America and Russia both lose in a more plural world, why should they not cooperate to prevent it? A special relationship of the superpowers, it may be argued, could control not only the bipolar rivalry that hastens the decline of each, but also the global pluralism that devalues the significance of both together. The idea of a U.S.–Soviet special relationship is at least useful in challenging conventional assumptions about an absolute conflict of interests, even if, at bottom, it suffers from the same flaws that undermine the hegemonic world view. The idea is less unfamiliar than it may, at first, seem. In its periodic revivals, American détente policy has sometimes flirted with the notion of a Soviet-American world condominium. A certain condominial bias has always weighed heavily on American thinking about arms control. Both nuclear superpowers, it is often said, have a special responsibility, indeed vocation, for global order. Fulfilling that responsibility requires a concentration of strategic power in their hands. Nuclear pluralism creates a world system incapable of being managed. Neither superpower, therefore, wants nuclear proliferation.

The geopolitical case for a world condominium can be carried well beyond these special concerns of the nuclear age. Both superpowers can be seen to have fundamental and long-term national interests that make them global conservatives.[34] Each has much more to lose than to gain from a revolutionary upheaval of the global status quo. Both are among the world's richest states, and neither, therefore, has any interest in the global repartition of wealth on a grand scale. Both, it has even been said, are Western and European in comparison with the Chinese, Indians, Moslems, or even Japanese and Latin Americans. From this perspective, their long-range interest ought to drive the superpowers, and the Europeans, into a common conservative front against what will eventually become a major challenge from the have-not countries.

Logically, this line of reasoning can be used to propose a calculated Western policy of Soviet appeasement. The United States, it may be argued, should not repeat Britain's historic mistake in dealing with Imperial Germany. Since Russia is determined to be admitted into the circle of world powers, timely appeasement is the only way to avoid a mutually destructive conflict. Sharing the world with the Russians would be a far better outcome for American interests, according to this view, than a struggle that exhausts both sides, to the eventual advantage of the Chinese and other rising powers in the Third World. Uncongenial as the backward and authoritarian Soviets may seem to Western sensibilities, they are far less alien than the great cultures of the East, whose notions of the individual and society are fundamentally incompatible with those of the West. Only a suicidal Western sentimentality refuses to recognize how alien and fundamentally hostile most Third World civilizations actually are to the West.

Appeasement can also be seen as the way to bring out the best in Soviet society. Internal liberalization will come, it may be argued, only as the Soviets expand globally. Like Western societies in the nineteenth century, Soviet domestic society will open up and "decompress" as the USSR finds an outlet for its energies in the world at large. If the Russians continue to be frustrated abroad, they will merely grow more and more repressive and paranoid at home.

Arguments of this sort are obviously highly controversial at every stage. But they raise questions about the future that should not be ignored. In a world growing more plural, a sound national strategy must always be alert to the dangers of hostile politico-economic combinations in the future. American policy has rather recklessly broken economic engagements with the Soviets in recent years and seems determined to stunt U.S.–Soviet trade. Such a policy seems inconsistent with America's long-range interests. American policy ought not to indulge its distaste for the Soviets to the point of abandoning the possibilities for economic collaboration entirely to others. It seems no more in the Soviet interest than in the American that the Western Europeans and Japanese should come to dominate Soviet trade and investment. Today, the need to contain the Soviet Union keeps Western Europe united and Russia's Eurasian neighbors tied to the United States. Tomorrow, a strong Soviet Union may also be needed to contain those same neighbors. The United States should not grow so obsessed with its present rivalry with the Soviets that it loses sight of the longer-range requirements of the Eurasian balance. It is upon this balance, today and tomorrow, that any *Pax Americana* depends.

But while the volatile complexity of relationships among allies and adversaries should never be underestimated, the broader argument for orienting American policy around a Soviet-American condominium is unconvincing. For a start, nothing suggests the Soviets would be willing or able to accept the discipline of a cooperative condominium on any terms the United States would conceivably offer. In any event, the case for condominium is simply a refined version of the hegemonic world view. While its premise is a critique of bipolar competition, its conclusion is a proposal for bipolar hegemony. It is simply duopoly turned on its head. Geopolitically, the case against condominium is the case against hegemony. The world is moving into not a hegemonic but a pluralist phase of its history. Two hegemons in decline, allied together, are unlikely to reverse the trend toward pluralism. In a more plural world, so exclusive a preoccupation with bipolar cooperation is as obsolescent as the old Cold War preoccupation with bipolar rivalry.

The United States, moreover, seems far better situated than the Soviet Union to adapt to a more plural world. For obvious reasons of geography and history, the United States has a very great comparative advantage in any game of competitive devolution. On the one hand, pluralism poses a far greater danger to the Soviets in Eurasia than to the United States in North America. On the other, Americans have far more promising prospects for conserving their own resources through devolution. America's European allies are a group of prosperous, powerful, stable, and closely linked states—the principal members of which have the collective demographic, economic, and military resources to maintain an adequate regional balance against the Soviets, even with the Americans playing a much less direct role. By contrast, the Russians can have little confidence that an Eastern Europe over which they no longer exercise an iron restraint will remain internally stable or reliably allied against the blandishments of a powerful West.

The Western Europeans, of course, have not been interested in relieving American overextension, despite their dismay at some of the consequences. Europe's own détente policies have, in effect, been aimed at encouraging the Soviets, not the Americans, to adjust to a more plural world. By cultivating a multiplicity of peaceful economic and cultural relations, continuous political dialogue, and arms talks aimed at mutual security, Europeans have tried to reconcile the Soviets to a more powerful and independent Western Europe, together with more national freedom and development in Eastern Europe.

For reasons already discussed at length, while Western Europeans have insisted on increasing independence for their own Soviet diplomacy, they have been quite content to remain an American military protectorate. Indeed, their Eastern policy has depended on it: rigidity toward NATO complements flexibility toward the Soviets. Defense is to be left to the Americans, with diplomacy and trade reserved for the Europeans.

While America's allies can doubtless be expected to exploit their advantages, why has the United States so long permitted itself to be manipulated in this fashion? Americans, it may be argued, have not been very imaginative in perceiving either the costs of the present situation, or the ways it might be altered to their advantage. Instead, the American imagination seems to have been paralyzed by the hypothetical risks of change.

One obvious risk is that an American protectorate would be replaced not by a more self-reliant Western Europe, but by a Soviet hegemony that would alienate Western Europe from America. As discussed earlier, however, the Soviet Union's own systemic inadequacies greatly limit what it has to offer Western Europe. Given Russia's brutal repression, backward economy, and timid diplomacy, European détente is unlikely to progress so rapidly that a more independent Western Europe would fling away either its own unity or its military and economic ties with the Americans. In a world with nuclear arms, there seems no reason why the Soviet Union should overawe a Western European coalition.

Another risk is that military devolution requires an enhanced indigenous European nuclear deterrent, perhaps even a national German deterrent—all of which may frighten and provoke the Russians or otherwise destabilize the nuclear balance.[35] Chapter 9 discussed the problems of a European deterrent in some detail, including the "worst-case" scenario of a national German deterrent. Here it seems appropriate to examine the nuclear issue within its triangular and Eurasian context.

Duopoly has always had its firmest hold in the military sphere, above all in the nuclear arena. While the wars in Vietnam and even Afghanistan have substantially devalued duopoly in conventional military terms, it lingers in the realm of strategic nuclear force. Here, numbers alone seem to confirm the special position of the two superpowers.[36] In reality, those numbers have grown increasingly meaningless as indicators of strategic positions. While superpower parity has radically devalued the credibility of extended nuclear deterrence, it has not detracted from the effectiveness of indigenous nuclear forces. Nor, it seems, will the new defensive technologies easily devalue Europe's national deterrents.[37] The pluralist trend, long established in the political and economic spheres, has now reached the strategic nuclear sphere. The result is bound to affect the triangular relationship of America, Europe, and Russia; the Eurasian politico-military balance; and the traditional questions at issue in Soviet-American arms control. It ought, in turn, to favor an American policy of devolution within NATO.

Logically, an America bent on devolution should stand ready to encourage rather than discourage Europe's nuclear deterrents. To make over conventional leadership in Europe without changing Europe's nuclear role is unrealistic, for all the reasons suggested earlier.[38] If America's front-line nuclear role in Eurasia is to be assumed by the Eurasians, the major states require their own second-strike capability. That second-strike deterrence, which already exists for Britain and France, must also effectively cover the Federal Republic of Germany. If the United States should not take the lead in developing European nuclear arrangements, it should at least make clear its vital interest in their success.

American encouragement should include sharing whatever technology becomes necessary to counteract Soviet progress in antiballistic missile defense. The United States should also be prepared to help resist the Soviet pressure that may be expected until a European nuclear arrangement is in place. Once European deterrence is organized, American commitments and forces may still provide that additional "uncertainty" so prized in European strategic theories. But the proper American role would lie in backstopping and reinforcing the nuclear forces maintained by the Europeans themselves, not in providing a front-line substitute for them.

Do European nuclear forces threaten the stability of the Eurasian political and military balance? Indigenous deterrents in Europe seem no more likely to provoke a nuclear war than does an extended deterrent from America. Arguably, because European deterrents are more credible politically, they are more stable militarily. European nuclear forces used to be thought an invitation to a Soviet preemptive strike. But at the present state of its technology, a Europe with nuclear arms is unlikely to be deprived of its second-strike capability.[39] Geographically, however, Europe remains so vulnerable to a counter-strike that the Soviets cannot easily count it a more aggressive military threat than the United States.

Encouraging second-strike capabilities among our European allies does have obvious implications for arms control. Many of these implications have already been absorbed into American policy. In the 1968 Non-Proliferation Treaty, the Western signatories explicitly reserved the right to form a European deterrent.[40] In recent years, the United States has resolutely refused to sign any agreement with the Soviets that would inhibit expanding the British and French nuclear arsenals.[41] In the long run, moreover, nuclear devolution in Eurasia might be expected to have significantly positive implications for intercontinental arms reductions between the Soviets and ourselves. With the European balance no longer exclusively, or even primarily, dependent on the intercontinental balance, the way would lie open for radical reductions in intercontinental missiles. The pressure for antiballistic defense to protect counterforce capabilities might also diminish.

This line of argument, although perfectly logical, has never had much appeal among traditional American partisans of arms control. In effect, they would prefer to see the control of strategic force remain in the hands of the two superpowers, rather than dispersed among America's own allies. American interest, defined in this traditional fashion, aligns itself with Soviet interest. Both superpowers work to inhibit Eurasian pluralism. Duopoly is defended as more stable. Each superpower is said to be highly conscious of its awesome vulnerability to the other; no mutual conflict of interest seems sufficiently vital to risk a nuclear conflict. Proliferation to Russia's neighbors, it is argued, would greatly augment the range of potential conflicts, as well as the danger of accidental or irrational provocation.

This traditional American view was certainly far more convincing in the 1950s and the 1960s. Serious nuclear capabilities were limited to the Americans and the Soviets. And America's relative invulnerability made its extended deterrence for Europe and Japan plausible, despite apprehensions about the future. Hopes for superpower détente based on a common interest in preventing nuclear war made effective arms-control agreements appear likely. Proliferation seemed neither necessary nor welcome.

Whether this same logic of cooperative duopoly remains convincing in an age of parity and proliferation is another matter. The Soviets certainly do not appear to believe so. They have repeatedly exploded American hopes for cooperative détente. Neither Soviets nor Americans, nor both together, have succeeded in stopping Britain, France, or China from developing independent nuclear forces. Others, like India, Israel, South Africa, Pakistan, or Sweden, may well be following.[42] Under the circumstances, the Soviets could not have been expected to base their strategic planning on duopoly and condominium but rather on the reality of nuclear proliferation and strategic pluralism. Their initial reaction was to develop ostentatious theater nuclear forces, combined with a relentless buildup of their already massive conventional forces. Under Gorbachev, a more subtle tactic appears to be an attempt to parlay reduction of Soviet theater nuclear forces—militarily redundant in any case—into a denuclearization of Western Europe. It remains to be seen how much dissension this will sow in NATO, particularly among the Western Europeans.

While the erosion of nuclear duopoly explains Soviet behavior, it has not had a corresponding influence on American policy. The consequences are increasingly destabilizing—not only economically and politically, but militarily as well. Logically, the United States, having lost its own relative invulnerability but continuing to have a vital interest in preventing Soviet domination of Eurasia, ought to foster independent nuclear capacities among its own European allies. In effect, strategic pluralism is the only way to preserve classic deterrence. Otherwise, faced with Soviet regional superiority, America's Eurasian commitments will inevitably grow less convincing and, therefore, more dangerous. Trying to sustain these commitments without European nuclear forces inevitably pushes the United States toward policies that actually destabilize the regional deterrence we are presumably trying to preserve.

Logically, we are driven toward either conventional deterrence for Eurasia or nuclear invulnerability for ourselves. In effect, No First Use and Star Wars are two sides of the same coin. The coin is devalued duopoly. The chances that either course can resolve the dilemmas of extended deterrence are extremely slim. Meanwhile, American policy, twisting around the dilemma of extended deterrence, risks seriously undermining classic deterrence, which has kept the European peace for several decades. Under the circumstances, partisans of arms control might seem well-advised to reconsider their traditional diffidence toward European deterrents. Only if the European leg of the nuclear triangle is properly developed can the superpowers maintain their strategic balance on a more reasonable scale. Until then, the needs of extended deterrence will continue to drive the arms race.[43] Arms-control negotiations will probably remain what they have become—the diplomatic obbligato to the relentless Soviet-American buildup of arms.

In summary, arms control has to base itself on the military realities. Both military and economic factors ordain that only Western Europe can sustain the European military balance. The Soviets are sufficiently threatening to make the need for that balance eminently clear. It remains for the Americans to make equally clear where the principal responsibility for European defense must lie. As it is, America's decaying hegemony, by undermining Western prosperity while it subsidizes European disunity, appears the principal obstacle to America's own vital interest.

12

The American Interest
in a Plural World

CHAPTER 1 asked two fundamental questions about the Atlantic Alliance: Is it viable in its present form? And, if not, is there a viable alternative? The answers that have emerged are as unequivocal as the subject permits. The alliance grows less and less viable in its present form, but a viable alternative seems possible. These conclusions reverse the conventional view. For years, NATO's problems have been regarded with a certain complacent pessimism, according to which NATO's traditional dilemmas can never be resolved but remain satisfactorily manageable. In my view, which takes economic as well as military consequences into account, NATO's problems are, in fact, growing seriously unmanageable, but they can also be resolved. This view gives today's policy makers a very special historic responsibility. Before policy can evolve, however, there must be a broad evolution of political mentality on both sides of the Atlantic.

The reasons for these conclusions have been explored at length. It has been shown how America's role in NATO has grown more onerous and less effective militarily, while encouraging nationalism and neutralism within Europe itself. Above all, America's oversized military commitments, of which NATO is the biggest single component, have pressed the United States into fiscal and financial practices destructive to American, European, and global prosperity. Much of the world economy has been depressed since the early 1970s, a situation for which American economic policy deserves a good part of the blame. The American economy has been unbalanced internally and externally since at least the late 1960s. The practices of the Reagan administration have simply brought into bold relief the systemic crisis that has long been brewing. The current American practice of heavy foreign borrowing seems particularly damaging and unsustainable.

For the reasons explored earlier, any serious attempt to remedy the American fiscal and monetary disorder must confront America's budgetary crisis. To do so, it must bring America's runaway military budget under control. That is unlikely so long as the NATO military commitment remains in its present form. The United States is now trying to provide Western Europe with not only a nuclear but also a conventional protectorate. While the United States is increasingly unable to maintain the forces adequate for such a commitment, the costs are nevertheless astronomical, particularly by comparison with what it would cost the Europeans to manage their own defense.

America's economic imbalances, linked as they are to swollen military budgets and overextended foreign commitments, suggest a broader geopolitical diagnosis. The general postwar trend has been toward a more plural distribution of resources and power around the globe. A more plural world almost inevitably diminishes America's capacity to control events unilaterally. Ironically, this pluralist trend, with its relative weakening of American power, results not from the failure of American postwar policy, but from its success. The United States promoted the recovery of Western Europe and Japan. That recovery has inevitably given them greater weight vis-à-vis the Americans today than at the end of the 1940s. Similarly, peaceful containment of Russia has almost inevitably meant a relative strengthening of the Soviets since Stalin's time. At the same time, Third World independence and development has led to a world system far less amenable to anyone's global hegemony, America's included. In other words, America's relative weakening seems a natural and almost inevitable result of trends that the United States itself has fostered. In a more plural world, the United States remains the world's most powerful country, but it is no longer an Atlas able to carry the global system on its own shoulders.

As I observed at the outset, the fundamental challenge to American foreign policy has become what to do about this decline of American power in relation to the rest of the world. American supremacy at the end of World War II gave the United States the central role in organizing the postwar order. The supremacy has been slowly waning but the central role has remained too much the same. As a result, the viability of the postwar order has been placed in serious jeopardy. Since the late 1970s, the United States has been caught up in a major new effort to regain its old supremacy—one of several such efforts since World War II. But for all the reasons made clear by the American experience in NATO, success in reaffirming the old supremacy has been more apparent than real. Under Reagan particularly, the whole effort appears more and more self-defeating.

If the United States cannot return to 1950, if it cannot reaffirm its old global supremacy, is there some way the *Pax Americana* can be run on a more plural and less hegemonic basis? Logically, the United States should serve its own and the general interest by learning how to make use of the strengths and interests of others. Given America's present and predictable degree of overextension, something beyond traditional burden-sharing is required. An intelligent policy of geopolitical devolution seems an urgent necessity. And given the significance of the NATO commitment in our fiscal overextension, and the great resources of the Western Europeans themselves, NATO seems the logical place for devolution to be employed. If devolution cannot succeed in Europe, it seems unlikely to succeed elsewhere.

America's European policy, however, seems caught in a vicious circle. The hegemony that has been underwriting Europe's dependence can never be ended, it is said, because Europeans have grown so dependent on it. NATO has made it unnecessary for European states either to acquire the military resources they might otherwise have been expected to maintain or to develop the security relationships with each other that their interests might otherwise have commanded. Over the years, nuclear weapons have greatly reinforced this tendency to rely on the Americans. Faith in nuclear deterrence has assuaged concern over NATO's lack of a serious conventional deterrent, something the American protectorate cannot easily provide.

Thus, under NATO's present arrangements, the Europeans have been militarily underdeveloped while the United States has been militarily overextended. The gradual evolution toward Soviet-American parity in the global nuclear balance has compounded the U.S.–European imbalance. Superpower strategic parity logically indicates a NATO strategy emphasizing indigenous regional deterrence and conventional defense. The American protectorate blocks progress in either direction. On the one hand, American missiles on or off European soil cannot effectively substitute for European nuclear forces. On the other hand, providing a serious European conventional defense is clearly beyond American military means.

So far, no American administration has been able to find a way out of this NATO dilemma. Given Western Europe's resources and military traditions, the remedy might seem obvious. "Why," it might be asked, "should the United States still be running Europe's defense anyway?" Small wonder the burden strains the American budget. European diffidence toward change seems, of course, quite understandable. European states have used NATO to liberate themselves from a substantial part of the burden of self-defense, to the profit of other domestic or foreign policy goals. American behavior is somewhat more surprising. Despite rhetoric about free-riding allies, successive U.S. administrations have been eager to continue America's hegemonic role in Europe's defense. This American tenacity seems difficult to justify from any broad calculation of national interest. Devolution in NATO seems the ideal way to adapt to and, indeed, take advantage of the global pluralization of power. For the evolution to pluralism, while it has reduced American supremacy, also gives the United States a potentially great comparative advantage over the Soviets. With a Europeanized NATO, not to mention the gradual rise of Asian great powers, the Soviets could be contained to a large degree by their own Eurasian neighbors, while American commitments could be brought into balance with American resources. Naturally, a policy of devolution carries risks, but its long-range prospects seem a good deal more promising than those of the status quo.

The risks, moreover, could be considerably reduced by timely leadership. Devolution, if carefully prepared, does not have to be traumatic or undertaken in circumstances that suggest a collapsing American commitment to Europe. The United States could quietly inform its principal NATO allies that it was determined to put its own fiscal house in order, and that to do so would inevitably require a reformation of its NATO role. It could, at the same time, affirm its intention to remain in the alliance but invite the Europeans to take over the major responsibility. It could set a firm, but not unreasonable, timetable.

On its face, devolution in NATO seems so self-evidently in America's interest that it might be assumed that truly formidable reasons must exist to deter the U.S. from pursuing it. In fact, the arguments against devolution are far from convincing. Europeans are said to lack the military means or to be incapable of organizing themselves to cooperate. The Soviets are said to be too great a political threat or economic attraction. Each of these arguments has been examined at length. None has been found compelling. Time, meanwhile, is obviously running out for the status quo. Why does American policy remain paralyzed?

Obvious answers come to mind. It is tempting, for example, to blame a political system that inhibits even examining long-range policies, let alone carrying them out consistently. But if the American political system makes major foreign policy initiatives difficult to conceive and carry through, it is, after all, the same political system that led the world to the *Pax Americana* a few decades ago. Since Vietnam, it has grown fashionable to blame the limitations of our foreign policy on the American public. America's postwar foreign policy consensus is said to have evaporated. No stable constituency remains adequate for America's old global role, or for any new one. But this formulation, fashionable among political elites, obscures a rather more significant reality. The masses are not blocking the leadership from a policy of devolution. The truth is that there is no leadership for a genuinely new foreign policy. Among the political elites, the old consensus remains. It is not the consensus but the policy that has failed. In a world that has changed drastically, American leadership remains enthralled by hegemony and duopoly.

Mass opinion, to be sure, is equally undeveloped. The American public is not so much opposed to an imperial role as unwilling to pay the escalating costs. That, in the end, seems the overriding lesson not only of the Reagan experiment with reaffirmation, but also of the Vietnam War itself. Opposition to the war grew decisive only after its futility and terrible costs had become almost invincibly obvious. The subsequent effect of this lesson on either public opinion or the elites has been greatly exaggerated. By the mid-1980s, the great majority in Congress and the country had no grave objections to intervention in Central America, the Caribbean, the Middle East, or elsewhere—so long as the interventions were quickly and painlessly successful. Nor does the same majority object to the Reagan military establishment. Even after the Reagan supply-side fantasy had been thoroughly exploded, and fiscal policy lay in ruins, Congress, half-controlled by the Democrats, could not bring itself to prevent a defense budget almost universally acknowledged to be preposterously and uselessly bloated. The same Congress proved equally incapable of raising taxes significantly. Apparently nothing can correct American fiscal policy short of a general financial catastrophe. With the budget as with Vietnam, disaster alone seems capable of jolting American policy back to reality. The traditional international role is untouchable—so long as it does not have to be paid for in blood or taxes.

The practical differences between the liberals and the Right in this matter are more apparent than real. Since the Right remains preoccupied with the Soviet threat, to the exclusion of more significant global changes, its foreign-policy vision remains firmly in a bipolar time warp. Given its present aversion to appeasement, the Right's logical response is the arms race. SDI, in part at least, is merely the latest phase in the vain effort to return to America's global invulnerability of 1950. In the face of a world that refuses to correspond to its vision, the Right's response is defiance.

Conventional liberals, though disturbed by the militarization of the political economy, are nevertheless equally bipolar in their geopolitical view. In place of a bipolar arms buildup, they would substitute a bipolar arms control. Increasingly, the differences are only rhetorical. While the liberals accept rearmament as necessary for arms-control bargaining, the Right accepts negotiations as necessary for a consensus on rearmament. Each complements the other within a mutually obsolescent bipolarity. This fixation on bipolarity not only prevents American policy from adapting to the real world, but also poisons relations between the superpowers. For the trend toward pluralism has already created strategic and political conditions that make obsolescent both the bipolar arms race and bipolar arms control. Even in the nuclear realm, pluralism is already a reality. The question is not whether it can be reversed, but how it can be channeled to sustain a more stable Eurasian military balance. Meanwhile, however, American policy remains locked in an increasingly redundant arms race with the Soviets.

In summary, the American political system finds it very difficult to face the reality of a plural world in which the United States is no longer supreme. It seems unjust to blame the general public for this state of affairs. Throughout the postwar administrations, the public has never been presented with a serious alternative to hegemonic foreign policy. No such alternative has ever been taken seriously among foreign policy elites or in the political class generally. American history does not furnish much guidance for our present circumstances, and American elites seem unable to learn from the experience of anyone else. Instead, the prevalent historical consciousness seems ensnared in the fantasy of a reborn *Pax Britannica*—oblivious to the completely different global context. To find a foreign policy appropriate for a plural world would require a powerful and sustained exercise of collective imagination. Despite the presence of an occasional Kennan, such a collective consciousness has never evolved. As a consequence, the American consensus has grown into a conspiracy to avoid reality. American policy, requiring a supremacy that cannot be sustained, lacks the guiding principles needed to determine priorities. Despite its colossal military means, America feels perpetually threatened and overextended. It is difficult to exaggerate the dangers of such a condition—either for the world or for democracy in America itself. The United States has become a hegemon in decay, set on a course that points to an ignominious end. If there is a way out, it lies through Europe. History has come full circle: the Old World is needed to restore balance to the New.

NOTES

Chapter 1: NATO and American Foreign Policy

1. See, for example, West German Foreign Minister Hans-Dietrich Genscher, "Toward an Overall Western Strategy for Peace, Freedom and Progress," *Foreign Affairs* 61, no. 1 (Fall 1982): 42–46. For transatlantic differences, see Pierre Hassner, "The Shifting Foundation," *Foreign Policy* no. 48 (Fall 1982): 3–20; and William E. Griffith, *The Superpowers and Regional Tensions: The USSR, the United States, and Europe* (Lexington, Mass.: Lexington Books, 1982), 36–40.

2. For an influential "hard-line" view in the Reagan administration, see Richard Pipes, "Soviet Global Strategy," *Commentary* 69, no. 4 (April 1980): 31–39. For the hard line applied to Europe's participation in the Siberian natural-gas pipeline project, see U.S. Ambassador to France Evan Galbraith, "An Official U.S. View on Moves to Stop the Pipeline," *International Herald Tribune*, 24–25 July 1982. More conciliatory approaches, embedded in the bureaucracy and represented in various other elements of the Reagan camp, coexisted uneasily and often moderated actual policy. For a European analysis, see Michel Tatu, "U.S.–Soviet Relations: A Turning Point?," *Foreign Affairs* 61, no. 3 (America and the World 1982): 591–610.

3. For postwar oscillations of U.S. security policy, see John Lewis Gaddis, *Strategies of Containment: A Critical Appraisal of Postwar American National Security Policy* (New York: Oxford University Press, 1982); and Robert E. Osgood, "The Revitalization of Containment," *Foreign Affairs* 61, no. 3 (America and the World 1982): 465–502.

4. For a distinguished example of this "complacent model," see A. W. DePorte, *Europe between the Superpowers: The Enduring Balance* (New Haven: Yale University Press/Council on Foreign Relations, 1979).

5. For an earlier version of this argument, see David P. Calleo, "The Alliance: An Enduring Relationship?," *SAIS Review*, no. 4 (Summer 1982): 27–39.

6. For differing reactions to the oil crisis, see Robert J. Lieber, *Oil and the Middle East War: Europe in the Energy Crisis*, Harvard Studies in International Affairs, no. 35 (Cambridge, Mass.: Center for International Affairs, Harvard University, 1976); see also Horst Mendershausen, *Coping with the Oil Crisis: French and German Experiences* (Baltimore: Johns Hopkins University Press, 1976). For the American attempt to use the oil crisis to reinforce its Western hegemony, see David P. Calleo, "The European Coalition in a Fragmenting World," *Foreign Affairs* 54, no. 1 (October 1975): 103–12.

7. Helmut Schmidt, "The World Economy at Stake," *The Economist*, 26 Feb. 1983, p. 21; or, for a stronger version, *International Herald Tribune*, 23 Apr. 1984, p. 1.

8. See David P. Calleo, *The Imperious Economy* (Cambridge, Mass.: Harvard University Press, 1982), pt. 2.

9. For earlier elaborations of this argument, see Ibid., especially 94–95, 167–73; and David P. Calleo, "Inflation and American Power," *Foreign Affairs* 59, no. 4 (Spring 1981): 781–812. See also Lester Thurow, "How to Wreck the Economy," *The New York Review of Books*, 14 May 1981, pp. 3–8; and Emma Rothschild, "Reagan and the Real America," *The New York Review of Books*, 5 Feb. 1981, pp. 12–18.

10. For the emergence of Soviet strategic parity with the United States, see chap. 4, n. 13. The following charts give a rough indicator for other measures of the relative U.S. decline.

Defense Share of GNP (percentage)

	1970	1979	1980	1981
U.S.[a]	8.2	4.7	5.0	5.3
USSR[b]	15.1	14.2	14.5	15.2

[a] U.S. Bureau of the Census, *Statistical Abstract of the United States 1987* (Washington, D.C.: U.S. Government Printing Office, 1986), table 521, p. 317.
[b] Calculated from estimates (in 1983 dollars) of Soviet real GNP in National Foreign Assessment Center, *Handbook of Economic Statistics, 1984* (Washington, D.C.: Central Intelligence Agency, 1984), 33; and estimates (also in 1983 dollars) of Soviet defense expenditures in Organization of the Joint Chiefs of Staff, *Military Posture for FY 1983* (Washington, D.C.: U.S. Government Printing Office, 1982), 16. See chap. 7, n. 23, for a discussion of varying approaches to estimating Soviet defense expenditures.

Average Annual Growth of Real GDP at Market Prices in the OECD Area (percentage changes)

	1958–67	1965–69	1970–74	1975–79	1980–84
U.S.	4.75	4.34	2.62	3.34	2.02
Japan	10.7	10.32	6.2	4.6	4.26
W. Germany	4.8	4.28	3.44	2.78	0.96
France	5.8	5.2	5.12	3.12	1.08
Italy	6.0	5.82	4.24	2.36	1.16
Britain	3.3	2.46	2.78	1.98	0.6
Canada	—	5.6	5.28	3.34	1.78
Other OECD	6.0	4.92	4.76	2.3	1.7

SOURCES: 1958–67, *OECD Economic Outlook* no. 7 (July 1970), 1. All others, *OECD Economic Outlook* no. 38 (December 1985), 172.

Weight of GNP/GDP in OECD Totals

	1964	1973	1979	1982
U.S.	52.9	40.0	34.6	40.4
Japan	5.7	12.9	15.0	14.0
W. Germany	8.6	10.6	11.2	8.5
France	7.3	8.0	8.4	7.1
Italy	4.1	4.3	4.7	4.6
Britain	7.6	5.4	5.8	6.4
Canada	3.6	3.7	3.3	3.8
Other OECD	10.2	14.7	17.0	15.2

SOURCES: 1964, *OECD Economic Outlook* no. 1 (July 1967), 6; 1973, *OECD Economic Outlook* no. 17 (July 1978), 13; 1979, *OECD Economic Outlook* no. 27 (July 1980), 12; 1982, *OECD Economic Outlook* no. 38 (December 1985), 19.

Chapter 2: The Atlantic Alliance and the Global System

1. *Pax Americana* is used in this book with some pride. The term, however, is often used derisively or with implications of exploitation and domination. In June of 1963, for example, President Kennedy used it to describe a hypothetical world order imposed by American arms and denounced the idea as contrary to America's idealistic desire for a lasting peace benefiting the entire world. "Toward a Strategy of Peace: Commencement Address by President Kennedy at American University, Washington, D.C., June 10, 1963," in *Documents on American Foreign Relations, 1963*, ed. Richard P. Stebbins (New York: Harper and Row/Council on Foreign Relations, 1964), 116. For a more comprehensive view, see Ronald Steel, *Pax Americana* (New York: Viking Press, 1967).

2. For a development of the "free-rider" thesis, see Charles P. Kindleberger, *The World in Depression 1929-1939* (Los Angeles: University of California Press, 1973), 301-8; and, by the same author, "Systems of International Economic Organization," in *Money and the Coming World Order*, ed. David P. Calleo (New York: New York University Press/Lehrman Institute, 1976), 15-39.

3. See chap. 9 for a discussion of the U.S. military role in NATO. In 1985, the United States had 353,100 men and 725 combat aircraft stationed in Europe. The Mediterranean Fleet consisted of 27,200 men and 31 vessels. The International Institute for Strategic Studies (IISS), *The Military Balance 1985-1986* (London: IISS, 1985), 13-14.

4. For French dissatisfaction with their initial role in NATO, see General André Beaufre, *L'Otan et l'Europe* (Paris: Calmann-Levy, 1966). For a thorough analysis of the gradual disengagement, see Michael M. Harrison, *The Reluctant Ally: France and Atlantic Security* (Baltimore: Johns Hopkins University Press, 1981), 134-63.

Britain has always retained substantial national control of its armed forces. Only the 55,000-man British Army of the Rhine and its reinforcements are under the American-led Supreme Headquarters Allied Powers Europe command. NATO's Channel command is British-led. Much of Britain's military force is, however, responsible to the American SACEUR, including the Channel command and British nuclear forces.

5. See chap. 6. See also David P. Calleo, *The Imperious Economy* (Cambridge, Mass.: Harvard University Press, 1982); and Susan Strange, "International Monetary Relations," in *International Economic Relations of the Western World, 1959-1971*, vol. 2, ed. Sir Andrew Shonfield (London: Oxford University Press, 1976). Also see n. 8.

6. Since the war, Japan has spent less than 1 percent of its GNP annually on defense and greatly prospered thereby according to Isaiah Frank, ed., *The Japanese Economy in International Perspective* (Baltimore: Johns Hopkins University Press/Committee for Economic Development, 1975), 3.

According to one estimate, if Japan, like the United States, had spent 6 or 7 percent of its GNP on defense from 1954 to 1974, the size of its economy in 1974 would have been about 30 percent smaller. See Hugh Patrick and Henry Rosovsky, eds., *Asia's New Giant: How the Japanese Economy Works* (Washington, D.C.: Brookings Institution, 1976), 45.

For U.S. pressure and actual Japanese rearmament, see the essays by Shinichiro Asao and William V. Kennedy, *International Herald Tribune*, 2 Mar. 1984. For Kennedy, the more the Americans pressure Japan for military effort, "the greater the likelihood that the prestige of the pro-U.S. leadership will decline and that of the militant nationalists revive." See also Congressman Stephen Solarz, "A Search for Balance," *Foreign Policy*, no. 49 (Winter 1982/83): 75-92.

7.

Relative Size of Economies and Trade: 1982

	GNP/GDP	Exports	Imports
		(billions of dollars)	
U.S.	3021.3	212.3	254.9
USSR	1787.0	32.0	27.5
W. Germany	666.8	176.4	155.4
France	540.7	96.7	115.7
Britain	482.6	97.0	99.6
Italy	348.7	73.5	86.2
Japan	1060.7	138.4	131.6

SOURCES: Soviet figures from National Foreign Assessment Center, *Handbook of Economic Statistics, 1984* (Washington, D.C.: Central Intelligence Agency, 1984), 33, 71; GNP/GDP figures for all other countries calculated using period average market rates from International Monetary Fund, *International Financial Statistics* (Washington, D.C.: IMF, 1984), Yearbook 1984, 274, 276, 286, 288, 350, 352, 362, 364, 588, 590, 592, 594; trade figures from *Direction of Trade Statistics* (Washington, D.C.: IMF, 1985), Yearbook 1985, 178, 185, 234, 241, 396, 399.

8.

Trade with the Soviet Union and Eastern Europe
(millions of 1986 dollars)

	Imports	% of total	Exports	% of total
U.S.	2,157	0.6	2,342	1.1
W. Germany	10,247	5.0	10,272	4.1
France	4,627	3.7	2,787	2.4
Britain	2,201	1.8	1,828	1.7
Italy	4,593	4.6	2,800	2.9

SOURCE: *OECD Economic Outlook* (Paris: OECD, December 1986), 144–45.

For the somewhat cyclical history of American efforts to control European trade with the Eastern bloc, see Angela Stent, *From Embargo to Ostpolitik: The Political Economy of West German–Soviet Relations 1955–1980* (New York: Cambridge University Press, 1981).

9. French fears of a new German-Soviet Rapallo and German worries about a Franco-Soviet entente have recurred throughout the postwar era. France's tendency to side with Russia in calling for a hard peace fed German fears immediately after the war. See Hans-Peter Schwarz, *Vom Reich zur Bundesrepublik: Deutschland im Widerstreit der Aussenpolitischen Konzeptionen in den Jahren der Besatzungsherrschaft* (Neuweid: Luchterhand, 1966). For German suspicions of de Gaulle's 1963 opening to the Soviets, see Wolfram Hanrieder, *The Stable Crisis: Two Decades of German Foreign Policy* (New York: Harper and Row, 1970), especially 72–75. For corresponding French suspicions of Ostpolitik, see Maurice Couve de Murville, *Une politique étrangère 1953–1969* (Paris: Plon, 1971). See also Robert Legvold, "Finlandization and Franco-Soviet Relations," in *Soviet Foreign Policy Toward Western Europe*, ed. George Ginsburgs and Alvin Z. Rubinstein (New York: Praeger, 1978), 86–101; and

William E. Griffith, *The Superpowers and Regional Tensions: The USSR, the United States and Europe* (Lexington, Mass.: Lexington Books, 1982), on the 1970s.

Chap. 10 also discusses later Franco-German tensions over relations with the Eastern bloc.

10. See chap. 11.

11. For declining superpower détente and West Germany's *Ostpolitik*, see Griffith, *Superpowers and Regional Tensions*, 32–40.

12. For my analysis of American postwar liberal internationalism, including support for decolonization, see David P. Calleo and Benjamin M. Rowland, *America and the World Political Economy: Atlantic Dreams and National Realities* (Bloomington: Indiana University Press, 1973), 20–43. See also n. 16.

13. See John Gallagher and Ronald Robinson, *Africa and the Victorians: The Climax of Imperialism* (New York: Doubleday, 1968); and Julian Amery, *The Life of Joseph Chamberlain* (London: St. Martin's Press, 1969), vols. 5, 6.

14. For the classic expression of protectionist doctrine, including an attack on British free-trade imperialism, see Friedrich List, *The National System of Political Economy*, 1885 edition (New York: Kelley, 1966).

15. See William Roger Louis, *Imperialism at Bay: The United States and the Decolonization of the British Empire, 1941–1945* (New York: Oxford University Press, 1978). For French reactions to American efforts at decolonization, see Guy de Carmoy, *Les politiques étrangères de la France: 1944–1966* (Paris: La Table Ronde, 1967).

16. For an early sketch of the American model for "liberal-national" Third World development, see Cordell Hull, *The Memoirs of Cordell Hull* (New York: Macmillan, 1948), vol. 2, 1477–78, 1599–1601. For a later sophisticated and highly influential treatise on the link between self-sustaining liberal economic development and democratic institutions in the Third World, see W. W. Rostow, *The Stages of Economic Growth, a Non-Communist Manifesto* (Cambridge: Cambridge University Press, 1960). See also n. 12.

17. For French designs under the Fourth Republic, see Harrison, *The Reluctant Ally*, 12–20. For de Gaulle's 1958 proposals, see Ibid., 86–101; and David Schoenbrun, *The Three Lives of Charles de Gaulle* (New York: Atheneum, 1966), 292–317.

18. See chap. 1, n. 6.

Chapter 3: The Founding Cycle: NATO from 1948 to 1960

1. For studies of the various recurring phases of American policy, see Robert E. Osgood, "The Revitalization of Containment," *Foreign Affairs* 61, no. 3 (America and the World 1982): 465–502; Henry Kissinger, *American Foreign Policy*, 3d ed. (New York: W. W. Norton, 1977); and John Lewis Gaddis, *Strategies of Containment: A Critical Appraisal of Postwar National Security Policy* (New York: Oxford University Press, 1982). While Gaddis admirably recounts the intellectual strategic debate in the development of American national security policy, his analysis gives less weight to the economic context. This approach makes it difficult to explain why neither symmetrical nor asymmetrical strategies of containment were permanently accepted. (Osgood sees the alternation resulting from electoral politics, which perhaps begs the question.) Symmetrical deterrence has, in fact, always been dropped when it cost the economy more than the politico-economic system was willing or able to sustain. Gaddis confesses surprise at "the *primacy* that has been accorded economic considerations in shaping strategies of containment, *to the exclusion of other considerations*" (p. 356, emphasis in original). But economic cost can be seen as less a parochial interference with strategic debates than a central concern of the very world system that military arrangements are meant to sustain. If Gaddis's scope is sometimes too narrow for the subject, his narration, documentation, and interpretation are often superb; this study owes much to his work.

2. For an earlier and somewhat more detailed treatment, see David P. Calleo, "Early American Views of NATO: Then and Now," in *The Troubled Alliance: Atlantic Relations in the 1980s*, ed. Lawrence Freedman (London: Heineman/Royal Institute of International Affairs, 1983).

3. Memorandum from the director of the Policy Planning Staff (Kennan), "Considerations Affecting the Conclusion of a North Atlantic Security Pact," in U.S. Department of State, *Foreign Relations of the United States 1948* (Washington, D.C.: U.S. Government Printing Office, 1974), vol. 3, 284–85.

4. Memorandum from the director of the Policy Planning Staff (Kennan) to the under secretary of state (Acheson), "Policy with Respect to American Aid to Western Europe, Views of the Policy Planning Staff," in U.S. Department of State, *Foreign Relations of the United States 1947*, vol. 3, 224–25.

5. Memorandum from Kennan, "North Atlantic Security Pact," vol. 3, 285.

6. Ibid., 287.

7. Memorandum from the director of the Policy Planning Staff (Kennan) to the secretary of state and the under secretary of state, "Policy Questions Concerning a Possible German Settlement," in U.S. Department of State, *Foreign Relations of the United States 1948*, vol. 2, 1287–97; Memorandum from the director of the Policy Planning Staff (Kennan) to the secretary of state, U.S. Department of State, *Foreign Relations of the United States 1948*, vol. 2, 1324–25; and "A Program Prepared by the Policy Planning Staff," Ibid., 1325–38.

8. Memorandum from Kennan, "North Atlantic Security Pact," 285–86.

9. Ibid., 287.

10. Ibid., 284; see also George F. Kennan, *Memoirs 1925–1950* (New York: Pantheon, 1967), 406–7.

11. As Marshall put it, "If Europe is restored as a solvent and vigorous community . . . the disturbing conflict between ourselves and the Soviets, insofar as Europe is concerned, will lessen." Cited in Hadley Arkes, *Bureaucracy, the Marshall Plan and the National Interest* (Princeton: Princeton University Press, 1972), 57.

For Kennan in July of 1947, Marshall aid was "to render principal European countries able to exist without outside charity. Necessity of this: a) So that they can buy from us; b) So that they will have enough self-confidence to withstand outside pressures." Cited in Richard J. Barnet, *The Alliance: America–Europe–Japan: Makers of the Postwar World* (New York: Simon and Schuster, 1983), 114. Kennan also insisted that aid be administered by the Europeans themselves, both to avoid a long-term American involvement in European affairs, and to "force the Europeans to begin to think like Europeans, and not like nationalists." Cited in Arkes, *Bureaucracy*, 51.

12. For a recent appraisal, see "The Truman Doctrine," *Economist* 302, no. 7489 (14 March 1987): 19–22. Much of the substance of NSC-68 can be found in earlier internal memoranda. See Clark M. Clifford's report to Truman, "American Relations with the Soviet Union," 24 Sept. 1946, in Arthur Krock, *Memoirs: Sixty Years on the Firing Line* (New York: Funk and Wagnall's, 1968), 419–82. See also John Lewis Gaddis, *Strategies of Containment*, 21–24. For the actual text, see NSC-68, 14 Apr. 1950, U.S. Department of State, *Foreign Relations of the United States 1950* (Washington, D.C.: U.S. Government Printing Office, 1977), vol. 1, 236–90. For the Korean War's role in promoting NSC-68 and tipping support in favor of rearmament, see Paul Y. Hammond, "NSC-68: Prologue to Rearmament," in Warner R. Schilling, Paul Y. Hammond, and Glenn H. Snyder, *Strategy, Politics, and Defense Budgets* (New York: Columbia University Press, 1962), 267–330. See also Dean Acheson's memoirs, *Present at the Creation* (New York: W. W. Norton, 1969).

13. John Lewis Gaddis, *Strategies of Containment*, 89–126.

14. Kennan's "realism" about the Soviet Union is best known from his celebrated Long Telegram, sent from the Moscow embassy, and published "Mr. X" article; see respectively "The Chargé in the Soviet Union to the Secretary of State," 22 Feb. 1946, in U.S. Department of State, *Foreign Relations of the United States 1946* (Washington, D.C.: U.S. Government Printing Office, 1969), vol. 6, 696–709; and "The Sources of Soviet Conduct," *Foreign Affairs*, 25, no. 4 (July 1947): 556–82.

On Kennan's eclipse, see Daniel Yergin, *Shattered Peace: The Origins of the Cold War and the National Security State* (Boston: Houghton Mifflin, 1977), 170–71, 322–24. Kennan says he felt like Acheson's "court jester" and observes: "The greatest mystery of my own role in Washington in those years . . . was why so much attention was paid in certain instances, as in the case of the telegram of February 1946 from Moscow and the X article, to what I had to say, and so little to others." Kennan, *Memoirs 1925–1950*, 427, 403. The X article elicited diverse and confused interpretations at the time. Walter Lippmann, for example, criticized Mr. X on grounds with which Kennan himself could presumably only have agreed, as seems clear from Kennan's internal memoranda at the time; see Walter Lippmann,

The Cold War, a Study in United States Foreign Policy (New York: Harper and Brothers, 1947); and Kennan's *Memoirs 1925–1950*, 359–60. Dean Acheson, unlike Lippmann, was one of the many impressed by Kennan's Long Telegram and wrote later that "his predictions and warnings could not have been better," referring to the immediate postwar years; see *Present at the Creation*, 151. By the late fifties, after Kennan had clarified his meaning, Acheson was to say: "Mr. Kennan has never, in my judgement, grasped the realities of power relationships, but takes a rather mystical attitude toward them. To Mr. Kennan there is no Soviet military threat in Europe." For the full text of Acheson's reply to Kennan, see *New York Times*, 12 Jan. 1958, p. 25.

15. For my earlier analysis, see David P. Calleo, *The Atlantic Fantasy: The U.S., NATO, and Europe* (Baltimore: Johns Hopkins University Press, 1970), 25–26, 64–65; see also "Agreement Between the Parties to the North Atlantic Treaty Regarding the Status of Their Forces" (19 June 1951); and "Agreement on the Status of the North Atlantic Treaty Organization, National Representatives and International Staff" (20 Sept. 1951); both in North Atlantic Treaty Organization, *NATO Facts and Figures* (Brussels: NATO Information Service, 1969), apps. 6, 7: 244–65.

16. The concept of asymmetrical versus symmetrical containment is central to John Lewis Gaddis's argument in *Strategies of Containment*. For its application to NSC-68 in particular, see 101–6. See also n. 1.

17. For my earlier analysis of the economic dimension of U.S. foreign policy in this period, see David P. Calleo and Benjamin M. Rowland, *America and the World Political Economy: Atlantic Dreams and National Realities* (Bloomington: Indiana University Press, 1973), 87–94.

18. See William A. Brown, *The International Gold Standard Reinterpreted, 1914–1934* (New York: National Bureau of Economic Research, 1940), 554; Brown talks of London's supremacy as a financial center before World War I, when New York was not yet a full-fledged international market. See also Herbert Feis, *Europe the World's Banker, 1870–1940* (New York: Yale University Press, 1930).

19. George F. Kennan, *The Decline of Bismarck's European Order: Franco-Russian Relations, 1875–1890* (Princeton: Princeton University Press, 1979). For a contrasting perspective on international order, reflecting views influential among American financial and business elites, see Clarence Streit, *Union Now* (New York: Harper, 1939).

20. The United States held 60 percent of the world's monetary gold stock in 1947 ($20.1 billion out of $33.3 billion), whereas the European powers were left economically exhausted. Britain was forced to negotiate a $3.75 billion loan from the Americans in 1945, and on conditions that proved ruinous. For a detailed account, see Sir Roy Forbes Harrod, "The U.S. Loan to Britain," in *The Life of John Maynard Keynes* (New York: St. Martin's Press, 1963), chap. 6; Richard N. Gardner, *Sterling-Dollar Diplomacy in Current Perspective: The Origins and the Prospects of Our International Economic Order* (New York: McGraw-Hill, 1980), 208–36. Many feared that the scarcity of usable reserves, the dollar gap, would prevent European recovery. American capital rushed into the breach: "Of the $8.5 billion increase in world reserves in the years 1949–1959, the United States provided $7 billion through the increase in its liabilities to foreign monetary authorities." See Robert Solomon, *The International Monetary System 1945–1976* (New York: Harper and Row, 1977), 31.

21. On the growth of international corporations and American investment in Europe, see David P. Calleo and Benjamin M. Rowland, *America and the World Political Economy*, 162–91; Raymond Vernon, "The Multinational Enterprise in Transatlantic Relations," in *America and Western Europe: Problems and Prospects*, ed. Karl Kaiser and Hans-Peter Schwarz (Lexington, Mass.: Lexington Books, 1977), 148–64. For a broad view of American corporate growth in this period, see John Kenneth Galbraith, *The New Industrial State*, 3d ed. rev. (Boston: Houghton Mifflin, 1978). Many studies concentrate on American direct investment in Europe, which, from 1950 to 1970, rose from $1.7 billion to $24.5 billion. See, for example, Raymond Vernon, *The Economic and Political Consequences of Multinational Enterprise: An Anthology* (Boston: Division of Research, Graduate School of Business Administration, Harvard University, 1972). For a popular French reaction, see J. J. Servan-Schreiber, *The American Challenge* (New York: Atheneum, 1968). For a favorable European view, see Christopher Layton, *Trans-Atlantic Investments*, 2d ed. (Boulogne-sur-Seine: The Atlantic Institute, 1968). For the more extreme possibilities for the international political economy, see George Ball, "COSMOCORP: The Importance of Being Stateless," *Atlantic Community Quarterly* 6, no. 2 (Summer 1968), 163–70.

22. See chap. 2, n. 4. See also David P. Calleo, *Britain's Future* (New York: Horizon Press, 1968), 92–94.

23. See Michael M. Harrison, *The Reluctant Ally: France and Atlantic Security* (Baltimore: Johns Hopkins University Press, 1981). For subsequent French disillusionment, see General André Beaufre, *NATO and Europe* (New York: Knopf, 1966). See also n. 36.

24. For a comprehensive study of early German views of the Atlantic relationship, see Hans-Peter Schwarz, *Vom Reich zur Bundesrepublik: Deutschland in Widerstreit der aussenpolitischen Konzeptionen in den Jahren der Besatzungsherrschaft* (Neuweid: Luchterhand, 1966). For an overview of Adenauer's influence with Americans, see Waldemar Besson, *Die Aussenpolitik der Bundesrepublik: Erfahrungen und Masstäbe* (Munich: Piper Verlag, 1970); for Adenauer as a manipulator, see Richard J. Barnet, *The Alliance: America–Europe–Japan; Makers of the Postwar World* (New York: Simon and Schuster, 1983), 15–58, especially 56–58. For Adenauer's handling of the EDC, see Arnulf Baring, *Aussenpolitik in Adenauers Kanzlerdemokratie: Bonns Beiträge zur Europäische Verteidigungsgemeinschaft,* [Schriften des Forschungsinstituts der deutschen Gesellschaft für Auswärtige Politik,] vol. 28 (Munich: R. Oldenbourg Verlag, 1969).

25. For European promotion of the alliance, see Alfred Grosser, *The Western Alliance: European-American Relations Since 1945,* trans. Michael Shaw (New York: Continuum, 1980), 82–89. For an important and characteristically American reaction, see Henry L. Stimson, "The Challenge to Americans," *Foreign Affairs* 26, no. 1 (October 1947): 5–14; and Henry L. Stimson and McGeorge Bundy, *On Active Service in Peace and War,* 1st ed. (New York: Harper and Brothers, 1948), 652–55. For a later and more enthusiastic acceptance of hegemony, see Walter Lippmann, *Western Unity and the Common Market* (London: H. Hamilton, 1962).

26. For U.S. encouragement for European unity during the Marshall Plan, see n. 2; see also Ernst Hans van der Beugel, *From Marshall Aid to Atlantic Partnership: European Integration as a Concern of American Foreign Policy* (New York: Elsevier, 1966); and Alfred Grosser, *The Western Alliance,* 101–5, 119–28. For the Kennedy administration, the multilateral nuclear force (MLF), and European unity, see Seyom Brown, *The Faces of Power: Constancy and Change in United States Foreign Policy from Truman to Reagan* (New York: Columbia University Press, 1983), 165–68. For a broad look at the links between American postwar enthusiasm for liberal trade, federalism, and European union, see David P. Calleo and Benjamin M. Rowland, *America and the World Political Economy,* pts. 1, 2.

27. For Taft's own exposition, see Robert A. Taft, *A Foreign Policy for Americans* (Garden City, N.Y.: Doubleday, 1951); also Taft's speech of 11 July 1949, *Congressional Record,* U.S. Senate 81st Congress 1st session (Washington: U.S. Government Printing Office, 1949), S2905–6. See also John Lewis Gaddis, *Strategies of Containment,* 119–20.

28. For Eisenhower's motives in seeking nomination, see Dwight D. Eisenhower, *The White House Years: Mandate for Change, 1953–1956* (Garden City, N.Y.: Doubleday, 1963), 13–22; also John Lewis Gaddis, *Strategies of Containment,* 127; and Samuel P. Huntington, *The Common Defense: Strategic Programs in National Politics* (New York: Columbia University Press, 1961), 85.

29. The Eisenhower administration actually expanded U.S. treaty commitments by only four nations beyond the forty-one inherited from Truman. But it did emphasize these alliances as the cornerstone of its foreign policy. U.S. commitments were bolstered by aid to local forces who were to deal with minor aggression. John Lewis Gaddis, *Strategies of Containment,* 152–53, 171–72.

30. On the military buildup's Keynesian rationale, and especially the influence of Leon Keyserling as head of the Council of Economic Advisers, see Paul Y. Hammond, "NSC-68: Prologue to Rearmament," in Warner R. Schilling, Paul Y. Hammond, and Glenn H. Snyder, *Strategy, Politics, and Defense Budgets* (New York: Columbia University Press, 1962), 267–330; see also John Lewis Gaddis and Paul Nitze, "NSC-68 and the Soviet Threat Reconsidered," *International Security,* 4, no. 4 (Spring 1980): 164–76; and John Lewis Gaddis, *Strategies of Containment,* 93–95.

31. For a more thorough discussion, see John Lewis Gaddis, *Strategies of Containment,* 145–61.

32. The Eisenhower administration's strategy of massive retaliation did not preclude the notion of flexible retaliation; the distinction between strategic and tactical weapons was blurred to allow a variety of nuclear responses. See Lawrence Freedman, *The Evolution of Nuclear Strategy* (London: Macmillan/International Institute for Strategic Studies, 1983), 76–77, 83–88.

33. For the Eisenhower administration's policy toward national liberation movements, see John Lewis Gaddis, *Strategies of Containment*, 175–82. For the reasons behind the founding of SEATO and the beginning of U.S. involvement in Indochina, see Ibid., 79–83.

34. For the administration's reasoning in intervening in Lebanon but not Syria, see Seyom Brown, *The Faces of Power*, 125–28.

35. In 1946, Congress passed the MacMahon Act to prevent any export of atomic materials or information. The Soviets detonated their first nuclear device in 1949, the British in 1952, the French in 1960. At Eisenhower's insistence, U.S. policy was redrafted to favor sharing with Britain in 1954 and amended further in 1957 and 1958. The Atomic Energy Act loosened restrictions with allies, though in practice almost exclusively with Great Britain. Kennedy, though instigating the Test Ban and Non-Proliferation Treaties, acceded to British demands to buy U.S. Polaris missiles in the Nassau Agreements of 1962 and offered a similar arrangement with France. He also proposed the Multilateral Nuclear Force. None of these arrangements, however, initially contemplated relinquishing American control of the missiles themselves. MLF missiles were to be committed to NATO, commanded by an American general, and subject to U.S. as well as European vetoes. In the only nuclear cooperation scheme actually carried out, the British wrested the right to use their Polaris missiles only in cases of supreme national interest. Kennedy's nuclear strategy is discussed further in chap. 4. For the British deterrent, see Lawrence Freedman, *Britain and Nuclear Weapons* (London: Macmillan/Royal Institute for International Affairs, 1980); for the French, see chap. 4; and Michael Harrison, *The Reluctant Ally*; and Wilfrid Kohl, *French Nuclear Diplomacy* (Princeton: Princeton University Press, 1971).

36. Most egregious were the French, who dedicated 40 to 45 percent of their defense budgets after 1950 and one-quarter of their officer corps to the colonial war in Indochina. NATO plans called for between fourteen and twenty active French divisions for European defense. Yet in 1953, probably only six divisions at 70 percent strength were available. By 1960, France had 418,000 men in Algeria and only 50,000 in Germany. Michael Harrison, *The Reluctant Ally*, 34–35. Accustomed to Eisenhower's nuclear strategy, Europeans were reluctant to increase spending for conventional defense as the Kennedy administration promoted its new flexible-response strategy. See Lawrence Freedman, *The Evolution of Nuclear Strategy*, 285–302, 326–27.

37. Sputnik triggered widespread apprehension across America, heightened shortly thereafter by a presidential commission on strategy known as the Gaither Commission, whose report warned of an imminent American vulnerability to Soviet nuclear attack and recommended accelerated production of missiles, increased defense of nuclear forces, and a huge civil defense effort. John Lewis Gaddis, *Strategies of Containment*, 184.

38. At first the Eisenhower administration pressed for German rearmament within the cadre of a supranational European Defense Community, itself to be placed under NATO—the Pleven Plan proposal of 1950. Initially, the United States had doubted the Pleven Plan. Acheson and Marshall both disapproved and an alternative, the Spofford Plan was proposed to permit German participation in NATO without waiting for a European Army. In June 1951, however, Jean Monnet convinced Eisenhower, at this time SACEUR, of the plan's value and thus shifted the U.S. position toward EDC. Richard Mayne, *Postwar: The Dawn of Today's Europe* (New York: Schocken Books, 1983), 311–16. By 1953, Secretary of State John Foster Dulles threatened an "agonizing reappraisal" if the EDC failed and declared a European Economic Community linking France and Germany essential for the survival of European civilization. See "Dulles Cautions Europe to Ratify Arms Treaty Soon," *New York Times*, 15 Dec. 1953, pp. 1, 15. Though the EDC was to be integrated into NATO, and so presumably under American command, some backers saw in it the basis for an independent European defense in the future as well as the motor for Europe's federal integration. Daniel Lerner and Raymond Aron, eds., *France Defeats EDC* (New York: Praeger, 1957); and David P. Calleo, *Europe's Future: The Grand Alternatives* (New York: Horizon Press, 1965), 49–51.

39. For the detailed reactions, see Alfred Grosser, *The Western Alliance*, 140–45; Michael Harrison, *The Reluctant Ally*, 41–45; and David P. Calleo. *Britain's Future*, 94–95.

40. On the Eisenhower administration's support for European unity, see Ernst Hans van der Beugel, *From Marshall Aid to Atlantic Partnership*, 305–49.

41. "Liberation" as a Republican election slogan reflected Dulles's need to assuage Senator McCarthy

and the extreme right by rejecting Acheson's mere containment. Dulles also expected his strident rhetoric would restrain the Soviets. In January 1953, he addressed "all those suffering under Communist slavery" and promised, "You can count on us." John Foster Dulles, "A Survey of Foreign Policy Problems," a radio-television address on 27 Jan. 1953, in *Department of State Bulletin* 28, 9 Feb. 1953, 212–16. Uprisings in Berlin in June 1953 and in Poland and Hungary in the fall of 1956 disproved his expectations and revealed American impotence. See also Seyom Brown, *The Faces of Power*, 107–12; and Coral Bell, *Negotiation from Strength: A Study in the Politics of Power* (New York: Knopf, 1963), 67–84.

42. In March 1952, Stalin himself proposed a neutralized, rearmed, and unified Germany within the Potsdam frontiers—an offer seen as a device to delay the EDC Treaty and left unexplored. After Stalin's death, Georgii Malenkov announced a less bellicose policy and pursued various initiatives. In 1955, Nikolai Bulganin invited Adenauer to Moscow. In 1957, the Polish Rapacki Plan offered, with Soviet backing, a nuclear-free zone in Central Europe. Adam Ulam, *Expansion and Coexistence, Soviet Foreign Policy 1917–73*, 2d ed. (New York: Praeger, 1974), 611. See also Coral Bell, *Negotiation from Strength*. Both Ulam and Bell believe the Soviets, if pressed, would have made considerable concessions to avoid German rearmament.

43. For Eisenhower on détente, arms control, and the abortive Paris summit, see Dwight D. Eisenhower, *The White House Years*, 506–30. See also Seyom Brown, *The Faces of Power*, 89–98; and John Lewis Gaddis, *Strategies of Containment*, 192.

44. For a trenchant review of new evaluations of Eisenhower, see Ronald Steel, "Two Cheers for Ike," *The New York Review of Books*, 24 Sept. 1981, 54–57.

Chapter 4: The Second Cycle:
From Kennedy to Ford, 1961–1976

1. The missile gap was actually seen to favor the United States. Lawrence Freedman, *The Evolution of Nuclear Strategy* (London: Macmillan Press/International Institute for Strategic Studies, 1981), 139–54; see also Arnold Horelick and Myron Rush, *Strategic Power and Soviet Foreign Policy* (Chicago: University of Chicago Press, 1966).

In due course, estimates of Soviet conventional forces in Europe were also reduced. Alain C. Enthoven and K. Wayne Smith, *How Much Is Enough?* (New York: Harper and Row, 1971). For a broad view, see John Lewis Gaddis, *Strategies of Containment: A Critical Appraisal of Postwar American National Security Policy* (New York: Oxford University Press, 1982), 207.

2. For the evolution of the flexible-response doctrine, see Lawrence Freedman, *The Evolution of Nuclear Strategy*, 227–56 and 285–302; see also Alain C. Enthoven and K. Wayne Smith, *How Much Is Enough?*; Desmond Ball, *Policies and Force Levels: The Strategic Missile Program of the Kennedy Administration* (Berkeley: University of California Press, 1980); William Kaufman, *The McNamara Strategy* (New York: Harper and Row, 1964); and John Lewis Gaddis, *Strategies of Containment*, chap. 7.

3. The United States adopted flexible response in 1962, but it was not formally accepted by the rest of the alliance until 1967. *Communiqué*, ministerial meeting of the North Atlantic Council, 14 Dec. 1967. For European resistance to the concept of flexible response, see Lawrence Freedman, *Evolution of Nuclear Strategy*, 293–302; William Kaufman, *The McNamara Strategy*, 102–34; for the German response, see Catherine McArdle Kelleher, *Germany and the Politics of Nuclear Weapons* (New York: Columbia University Press, 1975), 156–79. For Helmut Schmidt's impressive but rather unique European support, see Helmut Schmidt, *Defense or Retaliation* (New York: Praeger, 1972), 211; and Lawrence Freedman, 288.

4. Given the Federal Republic's resources and location, and American, British, and French preoccupations elsewhere, West Germany was logically the principal source for new conventional forces.

The Radford Plan of 1956 hoped German forces might permit U.S. withdrawal or reduction. See Catherine McArdle Kelleher, "Germany and NATO: The Enduring Bargain," in *West German Foreign Policy: 1949–1979*, ed. Wolfram Hanrieder (Boulder, Colo.: Westview Press, 1980), 46–47. For German objections, see Kelleher, *Germany and the Politics of Nuclear Weapons*, 169–71; and Alastair Buchan, *NATO in the 1960s* (New York: Praeger, 1963), 83–84.

5. For a general survey, see Lawrence Freedman, *Evolution of Nuclear Strategy*, 307–8. During the 1960s, British strategists, such as Sir Basil Liddell Hart, Patrick Blackett, and Rear Admiral Anthony Buzzard, developed important critiques of massive retaliation but, unlike the French, were uninterested in a general European alternative to dependence on the United States.

De Gaulle articulated general French policy thus: "our independence requires, in the atomic age we live in, that we have the necessary means to deter a possible aggressor ourselves, without detriment to our alliances, but without our allies holding our fate in their hands." *Major Addresses, Statements, and Press Conferences of General Charles De Gaulle, March 17, 1964–May 16, 1967* (New York: Ambassade de France, Service de Presse et d'Information, 1967), 88.

For the development of French strategic doctrine, see chap. 10, nn. 31, 34, 35.

6. See chap. 10, nn. 34, 35.

7. The United States offered de Gaulle technical assistance and equipment in exchange for concessions from him on NATO, British EEC entry, and the Test Ban Treaty. De Gaulle refused and was punished by a U.S. embargo on uranium and advanced computers. As a result, French nuclear weapons are produced without American assistance. Michael Harrison, *The Reluctant Ally* (Baltimore: Johns Hopkins University Press, 1981), 80–81. See also, John Newhouse, *De Gaulle and the Anglo-Saxons* (New York: Viking Press, 1970).

8. Catherine McArdle Kelleher, *Germany and the Politics of Nuclear Weapons*, 122–43; also Alfred Grosser, "France and Germany: Divergent Outlooks," *Foreign Affairs* 44, no. 1 (October 1965): 25–26.

9. In 1964, German Defense Minister Franz-Josef Strauss proposed a nuclear-armed European defense community in place of an MLF. In his *The Grand Design: A European Solution to German Reunification* (New York: Praeger, 1965), Strauss proposed a six-year transition to European confederation. Britain and France were to pool their nuclear forces, which would initially remain under national control. As integration progressed toward a federal political structure and a formal defense community, a European nuclear council of defense ministers would create common defense policy for an integrated European nuclear force, closely coordinated with the U.S. nuclear arsenal in NATO. Germany would have no national control over the nuclear weapons, which would rest with the European federal authority. Strauss opposed exchanging the American nuclear umbrella for the French *force de frappe*: "Germany does not want atom patronage, but atom partnership. . . ." Ibid., 64. See Wilfrid L. Kohl, *French Nuclear Diplomacy* (Princeton: Princeton University Press, 1971), 306–8. Baron Guttenberg, a CSU deputy in the Bundestag who helped engineer the Grand Coalition that supplanted Erhard, proposed a European atomic force with the French atomic arsenal as its nucleus. See interview on Bayerischer Rundfunk, 10 June 1964, and *Die Welt*, 11 June 1964, cited in Kohl, 289. The French had earlier hinted a certain interest in using their nuclear forces as the basis of a European force. For example, French Defense Minister Pierre Messmer stated: "In order for Europe to exist, it will be necessary that she assume the burden and the responsibility of her defense, and that she possess nuclear arms for that purpose." The French nuclear arsenal was, in his view, "*à pièce maîtresse*" in the future construction of Europe. Pierre Messmer, "Notre politique militaire," *Revue de défense nationale* (May 1963): 761, cited in Kohl, 283.

10. For the principal schemes for a NATO deterrent, see Lawrence Freedman, *Evolution of Nuclear Strategy*, 327–28; and idem, *Britain and Nuclear Weapons* (London: Macmillan Press, 1980). See, in addition, Alastair Buchan, *The Multilateral Force: A Historical Perspective* (London: International Institute for Strategic Studies, 1964); Robert Bowie, "Strategy and the Atlantic Alliance," *International Organization* 27, no. 3 (Summer 1963); Albert Wohlsletter, "Nuclear Sharing: NATO and the N+1 Country," *Foreign Affairs* 39, no. 3 (April 1961); Pierre Gallois, "U.S. Strategy and the Defense of Europe," *Orbis* 7, no. 2 (Summer 1983). Buchan, Wohlsletter, and Gallois were critics of MLF, and Bowie a proponent.

11. As early as 1957, the Eisenhower administration emplaced Thor and Jupiter IRBM's in Britain, Italy, and Turkey, with national veto rights over their use more to plug the "missile gap" than to meet demands for a more European nuclear defense. Upon entering office and discovering that the missile gap was an illusion, Kennedy ordered the missiles out of Europe. This order was never fully carried out, and the missiles in Turkey were not removed until after the Cuban missile crisis. The MLF was proposed as a political rather than military substitute. John Lewis Gaddis, *Strategies of Containment*, 221–22.

Currently the United States maintains "positive two-man control" over all U.S. NATO nuclear weapons. All are "locked" with coded devices (Permissive Action Links) that can, theoretically, be released solely on the order of the U.S. president. Where earmarked for use by allied troops, the exact details of nuclear sharing are governed by secret agreements. A "two-key" system is thought to give the United States control over the warhead and the host country control over the delivery vehicle. See Jeffrey Record, with the assistance of Thomas I. Anderson, *U.S. Nuclear Weapons in Europe—Issues and Alternatives* (Washington, D.C.: The Brookings Institution, 1974), 28–31.

Much of the impetus to develop and install the Permissive Action Links (PALs) came from a visit of the Joint Committee on Atomic Energy to Europe in 1960. The Committee discovered German-manned aircraft, armed with nuclear weapons, sitting on the edge of a runway with their starting plugs in. "Control" came from an American officer armed with a revolver somewhere in the vicinity. John D. Steinbruner, *The Cybernetic Theory of Decision: New Dimensions of Political Analysis* (Princeton: Princeton University Press, 1974), 180–81.

12. In December of 1966, NATO's Defense Planning Committee created a two-tiered forum for discussing nuclear issues. The first tier, the Nuclear Defense Affairs Committee (NDAC), was open to all interested members. The second tier, the Nuclear Planning Group (NPG), set up for detailed consultation, included the United States, West Germany, Great Britain, Italy, and three other NDAC members who served in rotation.

The NPG has since met twice yearly on the ministerial level and taken up matters such as ABM systems for Europe, guidelines for tactical nuclear weapons, SALT, and MBFR negotiating positions. David N. Schwartz, *NATO's Nuclear Dilemmas* (Washington, D.C.: The Brookings Institution, 1983), 185–87.

13. Nuclear parity, elusive to define and measure, involves the number of launchers, deliverable warheads, and their accuracy in relation to the targets. Parity in the number of strategic launchers (ICBMs, SLBMs, and strategic bombers) was reached between 1971 and 1973.

Strategic Launcher Parity

	1969		1971		1975	
	U.S.	USSR	U.S.	USSR	U.S.	USSR
ICBMs	1,054	1,028	1,054	1,513	1,054	1,527
SLBMs	656	196	656	448	656	628
Bombers	560	145	505	145	422	140
Total	2,270	1,369	2,215	2,106	2,132	2,295

Superior U.S. technology, in particular the earlier development of the Multiple Independently Targeted Re-entry Vehicles (MIRV), continued, until the early 1980s, to give the United States a huge advantage in deliverable warheads.

Warheads (ICBMs and SLBMs)

	1971		1977		1983	
	U.S.	USSR	U.S.	USSR	U.S.	USSR
ICBM	1,254	1,510	2,154	2,647	2,145	5,654
SLBM	1,236	440	5,120	909	5,145	2,688
Total	2,490	1,950	7,274	3,556	7,290	8,342

COMPILED FROM: *The Military Balance 1977–78, 1979–80, 1983–84* (London: International Institute for Strategic Studies), 79, 88–89, 118–19.

As late as 1985, the United States was still thought to have a continuing advantage in accuracy, with its most accurate ICBM having a Circular Error Probable (CEP) of 220 meters and the Soviet equivalent a CEP of some 300 meters.

14. Interestingly, in the 1980s, two principal defense planners of the Kennedy-Johnson era, McGeorge Bundy and Robert McNamara, joined with George Kennan and Gerard Smith to advocate a NATO No-First-Use policy on nuclear weapons with substantially improved conventional forces. See "Nuclear Weapons and the Atlantic Alliance," *Foreign Affairs* 60, no. 4 (Spring 1982): 753–68.

15.

U.S. Troop Levels in Europe (thousands)

1950	1955	1960	1964	1965	1968	1970	1975	1981
145	405	379	436	363	314	291	303	328

West German Troop Levels and Constraints (thousands)

	1955	1962	1966	1970	1974	1978	
	—	368	461	455	475	491	

SOURCE: All figures, except those for 1964 and 1968, are from the U.S. Department of Defense, reprinted in *Congressional Record*, 21 May 1982, S5892–93; for the latter two years, see U.S. Department of Defense, *Annual Report to the Congress FY 1983*, c–5.

The 1955 plans for a 500,000-man German Army dropped to 320,000 in 1956—a result of cutting the conscription period from 18 to 12 months. For an analysis, see Wolfram Hanreider, *The Stable Crisis: Two Decades of German Foreign Policy* (New York: Harper and Row, 1970), chap. 1.

16. Diego A. Ruix Palmer, "The Front Line in Europe—The Forces: National Contributions," *Armed Forces Journal* (May 1984), 55–58. For further discussion, see chap. 9, nn. 5, 15.

17. For the impact of the French withdrawal on NATO military capabilities, see David P. Calleo, *The Atlantic Fantasy: The U.S., NATO and Europe* (Baltimore: Johns Hopkins University Press, 1970), 33–35, 154–55. For a contrary view, see Brigadier Kenneth Hunt, "NATO Without France:

The Military Implications," *Adelphi Papers*, no. 32 (London: International Institute for Strategic Studies, 1966).

18. By the late 1950s, a deliberate all-out attack seemed less likely than a miscalculation or momentary rashness. Accordingly, the primary purpose of NATO conventional forces would be to enforce a pause in the fighting, during which a diplomatic solution could be reached before escalation grew uncontrollable. This view was first propounded in 1957 by the SACEUR, General Lauris Norstad. Germans criticized it for implying a de facto threshold below which the Soviets might attack Germany without risking a nuclear conflagration, a notion that would weaken deterrence. James L. Richardson, *Germany and the Western Alliance* (Cambridge, Mass.: Harvard University Press, 1966), 74–78. See also General Lauris Norstad, "NATO Strength and Spirit," *NATO Letter* (January 1960), 7–11; and Lawrence Freedman, *Evolution of Nuclear Strategy*, 292–93.

19. David N. Schwartz, *NATO's Nuclear Dilemmas*, 186–92.

20. For the Kennedy administration's hopes for détente, see Arthur Schlesinger, *A Thousand Days: John F. Kennedy in the White House* (Boston: Houghton Mifflin, 1965), 891–92. In the late 1950s and early 1960s, an academic theory of convergence encouraged such hopes. For a classic examination of convergence, see Zbigniew Brzezinski and Samuel P. Huntington, *Political Power: USA/USSR* (New York: Viking Press, 1965), 419–36.

21. As early as 1961, Walt Rostow had tried to link Soviet moderation in Vietnam to détente. John Lewis Gaddis, *Strategies of Containment*, 249.

For Kissinger's "linkage" to Vietnam, see his memoirs, *The White House Years* (Boston: Little, Brown, 1979), 128; and idem, *American Foreign Policy*, 3d ed. (New York: W. W. Norton, 1977). For an assessment of his success, see Seyom Brown, *The Faces of Power: Constancy and Change in the United States Foreign Policy from Truman to Reagan* (New York: Columbia University Press, 1983), 354–76.

22. See de Gaulle's speech, Lille, 29 June 1947, microfilm. For an analysis of de Gaulle's perspectives and policies, see Edward A. Kolodziej, *French International Policy under de Gaulle and Pompidou: The Politics of Grandeur* (Ithaca: Cornell University Press, 1974). For the author's view at the time, see David P. Calleo, *Europe's Future: The Grand Alternatives* (New York: Horizon Press, 1965), chap. 4; and later, *The Atlantic Fantasy*, chap. 6. For a sample of de Gaulle's vision of a pan-European system, see his *War Memoirs* vol. 3 (New York: Simon and Schuster, 1960). For a summary of its public development, see Guy de Carmoy, *Les politiques étrangères de la France 1944–66* (Paris: La Table Ronde, 1967), 353–55.

23. For a discussion, see Susan Strange, "International Monetary Relations," in *International Economic Relations of the Western World 1959–1971*, ed. Andrew Shonfield (New York: Oxford University Press, 1976), vol. 2, 281–99. See also David P. Calleo, *The Imperious Economy* (Cambridge, Mass.: Harvard University Press, 1982), chaps. 3, 5.

24. For the text of the treaty, see the appendix to Robert Picht, ed., *Das Bündnis im Bündnis: Deutsch-französische Beziehungen im internationalen Spannungsfeld* (Berlin: Severin and Siedler, 1982). On Adenauer's motives in signing the treaty, see the final volume of his memoirs, *Erinnerungen: 1959–1963* (Stuttgart: Deutsche Verlags-Anstalt, 1968), 205. For an analysis of de Gaulle's German campaign and Adenauer's encouragement of Franco-German cooperation from a German perspective, see Waldemar Besson, *Die Aussenpolitik der Bundesrepublik: Erfahrungen und Maßstäbe* (Munich: Piper Verlag, 1970), 304–9.

25. For a description of Adenauer's fall and his relations with de Gaulle, see Aidan Crawley, *The Rise of Western Germany 1945–72* (London: William Collins Sons & Co., 1973), chap. 14, particularly 257–63.

For Erhard's economic views, see Reinhard Blum, *Soziale Markt-Wirtschaft* (Tübingen: J. C. B. Mohl, 1969). For Erhard's Atlanticism and early opposition to the EEC, see Wolfram Hanrieder, *The Stable Crisis: Two Decades of German Foreign Policy* (New York: Harper and Row, 1970), 62–69; and Waldemar Besson, *Die Aussenpolitik der Bundesrepublik*, 322–28.

26. For tensions between de Gaulle and Erhard, and de Gaulle and Kiesinger, see Wolfram Hanrieder, *The Stable Crisis*, 75–76. For German *Ostpolitik* under Kiesinger and Brandt, see William Griffith,

The Ostpolitik of the Federal Republic of Germany, (Cambridge, Mass.: MIT Press, 1978); Karl Kaiser, "The New Ostpolitik," in *West German Foreign Policy 1949–1979—Necessities and Choices*, ed. Wolfram Hanrieder; and Boris Meissner, *Die Deutsche Ostpolitik 1961–1970* (Cologne: Verlag Wissenschaft und Politik, 1970).

27. For foreign policy and Erhard's fall, see Waldemar Besson, *Die Aussenpolitik der Bundesrepublik*, 322–28, 348–64. See also David P. Calleo, *The German Problem Reconsidered*, 171–73.

28. At the 1960 conference of the SPD, Willy Brandt explained his approach thus: "The problem is to fix the status quo militarily in order to get the necessary freedom of movement to overcome the political status quo." From Harold Kent Schellinger, Jr., *The SPD in the Bonn Republic: A Socialist Party Modernizes* (The Hague: Martinus Nijhoff, 1968), 176. For my earlier views, see David P. Calleo, *The Atlantic Fantasy*, 134–40; and *The German Problem Reconsidered*, chap. 7.

29. In a speech on 7 October 1966, for example, Johnson exhorted the Europeans to improve East-West relations, a call welcomed in Bonn as the more active *Ostpolitik* was launched. See Waldemar Besson, *Die Aussenpolitik der Bundesrepublik*, 368–73. Johnson's encouragement of European détente was followed by U.S. Undersecretary of State for Political Affairs Eugene V. Rostow in a speech on 24 November 1966 to the Ministerial Council of the OECD in Paris. Rostow observed: "Two facts about the situation are plain, as the President made clear: there can be no détente in Europe without German reunification, but no peaceful reunification of Germany can be imagined without détente, without the consent of the Soviet Union and Eastern Europe. . . . We are not suggesting, I emphasize, that we should promote a common position with which to confront the countries of Eastern Europe. Rather we should work for a shared view about separate steps which might be taken separately and together to extend and advance the area of peaceful economic engagement." *Department of State Bulletin*, 56, no. 1,436 (2 January 1967): 24.

30. As détente was growing fashionable and after French withdrawal, the NATO Ministerial Meeting of December 1966 commissioned a new study of NATO's role. The report became known after the study group's chairman, Belgian Foreign Minister Pierre Harmel. For the text, see *Texts of Final Communiques Issued by Ministerial Sessions of the North Atlantic Council, the Defence Planning Committee, and the Nuclear Planning Group* (Brussels: NATO Information Service, 1975), 198–202. For a discussion, see Roger Morgan, *The United States and West Germany: A Study in Alliance Politics* (London: Oxford University Press, 1974), 179–80.

31. For Soviet policy toward West Germany, see Angela Stent Yergin, "Soviet–West German Relations: Finlandization or Normalization?" in *Soviet Foreign Policy Toward Western Europe*, ed. George Ginsburgs and Alvin Z. Rubinstein (New York: Praeger, 1978), 102–33; for Soviet policy toward Czechoslovakia and interest in finding a legal basis for intervention in 1968, see Pavel Tigrid, *Why Dubcek Fell* (London: MacDonald, 1971), 124–36.

32. De Gaulle's successor, Georges Pompidou, initially welcomed Brandt's *Ostpolitik* as a contribution to détente and a hindrance to unwelcome pressure for further EEC integration. But Pompidou soon grew worried that *Ostpolitik* might ultimately neutralize and reunify Germany. He also criticized the arms-control talks, SALT and MBFR, both supported by West Germany. German bullying of the French to devalue in 1969 revealed their uncomfortable economic power. France sought closer ties with England to compensate. See F. Roy Willis, "Germany, France and Europe," in *West German Foreign Policy 1949–1979*, ed. Wolfram Hanrieder, 93–126; and Edward Kolodziej, *French International Policy*, 391–443.

33. Kissinger feared Brandt's *Ostpolitik* was a revival of traditional German power politics, more dangerous for its long-range rather than immediate consequences. Henry A. Kissinger, *The White House Years* (Boston: Little, Brown, 1979), 529–30, 408–12. For his general critique of European diplomatic independence, see Henry A. Kissinger, *American Foreign Policy*, 3d ed. (New York: W. W. Norton, 1977), 99–113.

34. See Walt W. Rostow, *The Stages of Economic Growth: A Non-Communist Manifesto* (Cambridge: Cambridge University Press, 1960).

35. For an analysis of Kennedy's development policies, see Seyom Brown, *The Faces of Power*, 181–99. For the Alliance for Progress and the Agency for International Development in the general

context of the administration's emerging policies, see Arthur Schlesinger, A *Thousand Days*, chaps. 8, 22.

36. By 1966, Johnson's appeals for an allied "presence" in Vietnam had produced twenty-three professors from Germany, two Dutch surgical teams, and eleven British police instructors. See Richard Barnet, *The Alliance—America, Europe, and Japan: Makers of the Postwar World* (New York: Simon and Schuster, 1983), 265. Opposition varied from country to country but was considerable even in Germany, the most supportive, and virulent in France, the most critical. Alfred Grosser, *The Western Alliance: European-American Relations Since 1945* (New York: Continuum, 1980), 237–43, 246–47.

In 1966, de Gaulle flew to the Cambodian city of Phnom Penh to denounce the American involvement in Vietnam. See his address of 1 September 1966 in *Major Addresses, Statements, and Press Conferences of General Charles de Gaulle, March 17, 1964–May 16, 1967*, 142.

37. Michael Harrison, *The Reluctant Ally*, 174–75.

38. From 1970–1976, congressional cuts in defense budgets averaged $6 billion annually, so that by 1977 defense spending was only 24.3 percent of the budget, compared to 40.8 percent in 1970. John Lewis Gaddis, *Strategies of Containment*, 322. For the effects, see Henry Kissinger, *The White House Years*, 939–49.

Conscription was replaced by an all-volunteer force in 1973 resulting in a cut of 600,000 in standing forces, further manpower cuts of 20 percent in the selected reserves, and 60 percent in standby reserves. For the significance for U.S. defense posture and capability, see Kenneth Coffey, *The Strategy Implications of the All-Volunteer Forces* (Chapel Hill: University of North Carolina Press, 1980), 51ff.

39. For my more detailed discussion, see chap. 6 and David P. Calleo, *The Imperious Economy*, chaps. 4, 5.

40. See n. 13.

41. For the Nixon administration's motives for arms control, see Henry Kissinger, *The White House Years*, 539–51; and *Years of Upheaval* (Boston: Little, Brown, 1982) chaps. 7, 8. For the U.S.–Soviet arms negotiations, see John Newhouse, *Cold Dawn: The Story of SALT* (New York: Holt, Rinehart and Winston, 1973).

42. See Seyom Brown, *The Faces of Power*, 396–413. On the effect of the Yom Kippur War on European diplomacy, see Henry Kissinger, *Years of Upheaval*, 707–22.

43. *Congressional Record*, 4 Oct. 1972, S–33658–59. For the consequences, see John Lewis Gaddis, *Strategies of Containment*, 314–16. For his bitter dismay, see Henry Kissinger, *Years of Upheaval*, chap. 7. See also his comment, quoted in Seyom Brown, *The Faces of Power*, 358.

44. Between 1970 and 1982, American food exports to the Soviet Union rose from $76 million to $2.13 billion. The theory behind improving trade with the Soviets was summed up by Kissinger: "Over time, trade and investment may leaven the autarkic tendencies of the Soviet system, invite gradual association of the Soviet economy, and foster a degree of interdependence that adds an element of stability to the political equation." Quoted in John Lewis Gaddis, *Strategies of Containment*, 294. Moderating Soviet behavior through trade proved exceedingly difficult, especially as the issue of trade itself became politicized, Ibid., 313–15.

45. Ibid., chap. 10. For my own contemporary analysis of Kissinger's strategy and its implications for the alliance, see "The Political Economy of Allied Relations: The Limits of Interdependence," in *Retreat from Empire? The First Nixon Administration*, ed. Robert E. Osgood (Baltimore: Johns Hopkins University Press, 1973).

46. Nixon's intention to open relations with China was already clear in his administration's first annual foreign policy statement of 18 Feb. 1970. *Public Papers of the Presidents: Richard M. Nixon 1970* (Washington, D.C.: U.S. Government Printing Office, 1971), 181. See also Henry Kissinger, *Years of Upheaval*, chap. 3.

47. Henry Kissinger's own account of the "Year of Europe" reveals its conceptual flaws and is unintentionally funny about its execution. Henry A. Kissinger, *Years of Upheaval*, chap. 5. For the text of the "Year of Europe" speech, see Kissinger, *American Foreign Policy*, 3d ed., 99–113.

48. For an informative general study of U.S. Middle East policy, see William B. Quandt, *Decade of Decisions: American Policy Toward the Arab-Israeli Conflict, 1967–1976* (Berkeley: University of

California Press, 1977). For his own detailed, absorbing, and highly revealing account, see Henry Kissinger, *The White House Years*, 567–631; and *Years of Upheaval*, chap. 11.

49. See David P. Calleo, "The European Coalition in a Fragmenting World," *Foreign Affairs* 54, no. 1 (Oct. 1975): 98–112.

50. For official French perspectives, see Thierry de Montbrial, "For a New World Economic Order," *Foreign Affairs* 54, no. 1 (Oct. 1975): 61–78.

Chapter 5: The Carter-Reagan Turnaround, 1977–1983

1. For a more detailed breakdown of the growth of U.S. and Soviet strategic arsenals, see chap. 4, n. 13.

2. A good summary of the window-of-vulnerability argument is found in Lawrence Freedman, *Evolution of Nuclear Strategy* (London: Macmillan, 1982), 388. For the Carter administration's concern, see the statement of Harold Brown, secretary of defense, in *Hearings Before the Committee on Foreign Relations, United States Senate, Ninety-sixth Congress, First Session, on the SALT II Treaty, July 9, 1979* (Washington, D.C.: U.S. Government Printing Office, 1979), pt. 1, 348; also Harold Brown, *Thinking About National Security: Defense and Foreign Policy in a Dangerous World* (Boulder, Colo.: Westview Press, 1983), 66–71.

3. Some military experts, including former Joint Chiefs of Staff Chairman Maxwell D. Taylor, argued that other defense requirements were more urgent. See Richard Halloran, "Former Leader of Military Chiefs Unsure Nation Needs MX Missile," *New York Times*, 12 May 1980, p. A16. Other critics argued that sea-basing would be more feasible. See Richard Halloran, "Pentagon Analysts See MX Alternative in Seaborne Missile," *New York Times*, 19 Apr. 1980, p. 1; and Richard Burt, "Brown Admits Aides Distorted MX Issue," *New York Times*, 5 Oct. 1980, p. 15. For environmental and military fears among residents of Utah and Nevada, see Richard Burt, "Two Governors Say Missile Plan Will Hurt State," *New York Times*, 27 Mar. 1980, p. 1; and "Pentagon Favors Curb on Missiles in Utah, Nevada," *New York Times*, 24 May 1980, p. 8.

4. See Seyom Brown, *The Faces of Power: Constancy and Change in United States Foreign Policy from Truman to Reagan* (New York: Columbia University Press, 1983), 541–48.

5. Helmut Schmidt, "The 1977 Alastair Buchan Memorial Lecture," *Survival* 20, no. 1 (January/February 1978): 2–10; also see *Financial Times*, 7 Mar. 1979, 5 June 1979.

6. Michael Mandelbaum, "The Anti-Nuclear Weapons Movements," *PS* 17, no. 1 (Winter 1984): 24–32.

7. The NATO "two-track" decision was taken at the special meeting of NATO foreign and defense ministers on 12 December 1979, and reaffirmed in the ministerial session on 13–14 December 1979. See *Final Communiqué* (Brussels: NATO Press Service, 14 December 1979).

8. See McGeorge Bundy, George Kennan, Robert McNamara, Gerard Smith, "Nuclear Weapons and the Atlantic Alliance," *Foreign Affairs* 60, no. 4 (Spring 1982): 753–68. From 1973 to 1975, as U.S. spending declined 3.8 percent annually, non–U.S. NATO defense spending rose by an annual average of 2.1 percent in real terms, led by France and Germany with 2.7 percent average real increases. Nevertheless, European members of NATO were still spending only 3.7 percent of GNP annually on defense from 1972 to 1976, whereas the United States was spending an average of 6 percent. Figures from *Congressional Record–Senate*, 21 May 1982, S5892–93; and *World Military Expenditures and Arms Transfers 1969–1978* (Washington, D.C.: United States Arms Control and Disarmament Agency, 1980), 32–34, 48–49, 71. From 1972 to 1976, German military manpower increased by 7.8 percent and French by 2 percent; total U.S. active-duty manpower declined by 16.5 percent, but U.S. ground forces stationed in Europe remained roughly constant while naval forces assigned to NATO Europe increased, bringing the total U.S. military presence in Europe up by 17.5 percent. See U.S. Department of Defense, *Annual Report to the Congress 1983*, (Washington, D.C.: U.S. Government Printing Office, 1982), c-5. See also n. 10.

9. For analysis of NATO's Long-Term Development Plan and the "3 percent solution," see Simon Lunn, *Burden-Sharing in NATO*, Chatham House Paper (London: Routledge and Kegan Paul/Royal Institute of International Affairs, 1983), 16–18, 29–32. For a critical appraisal, see David Greenwood, "NATO's 3% Solution," *Survival* 23, no. 1 (November/December 1981): 252–60.

10. See, for instance, *Defense White Paper 1979: The Security of the Federal Republic of Germany and the Development of the Federal Armed Forces* (Bonn: Federal Ministry of Defense, 1979), 149–62; and the French "Loi de la programmation militaire, 1984–1988," *Journal Officiel*, Lois et Decrets, 9 Juillet 1983, 2,114–21.

11. See General Bernard W. Rogers, "Greater Flexibility for NATO's Flexible Response," *Strategic Review* 11, no. 1 (Spring 1983): 11–19; For an analysis, see Boyd D. Sutton et al., "Deep Attack Concepts and the Defence of Central Europe," *Survival* 26, no. 2 (March/April 1984): 50–69. For the proposed "Follow on Force Attack" (FOFA) doctrine, see chap. 9, n. 16 and text.

12. See Thomas A. Callaghan, Jr., "The Unbuilt Street—Defense Industrial Cooperation within the Alliance," *NATO's Fifteen Nations* (October/November 1982), 26; and Keith Hartley, *NATO Arms Cooperation—A Study in Economics and Politics* (London: Allen and Unwin, 1983).

13. For the inside account, see Cyrus Vance, *Hard Choices: Critical Years in America's Foreign Policy* (New York: Simon and Schuster, 1983), 232–55; also Zbigniew Brzezinski, *Power and Principle: Memoirs of the National Security Advisor, 1977–1981* (New York: Farrar, Straus and Giroux, 1983), 437–43.

14. See William B. Quandt, "The Western Alliance in the Middle East," in *The Middle East and the Western Alliance*, ed. Steven L. Spiegel (London: Allen and Unwin, 1982). See also André Fontaine, "Transatlantic Doubts and Dreams," *Foreign Affairs* 59, no. 3 (America and the World 1980): 578–93.

15. For an account of French and Soviet roles in arming Iraq, see Francis Fukuyama, "New Directions for Soviet Middle East Policy in the 1980's: Implications for the Atlantic Alliance," in *The Middle East and the Western Alliance*, 133–36.

16. Jimmy Carter, "Address to the Nation, January 4, 1980," *Department of State Bulletin* 80, no. 2034 (January 1980), special section on Soviet invasion of Afghanistan, p. A.

17. For the Carter Doctrine, see *Department of State Bulletin* 36, no. 2035 (February 1980), special section, p. B. See also Jimmy Carter, *Keeping Faith: Memoirs of a President* (New York: Bantam Books, 1982), 471–83. For the Carter rearmament, see Seyom Brown, *The Faces of Power*, chap. 32.

18. See the Franco-German summit communiqué of February 5, 1980, *Europe: Political Day* (Paris: Agence Internationale d'Information, February 6, 1980). For alliance differences and irritations, see also "The Split in the Western Alliance," *Financial Times*, 2 Feb. 1980; "US Irritated with France over Afghanistan Shifts," *International Herald Tribune*, 11 Feb. 1980; and "US Afghan Policy is Seen Unsettling European Allies," *International Herald Tribune*, 18 Feb. 1980. See too James Reston, "A Talk with Schmidt," *International Herald Tribune*, 8–9 Mar. 1980.

19. "Will Europe Help America Help Europe?" *Economist* 285 (11 December 1982): 62–64.

20. For U.S. policy and the Polish situation, see Dimitri K. Simes, "Clash Over Poland," *Foreign Policy*, no. 46 (Spring 1982): 49–66.

21. See Heinrich Bechtol, "Bonn nach dem Entscheid in der Polen-Krise," *Aussenpolitik* 33, no. 2 (1982): 111–12; and Ernst-Otto Czempiel, "Deutschland-USA: Kooperation und Irritationen," *Aussenpolitik* 33, no. 1 (1982): 19–27.

22. Defense spending in 1984 was 81 percent higher than in 1980, 40 percent in real terms. Defense spending rose from 5.2 to 6.5 percent of GNP and from 23 to 27.1 percent of federal outlays, which also increased from 22.4 to 24.0 percent of GNP.

U.S. Defense Spending (millions of dollars)

	1972	1976	1980	1982	1984
Current dollars	75,006	95,508	142,621	213,751	258,151
1985 dollars	193,170	181,475	192,133	242,230	269,872

Weapons versus Manpower (Percentage of Defense Budget)

	1976	1980	1983	1984	1985 (proposed)
Manpower	26.6	21.7	19.1	18.8	—
Procurement	22.0	24.7	33.6	33.3	35.3

SOURCE: Caspar W. Weinberger, *Annual Report to the Congress, Fiscal Year 1985* (Washington, D.C.: U.S. Government Printing Office, 1984), 279–80.

23. See John F. Lehman, "Rebirth of a U.S. Naval Strategy," *Strategic Review* 9, no. 3 (Summer 1981): 9–15; and *Aircraft Carriers: The Real Choices*, Washington Papers, vol. 6, no. 52 (Washington, D.C.: Center for Strategic and International Studies, 1978), chaps. 2, 3. See also chap. 7, n. 33. Between FY 1980 and FY 1985 spending on the navy increased from $47.2 billion to $102.3 billion, a 61 percent real increase. *Annual Report to the Congress*, 279.

24. For the administration's evolving plans for the MX missile, rechristened "the Peacekeeper," see Caspar W. Weinberger, *Annual Report(s) to the Congress Fiscal Year(s) 1983, 1984, 1985* III: 57–58, 220–21, 186–87, respectively. During 1982, the administration toyed with deploying the missiles in a "dense pack"—so close together that incoming missiles would commit "fratricide" and destroy each other, an option subsequently rejected.

25. See Brent Scowcroft, "Final Report of the President's Commission on Strategic Forces," *Atlantic Community Quarterly* 22, no. 1 (Spring 1984): 14–22. A good summary is found in "A sober look at US strategy," *Financial Times*, 18 Apr. 1983. For the administration's reaction, see Caspar W. Weinberger, *Annual Report to the Congress Fiscal Year 1985*, 186–87. See also Fred Charles Iklé, "The Reagan Defense Program: A Focus on Strategic Imperatives," *Strategic Review* 10, no. 2 (Spring 1982): 11–18.

26. Carter's Presidential Directive 59 (July 1980) contemplated limited, counterforce exchanges. On Carter's strategy, see Lawrence Freedman, *The Evolution of Nuclear Strategy*, 393–94. The first Reagan administration made no formal changes but gave nuclear war-fighting greater emphasis. "National Security Decision Document 13" (Fall 1981) declared, for example, that the U.S. planned to prevail in a nuclear war. Many known "war fighters" were appointed to advisory or official positions. For a critique, see Theodore Draper, "Nuclear Temptations," *New York Review of Books*, 19 Jan. 1984, pp. 42–46; and Robert Scheer, *With Enough Shovels—Reagan, Bush and Nuclear War* (New York: Random House, 1982).

Perhaps the most damaging public statement for European relations came from the president himself, on 16 October 1981, in an interview with out-of-town newspaper editors: "I could see where you could have the exchange of tactical weapons against troops in the field without it bringing either one of the major powers to pushing the button." Richard Halloran, "Weinberger Seeks to Assure Allies on Reagan Remark on Atom War," *New York Times*, 21 Oct. 1981, p. 1.

27. For the difficulties of the two-track decision, see Strobe Talbott, "Buildup and Breakdown," *Foreign Affairs* 62, no. 3 (America and the World 1983): 591–92; and *Deadly Gambits—The Reagan Administration and Stalemate in Nuclear Arms Control* (New York: Knopf, 1984), 47–48.

28. For the causes and consequences of the peace movement in Europe, see Lawrence Freedman, "Limited War, Unlimited Protest"; Morton Halperin, "NATO and the TNF Controversy: Threats to the Alliance"; and William E. Griffith "Bonn and Washington: From Deterioration to Crisis?" *Orbis* 26, no. 1 (Spring 1982): 89–117. For the problem in a generational perspective, see *The Successor Generation: International Perspectives of Postwar Europeans*, ed. Stephen F. Szabo (London: Butterworth, 1983).

29. See Jeffrey Boutwell, "Politics and the Peace Movement in West Germany," *International Security* 7, no. 4 (Spring 1983): 72–92; and Lawrence Whetten, "The West German Left in Opposition," *World Today* (June 1983), 216–23. For an analysis of the 1983 German election, see Rainer Eisfeld, "The West German Elections: Economic Fears and the Deployment Debate," *Government and Opposition* 18, no. 3 (Summer 1983): 291–303.

30. David Richardson, "On the March—U.S. Version of Peace Crusade," *U.S. News and World Report*, 22 Mar. 1982, pp. 24–26; James Wallace, "Nuclear Freeze Crusade: Gaining or Waning?" *U.S. News and World Report*, 25 Apr. 1983, pp. 18–21; and William Isaacson, "A Blast from the Bishops," *Time*, 8 Nov. 1982, pp. 6–8.

31. See n. 8.

32. For the issue of French and British nuclear forces in the INF negotiations, see Strobe Talbott, *Deadly Gambits*, pt. 1, passim; and Pierre Lellouche, "France and the Euromissiles," *Foreign Affairs* 62, no. 2 (Winter 1983/84), 318–34.

33. See the transcript of Reagan's initial SDI speech of 23 March 1983, *New York Times*, 24 Mar. 1983, p. A20. For a critique of the Reagan SDI initiative and its implications for the ABM Treaty, see Sidney D. Drell, Philip J. Farley, and David Holloway, "Preserving the ABM Treaty: A Critique of the Reagan Strategic Defense Initiative," *International Security* 9, no. 2 (Fall 1984):˙57–91. For discussions on the scientific and security issues of SDI, see *Weapons in Space Vol. I: Concepts and Technologies, Daedalus* 114, no. 2 (Spring 1985); and *Weapons in Space Vol II: Implications for Security, Daedalus* 114, no. 3 (Summer 1985).

34. Unlike the United States, Europe is threatened not merely by ICBMs, but also by an extensive array of shorter-range weapons—nuclear-armed bombers, short-range ballistic missiles (the SS-21, SS-22, SS-23), cruise missiles, and even nuclear artillery. The wide array of potential threats, combined with the short flight times to Western European targets makes a leak-proof defense against nuclear weapons impossible. Furthermore, a point-defense system to protect European missiles is viewed as inappropriate because most European targets are "soft," and because Europe's high population density means even an attack against military targets will result in widespread civilian destruction. William J. Broad, "Allies in Europe Are Apprehensive About Benefits of 'Star Wars' Plan," *New York Times*, 13 May 1985, pp. A1, A6. Europe's vulnerability was, of course, shared by the Soviets in respect to an attack for Eurasia. The ostentatious deployment of Soviet missile submarines off the American coastline in 1983 was, presumably, meant to establish a parallel U.S. vulnerability.

35. For Soviet ABM programs, see Sayre Stevens, "The Soviet BMD Program," in *Ballistic Missile Defense*, ed. Ashton B. Carter and David N. Schwartz (Washington, D.C.: Brookings Institution, 1984); and Clarence A. Robinson, Jr., "Soviets Accelerate Missile Defense Efforts," *Aviation Week and Space Technology*, 16 Jan. 1984, 14–16.

36. Early European reaction to both SDI and Eureka was mixed. At a meeting of the Western European Union in April 1985, the defense and foreign ministers of Britain, France, West Germany, Italy, the Netherlands, Belgium, and Luxembourg failed to agree on a joint response to Reagan's proposal to share SDI research. Great Britain was the first European government to reach a formal agreement with the United States, which was supposed to serve as a precedent for the other allies; see "U.S., Britain Agree on SDI Participation," *Washington Post*, 31 Oct. 1985, p. A21. West Germany officially favored cooperation with SDI if no tax money were spent on research, but only with considerable dissension within the CDU/FDP coalition; France rejected official participation in SDI outright but seemed not to reject participation for particular French firms. See "Allies in Europe Are Apprehensive About Benefits of 'Star Wars' Plan," *New York Times*, 13 May 1985, pp. A1, A6.

37. See Richard Pipes, a distinguished historian of the Soviet Union and a Reagan National Security Council member during 1981–82, "Can the Soviet Union Reform?" *Foreign Affairs*, 63, no. 1 (Fall 1984); 47–61. For analyses, see Samuel P. Huntington, "The Defense Policy of the Reagan Administration," and I. M. Destler, "The Evolution of Reagan Foreign Policy," in *The Reagan Presidency— An Early Assessment*, ed. Fred I. Greenstein (Baltimore: Johns Hopkins University Press, 1983). See also Michel A. Tatu, "U.S.–Soviet Relations: A Turning Point," *Foreign Affairs* 61, no. 3 (America and the World 1982): 591–610. For the problems plaguing the Soviet system, see Marshall I. Goldman, *The U.S.S.R. in Crisis* (New York: W. W. Norton, 1983).

38. See David P. Calleo, "SDI, Europe, and the American Strategic Dilemma," in *SDI and U.S. Foreign Policy* (Washington, D.C.: Johns Hopkins Foreign Policy Institute, School of Advanced International Studies, 1987), 101–26. See also Robert E. Osgood, "The Implications of SDI for U.S.– European Relations," Ibid., 60–100.

39. See n. 37.

40. For a historical examination of U.S. energy-related trade with the Soviet Union, see Jan Braathu,

"Unilateralism and Alliance Cohesion: The United States, Western Europe, and the Regulation of Energy-Related Trade with the Soviet Union," *Cooperation and Conflict* 18, no. 1 (March 1983): 21–41. On the rapid growth of lending to the Soviets and Eastern Europe generally, see Jan Vanos, "Convertible Currency Indebtedness of the CMEA Countries, Its Implications, and Outlook for 1983–87," in *External Economic Relations of the CMEA Countries: Their Significance and Impact in a Global Perspective* (Brussels: NATO Economics and Information Directorates, 1983), 243–273. For reactions to, and accounts and analyses of, the actual pipeline deal and dispute, see Thomas Blau and Joseph Kirchheimer, "European Dependence and Soviet Leverage: The Yamal Pipeline," *Survival* 23, no. 5 (September/October 1981): 209–14. See also Charles Maechling, Jr., "Outreaching the Law to Hurt the Allies," *International Herald Tribune*, 31 July–1 Aug. 1982; Wolfgang Wagner, "A Friendly Visit Wasted"; Otto Graf Lambsdorff, "A Family Dispute to Settle Patiently," *International Herald Tribune*, 31 July–1 Aug. 1982; John P. Schutte, Jr., "Pipeline Politics," *SAIS Review*, no. 4 (Summer 1982): 137–48; Tom Blau, "Stricter Controls on U.S. Technology Exports," *Journal of Defense and Diplomacy* 1, no. 4 (July 1983): 17–22, 63; and, in general, *The Economist*, July–September, 1982. For the Reagan administration's case, see Richard N. Perle, "The Strategic Implications of the West-East Technology Transfer," *Adelphi Papers*, no. 190 (London: International Institute for Strategic Studies, 1984), 20–27, "The Eastward Technology Flow: A Plan of Common Action," *Strategic Review* 17, no. 2 (Spring 1984), 24–32; Caspar W. Weinberger, *Annual Report to Congress Fiscal Year 1985*, 177–84.

41. See, for example, James Chace, *Endless War: Why We Are in Central America* (New York: Vintage Books, 1984). Also, Christopher Dickey, "Central America: From Quagmire to Cauldron," *Foreign Affairs* 62, no. 3 (America and the World 1983), 659–94; and "The U.S. and Latin America," *Foreign Affairs* 63, no. 3 (America and the World 1984), 560–80; Richard H. Ullman, "At War with Nicaragua," *Foreign Affairs* 62, no. 1 (Fall 1983), 39–58. For the European reaction, see Stanley Hoffmann, "The U.S. and Western Europe: Wait and Worry," *Foreign Affairs* 63, no. 3 (America and the World 1984), 631–52.

42. See Larry L. Fabian, "The Middle East: War Dangers and Receding Peace Prospects," *Foreign Affairs* 62, no. 3 (America and the World 1983), 632–58; and Dankwart A. Rustow, "Realignments in the Middle East," *Foreign Affairs* 63, no. 3 (America and the World 1984), 581–601.

43. See n. 38.

Chapter 6: The Atlantic Alliance and the World Economy

1.

U.S. Balance of Payments 1950–1982 (in millions of dollars)

	1950[a]	1955[a]	1960[c]	1965[c]	1970[c]	1975[c]	1980[d]	1984[d]
Current Account	−1,943	298	2,824	5,435	2,360	18,445	1,870	−107,360
"Basic Balance"*	−3,432	−1,461	−1,138	−1,923	−3,891	666	−882	−65,560
Balance on Official Settlements	−3,468	−983	−3,406	−1,290	−10,701	−3,022	−7,870	140
Change in Reserves	180[b]	−870[b]	−2,145	−1,222	−2,477	607	8,160	3,140

* Current account plus long-term capital flows

SOURCES:

[a] *Statistics of Balance of Payments 1950–1961* (Paris: Organization for Economic Cooperation and Development, 1964), 16, 18.

[b] *International Financial Statistics Yearbook 1984* (Washington, D.C.: International Monetary Fund, 1984, 594–95.

[c] *Balance of Payments of OECD Countries 1960–1977* (Paris: Organization for Economic Cooperation and Development, 1979), 10–11.

[d] *Balance of Payments of OECD Countries 1965–1984* (Paris: Organization for Economic Cooperation and Development, 1986), 10, 11.

2. (Cambridge, Mass.: Harvard University Press, 1982).

3. For the arrangements, and early disputes over them, see Gerald M. Meier, *Problems of a World Monetary Order* (London: Oxford University Press, 1974), 18–48; and Richard N. Gardner, *Sterling-Dollar Diplomacy in Current Perspective* (New York: Columbia University Press, 1968), 71–100.

4. Alan S. Milward, *The Reconstruction of Western Europe, 1945–1951* (Berkeley: University of California Press, 1984), 17–42, sees the dollar gap resulting less from Europe's needs for recovery than from its heroic effort to restructure for rapid future growth.

5. Jacques Rueff's, "Le problème monétaire international" and "Le déficit de la balance des paiements des États-Unis," in *Oeuvres complètes*, ed. E. M. Claassen and G. Lane, Tome III, vol. 2, *Politique Économique*, (Paris: Plon, 1980), 180–85, 196–225, respectively. De Gaulle's press conference of 4 February 1965, which charged the United States with abusing the international monetary system, is reproduced in English in *Major Addresses, Statements and Press Conferences of General Charles de Gaulle* (New York: French Embassy, Press and Information Division, 1967), 77–86. For the critique of the gold standard by Rueff and others at the Bank of France in the 1920s, see Judith L. Kooker, "French Financial Diplomacy: The Interwar Years," in *Balance of Power or Hegemony: The Interwar Monetary System*, ed. Benjamin M. Rowland (New York: Lehrman Institute/New York University Press, 1976), 83–145. For an analysis of how Rueff's duplicating mechanisms of the gold-exchange standard characterize big private banks as well, see Paul Fabra, *Mutations dans la structure financière après Bretton Woods* (Amsterdam: Fondation Européene de la Culture, 1980).

6. For international monetary events, policies, and perspectives in the 1960s and 1970s, see Susan Strange, "International Monetary Relations," *International Economic Relations of the Western World, 1959–1971*, ed. Andrew Shonfield (London: Oxford University Press/Royal Institute of International Affairs, 1976) vol. 2, 263–99; and Robert Solomon, *The International Monetary System 1945–1981* (New York: Harper and Row, 1982). For my own extended analysis of the dollar's problems throughout the postwar era, see David P. Calleo, *The Imperious Economy* (Cambridge, Mass.: Harvard University Press, 1982).

7.

U.S. 'Imperial Balance' (1960–1970)

	Current Account (Less Travel and Government)*	Long-Term Capital, Government, Travel, Transfer Payments, and Government Long-Term Capital
	(in millions of dollars)	
1960	5,767	−9,983
1961	9,821	−9,671
1962	9,388	−10,008
1963	10,441	−11,271
1964	12,800	−11,727
1965	11,441	−13,064
1966	10,667	−12,726
1967	11,027	−14,630
1968	8,550	−10,399
1969	4,988	−12,189
1970	6,938	−14,299

* Less net of travel and government, including military, trade in goods and services.
SOURCES: For 1960–1961, *I.M.F. Balance of Payments Yearbook*, vol. 16 (Washington, D.C.: International Monetary Fund, 1965), United States section, 5. For 1962–1963, *I.M.F. Balance of Payments Yearbook*, vol. 19 (1968), 1. For 1964–1968, *I.M.F. Balance of Payments Yearbook*, vol. 21 (1970), 1. For 1969–1970, *I.M.F. Balance of Payments Yearbook*, vol. 26 (1975), 1.

8. For the monetarist model, see William M. Corden, *Inflation, Exchange Rates and the World Economy* (Chicago: University of Chicago Press, 1977), 7–19.

9. For a broad account of the decline of the dollar and its impact on short-term capital markets and the Eurodollar market, see Susan Strange, "International Monetary Relations." See also Robert Solomon, *The International Monetary System*; and Harold van Buren Cleveland, "How the Dollar Standard Died," *Foreign Policy* 5 (Winter 1971–72): 41–51.

10. There was also the analysis based on the postwar need for international liquidity, impossible to meet under postwar arrangements without a degree of American credit creation incompatible with monetary stability. See Robert Triffin, *Gold and the Dollar Crisis* (New Haven: Yale University Press, 1960), and *The World Money Maze* (New Haven: Yale University Press, 1966). For my more extended discussion of these analyses, see David P. Calleo, *The Imperious Economy*, chaps. 3–6.

11.

U.S. Federal Budget Deficit (in billions of dollars)

Year	Level	Year	Level	Year	Level	Year	Level	Year	Level
1961	−3.4	1966	−3.8	1971	−23.0	1976	−73.7	1981	−78.9
1962	−7.1	1967	−8.7	1972	−23.4	1977	−53.6	1982	−134.2
1963	−4.8	1968	−25.2	1973	−14.8	1978	−59.2	1983	−230.8
1964	−5.9	1969	+3.2	1974	−6.1	1979	−40.2	1984	−185.3
1965	−1.6	1970	−2.8	1975	−53.2	1980	−73.8	1985	−212.3
								1986, est.	−202.8

SOURCE: For 1961–1973, *Statistical Abstract of the United States: 1984* (Washington, D.C.: U.S. Department of Commerce, 1983), table 498, 315. For 1974–1986, *Statistical Abstract of the United States: 1987* (1987), table 479, p. 292.

12.

Federal Budget Outlays, by Function: 1970–1985
(percentage distribution)

	1970	1975	1980	1985
National Defense	41.8	26.0	22.7	26.5
Social Security and Medicare	18.7	23.3	25.5	26.8
Income Security	8.0	15.1	14.6	13.3
Health	3.0	3.9	3.9	3.5
Veterans Benefits and Services	4.4	4.8	5.4	2.8
Education, Training, and Employment	4.4	4.8	5.4	3.2
Commerce and Housing Credit	1.1	3.0	1.6	1.0
Transportation	3.6	3.3	3.6	2.8
Natural Resources and Environment	1.6	2.2	2.4	1.4
Energy	0.5	0.9	1.7	0.6
Agriculture	2.7	0.9	1.5	2.1
International Affairs	2.2	2.1	2.1	2.0
Net Interest	7.4	7.0	8.9	13.6
Other	—	4.6	4.4	1.7

SOURCE: *Statistical Abstract of the United States: 1986* (Washington, D.C.: 1985), table 493, pp. 306–7.

*Total Government Revenue as a Percentage
of GDP*[a]

1955	1960	1965	1970	1975	1980	1983
32.6	26.6	26.5	30.1	30.2	30.7	35.7

*Federal Revenue as a Percentage of
Total Taxes*[b]

1955	1979	1983
63.0	44.0	57.4

SOURCES: [a]*Long-Term Trends in Tax Revenues*
(Paris: Organization for Economic Cooperation and
Development, 1981), table 1, p. 11.
[b] Ibid., table 11, p. 21.
Except 1983: *Statistical Abstract of the United States:
1986*, table 540, p. 331.

Defense Spending in Constant (1972) Dollars: 1960–1985

	Outlays (billions)	Percentage of Total Federal Outlays
1960	78.4	52.2
1965	74.1	42.8
1970	94.0	41.8
1975	69.2	26.0
1980	71.3	22.7
1985	96.8	26.5

SOURCE: *Statistical Abstract of the United States: 1986*, table 540, p. 331.

Since 1955 total taxes have increased their share of GDP, but the proportion to federal general revenue has declined sharply with the slack taken up mostly by increased state and local taxes (up from 26 to 30 percent of total taxes) and increased contributions to social security (from 11 to 25 percent). Defense outlays as a proportion of total federal budget outlays were cut roughly in half, most sharply in the 1970s.

13. On economic policy under Eisenhower, see Herbert Stein, *The Fiscal Revolution in America* (Chicago: University of Chicago Press, 1969), 281–308; for the New Deal under Roosevelt, Ibid., 55–130; for the influence of Keynesian theory, Ibid., 131–68.

14. On Kennedy's initiation into the "New Economics," see Seymour E. Harris, *Economics of the Kennedy Years* (New York: Harper and Row, 1964), 55–77; for the fiscal policies of the Kennedy and Johnson administrations and the tax cut of 1964, see Herbert Stein, *The Fiscal Revolution in America*, chaps. 15, 16; for evaluations, see James Tobin, *The New Economics One Decade Older* (Princeton: Princeton University Press, 1979), 1–39; or David P. Calleo, *The Imperious Economy*, 9–24.

15. For the slump of 1969–70, see *Economic Report of the President* (Washington, D.C.: U.S. Government Printing Office, 1970), 21–71.

16. For Nixon's success in manipulating the economy to his own electoral advantage and his post-election policies, see Otto Eckstein, *The Great Recession* (Amsterdam: North Holland, 1978), 39–60.

17. For my more extended analysis of the Nixon revolution, see David P. Calleo, *The Imperious Economy*, chaps. 4–6.

18. See the "Peterson Report," *The United States in the Changing World Economy*, vol. 1 (Washington, D.C.: U.S. Government Printing Office, 1971).

19. Many American monetarists, notably Milton Friedman, preferred floating rates. A free market for money would constantly adjust exchange rates without the violent extreme disruptions characteristic of changes in a fixed-rate system. See Milton Friedman's testimony before the Joint Economic Committee of the 88th Congress, cited in G. M. Maier, *Problems of a World Economic Order*, 236–42. See also Harry G. Johnson, "The Case for Flexible Exchange Rates," *Federal Reserve Bank of St. Louis Review* 51, no. 6 (June 1969): 12–24; and Gottfried Haberler and Thomas D. Willek, *A Strategy for U.S. Balance of Payments Policy* (Washington, D.C.: American Enterprise Institute, 1971), 7–16.

20. For the theory of "free riders," see Charles P. Kindleberger, *The World in Depression, 1929–1939* (Los Angeles: University of California Press, 1973), 301–8; also his essay, "Systems of International Economic Organization," in *Money and the Coming World Order*, ed. David P. Calleo (New York: New York University Press/Lehrman Institute), 15–39.

21. "Remarks of the Honorable John B. Connally, Secretary of the Treasury, at the International Banking Conference of the American Bankers Association, Munich, Germany," *Department of the Treasury News* (Washington, D.C.: U.S. Government Printing Office, 28 May 1971). The link was plausible, as the comparison of the "basic balance" and net military transaction figures from 1960–70 suggests. See U.S. Department of Commerce, *Survey of Current Business, June 1971*, (Washington, D.C.: U.S. Government Printing Office, 1971), table 1.

22. For relative contributions to allied defense, see the tables in chaps. 7 and 9.

23.

Federal Budget Outlays 1970–1975
(in billions of constant (1972) dollars)

	Total	Defense	Nondefense	Deficit
1970	220.2	90.1	130.1	−2.8
1972	230.7	76.6	154.1	−23.4
1973	233.3	70.0	163.3	−14.8
1974	236.9	68.4	168.5	−4.7
1975	260.2	68.7	191.5	−45.2

SOURCE: *Statistical Abstract of the United States 1984*, tables 498, 505; pp. 315, 319.

24. For my analysis of European grievances, see *The Imperious Economy*, chaps. 4–6.

25. See Harold van Buren Cleveland and W. H. Bruce Brittain, *The Great Inflation: A Monetarist View* (Washington, D.C.: National Planning Association, 1976), 26 ff.

26. For the shocks on the United States, see Otto Eckstein, *The Great Recession*, 61–65; for a longer-range view, see W. W. Rostow, *The World Economy: History & Prospect* (Austin: University of Texas Press, 1982), 591–609. See also John M. Blair, *The Control of Oil* (New York: Pantheon, 1976), 261–75.

27. See Otto Eckstein, *The Great Recession*, 1–4. For monthly figures of changes in consumer price indexes over the period 1973–74, see *Economic Report of the President 1975*.

28. W. W. Rostow, *The World Economy*, 635–43.

29. See John M. Blair, *The Control of Oil*, 169–204. For an international comparison of retail oil prices and of taxes as a percentage of the total retail price of oil, see *Economist*, (1 March 1980), 73. For my argument in more detail, see *The Imperious Economy*, 110–47.

30. See Robert N. Dunn, Jr., "Exchange Rates, Payments Adjustment, and OPEC: Why Oil Deficits Persist," *Princeton Essays in International Finance*, no. 137 (September 1979); also U.S. Senate Committee on Foreign Relations, Subcommittee on International Economic Policy, *International Debt*,

The Banks and U.S. Foreign Policy (Washington, D.C.: U.S. Government Printing Office, 1977); and Paul Volcker, "The Recycling Problem Revisited," *Challenge* (July/August 1980), 3–14.

31. See Richard S. Weinert, "International Finance: Banks and Bankruptcy," *Foreign Policy* no. 50 (Spring 1983) 138–49; also William R. Cline, *International Debt: Systemic Risk and Policy Response* (Cambridge, Mass.: M.I.T. Press/Institute for International Economics, 1984).

32. For the erosion of the 1973 OPEC price hike, as well as the 1979 hike that reversed virtually all the real price decline post 1974, see *OECD Economic Outlook* (Paris: Organization for Economic Cooperation and Development, July 1979) 56–65.

33. For a defense of the locomotive theory, see *Towards Full Employment and Price Stability*, ed. Paul McCracken (Paris: Organization for Economic Cooperation and Development, 1977), 179–88. For an American critique, see Geoffrey E. Wood and Nancy Ammon Jianakoplos, "Coordinated International Expansion: Are Convoys or Locomotives the Answer?," *Federal Reserve Bank of St. Louis Review* 60, no. 7 (July 1978): 11–19.

34. For pressures on OPEC for a price rise, see "OPEC Debt on the Rise," *Economist* (7 October 1978), 100. For the effects of Iranian events and Saudi production cuts, see "Not Over a Barrel," *Economist* (6 June 1979), 50; and "The Oil Price Outlook's Bad—and a Saudi Decision did It," *Economist* (26 May 1979), 101–2. For the explosion of oil prices on the spot market and OPEC's subsequent stabilization at $30 a barrel, see "OPEC's Expensive Game of Leapfrog," *Economist* (3 November 1979), 57–58; and "$30 Oil," *Economist* (22 December 1979), 7–8.

35. Expenditures for strategic forces between fiscal 1977 and 1980 increased from $9.4 billion to $10.8 billion, while expenditures for General Purpose Forces jumped from $40.2 billion to $50 billion (current dollars). *Department of Defense Annual Reports, FY 1977* (Washington, D.C.: U.S. Department of Defense, 1976), A13; and *FY 1980* (Washington, D.C.: U.S. Department of Defense, 1979), 320. Overall U.S. defense expenditures relative to budget deficits for the period 1975–81 (in millions of dollars) were:

Year	Defense Expenditure	Budget Deficit
1975	85,552	−45,154
1976	89,430	−66,413
Transition Quarter	22,307	−12,956
1977	97,501	−44,948
1978	105,186	−48,807
1979	117,681	−27,694
1980	135,856	−59,563
1981	161,088	−55,215

SOURCE: *Economic Report of the President 1981*, 314–15.

36.

Federal Republic of Germany

	1974	1975	1976	1977	1978	1979
Government Deficit (billions of DM)	−10.11	−34.04	−30.16	−22.24	−25.61	−26.13
Deficit as % of GDP (1980 prices)	0.8	2.7	2.3	1.6	1.8	1.8
GNP Deflator (Increase from last period)	5.0	4.7	2.8	3.1	3.7	3.7

SOURCE: *International Financial Statistics Yearbook 1984* (Washington, D.C.: International Monetary Fund, 1984), 289.

37. See Paul Volcker, "Statements to Congress on October 17, 1979," *Federal Reserve Bulletin* 65, no. 11 (November 1979): 888–89; and *Economic Report of the President, 1980*, 54–55.

38. On the recession of 1980–82 and the administration's policy for recovery, see *Economic Report of the President, 1983*, 17–28.

39. See *Debt and the Developing World* (Washington, D.C.: IBRD, 1984).

40. Analysts at the Federal Reserve Bank of St. Louis reckoned that, had the pace of rearmament stayed at Carter's level, the rising trend in federal revenue would have permitted Reagan's tax cuts without serious deficits. Keith M. Carlson, "Trends in Federal Revenues 1955–86," *Federal Reserve Bank of St. Louis Review* 63, no. 5 (May 1981): 31–39.

41. For the administration's proposals and rationalizations of the ensuing deficits, see *The United States Budget in Brief: Fiscal Year 1982 and Fiscal Year 1983* (Washington, D.C.: Executive Office of the President/Office of Management and Budget, 1981 and 1982). Fiscal 1983 had a $207.8 billion shortfall, and by the Fiscal 1984 budget, the administration was admitting a "structural" fiscal deficit. *U.S. Budget in Brief: Fiscal Year 1984*, 18. Interviews with Office of Management and Budget Director David Stockman, plus various leaks, suggested that the deficits were actually a conscious strategy to reshape the U.S. fiscal profile by forcing drastic civilian cuts. Stockman faults Reagan for lacking the revolutionary courage to cut civilian entitlements. See William Greider, "The Education of David Stockman," *Atlantic Monthly* (December 1981), 27–40. For his own remarkable account of how the administration miscalculated and refused to face the consequences, see David A. Stockman, *The Triumph of Politics: Why the Reagan Revolution Failed* (New York: Harper and Row, 1986). Chap. 12 captures the essence of the story. The analytical Epilogue blames the welfare state, although Stockman severely criticizes the defense budget throughout. See, for example, 282–99.

42. See *Grace Commission Final Report and Summary Report* (Washington, D.C.: U.S. Government Printing Office, 1984). The administration estimated "quantifiable one-time cost savings of over 3 billion dollars and recurring annual savings of nearly 2 billion dollars," from deregulation. *The U.S. Budget in Brief: Fiscal Year 1983*, 5. For details, see *Economic Report of the President* (Washington, D.C.: U.S. Government Printing Office, 1982), 134–66.

43. For a critique of the Reagan model, see Robert L. Heilbroner, "The Demand for the Supply-Side," *New York Review of Books* (11 June 1981), 37–41. For a critique of the "equilibrium price-auction view of the world" on which it is based, see Lester C. Thurow, *Dangerous Currents: The State of Economics* (New York: Random House, 1983), 124–41. For my own early analysis, see *The Imperious Economy*, chap. 9.

44. It was not without irony that the country's most illustrious conservative economists had made their reputations by pointing out the fallacies of neo-Keynesian growth policies. Keynes himself might well have disowned some of his postwar offspring. He had, after all, promoted deficit financing under quite different circumstances—to nudge the stagnant economies of the 1930s out of their deep depression. After the war, the Keynesian formula had often been used for a different end—to legitimate expansive macroeconomic policies in chronically overheated economies. Normally these included not only fiscal deficits but also monetary accommodation: hence, the seemingly inexorable postwar tendency toward inflation. For postwar politicians and economists, inflation seemed the easiest way not only to ensure full employment but also to reconcile ambitious policies with inadequate revenues. Economists believed they had found a "Phillips Curve," which demonstrated how a little inflation could be traded for a higher rate of employment and growth. And thanks to "bracket creep" and continually depreciating debt, inflation levied by stealth the taxes that democratic legislatures, at home and abroad, could not be persuaded to lay on directly. So long as the public's imagination failed to grasp how much the value of money was depreciating, "money illusion" continued to deceive both labor and capital in what hard-pressed governments could easily convince themselves was in the general interest. Conservative monetarists argued that money illusion could not persist in keeping unemployment below its "natural rate," and that inflation would naturally grow ever-more extreme.

Money illusion is said to exist when economic behavior is guided by nominal values of money unadjusted for changing prices. See Charles P. Kindleberger, "Money Illusion and Foreign Exchange," in *Leading Issues in International Economic Policy*, ed. C. Fred Bergsten and William G. Tyler (Lexington, Massachusetts: Lexington Press, 1973), 51–63. For the link with the Phillips Curve, see Milton Friedman, "The Role of Monetary Policy," *American Economic Review*, no. 1 (1968). For my own discussion, see *The Imperious Economy*, 35–44.

45.

U.S. Economy 1979–1984

	1978	1979	1980	1981	1982	1983	1984
GNP (billions of dollars)	2,164	2,418	2,632	2,958	3,069	3,305	3,363
Annual Percentage Change[a]	12.8	11.7	8.8	12.4	3.8	7.7	10.8
Implicit Price Deflator[b]	150.4	163.4	178.4	195.6	207.4	215.3	223.4
GNP (constant dollars)[b]	1,439	1,479	1,475	1,512	1,480	1,535	1,639
Annual Percentage Real Change[a]	5.0	2.8	−0.3	2.5	−2.1	3.7	6.8
Money Stock Growth[a]							
M1	8.3	7.2	6.7	6.5	8.8	9.8	5.9
M2	8.0	17.4	—	10.0	8.9	12.0	8.4
M3	11.8	9.6	10.3	12.4	9.4	10.4	10.8
L	12.1	10.8	9.9	11.7	9.9	11.2	11.5
Unemployment[c]	6.1	5.8	7.1	7.6	9.7	9.6	7.5

[a] Percentage change from preceding period.
[b] Based on 1972 dollars, price deflator—1972 = 100.
[c] Percentage of total work force. Average for year.
SOURCE: *Statistical Abstract of the United States: 1986*, tables 719, 850, 684; pp. 432, 504, 406.

46.

Decrease in Expected US Inflation Rates and Increases in Real Interest Rates, 1980–1983

	1980 average	November 1983
Long-term Government bond rate	11.39	11.92
1-year inflation[a]	13.54	3.19
Real interest rate 1	−2.16	8.73
3-year distributed lag inflation[b]	11.67	4.90
Real interest rate 2	−0.28	7.02

[a] Change in the consumer price index (CPI) over the preceding 12 months.
[b] Weights beginning with the immediately preceding 12-month change in the CPI are .5, .3, and .2.
SOURCE: *Economic Report of the President 1984*, 52.

47. The president's Council of Economic Advisers held the higher U.S. real interest rates between 1980 and 1983 simply as typical of monetary disinflation, characteristic also of other countries but, in the present situation, having a disproportional effect on dollar assets. Ibid., 52–53.

Volcker's explanation focused on the fiscal and trade deficits; see his congressional statements reprinted in *Federal Reserve Bulletin* 71 (April 1985): 204–24; 72 (June 1986): 398–403.

48. See, for example, Samuel Brittan, "A Very Painful World Adjustment," *Foreign Affairs* 61, no. 3 (America and the World 1982): 541–68.

49.

Money Stock Measures
(percentage change from previous period)

	M1	M2	M3	L
1970	5.2	—	7.1	6.8
1971	6.4	—	11.3	13.3
1972	9.0	—	11.2	13.7
1973	5.5	7.0	11.2	11.7
1974	4.3	5.6	8.5	9.3
1975	6.0	10.3	11.6	10.9
1976	6.6	13.7	11.9	10.8
1977	8.1	10.6	12.3	12.4
1978	8.3	8.0	11.8	12.1
1979	7.2	17.4	9.6	10.8
1980	6.7	—	10.3	9.9
1981	6.5	10.0	12.4	11.7
1982	8.8	8.9	9.4	9.9
1983	9.8	12.0	10.4	11.2
1984	5.9	8.4	10.8	11.5

SOURCE: For 1970–1972, *Statistical Abstract of the United States: 1977*, table 856, p. 533. For 1973–1974, *Statistical Abstract of the United States: 1980*, table 902, p. 543. For 1975–1984, *Statistical Abstract of the United States: 1986*, table 850, p. 504.

50. The administration predicted the most robust economic recovery in more than a decade, with real GNP growth of 4.9 percent in 1984, 4.6 percent in 1985, and 4.3 percent in both 1986 and 1987. See *U.S. Budget in Brief: FY 1983*, 20. The 1984 target was far exceeded, with real growth at 6.8 percent, the highest since 1955. The outsized federal deficit continued, however, with federal debt growing at an unprecedented rate:

U.S. Federal Deficit and Debt, 1980–1984 *(billions of dollars)*

	1980	1981	1982	1983	1984
Total Deficit	−73.8	−78.9	−127.9	−207.8	−185.3
Outstanding Gross Federal Debt	−914.3	−1,003.9	−1,147.0	−1,381.9	−1,576.7

SOURCE: *Economic Report of the President 1985*, 317. For a comparison of the 1983 recovery with a "typical" postwar recovery, see *Economic Report of the President 1985*, 177.

51.

U.S. Trade Balance (billions of dollars)

1980	−25.5
1981	−28.1
1982	−36.7
1983	−67.6
1984	−114.3
First 3 Quarters of 1985	−86.6

SOURCE: *Balance of Payments Statistics* 37, no. 2, p. 24.

52.

Net Capital Flows to U.S. (billions of dollars)

1980	−35.9
1981	−27.1
1982	−23.0
1983	25.7
1984	76.7
First 3 Quarters of 1985	60.8

SOURCE: *Balance of Payments Statistics* 37, no. 2, p. 24.

Multilateral Trade-Weighted Value of the Dollar (March 1973 = 100)

	Nominal	Real
1970	121.1	—
1971	117.8	—
1972	109.1	—
1973	99.1	98.8
1974	101.4	99.2
1975	98.5	93.9
1976	105.6	97.3
1977	103.3	93.1
1978	92.4	84.2
1979	88.1	83.2
1980	87.4	84.8
1981	102.9	100.8
1982	116.6	111.7
1983	125.3	117.3
1984	138.2	128.7

SOURCE: *Economic Report of the President 1985*, 345, 351.

53. Irving Kristol, "The Old World Needs a New Ideology," *Wall Street Journal* (1 Apr. 1985), p. 22.

54. Europe's recovery from the deep recession of the early 1980s was impeded by fear of an inflationary currency depreciation in the face of Reagan's strong dollar and widening budget deficits brought on by record unemployment. In December 1984, the OECD projected only very modest European GNP growth—perhaps up to 2.5 percent per annum. See *OECD Economic Outlook* (Paris: Organization for Economic Cooperation and Development, December 1984), 18. The projections assumed stable exchange rates and international oil prices. As the dollar began to fall significantly by mid-1985 and OPEC's divisions presaged a significant decline in oil prices, European policy had more elbow room; nevertheless, recovery remained modest, and unemployment very high. *OECD Economic Outlook: July 1985*.

55. *Debt and the Developing World: Current Trends and Prospects* (Washington, D.C.: World Bank, 1984), vii–xiii, 2–5. For rescheduling agreements with international banks, see *IMF Annual Report 1984* (Washington, D.C.: International Monetary Fund, 1984), 91–92; and *The World Bank Annual Report 1984* (Washington, D.C.: World Bank, 1984), 37–42.

56. For particularly prescient foreign analysis, see Kurt Richebächer, *Currency and Credit Markets*, no. 135 (Zurich: Utilitas Verlag Für Währungen und Kreditmärkte, June 1984).

57. See, for example, Anatole Kaletsky, "The Outlook for the Dollar: Prepare for a Crash Landing," *Financial Times*, 6 June 1985. For further analysis of "soft" vs. "hard" landings, see Stephen Marris, "The Dollar Problem," *Statement before the Subcommittee on Domestic Monetary Policy of the Committee on Banking, Finance and Urban Affairs, U.S. Congress, House of Representatives, Ninety-eighth Congress, August 9, 1984* (Washington, D.C.: U.S. Government Printing Office, 1984); and his *Deficits and the Dollar: The World Economy at Risk* (Washington, D.C.: Institute for International Economics, 1985). From March 1985 to March 1986, the dollar had depreciated 31 percent against the DM and the Yen, falling even more sharply against the latter in subsequent months.

58. See the analysis of the post-1973 European deceleration by Andrea Boltho, "Growth," in *The European Economy: Growth and Crisis*, ed. Andrea Boltho (Oxford: Oxford University Press, 1982), particularly 20–28. For a sober look at long-range prospects, see also *Europe's Stagflation*, ed. Michael Emerson (Oxford: Clarendon Press/Centre for European Policy Studies, 1984).

59. The following charts help illustrate major elements of the European economic situation since 1975:

Gross Fixed Capital Formation
(percentage of GNP)

	1975	1976	1977	1978	1979	1980	1981	1982	1983	1984	1985
U.S.	17.0	17.1	18.3	19.5	19.8	18.5	17.8	16.5	16.8	18.1	18.6
W. Germany	20.4	20.2	20.3	20.8	21.9	22.8	21.9	20.7	20.8	20.2	19.5
France	23.3	23.3	22.3	21.4	21.5	21.9	21.4	20.5	19.6	19.0	18.9
Britain	20.1	19.5	18.6	18.6	18.8	18.1	16.5	16.6	16.5	17.4	17.2
Italy	20.6	20.0	19.6	18.7	18.8	19.8	20.2	19.0	18.0	18.2	18.2

SOURCE: (1975–1983) *OECD Economic Outlook*, June 1985, 158; (1984–1985) *OECD Economic Outlook*, December 1986, 158.

Gross Saving
(percentage of GNP)

	1975	1976	1977	1978	1979	1980	1981	1982	1983	1984	1985
U.S.	17.4	17.9	18.9	20.2	20.3	18.3	19.0	15.9	15.2	17.4	16.5
W. Germany	20.8	22.2	21.8	22.8	23.0	22.3	20.7	20.9	21.8	21.5	22.2

Gross Saving (continued)
(percentage of GNP)

	1975	1976	1977	1978	1979	1980	1981	1982	1983	1984	1985
France	23.0	23.0	22.7	22.6	22.8	22.2	19.8	18.6	18.6	18.5	18.0
Britain	15.9	16.2	19.7	19.8	20.2	18.5	17.5	18.6	18.1	18.5	19.2
Italy	20.1	22.1	22.6	22.4	23.0	22.5	19.0	18.5	17.5	18.1	17.7

SOURCE: (1975–1983) OECD *Economic Outlook*, June 1985, 159; (1984–1985) OECD *Economic Outlook*, December 1986, 159.

Productivity (GDP/Employment)
(percentage change from previous period)

	1975	1976	1977	1978	1979	1980	1981	1982	1983	1984	1985
U.S.	−0.5	2.7	1.3	0.1	−0.4	−0.6	1.4	−1.3	2.4	2.2	0.7
W. Germany	0.1	6.7	2.7	3.3	3.1	0.9	0.6	0.7	3.1	2.9	1.7
France	1.2	4.4	2.4	3.0	3.3	0.9	1.0	1.8	1.5	2.6	1.5
Britain	−1.2	2.8	0.6	2.3	0.8	0.2	2.0	4.1	3.6	1.1	2.2
Italy	−4.0	5.0	1.0	2.1	3.8	3.1	−0.3	0.0	−1.3	2.5	1.8

SOURCE: OECD *Economic Outlook*: July 1977, 33; July 1978, 14; July 1979, 26; July 1980, 22; July 1981, 23; December 1984, 50, December 1986, 127.

Growth of Real GNP/GDP
(percentage changes from previous half-year)

	1981		1982		1983		1984		1985
	I	II	I	II	I	II	I	II	I
U.S.	5.7	−0.1	−3.9	−0.5	4.1	7.2	8.3	3.6	1.7
W. Germany	0.3	1.1	−2.2	0.6	2.1	2.6	2.4	3.5	−0.2
France	−0.2	3.2	1.1	0.8	0.6	0.8	2.0	1.7	0.0
Britain	−1.9	−0.3	2.6	1.3	4.8	2.8	1.4	1.6	4.7
Italy	2.9	−1.7	1.7	−3.7	−0.1	2.4	2.8	2.2	1.9

SOURCE: OECD *Economic Outlook*, July 1985, 173.

Unemployment
(percentage of total labor force)

	1981	1982	1983	1984	1985
U.S.	7.5	9.5	9.5	7.4	7.1
W. Germany	4.4	6.1	8.0	8.5	8.6
France	7.3	8.1	8.3	9.7	10.1
Britain	9.9	11.4	12.6	13.0	13.0
Italy	8.3	9.0	9.8	10.2	10.5

SOURCE: OECD *Economic Outlook*, July 1985, 183; December 1986, 167.

The 1984 German unemployment rate was comparable to 1935–36, the British to 1936–37. See B. R. Mitchell, *European Historical Statistics 1750–1975*, 2d rev. ed. (New York: Facts on File, 1981), 178–79.

60. See Lawrence A. Fox and Stephen Cooney, "Protectionism Returns," *Foreign Policy*, no. 53 (Winter 1983/84), 74–90.

61. U.S. trade with the Pacific rim surpassed trade with the European Community by 1975, and with Western Europe as a whole by 1981:

	1975	1980	1981	1982	1983
Total trade with EC*	40.1	91.0	94.0	90.4	88.2
Percentage of total U.S. trade	19.6	19.5	19.0	19.8	19.2
Total trade with Western Europe*	50.8	114.1	116.3	112.4	109.9
Percentage of total U.S. trade	24.9	24.5	23.5	24.6	24.0
Total trade with East Asia, South Asia, and Oceania*	45.2	113.4	126.7	125.8	137.8
Percentage of total U.S. trade	22.1	24.3	25.6	27.6	30.1
Total trade with Japan*	21.0	51.5	59.4	58.7	63.1
Percentage of total U.S. trade	10.2	11.1	12.0	12.9	13.8

* Trade figures in billions of dollars.
SOURCE: Calculated from data in *Statistical Abstract of the United States 1985*, 816–17.

U.S. Agricultural Trade with the European Community 1983 (in millions of dollars)

	Imports	Exports
Live animals chiefly for food	292.0	128.2
Meat and meat preparations	292.0	207.5
Dairy products	212.1	22.1
Seafood	187.4	186.1
Cereals and cereal preparations	96.7	1,093.1
Vegetables and fruit	178.0	497.1
Sugar and sugar preparations	90.2	17.8
Coffee, tea, spices, etc.	219.2	13.4
Animal feeds	18.9	1,849.4
Miscellaneous edible products and preparations	30.6	49.6
Total food and live animals	1,617.1	4,064.3

SOURCE: *Foreign Trade by Commodities* (Paris: Organization for Economic Cooperation and Development, 1985), 94–116.

62. David Watt cites the Gallup poll of February 1983, according to which 70 percent of the British people lacked any confidence in the judgment of the American administration. "The Conduct of American Foreign Policy As a European Saw It," *Foreign Affairs* 62, no. 3 (America and the World 1983): 521–33.

Chapter 7: America's Budgetary Dilemma: Fiscal Deficits and Geopolitical Strategies

1. See *The United States Budget in Brief FY 1986* (Washington, D.C.: Executive Office of the President/Office of Management and Budget, 1985), 79. More optimistic assumptions have reduced official projections for the FY 1989 deficit from $193 billion in FY 1983 to a mere $107 billion in FY 1986. With the economy apparently slowing and congressional action uncertain, official optimism may well prove unfounded.

The actual magnitude and significance of U.S. fiscal deficits is far from clear. Some expenditures are obviously productive capital investments. Off-budget spending and loan guarantees tend to understate actual outlays and obligations. The practice of regarding the social security "surpluses" as income to offset other current expenditures now distorts historical comparisons. For international comparisons, U.S. federal deficits are generally combined with state and local government balances, usually in surplus. This practice reduces the U.S. fiscal deficit for government at all levels, the obvious standard for international comparisons, but may understate the impact of U.S. deficits on policy. Since macroeconomic policy is made in Washington and not in the state capitals, federal financing requirements have greater impact on monetary policy than state surpluses. For general discussions of the significance of fiscal deficits, see Robert L. Heilbroner, "Economic Prospects," *New Yorker*, 29 Aug. 1983, 66–74. For the growth and impact of fiscal deficits since the New Deal, see Herbert Stein, *The Fiscal Revolution in America* (Chicago: University of Chicago Press, 1969), 74–90. See also Peter G. Peterson, "Social Security: The Coming Crash," *New York Review of Books*, 2 Dec. 1982, 34–38.

2. *The United States Budget in Brief, FY 1984* (Washington, D.C.: Executive Office of the President/Office of Management and Budget, 1983), 18.

3.

Comparative per Capita GNP
(in constant 1981 dollars)

	1975	1980	1982
U.S.	11,290	12,661	12,482
France	9,181	10,637	10,532
W. Germany	9,321	11,148	11,032

SOURCE: *Statistical Abstract of the United States 1985* (Washington, D.C.: U.S. Bureau of the Census, December 1984), 846.

4.

Overall Government Deficits (1982–1985) and Accumulated Debt (1984)
(as a percentage of GNP/GDP)

	Deficit[a]				Debt[b]
	1982	1983	1984	1985	1984
U.S.	3.8	4.1	3.4	3.7	49.7
of which: Federal[c]	4.2	6.4	5.6	5.0	
France	2.7	3.1	2.8	3.2	28.3
W. Germany	3.4	2.8	2.3	1.5	42.3

SOURCES:
[a] *OECD Economic Outlook* (Paris: Organization for Economic Cooperation and Development, June 1985), 3.
[b] *OECD Economic Outlook* (Paris: Organization for Economic Cooperation and Development, December 1983), 43.
[c] *Budget of the U.S. Government FY 1985* (Washington, D.C.: U.S. Government Printing Office, 1984), 9–60, table 24.

As the table makes clear, U.S. overall deficits were proportionately larger in 1982 and 1983, though rivaled by the Germans in 1982 and by the French in 1984 and 1985. By 1984, however, the United States was in sharp recovery while France was in a deep slump. In the United States, moreover, the federal deficit is much higher than the overall deficit and far more significant for macroeconomic policy.

5. Interestingly, if the income comparisons are made excluding social security contributions, the proportions of GDP are much more nearly equal. In 1980 they were: U.S. 22.6 percent, France (1979) 23.6 percent and Germany 24.5 percent. See *OECD Studies in Taxation: Long-Term Trends in Tax Revenues of OECD Member Countries, 1955–1980* (Paris: Organization of Economic Cooperation and Development, 1981), 13, 35. Also of interest is the percentage of revenues to central, state, and local governments and to social security, particularly in the two federally constituted countries. In 1980:

	Central	State and Local (in percentages)	Social Security Funds
U.S.	44	30	25
W. Germany	32	32	34
France (1979)	n.a.	n.a.	42.8

SOURCE: Ibid., 21, 35.

6. Between 1977 and 1982 twenty-five states adopted measures restricting either state or local government revenues and expenditures. The most famous local revolt, California's Proposition 13 (approved in June 1978), protested the resumption of higher state and local tax burdens after an exceptional period, following 1972, of federal revenue sharing with the states. See Charles R. Hutton and June A. O'Neill, "Tax Policy," and George E. Peterson, "The State and Local Sector," both in *The Reagan Experiment*, ed. John L. Palmer and Isabel N. Sawhill (Washington, D.C.: Urban Institute Press, 1982), 97–128, 157–217 (the latter containing a listing of local budget adjustments by state).

7. Chap. 6 develops this argument at length. See chap. 6, nn. 3, 5, 6.

8. See also my article "A European Solution to America's Budget Crisis," *Washington Post,* 22 May 1983, p. B1.

9. See "The Role of the Public Sector," *Background Paper for Working Party No. 1 of the Economic Policy Committee* (Paris: Organization for Economic Cooperation and Development, 1982), 80.

10. Ibid., 86.

11. Ibid., 24.

12. Ibid., 71.

13. Ibid., 73.

Cost Per Pupil Year by Level of Public Education
(in dollars at prevailing official exchange rates)

	Primary and Secondary		Higher	
	1970	1979	1978	1979
France	418	1,440	667	2,700
W. Germany	393	2,220	2,581	4,700
U.S.	1,068	2,540	3,150	8,200

All three countries show the same trend toward increased enrollments in more expensive higher-level education. For relative student contributions, see Edward B. Fiske, "Higher Education's New Economics," *New York Times Magazine,* 1 May 1983, pp. 46 ff.

14. In 1980 the U.S. public sector share of overall health expenditure was 41.7 percent, as against 77.5 percent in France and Germany; "The Role of the Public Sector," 75.

15. Reagan's fiscal policy followed a contrary strategy of attempting to reduce direct benefits rather than increasing them for the income groups yielding the major share of tax revenue. The FY 1986 budget proposals, for example, tried to slash middle-class oriented programs in education and health care. First-term budget cuts had already squeezed the bottom end of the income scale. For Reagan's freezes, reforms, and eliminations, see *New York Times*, 5 Feb. 1985, pp. A18–19. Reagan tax reform proposals went in the same direction. For the Treasury Department's blueprint, see "The Tax Plan Cometh," *Fortune* (24 Dec. 1984), 8.

16. Secretary of State for Defence (Britain), *Statement on the Defence Estimates 1985, No. 1* (London: Her Majesty's Stationery Office, 1985), 36.

17. For an interpretation of congressional voting on defense, see Robert E. Osgood, "The Revitalization of Containment," *Foreign Affairs* 60, no. 3 (America and the World 1981): 465–502.

18. See *The Forrestal Diaries*, ed. Walter Millis (New York: Viking Press, 1951), 298–335; also Robert S. McNamara, *The Essence of Security* (New York: Harper and Row, 1968), 90.

19. For a recent indictment, see Edward N. Luttwak, *The Pentagon and the Art of War* (New York: Simon and Schuster, 1984), 68–92.

20. A concise summary of General Jones's views is to be found in the introduction to Archie D. Barrett, *Reappraising Defense Organization* (Washington, D.C.: National Defense University, 1983), xxiii–xxv. In April 1986, the Senate mustered a powerful bipartisan coalition to pass a bill imposing some of the changes to consolidate the Joint Chiefs that reformers had long been advocating. Assuming support from the House and the administration, it would nevertheless take several years to assess the effects. See "Senate Armed Service Panel Votes to Revamp Joint Chiefs," *Washington Post*, 22 Feb. 1986, p. A1.

21.

Defense Expenditure
(as a percentage of GNP)

	1914[a]	1949	1954	1955	1965	1969	1974	1977	1980[b]	1983[b]	1984[c]
U.S.	—	5.1	12.7	11.0	8.3	9.6	6.6	6.0	5.6	7.4	6.4
W. Germany	4.6	—	4.7	4.8	5.0	4.1	4.1	3.4	3.3	3.4	3.3
France	4.8	6.2	8.5	7.4	6.1	4.9	4.1	3.6	4.0	4.2	4.1
Britain	3.4	7.0	9.9	9.2	6.6	5.8	5.8	5.0	5.0	5.5	5.5
Italy	3.5	3.9	4.5	4.1	3.7	3.0	3.0	2.4	2.4	2.8	2.7

SOURCE: Except where otherwise noted, NATO: *The Next Thirty Years*, ed. Kenneth A. Meyers, (Boulder, Colo.: Westview Press, 1980), 406.
[a] A. J. P. Taylor, *The Struggle for Mastery in Europe* (Oxford: Oxford University Press, 1954), xxix.
[b] *The Military Balance 1985–1986* (London: International Institute for Strategic Studies, 1985), 170.
[c] *The Military Balance 1986–1987* (London: International Institute for Strategic Studies, 1986), 212.

22. In terms of overall manpower and equipment, the French and Germans seem to get more value for their money than do the Americans. With an overall defense budget only 18.6 percent of the American budget, France and Germany together field, for example, an army 82.7 percent as large and equipped with 48.3 percent as many tanks.

Item-by-item comparison of military budgets is obviously tricky, since expense categories are defined differently from country to country. The broad conclusion about relative efficiency nevertheless seems difficult to deny.

23. Estimates of total defense expenditures cited from U.S. Department of Defense, *Report on Allied Contributions to the Common Defense*, 1984, 30.

Comparative Estimates of Soviet Defense Expenditures

Source	Price Base	1970	1980	1981	1983	1985	Annual growth rate 1970–80 (percentage)
Billions of Roubles							
USSR	Current	17.90	17.10	17.054	17.054	19.063	−0.4
CIA	1970	44–53	62–79	70–75	—	—	3.7
Britain	Current	—	61–89	64–92	—	—	4.0
Rosefielde	1970	43.5	—	—	—	—	8.5
Billions of Dollars							
USSR	Current	—	—	24.4	21.3	23.4	—
JCS	1983	188	250	267	—	—	2.8
Rosefielde	1970	104.5	—	—	—	—	4.9
CIA	1983	—	—	225	235	—	—

SOURCE: I.I.S.S., *Military Balance 1983–1984*, 13, *Military Balance 1985–1986*, 18.

For a critique of the CIA estimates, see Franklyn D. Holzmann, "Soviet Military Spending: Assessing the Numbers Game," *International Security* 6, no. 4 (Spring 1982): 78–101. For a general analysis stressing the continuity of the Soviet buildup, see David Fewtrell, "The Soviet Economic Crisis: Prospects for the Military and the Consumer," in *Adelphi Papers*, no. 186 (London: International Institute for Strategic Studies, 1983): 10–11.

24. On the Soviet Union's rapidly changing ethnographic composition and the resultant policy problems, see Jeremy R. Azrael, "Emergent Nationality Problems in the USSR," in *Soviet Nationality Policies and Practices*, ed. Jeremy R. Azrael (New York: Praeger, 1978), 363–90. A valuable, if now somewhat dated, reference work is *Handbook of Major Soviet Nationalities*, ed. Zev Katz (New York: Free Press, 1975). See too Teresa Rakowska-Harmstone's interesting essay, "The Soviet Army as the Instrument of National Integration," in *Soviet Military Power and Performance*, ed. J. Erickson and E. J. Feuchtwanger (London: Macmillan, 1979), 129–54. See also Helene Carrere d'Encausse, *Confiscated Power*, trans. George Holock (New York: Harper and Row, 1982), 297–305.

25. On the British 1981 *Defence Review* and the updated *Defence White Paper* released by the government after the Falklands War, see C. J. Bowie and A. Platt, *British Nuclear Policymaking* (Santa Monica, Cal.: Rand Corporation, 1984), 1–6. On the French government's modernization plans, particularly in the area of research and development, see Prime Minister Mauroy's speech of 20 Sept. 1983, "La stratégie de la France," reprinted in *Défense Nationale* (November 1983), 5–22. See also chap. 9, n. 40.

26. On Pakistan's nuclear intentions, see *Strategic Survey 1983–1984* (London: International Institute for Strategic Studies, 1984), 87. For India and Pakistan generally, Ibid., 82–90; for China, Ibid., 94–98. For further assessments of China's nuclear capacity and strategic position, see I.I.S.S., *The Military Balance 1985–1986*, 111–13; Justin Galen (pseud.), "U.S.' Toughest Message to the USSR," *Armed Forces Journal International* (February 1979). For an analysis of China's strategic role, see Jonathan D. Pollack, *The Sino-Soviet Rivalry and Chinese Security Debate* (Santa Monica, Cal.: Rand Corporation, 1982). For rumors and denials of a Swedish nuclear capability, see *New York Times*, 27 Apr. 1985, p. 6. See also chap. 11, n. 42.

27. By 1985, the Soviets had deployed some 543 IRBMs and MRBMs, roughly 336 of which were in western USSR and the rest in the central and eastern parts of the country. Of these, 423 were SS-

20 mobile IRBMs (of which 162 were in the Far East, 45 in Central Asia—being relocated to sites in the western USSR according to the I.I.S.S.—and 216 west of the Urals). The remaining 120 were SS-4 *Sandal* MRBMs, which are now being retired. See I.I.S.S., *Military Balance 1985–1986*, 21. For an analysis of Soviet deployments, see Harry Gelman, *The Soviet Far East Buildup and Soviet Risk-Taking Against China* (Santa Monica, Cal.: Rand Corporation, 1982).

28. For an analysis of Chinese conventional forces and their slow modernization, as well as Soviet forces deployed in opposition, see I.I.S.S., *The Military Balance 1985–1986*, 111–15; 29–30. For a discussion of the European balance, see chap. 9, especially n. 5.

29. Given America's vital political, economic, cultural, and moral interest in Western European and Japanese independence, the United States obviously should not disinterest itself totally in the Eurasian balance, as some advocate from a purely military perspective. Suggestions along these lines represent the sort of logical extremism that defeats any kind of reform by carrying it to a manifestly absurd degree. For the foreseeable future, some American forces should certainly continue to be stationed in Europe and Japan. There is a great difference, however, between taking charge of Eurasian territorial defense, with commensurate ground and naval forces, and stationing a few divisions to aid a defense essentially directed by our allies themselves. Even one or two American divisions would be an important contribution to territorial defense and an earnest gesture of continuing nuclear commitment. Here again, however, the U.S. nuclear deterrent should no longer pretend to be the sole deterrent. See chap. 9, n. 34.

30. On U.S. plans for fighting two wars, see John D. Mayer, *Rapid Deployment Forces: Policy and Budgetary Implications* (Washington, D.C.: Congress of the United States, Congressional Budget Office, 1983). For the current Defense Department view of U.S. national security commitments, see Caspar W. Weinberger, *Annual Report to the Congress*, especially pt. 1, section C, "U.S. National Security Objectives and Defense Strategy," and section D, "Conventional Capabilities Required by U.S. Strategy," 25–45.

31. In the mid-1980s the army is undergoing a reorganization moving in this direction. Two new light infantry divisions are being added and two heavy divisions are being lightened. When this process is completed at the end of FY 1986, the army will have 10 heavy and 8 light active divisions as well as 6 heavy and 4 light nondivisional maneuver brigades. The Defense Department acknowledges that the new light divisions will be inappropriate for reinforcing Europe's Central Front. See Caspar W. Weinberger, *Annual Report to the Congress*, 133–36.

32. For the Pentagon calculation, see Richard Halloran, "Europe Called Main U.S. Arms Cost," *New York Times*, 20 July 1984, p. A2. Overall manpower costs account for 41 percent of the defense budget. The most recent I.I.S.S. figures show 353,100 troops stationed in Europe (27,250 afloat), *The Military Balance 1985–1986*, 13. These figures do not include the 10 army divisions assigned to NATO in the United States, the 88 air force squadrons and one marine amphibious brigade, or the reserves regularly assigned to NATO. The United States is obligated to supply all of these as reinforcements within ten days of the outbreak of hostilities. All naturally require prepositioned material and lift programs. See U.S. Department of Defense, *Report on Allied Contributions to the Common Defense*, 76, 81; and Caspar W. Weinberger, *Annual Report to the Congress, FY 1986*, 224. See also chap. 9, n. 33.

33. For the official justification of a 600-ship navy, see the statement of the Honorable John F. Lehman, Jr., secretary of the navy, *Hearings Before the Committee on Armed Services, United States Senate, Ninety-Seventh Congress, Second Session, S. 2248* (Washington, D.C.: U.S. Government Printing Office, 1982), pt. 2, 1054–72. For a close analysis, see Peter F. Tarpgaard, *Building a 600-Ship Navy: Costs, Timing and Alternative Approaches* (Washington, D.C.: Congress of the United States, Congressional Budget Office, 1982). Critics disparage the maritime strategy behind the 600-ship navy, particularly the need for 15 carrier battlegroups. Fifteen carriers are said to be insufficient to attack the Soviet coast in an offensive operation to secure the sea lines of communication (SLOC). Without such a goal, a 12-carrier fleet, saving $54 billion in capital costs alone, would be sufficient. See Joshua M. Epstein, *The 1987 Defense Budget* (Washington, D.C.: Brookings Institution, 1986), 41–45. For a proposal to reduce the U.S. ground commitment and boost the air commitment in Europe, see Steven Canby and Ingemar Dörfer, "More Troops, Fewer Missiles," *Foreign Policy*, no. 53 (Winter 1983–84): 3–17. Current efforts to boost the mobility of U.S. forces, particularly the light forces of the new Central Command, seem likely to squeeze resources for the European-oriented divisions. Airlift

procurement costs have risen, for example, from $757 million in FY 1982 to $3.6 billion in FY 1986. Overall force projection outlays have risen from $5.2 billion in FY 1982 to $8.1 billion in FY 1986. See Deborah G. Meyer, "You Can't Be There Till You Get There!" *Armed Forces Journal*, July 1984, 76–91. See also the interview with Lt. Gen. Robert C. Kingston, commander-in-chief, U.S. Central Command, Ibid., 67–73.

34. See Herbert Stein, "A Reagan Economic Revolution?" *New York Times*, 16 Apr. 1985, p. A27.

35. See Edward N. Luttwak, *The Pentagon and Art of War*, 266–86 and Steven L. Canby, "Military Reform and the Art of War: Military Superiority at FY 82 Budget Levels," *International Security Review* 7, no. 3 (Fall 1982).

Chapter 8: The *Pax Americana* and the *Pax Britannica*

1. Immensely popular during and immediately after the war, Clarence Streit's tract *Union Now: A Proposal for an Atlantic Union of the Free* (New York: Harper and Brothers, 1940) spelled out the hegemonic view and America's responsibility therein. A similar view was widely disseminated through the Luce publications, which trumpeted the arrival of "the American Century"; see Henry Luce's editorial in *Life*, 17 Feb. 1941. For an erudite postwar version, see Eugene V. Rostow, *Law, Power and the Pursuit of Peace* (Lincoln: University of Nebraska Press, 1968). For Dean Acheson's broad views, as stated in his memoirs, see *Present at the Creation* (New York: W. W. Norton, 1969).

2. Reflection upon the course of former empires has led a number of writers to observe modern parallels. See, in particular, the works of my colleague, George Liska, who stresses the need for a maturing hegemon to appease rising powers to prevent systemic self-destruction. His earlier book, *Imperial America: The International Politics of Primacy* (Baltimore: Johns Hopkins University Press, 1967), focuses on the need to manage the Western alliance to accommodate European aspirations. Several later volumes have emphasized accommodating the Soviets in the interests of a broader balance against rising powers in the Third World. See, for example, his *Russia and the Road to Appeasement: Cycles of East-West Conflict in War and Peace* (Baltimore: Johns Hopkins University Press, 1982). For a concise statement, see "The West at the Crossroads: The Case for U.S.–Soviet Appeasement," *SAIS Review* 3, no. 1 (Winter-Spring, 1983): 169–81. His student, Edward N. Luttwak, in *The Grand Strategy of the Roman Empire* (Baltimore and London: Johns Hopkins University Press, 1976), notes the tendency for domestic turmoil within the hegemonic state to invite aggression against it. Robert J. A. Skidelsky notes that "a system which depends on the exertions of a preponderant power is inherently unstable in the long run." See "Retreat from Leadership: The Evolution of British Economic Foreign Policy, 1870–1939," in *Balance of Power or Hegemony: The Interwar Monetary System*, ed. Benjamin M. Rowland (New York: Lehrman Institute/New York University Press, 1976), 150–51. For a detailed study of the interwar economic crisis, explicitly informed by the hegemonic view and the inevitability of its decay, see Charles P. Kindleberger, *The World in Depression 1929–1939* (Los Angeles: University of California Press, 1973). For a concise statement of Kindleberger's views on hegemonic decay, with particular reference to the United States, see "International Economic Organization" in *Money and the Coming World Order*, ed. David P. Calleo (New York: Lehrman Institute/New York University Press, 1976), 31–38. For a broad survey of imperial economic decay throughout the ages, see Carlo M. Cipolla, *The Economic Decline of Empires* (London: Methuen, 1970).

A hegemonic position can also compensate for domestic weakness. For how imperial assets buttressed Britain's position well after its domestic economic base was eroding, see Paul Kennedy, *The Realities Behind Diplomacy: Background and Influence on British External Policy, 1865–1980* (London: Allen and Unwin, 1981), 165–70, 226–30.

3. Canning's famous phrase came in response to the French invasion of Spain in 1826: "I resolved that if France had Spain, it would not be Spain 'with the Indies.' I called the New World into existence, to redress the balance of the Old." The outcome of the Napoleonic wars—of Europe's inability to give birth to a dominant power—was all in Britain's favor: "indirectly, as a European balance of power, and

directly, in the shape of British supremacy beyond the seas. More clearly than ever before, the old Continent had bought the continuance of its free system of states at the price of the migration of its power"; Ludwig Dehio, *The Precarious Balance: The Politics of Power in Europe 1494–1945*, trans. Charles Fullman (London: Chatto and Windus, 1963), 174. Dehio's distinction between global and European balance is clear enough. More generally, however, the concept of the balance of power has lent itself to a notoriously diverse range of meanings—signifying variously a distribution of power, equilibrium, a preponderant hegemony, balanced hegemonies, peaceful stability, bellicose instability, "power politics," a universal law of history, a system guiding policymaking—see Ernst B. Haas's useful survey, "The Balance of Power: Prescription, Concept, or Propaganda," in *International Politics and Foreign Policy*, ed. J. N. Rosenau (New York: Free Press, 1961), 318–29. Here it means a system of interdependent powers or groupings of powers, no one of whom is dominant and whose individual mix of capacities and vulnerabilities reinforces adherence to a set of rules for interaction designed to maintain order while preventing domination and exploitation.

4. On European conduct of colonial operations and British technological superiority in arms, see Hew Strachan, *European Armies and the Conduct of War* (London: Allen and Unwin, 1983), 76–89. William H. McNeil remarks that imperial expansion was "so cheap that the famous phrase that Britain acquired its empire in a fit of absence of mind is a caricature rather than a falsehood"; see *The Pursuit of Power* (Chicago: University of Chicago Press, 1982), 256–61.

5. For my views on the Anglo-American "special relationship," see David P. Calleo, *Britain's Future* (New York: Horizon Press, 1968) and David P. Calleo and Benjamin M. Rowland, *America and the World Political Economy* (Bloomington and London: Indiana University Press, 1973), pt. 2.

6. German trade was particularly successful in displacing Britain within Europe. See W. W. Rostow, *The World Economy: History & Prospect* (Austin: University of Texas Press, 1980), 67–72. For general discussions of German economic development, see J. H. Clapham, *The Economic Development of France and Germany, 1815–1914*, 4th ed. (Cambridge: Cambridge University Press, 1936); Gustav Stolper, *The German Economy: 1870 to the Present* (New York: Harcourt Brace Jovanovich, 1967); Knut Borchardt, "The Industrial Revolution in Germany, 1700–1914," in *The Fontana Economic History of Europe*, vol. 4, pt. 1, ed. Carlo M. Cipolla (London: Fontana Books, 1973); and David Landes, *The Unbound Prometheus* (Cambridge: Cambridge University Press, 1969). For my own analysis of the historiographical issues involved in the relationship between economic development and German foreign policy, see David P. Calleo, *The German Problem Reconsidered* (Cambridge: Cambridge University Press, 1978), chaps. 3, 4.

7. On the complicated circumstances of the Franco-Russian Alliance, which initially was also hostile to the British, see William L. Langer, *The Diplomacy of Imperialism, 1890–1902* (New York: Knopf, 1951), especially 31–60.

For assorted views on the causes of World War I, see the essays by James Joll, Fritz Fischer, Imanuel Geiss, P. H. S. Hatton, and Gerhard Ritter in *The Origins of the First World War, Great Power Rivalry and German War Aims*, ed. H. W. Koch (New York: Taplinger, 1972). A brief assessment of the debate may be found in the conclusion of L. C. F. Turner's *Origins of the First World War* (London: Edward Arnold, 1970), 112–15. Turner argues that Britain's incoherence and indecision made its role more accidental than deliberate; see also Luigi Albertini, *Origins of the War of 1914* (London: Oxford University Press, 1957) vol. 3, 380–85. For the German view that the British egged on "French revanchism" and "Pan-Slav chauvinism," see Bethmann Hollweg's farewell to the British ambassador, cited in Konrad Jarausch, *The Enigmatic Chancellor: Bethmann Hollweg and the Hubris of Imperial Germany* (New Haven: Yale University Press, 1973); 176–77. For my analysis, see *The German Problem Reconsidered*, chap. 3.

8. For the development of these ideas by German historians, see Ludwig Dehio, "Ranke and German Imperialism," in his *Germany and World Politics in the Twentieth Century* (New York: Knopf, 1959).

9. France, widely perceived after the loss of Alsace-Lorraine as Europe's chief revisionist power, adopted an unambiguously defensive posture on the eve of the war in 1914 to avoid alienating British opinion. Luigi Albertini, *Origins of the War of 1914*, 647.

10. Britain's early export lead had come from consumer goods, principally textiles, and had diminished steadily as world trade shifted toward producer goods while British industry did not shift accordingly.

For how the industrial transformations of the prewar period favored German and American development, see W. W. Rostow, *The World Economy*, 177–93 (the German case is specifically treated in 403–8). For several decades, Britain compensated for a declining balance on tradable goods by achieving a large share of the world's shipping, insurance, and other commercial services. This stream of "invisible" income actually yielded a surplus on the current account until 1929. But during the years 1925–1929, the surplus was insufficient to finance the export of capital that prevailed over the period. "The difference was met by attracting short-term funds to London for reinvestment abroad, and this short-term borrowing was destined to cause trouble in 1931, when money was suddenly recalled"—all the more since exports and invisibles began in 1929 to shrink at a fantastic rate (by 28 million pounds that year, by 199 million pounds in 1931), abruptly throwing the current account into severe deficit. W. Arthur Lewis, *Economic Survey 1919–1939* (London: Allen and Unwin, 1949), 42–43, 74–89; and *European Historical Statistics*, 867.

11. In 1914 the United States was a debtor nation, owing $4 billion. By 1919, it had become a creditor nation, being owed $4 billion. By 1924, it alone held one-half the world's gold. On the effect of gold imports on the American economy in 1920–24, see William A. Brown, Jr., *The International Gold Standard Reinterpreted* (New York: National Bureau of Economic Research, 1940), vol. 1, 239–82.

12. For Weimar Germany's dependence on American credit and the implications for domestic economic policy, see Robert C. Dahlberg, *Heinrich Brüning, the Center Party and Germany's "Middle Way"* (Washington, D.C.: Johns Hopkins School of Advanced International Studies, unpublished Ph.D. dissertation, 1983).

13. For some of the effects on European relations, see, inter alia, Stephen A. Schuker, *The End of French Predominance in Europe: The Financial Crisis of 1924 and the Adoption of the Dawes Plan* (Chapel Hill: University of North Carolina Press, 1976); and W. Arthur Lewis, *Economic Survey 1919– 1939*. Lewis summarizes: "If 1919–25 was a period obviously dominated by the effects of the war, 1925–29 was just as much a period of readjustment to the effects of the war, though these effects were no longer visible on the surface. . . . So soon as America ceased to expand and lend, then underlying maladjustments were to come out and take charge" (p. 50).

14. On Britain's going off the gold-exchange standard, see Robert Skidelsky, *Politics and the Slump* (London: Humanities, 1967), especially 375–84. For the London Conference and Roosevelt's protectionist policy, see Benjamin M. Rowland, "Preparing the American Ascendancy: The Transfer of Economic Power from Britain to the United States, 1933–1944," in *Balance of Power or Hegemony: The Interwar Monetary System*, 195–207. On the impact of the economic crisis on German society and the return to protectionism there, see Francis Rome, *The German National Socialist Regime: Its Response to the World Economic Crisis, Its Ideas and Pre-War Economic Policies* (Washington, D.C.: Johns Hopkins School of Advanced International Studies, unpublished Ph.D. dissertation, 1975), 111– 29. See also Robert Dahlberg, n. 12.

15. Hitler's geopolitical thinking is considered at greater length in David P. Calleo, *The German Problem Reconsidered*, 85–121. Hitler's own writings, of course, set forth his views quite clearly; see particularly *Hitler's Secret Book* (New York: Grove Press, 1961) and *The Testament of Adolf Hitler*, ed. François Genoud (London: Cassel, 1961).

16. British interwar sympathy for German desires to revise the Versailles system peacefully were encouraged by John Maynard Keynes's *The Economic Consequences of the Peace* (New York: Harcourt, Brace and Howe, 1920). British vacillation encouraged Hitler to overreach himself and precipitate a war he had not planned, according to A. J. P. Taylor, *The Origins of the Second World War* (London: Hamish Hamilton, 1961), 134–36. For a view highlighting the limits of British sympathy and stressing concern over their own military weakness, see Simon Newman, *March 1939: The British Guarantee to Poland* (Oxford: Clarendon Press, 1976), 8–32. For a different interpretation, see Sidney Aster, *1939: The Making of the Second World War* (New York: Simon and Schuster, 1973).

17. For racist-versus-Europeanist views in the Nazi government, particularly in planning potential economic organization, see Jean Freymond, *Le troisième Reich et la réorganisation économique de l'Europe 1940–1942: Origines et projets* (Leiden: Sijthoff, 1974).

18. Principled opposition among Europeans to Nazi domination was not universal; in this regard,

see particularly Robert O. Paxton's important works on French collaboration, *Vichy France: Old Guard and New Order* (New York: Knopf, 1972) and (with Michael R. Marrus) *Vichy France and the Jews* (New York: Basic Books, 1981).

19. For an early balance-of-power argument that considers both economic and political aspects, see David Hume, "On the Balance of Trade," in *Writings on Economics*, ed. Eugene Rotwein (Madison: University of Wisconsin Press, 1970); and "On the Balance of Power," in *Essays Moral, Political and Literary* (London: 1889), vol. 1. Ernst Haas notes how most other opponents of mercantilism in Hume's age—for example, the elder Mirabeau—attacked the balance of power as well; "The Balance of Power: Prescription, Concept, or Propaganda," *International Politics and Foreign Policy*, 324. On the practice of balance of power in its golden age, see Sir Charles Webster, *The Foreign Policy of Castlereagh 1812–1815: Britain and the Reconstruction of Europe* (London: G. Bell and Sons, 1950). See also n. 29.

20. The Anglo-American-French dispute over the gold-exchange standard and the Bretton Woods system after World War II has its roots in the interwar period. For the French position and the debate over monetary organization between the wars, see Judith L. Kooker, "French Financial Diplomacy: The Interwar Years," in *Balance of Power or Hegemony*, 83–145. See also my own essay, "The Historiography of the Interwar Period: Reconsiderations," in Rowland, 227–60. For a concise summary of contemporary schools of thought on international monetary reform, see John Williamson, *The Open Economy and World Economy* (New York: Basic Books, 1983), 346–48.

21. See William A. Brown, *The International Gold Standard Reinterpreted 1915–1934*; Arthur I. Bloomfield, *Monetary Policy under the International Gold Standard* (New York: Federal Reserve Bank of New York, 1959); and Charles P. Kindleberger, *The World in Depression, 1929–1939* (Los Angeles: University of California Press, 1973), 28, 291–308. For my own analysis, see *Balance of Power or Hegemony*.

22. Rueff's analysis of the breakdown of the gold standard is contained in a well-known essay of 1932, "Défense et illustration de l'étalon-or," now reprinted in *Oeuvres complètes de Jacques Rueff*, Tome III, vol. 2, *Politique économique* (Paris: Plon, 1980), 105–27. For a contemporary American defense of Rueff's views, see Lewis Lehrman, "The Creation of International Monetary Order," in *Money and the Coming World Order*, 71–120.

23. Over the period 1900–1913, Britain was actually a slight net importer of bullion and specie; see the figures in A. K. Cairncross, *Home and Foreign Investment 1870–1913* (Cambridge: Cambridge University Press, 1953), 180. See too P. M. Oppenheimer, "Monetary Movements and Position of Sterling," and A. G. Kemp, "Long Term Capital Movements," in *The British Balance of Payments*, ed. D. J. Robertson and L. C. Hunter (Edinburgh and London: Oliver and Boyd, 1966), 90, 95–96, 138–42.

24. For French attitudes toward the postwar monetary system, see again Jacques Rueff, *The Age of Inflation* (Chicago: Regnery, 1964) and *The Monetary Sin of the West* (New York: Macmillan, 1971).

25. See the analysis of W. Arthur Lewis cited in n. 10. Robert Skidelsky, observing that by 1928 London's net liability to foreigners already probably exceeded 500 million pounds, concludes: "Britain's current account surplus was simply not sufficient to balance both its long-term lending and its short-term debts. Instead of appropriating part of the surplus to liquidate those debts, Britain in fact increased them in the years 1924–27 by using short-term inflows to finance a rate of long-term lending far in excess of the current account surplus of those years." "Retreat from Leadership," in *Balance of Power or Hegemony*, 176. Given the fragility of Britain's surplus, based as it was on liquidity-sensitive trade in invisibles, the flight from sterling after 1929 irresistably strengthened pressures for devaluation.

26. For a sharp critique of American monetary policy during the period, see Harold van Buren Cleveland, "The International Monetary System in the Interwar Period," in *Balance of Power or Hegemony*, 40–50. On the Federal Reserve's sterilization of American gold inflows, see Judith L. Kooker, "French Financial Diplomacy, The Interwar Years," in Ibid., 103–5.

The most concise review of the interactions of the entire period is to be found in W. A. Lewis, *Economic Survey 1919–1939*; the most comprehensive, in W. A. Brown, Jr., *The International Gold Standard Reinterpreted*, particularly books. 2, 3.

27. See Robert C. Dahlberg, *Heinrich Brüning, the Center Party and Germany's "Middle Way,"* 103–8.

28. J. A. Hobson gives a classic assertion of the deleterious effects of imperialist expansion on national life. Economic health is undermined by the decline of home industries deprived of investment capital sent abroad. Democratic politics are undermined as wealthy citizens press their government to defend interests in countries over which they have no political authority. "This is the largest, plainest instance history presents of the social parasitic process by which a moneyed interest within the State, usurping the reins of government, makes for imperial expansion in order to fasten economic suckers onto foreign bodies so as to drain them of their wealth in order to support domestic luxury. . . . But nature is not mocked; the laws which, operative throughout nature, doom the parasite to atrophy, decay, and final extinction are not evaded by nations any more than by individual organisms." *Imperialism: A Study* (London: Allen and Unwin, 1948; 1st ed., 1902), 367. For a view more sympathetic to the imperial power, if not optimistic about its fate, see also Charles P. Kindleberger, "Systems of International Economic Organization," in *Money and the Coming World Order.*

29. For an essentially similar analysis of "mercantilist" and "liberal" alternatives within the world political economy, see Barry Buzan, *Peoples, States, and Fear: The National Security Problem in International Relations* (Chapel Hill: University of North Carolina Press, 1983), 136–50. Buzan argues that continuing economic innovation is the condition of sustained hegemonic dominance, and that ascendancy tends to ossification rather than successful adaptation to changing conditions.

30. De Gaulle's nationalist vision, in which the weak have a duty to assert themselves, furnishes a celebrated recent example of this view. See David P. Calleo, *Europe's Future: The Grand Alternatives* (New York: Horizon Press, 1965), 81–133.

31. See V. I. Lenin, "Imperialism, the Highest Stage of Capitalism: A Popular Outline," in *Selected Works of Lenin* (Moscow: Progress Publishers, 1971), 169–263.

32. John Stuart Mill, *Principles of Political Economy* (London: Longmans, Green, 1940), bk. 4, chap. 4. For Hobson, see n. 28.

33. For an application of the Platonic formula to a theory of coexistence among modern capitalist states, see Bernard Bosanquet, *The Philosophical Theory of the State* (London: Macmillan, 1951). The Marxist picture of capitalism as a state of perpetual war continues to receive vigorous postwar expression; see, for example, Harry Magdoff and Paul Sweezy, *The Deepening Crisis of U.S. Capitalism* (New York: Monthly Review Press, 1981). Poised uneasily somewhere between Mill and Lenin are American liberal writers, of whom John Kenneth Galbraith may be taken as representative; see his more recent work, *The Anatomy of Power* (Boston: Houghton Mifflin, 1983), particularly the analysis of organization and the state, 144–59.

34. Vietnam and Afghanistan are obvious illustrations of the military difficulties of foreign intervention by the superpowers. So is the Iran-Iraq war of the 1980s. Iran, with two million men under arms and modern American equipment, cannot easily be coerced militarily. This war also demonstrates that Third World conflict need not intensify superpower conflict, since both the U.S. and the Soviets are backing Iraq.

35. For a somewhat different analysis, which sees a more plural distribution of world power increasing the probability of superpower conflict in the Third World, see Stanley Hoffmann, "Security in an Age of Turbulence: Means of Response," in *Third World Conflict and International Security,* ed. Christoph Bertram (London: International Institute for Strategic Studies/Macmillan, 1982), 59–78.

36. Walt W. Rostow gives a learned and brilliantly suggestive analysis of this transformation from heavy industries to "high energy" industries, and the implication for political economy; see *The World Economy: History and Prospects* (Austin: University of Texas Press, 1978). Without claiming to invoke his authority for my conclusions, I am much indebted to his work on the link between the nature of industry and the consequences for macroeconomic management and the nature of political economy generally.

37. Ibid., 91–99, 287–89.

38. The implications for Third World development have been hotly debated. The *dependecia* literature is now vast; for an early and influential example, see the report submitted to the Inter-American Bank

by Raúl Prebisch, *Change and Development: Latin America's Great Task* (New York: Inter-American Development Bank/Praeger, 1971).

39. In this connection, see W. W. Rostow on the problems of world political economy in the "fifth Kondratieff upswing," in *The World Economy: History and Prospects*, 625–58.

Chapter 9: Military Arrangements

1. Unless otherwise stated, figures cited are from *The Military Balance 1985–1986* (London: The International Institute for Strategic Studies, 1985). It should be noted that included in the current I.I.S.S. figures for total Soviet armed forces (5.3 million men) are 615,000 railroad construction and labor troops and 705,000 command and general support troops. Ibid., 21. In Western countries these forces would normally be civilian and not counted in the overall troop totals.

2. See John Mearsheimer, "Why the Soviets Can't Win Quickly in Central Europe," *International Security* 7, no. 1 (Summer 1982): 3–39.

3. Different statistical measures have been developed to compare the combat potential of ground forces. Most experts agree that straight numerical comparisons do not yield satisfactory results. Any comparison of manpower figures without considering equipment is clearly incomplete. Since 1971, official U.S. studies have used the armored division equivalent (ADE) which estimates force strength based on standard measures developed by the U.S. Army. Using the weapons effectiveness index (WEI) a weighted unit value (WUV) can be calcuated. The WUV for a U.S. armored division is defined as 1.0 ADE, and all other units are rated accordingly. See William P. Mako, *U.S. Ground Forces and the Defense of Central Europe* (Washington, D.C.: Brookings Institution, 1983), app. A, pp. 105–25. Evaluations of equipment, however, are notoriously complex and speculative. NATO estimates of the early 1980s gave the Warsaw Pact an advantage of approximately 2.1:1, or 16,620 vs. 8,050 Main Battle Tanks (MBT) on the Central Front. But putting this ratio in perspective requires considering antitank guided weapons. NATO's reckonings gave itself 12,340 crew-served and/or mounted antitank guided weapons vs. 18,400 for the Warsaw Pact. Helicopters capable of carrying antitank systems were another factor. NATO gave itself 605 vs. 1,360 for the Warsaw Pact. The question here, presumably, was not who had more antitank weapons, but whether NATO had sufficient to offset the Soviet MBT advantage. That would depend also on the quality of the weapons. Overall, NATO antitank guided weapons are believed superior. Data from *NATO and the Warsaw Pact: Force Comparisons* (Brussels: NATO Information Services, 1984). Tactical air power in a close air support (CAS) role could be the essential factor halting a conventional thrust. Some estimates have seen NATO CAS able to destroy 6,500 armored fighting vehicles in the first 14 days of a conflict and an additional 4,600 over the next 21 days, see Barry R. Posen, "Measuring the Conventional Balance: Coping with Complexity in Threat Assessment," *International Security* 9, no. 3 (Winter 1984–85): 70–73.

Artillery on the Central Front is subject to a similar refinement. Some Department of Defense qualitative evaluations have reduced the Warsaw Pact numerical advantage to 1.2:1. Robert L. Fischer, *Defending the Central Front, Adelphi Paper*, no. 127 (London: International Institute for Strategic Studies, 1977).

New Precision Guided Munitions (PGM) could radically alter all these calculations although considerable dissent exists about the overall effect of emerging technologies. For an extended discussion, see the various pieces in *New Technologies and Western Security Policy, Parts I–III, Adelphi Papers*, nos. 197–99 (London: International Institute for Strategic Studies, 1985).

Standardized measures for air power do not exist. For the Soviet air threat to Europe and the difficulties of assessing it, see Joshua M. Epstein, *Measuring Military Power—The Soviet Air Threat to Europe* (Princeton: Princeton University Press, 1984).

4. Edward Luttwak points out that the number of active U.S. divisions could be increased from 16 to 78 at present manpower levels by changing to "Soviet" style divisions. Soviet force structure, he

argues, maximizes the perceptible manifestations of power and reaps many psychological benefits. U.S. policy, which uses straight numerical comparisons such as number of divisions or tanks to ensure congressional support for defense merely reinforces the perception of Soviet advantage. Edward N. Luttwak, "Perceptions of Military Force and U.S. Defense Policy," *Survival* 19, no. 1 (January/February 1977): 2. Steven Canby has argued that NATO could solve many of its military problems simply by restructuring its divisions to increase the number deployed and by increasing the percentage of available manpower in combat and reserve forces. Steven L. Canby, "Military Reform and the Art of War: Military Superiority at FY 82 Budget Levels," *International Security Review* 7, no. 3 (Fall 1982).

5. The Southern theater, or Mediterranean flank, depends much more on naval and air balances than on ground forces. While a Soviet attack across the North Italian plain is sometimes treated as an imminent threat, it would have to traverse a well-armed Yugoslavia (with 241,000 men under arms and 500,000 men in a well-organized reserve) and presumably meet an Italian army of some 270,000. The Italians have, in addition, an excellent air force of 315 combat aircraft and additional army and navy air wings. A Russian threat to Thrace or the Dardanelles is more plausible. There, Soviet forces of 390,000 in the southern USSR plus a Bulgarian army of 105,000 confront Greek forces of 158,000 and Turkish forces of 520,000. The politics of Greco-Turkish military collaboration would obviously be complex. Presumably, the Soviets could also invade Eastern Turkey, although it is not clear what purpose such an invasion would serve in an intensive, decisive, and short confrontation across central Europe. The principal strategic danger of a Soviet victory in the Dardanelles would be the liberation of the Soviet Black Sea fleet, which, with its eighty-three principal combatants, could greatly increase the scope of Soviet offensive activity throughout the Mediterranean. Otherwise, the naval balance overwhelmingly favors the West. The French and Italian fleets contain 3 carriers, 36 other major surface combatants, and 21 submarines. The Sixth Fleet adds two carrier battle groups. The value of carriers is a subject of great controversy. In any conflict, the navy is expected to withdraw them to the open sea, since they would be highly vulnerable to Soviet land-based aircraft. The same vulnerability would presumably affect Soviet ships. Given the Italian air force, the Soviet naval threat seems eminently containable—at least until the decisive battle has taken place across the German plain. Certainly, the conventional military balance in the Mediterranean cannot offer the Soviets any realistic expectation of quick victory, at least without diverting resources that would presumably be applied more judiciously to the crucial German battle. I.I.S.S., *The Military Balance 1985–1986*.

The conventional situation on NATO's Northern Flank is greatly complicated by strategic nuclear issues and by the neutral status of Sweden and Finland. To date, Sweden has been the bulwark of Nordic security with its "extroverted" high-technology strategy. Currently, in the estimation of the military establishments of Norway, Sweden, and Finland, the Soviet Union does not possess the forces or the degree of specialization required for a successful ground campaign in the far North. This situation could change as Sweden reconsiders her extremely costly extrovert strategy. For an excellent discussion of the Nordic situation, see Steven L. Canby, "Swedish Defense," *Survival* 23, no. 3 (May/June 1981): 116–23; and Erling Bjøl, *Nordic Security, Adelphi Paper*, no. 181 (London: International Institute for Strategic Studies, 1983).

NATO attempts to strengthen conventional forces in Norway are complicated by the strategic nuclear situation. Currently, the Soviets station roughly two-thirds of their SSBN force in the Barents Sea, where it is protected by two-thirds of their SSN fleet and about one-quarter of their surface fleet and naval air arm. They apparently intend the Barents Sea to be a "sanctuary" for their sea-based deterrent. NATO efforts either to place tactical air wings in Northern Norway or to deploy U.S. carrier forces to threaten the Kola Penninsula would directly threaten this sanctuary. For a discussion of how current NATO plans for the Northern Flank might necessitate a Soviet ground attack in the region or lead to inadvertent nuclear escalation, see Barry R. Posen, "Inadvertent Nuclear War? Escalation and NATO's Northern Flank," *International Security* 7, no. 2 (Fall 1982): 28–54.

NATO's central front remains the main point of confrontation with the Warsaw Pact. The front comprises eight corps sectors divided into a Northern Army Group (NORTHAG) and a Central Army Group (CENTAG), each with four corps sectors aligned in a layer-cake fashion along the inner German border. (There are also German and Dutch forces located adjacent to the Central Front in Schleswig-

Holstein.) From north to south the corps sectors in NORTHAG are: I Dutch corps; I German; I British; I Belgian. In CENTAG the corps sector from north to south are: III German; V American; VII American; II German.

German and American forces are considered the strongest, and Dutch and Belgian forces the weakest. The I Belgian Corps includes two mechanized divisions. The corps headquarters and one division are in the Federal Republic; the other division is actually in Belgium. In a conflict, to reach full strength the corps would need sufficient warning not only to bring its second division from Belgium, but also to cover the considerable distance between its normal garrison in Germany and its assigned wartime deployment. The I Belgian Corps also is said to suffer from a lack of training, chronic shortages of spare parts, and a deficiency of main battle tanks.

The I Netherlands Corps is fairly well equipped but maintains only one armored brigade in Germany. Its remaining forces are in the Netherlands. Should they fail to reach their defensive positions in time, the I German Corps would be forced to defend two sectors, a major vulnerability. See Diego A. Ruix Palmer, "The Front Line in Europe—The Forces: National Contributions," *Armed Forces Journal* (May 1984), 55–58.

6. Robert Lucas Fischer, *Defending the Central Front: The Balance of Forces*. For a more recent attempt, see Barry R. Posen, "Measuring the European Conventional Balance."

7. For a summary of several studies on the effects of varying rates of mobilization on NATO/Warsaw Pact force ratios, see Fen Osler Hampson, "Groping for Technical Panaceas: The European Conventional Balance and Nuclear Stability," *International Security* 8, no. 3 (Winter 1983–84): 64–69. For the political problems of mobilization, see Richard K. Betts, "Surprise Attack: NATO's Political Vulnerability," *International Security* 5, no. 4 (Spring 1981): 117–49.

8. Robert L. Fischer, *Defending the Central Front*, 23–25. For a discussion of the origins of the 3: 1 ratio and its applicability to nuclear conflict, see Otto Heilbrunn, *Conventional Warfare in the Nuclear Age* (New York: Praeger, 1965), chap. 4.

9. A 1975 Defense Department study estimated 18.3 million fatalities following a Soviet counterforce attack on U.S. silos. A less optimistic study by the U.S. Arms Contol and Disarmament Agency estimated 50 million deaths. Desmond Ball, *Can Nuclear War Be Controlled*, Adelphi Paper, no. 169 (London: International Institute for Strategic Studies, 1981). Such estimates neglect the secondary effects of nuclear weapons. For dramatic estimates, see Solly Zuckerman, *Nuclear Illusion and Reality* (New York: Viking Press, 1982), chap. 2; and Jonathan Schell, *The Fate of the Earth* (New York: Knopf, 1982). In 1983, the National Academy of Sciences predicted a "nuclear winter" from such counterforce strikes, whose climatic effects would threaten the human species and planetary life in general. See Carl Sagan, "Nuclear War and Climatic Catastrophe," *Foreign Affairs* 62, no. 2 (Winter 1983–84): 257–92.

For a general critique both of counterforce strategies and of the strategic and political inferences drawn by Schell, see the articles by Theodore Draper, *The New York Review of Books*, 15 July 1982; 18 Aug. 1983; 19 Jan. 1984; and 31 May 1984.

10. For a history of the development of nuclear strategies, see Lawrence Freedman, *The Evolution of Nuclear Strategy* (New York: St. Martin's Press, 1981).

11. For a recent discussion, see Josef Joffe, "Can Europe Live with its Defense?" in *The Troubled Alliance*, ed. Lawrence Freedman (London: Heineman, 1983), 123–36. See also the remarks of French Defense Minister Charles Hernu before the West European Union, *Le Monde*, 2 Dec. 1982. For a critical analysis of European opposition to conventional deterrence, see Steven L. Canby, "NATO Defense: The Problem Is Not More Money," in *American Security Policy and Policy-Making: The Dilemmas of Using Military Force*, ed. Robert Harkavy and Edward A. Kolodziej (Lexington, Mass.: Lexington Books, 1980): 85–99.

For proposals from the European peace movement to substitute conventional for nuclear deterrence, see Ben Dankbaar, "Alternative Defense Policies and the Peace Movement," *Journal of Peace Research* 21, no. 2 (1984): 141–55.

12. Steven Canby and Ingemar Dörfer, for example, suggest NATO could achieve actual conventional superiority by a new division of labor within NATO and save money in the process. If the United States reassigned 450 more planes to NATO (from its existing inventory), European air forces could be

reduced, which could save European defense budgets 12 percent, which could go to more European troops and reserves. With the role of American reinforcements thus reduced, reductions in naval and transport capabilities would also bring the United States large savings. See Steven L. Canby and Ingemar Dörfer, "More Troops, Fewer Missiles," *Foreign Policy*, no. 53 (Winter 1983/84), 3–17. For recent proposals and German reactions, see *Der Spiegel*, 27 Aug. 1984, 97–98. See also Colonel T. N. Dupuy, "The Non-Debate over How Armies Should Fight," *Army*, June 1982, 34–35; and Paul Bracken, "West European Sprawl as an Active Defense Variable," *Military Strategy and Tactics* ed. R. Huber (New York: Plenum Press, 1975), 219–30.

13. Colonel T. N. Dupuy, "The Non-Debate over How Armies Should Fight," 34–45. Recent proposals call for a system of buried pipes along the border, which could be filled with liquid explosives and detonated to create a system of trenches to impede advancing of armored divisions. See "Buried Explosive System Creates Tank Ditch Quickly," *Defense News*, 17 Feb. 1986. Earlier NATO plans proposing Atomic Demolition Munitions (ADM) proved too contoversial, although the United States currently stockpiles some 350 ADMs in Europe for this purpose. See *Der Spiegel*, 27 Aug. 1984, 97–98.

For using urban sprawl near Germany's frontier to create a "super-Maginot line" against armored forces, see Bracken, "West European Sprawl," 219–30.

14. See n. 5. For the advantages of the Dutch "Rechstreeks Instromed Mobilisable (RIM)" system as a model for mobilization purposes, see Canby, "NATO Defense," 92–98.

15. The priority traditionally given nuclear weapons in French defense budgets has in the past left conventional forces somewhat neglected. Greater attention to European security under Giscard d'Estaing led to additional spending on conventional forces, but well over half of the budgeted funds went into operating expenses, and planned purchases of new equipment had to be stretched out; see Edward A. Kolodziej, "French Security Policy: Decision and Dilemmas," *Armed Forces and Society* 8 (Winter 1982): 194–95; and Yves Laulan, "France and her Army in the 1980's," in *The Internal Fabric of Western Society*, ed. Gregory Flynn (Totowa, N.J.: Allanheld, Osmun, 1981), 106. The *Force d'Action Rapide* grew out of this reorientation of strategic emphasis; for details of Defense Minister Charles Hernu's November 1982 presentation to the Army Chiefs of Staff, see *Le Monde*, 7 Dec. 1982, and Jacques Isnard's commentary of 16 Dec. 1982, "Du missile nucleaire Hadès aux helicoptères antichars." Hernu later affirmed the reorientation, saying that the new force was designed "to enhance our capacity . . . to engage conventional forces in Europe when and where we must." *Le Monde*, 22 Apr. 1983.

The new force was not unanimously welcomed by the French military command—witness the resignation in March 1983 of General Delaunay. The Five Year Military Plan of which the FAR is a part envisioned a total defense budget of 830 billion francs, or an average of 160 billion annually. This with an average annual increase of 11 billion francs, or just 8.3 percent higher than the 1985 defense budget. With inflation at over 8 percent per year, some members of the French opposition saw Mitterrand's plans as insufficient. For a defense of the government's proposals on strictly theoretical grounds, see General Lucien Poirier, "La greffe," *Défense Nationale* (April 1983), 5–32; for a warning against disassociating nuclear from conventional tactics, see General François Valentin, "L'arête étroite," *Défense Nationale* (May 1983), 45–56. Further details on the new intervention force are to be found in Jacques Isnard, "La force d'action rapide française pourra intervenir en Europe," *Le Monde*, 20–21 Nov. 1983. Currently the FAR has been built up to 43,600 men in five divisions, including one light armored division. I.I.S.S., *The Military Balance 1985–1986*, 46.

Using the FAR as operational reserves would help rectify what many analysts see as NATO's greatest deficiency. For the importance of such reserves, see, for example, Canby, "Military Reform and the Art of War;" Brigadier General Kenneth Hunt, "European Military Postures," paper given at Wilson Center, International Security Studies core seminar, session 5, 28 Feb. 1980; and Waldo D. Freeman, Jr., "NATO Central Region Forward Defense: Correcting the Strategy/Force Mismatch," *National Security Affairs, Issue Paper*, no. 81–83 (National Defense University, 1981).

16. For the Rogers proposals, see General Bernard W. Rogers, "Greater Flexibility for NATO's Flexible Response," *Strategic Review* 11, no. 2 (Spring 1983). The same emphasis on new weaponry is found in the report of the European Security Study (ESECS), *Strengthening Conventional Deterrence in Europe: Proposal's for the 1980's* (London: Macmillan Press, 1983). For a military critique, see

Steven L. Canby, "New Conventional Force Technology and the NATO-Warsaw Pact Balance: Part 1," *New Technology and Western Security Policy, Adelphi Paper,* no. 198. For negative European reactions, see Boyd D. Sutton et al., "Deep Attack Concepts and the Defense of Central Europe," *Survival* 26, no. 2 (March/April 1984): 55–56; or General (ret.) François Valentin, "L'arête étroite," 45–56.

German opponents stress the offensive nature of weapons designed for deep attack and, in veiled protest against reducing the role of nuclear weapons, criticize Airland Battle 2000 as a war-fighting, rather than a war-deterring tactic. See, for example, the controversy within the German military over the strategy as reported by *Suddeutsche Zeitung,* 13–15 Aug. 1983.

17. See, for example, T. N. Dupuy, "The Nondebate over How Armies Should Fight"; Edward N. Luttwak, "The Operational Level of War"; Steven L. Canby, "Territorial Defense in Central Europe."

18. John Mearsheimer, "Maneuver, Mobile Defense, and the NATO Central Front," *International Security* 6, no. 3 (Winter 1981/82): 104–22; and "Nuclear Weapons and Deterrence in Europe," *International Security* 9, no. 3 (Winter 1984/85): 19–46.

19. See Steven L. Canby, "Military Reform and the Art of War."

20. Steven L. Canby, "Territorial Defense in Central Europe," 57–67; Samuel Huntington, "Conventional Deterrence and Conventional Retaliation in Europe," *International Security* 8, no. 3 (Winter 1983/84): 32–56.

21. In 1982, officers formed 13 percent of the U.S. Army: during World War II, the U.S. proportion was 8 percent and the German 4 percent. Steven L. Canby, "Military Reform and the Art of War." See also Jeffrey Record, "Technology and Bureaucracy Don't Win Wars," *International Herald Tribune,* 20 Feb. 1984, p. 8; and Edward N. Luttwak, *The Pentagon and the Art of War* (New York: Simon and Schuster, 1984), chaps. 6, 7.

22. For the use of "Jaeger" (Hunter) infantry reserves, see Steven L. Canby, "Military Reform and the Art of War." For a review of suggestions for territorial defense, see Steven L. Canby, "Territorial Defense in Central Europe," 53–63; Waldo D. Freeman, "NATO Central Region Forward Defense"; and Edward Luttwak, "The Operational Level of War," *International Security* 5, no. 3 (Winter 1980/81): 61–79. For parallel German proposals, see, for example, Horst Afheldt, "Konzeption einer raumdeckenden Verteidigung für die Bundesrepublik," in *Sicherheitspolitik der Bundesrepublik Deutschland. Dokumentation 1945–1977,* ed. Klaus von Schubert (Köln: Verlag Wissenschaft und Politik, 1979).

23. See chap. 7, n. 31. For a critical analysis of the effect of the Rapid Deployment Force on the NATO commitment, see John D. Mayer, *Rapid Deployment Forces: Policy and Budgetary Implications* (Washington, D.C.: Congressional Budget Office, 1983), 19–28.

24. See Karl Kaiser et al., "Nuclear Weapons and the Preservation of Peace: A German Response," *Foreign Affairs* 60, no. 5 (Summer 1982): 1157–70. See also the discussion in Josef Joffe, "Can Europe Live with Its Defense?"

25. See n. 11.

26. See chap. 5, n. 11. For a trenchant critique of the quantative and materialistic bias of the American defense establishment, see Edward Luttwak, *The Pentagon and the Art of War,* chap. 4.

27. For a general analysis, see William Wallace, "European Defense Cooperation: Reopening the Debate"; Stanley R. Sloan, "In Search of a New Transatlantic Bargain"; and Gregory F. Treverton, "Economics and Security in the Atlantic Alliance," *Survival* 26, no. 6 (November/December 1984).

28. Henry A. Kissinger, "A Plan to Reshape NATO," *Time,* 5 Mar. 1984, 20–24. For the initial European reactions to the proposal, see Moshin Ali, "Kissinger Wants Europe to Take over NATO," *The Times* (London), 1 Mar 1984, p. 8; Freiderich Bonnart, "NATO Stunned by Kissinger," *The Times* (London), 2 Mar. 1984, p. 12. Former West German Chancellor Helmut Schmidt also has called for French forces to re-enter an integrated Western military structure, to be put under a French commander. See Helmut Schmidt, *A Grand Strategy for the West—The Anachronism of National Strategies in an Interdependent World* (New Haven: Yale University Press, 1985), 42.

29. In 1986, the United States had 340,000 short tons of equipment and supplies stored under the program for Prepositioning of Material Configured to Unit Sets (POMCUS), which it planned to raise to between 570,000 and 590,000 by 1992, entailing a growth of real operating costs of approximately

5 percent per year. The FY 1987 Budget proposal requested $152 million for the maintainence of POMCUS. Of this, $130.2 million was the theater operating cost for the storage, maintenance, and guarding costs for the equipment but did not include military pay. The U.S. Army contracted with the domestic government to guard the sites. In a war, these guard troops have assigned missions that they are supposed to carry out after the POMCUS supplies have been distributed.

30. For a general discussion of the command and control of nuclear forces in Europe, see Jeffrey Record with the assistance of Thomas I. Anderson, U.S. Nuclear Weapons in Europe—Issues and Alternatives (Washington, D.C.: Brookings Institution, 1974), 28–31.

31. For a distinguished group of former high U.S. officials advocating No First Use, see McGeorge Bundy, George F. Kennan, Robert S. McNamara, and Gerard Smith, "Nuclear Weapons and the Atlantic Alliance," Foreign Affairs 60, no. 4 (Spring 1982): 753–68. For a German response, see Karl Kaiser, et al., "Nuclear Weapons and the Preservation of Peace: A German Response"; and Josef Joffe, "Can Europe Live with Its Defense?"

For the initial Reagan announcements on the Strategic Defense Initiative and the ensuing debate see chap. 5, nn. 33, 38. For the neoconservative disaffection with NATO, see Melvyn Krauss, How NATO Weakens the West (New York: Simon & Schuster, 1986); and Irving Kristol, "NATO at a Dead End," Wall Street Journal, 15 July 1981, p. 26; "Reconstructing NATO: A New Role for Europe," Wall Street Journal, 12 Aug. 1982, p. 18; and " 'Global Unilateralism' and 'Entangling Alliances,' " Wall Street Journal, 3 Feb. 1986, p. 20.

32. Most significant of the attempts to build a European security system as the "European Pillar" for NATO was the European Defense Community, which would have formed a federal European army in the NATO framework. The failure of the EDC led to a national German army and German membership in NATO. Other attempts to build the European pillar have centered around the Western European Union, a product of the 1948 Brussels Treaty. Attempts to rejuvenate the WEU have been a particular favorite of the French since they left the integrated command structure. For an early work setting out the basic French arguments, see André Beaufre, NATO and Europe, trans. Joseph Green (New York: Knopf, 1966). On European Defense cooperation, see Trevor Taylor, European Defence Cooperation, Chatham House Paper, no. 24 (London: Royal Institute of International Affairs/Routledge and Kegan Paul, 1984). On the most recent attempt to build up the WEU, see "Learning to Crawl," Economist, no. 293 (3 Nov. 1984): 54.

33. Estimating the savings from cutting five divisions is, of course, extremely difficult. Earl Ravenal has estimated the cost of the U.S. force commitment to Europe, for general-purpose forces, to be $134 billion. Earl C. Ravenal, "Europe Without America: The Erosion of NATO," Foreign Affairs 63, no. 5 (Summer 1985): 1,026. For an extended, but older version of this argument, see Earl C. Ravenal, Defining Defense: The 1985 Military Budget (Washington, D.C.: Cato Institute, 1984). Therefore, one might reckon that cutting this commitment by approximately one-half would save around $67 billion, but naval and air forces, which would have to be committed to support U.S. ground forces in Europe, also need to be added to this calculation.

34. See Helmut Schmidt, A Grand Strategy for the West, 140.

35. See Steven L. Canby, "Military Reform and the Art of War."

36. For a discussion of the changes in French tactical nuclear and conventional forces since 1970, see David Yost, France's Deterrent Posture and Security in Europe, Part I: Capabilities and Doctrine, Adelphi Paper, no. 194 (London: International Institute for Strategic Studies, Winter 1984/1985): 48–64. See also n. 16.

37. In 1914 the French had a pool of nearly seven million men, four million men with some military training, to draw on, and the French command placed the strength of its first line troops and reserves at one million men. B. H. Liddell Hart, History of the First World War (London: Cassell and Company, 1970), 55–56. The I.I.S.S. currently lists the size of French reserves, in all services, at 393,000 men. The Military Balance 1985–1986, 46.

38. See William Drozdiak, "Schmidt Urges Unity of Paris, Bonn Forces," International Herald Tribune, 29 June 1984, p. 1.

39. Under current law, German armed forces are predicted to drop to 270,000 in the mid-1990s from a current level of 478,000, due to a falling birth rate in the mid-1960s. A variety of measures

could compensate, for example, increasing short-term volunteers, increasing the length of conscription, reducing exemptions, and increasing the role of non-Germans and women. John L. Mearsheimer, "Nuclear Weapons and Deterrence," 34ff. In the mid-1980s, the *Bundeswehr* has actually been expanding its wartime level to 1.27 million men. After 1987, when the Wartime Host Nation Support (WHNS) Programme is fully implemented, wartime strength is to rise to 1.34 million men. Federal Minister of Defense, *The Situation and the Development of the Federal Armed Forces, White Paper 1985* (Bonn: Federal Minister of Defense, 1985), 236.

40. Both France and Britain have major nuclear force modernization programs scheduled for completion in the mid-1990s. The British deterrent in the mid-1980s consists of 4 submarines, each carrying 16 missiles. Each missile carries 2 to 3 warheads, not independently targetable and, therefore, counted as 1 in the totals. Britain is retrofitting new motors on its A3TK Polaris missile force, having modernized the missile warhead under the Chevaline program.

In the modernization program, the Polaris fleet is being replaced with American Trident D-5 missiles. The four Trident boats projected will each carry 16 missiles, each with up to 10 independently targetable warheads, which will represent a force of 640 warheads, or a tenfold increase. Secretary of state for defence (Britain), *Statement on the Defence Estimates 1985*, no. 1, (London: Her Majesty's Stationery Office, 1985): 19–21, 54.

France, having completed the update of her land-based force in the early 1980s, deploys, in the mid-1980s, 18 SSBS land-based missiles, 4 submarines with 16 M-20 single warhead missiles, 1 submarine with 16 M-4 6-warhead missiles, and 22 Mirage bombers for a total of 200 strategic warheads. Further modernization plans call for refitting 4 of the older nuclear submarines with M-4 missiles by 1991, which would leave France able to deploy 5 submarines with 480 warheads, along with the 18 land-based missiles, for a total of 498 warheads. David S. Yost, *France's Deterrent Posture and Security in Europe, Part 1: Capabilities and Doctrine, Adelphi Paper*, no. 194, (London: International Institute for Stategic Studies, Winter 1984/85): 19–29.

41. See, for example, *Strengthening Conventional Deterrence in Europe, Proposals for the 1980s*, Report of the European Security Study (Boston: American Academy of Arts and Sciences, 1983): 153–54, 171–72, 180.

Chapter 10: Managing the European Coalition: The Franco-German Minuet

1. For a discussion of efforts by the foreign ministries of the nine European Community members (before the accession of Greece, Spain, and Portugal) to coordinate informally their foreign policies, see David Allen, Reinhardt Rummel, and Wolfgang Wessels, *European Political Cooperation: Towards a Foreign Policy for Western Europe* (London: Butterworth Scientific, 1982).

2. On the early hopes and theories of the European integrationists, see David P. Calleo, *Europe's Future: The Grand Alternatives* (New York: Horizon Press, 1965), 23–78. For reflections on the confederal arrangement that has evolved, see *The European Community: Past, Present and Future*, ed. Loukas Tsoukalis (Oxford: Basil Blackwell, 1983). On the persistence of national sovereignty in the community, see William Wallace, "Europe as a Confederation: The Community and the Nation-State," in Ibid., 57–68; and Stanley Hoffmann, "Reflections on the Nation-State in Western Europe Today," in Ibid., 30–37.

3.

Average Annual Percentage Growth Per Capita of Gross Domestic
Product (or Net Material Product) at Constant Prices

	France	W. Germany	Italy	Britain	U.S.	USSR*
1960–70	4.6	3.5	4.6	2.3	3.3	5.9
1970–75	3.4	2.0	2.3	2.3	1.8	4.9
1975–81	2.4	3.6	3.2	1.2	2.1	3.2

* Net Material Product, an indication of the total net value of goods and material services,
excluding such nonmaterial services as financing, insurance, real estate, social services, public
administration, and defense.
SOURCE: United Nations Statistical Yearbooks, 1975 and 1982 (New York: U.N. Statistical
Office, 1976, 1985).

4. For French motives in the European Defense Community question, see Michael M. Harrison, *The Reluctant Ally: France and Atlantic Security* (Baltimore: Johns Hopkins University Press, 1981), 28–29.

5. See Bernd Langeheine and Ulrich Weinstock, "Graduated Integration: A Modest Path Towards Progress," and William Nicoll, "Paths to European Unity," both in *Journal of Common Market Studies* 23, no. 3 (March 1985).

6. See chap. 7, n. 21.

7. See Robert Paxton, *Vichy France: Old Guard and New Order, 1940–1944* (New York: Knopf, 1972).

8. See Alan S. Milward, *The Reconstruction of Western Europe, 1945–51* (Berkeley: University of California Press, 1984), 18–21, 37–55, 462–77.

9. De Gaulle recounts his first inkling of Franco-German potential upon visiting Germany in 1945; Charles de Gaulle, *Salvation, 1944–1946* (New York: Simon and Schuster, 1960), 235.

10. On the extent of Franco-German leadership in forming the European Coal and Steel Community and the European Economic Community, see Richard Mayne, *The Recovery of Europe, From Devastation to Unity* (London: Weidenfeld and Nicolson, 1970), 214–57.

11. For a general account of the EEC's struggles in the de Gaulle era, see Richard Mayne, *The Recovery of Europe, From Devastation to Unity*, 272–76. For an analysis of de Gaulle's effort to make France's European partners choose between "European integration and Atlantic liberalization," see David P. Calleo and Benjamin M. Rowland, *America and the World Political Economy* (Bloomington: Indiana University Press, 1973), chaps. 5, 6. For a definitive French view, see Maurice Couve de Murville, *Une politique étrangère* (Paris: Plon, 1971), especially 285–346.

12. For converging Franco-German interests and the European Monetary System, see Tom de Vries, "On the Meaning and Future of the European Monetary System," *Princeton University Essays in International Finance*, no. 138 (September 1980): especially 9–13.

13. See chap. 4, nn. 26, 32.

14. See Wolfgang Wagner, "Aussichten der Ostpolitik nach dem Abschluss der Berlin-Verhandlungen," *Europa-Archiv*, 3 Folge 1972, 79–86. See also David P. Calleo, *The German Problem Reconsidered* (New York: Cambridge University Press, 1978), 174–77.

15. On French leadership in challenging American efforts to impose allied economic sanctions against the East, see Robert D. Putnam and Nicholas Bayne, *Hanging Together: The Seven-Power Summits* (Cambridge, Mass.: Harvard University Press, 1984), 150–70. See also chap. 5, n. 40.

16. For Mitterrand's reaffirmation to Schmidt of Franco-German friendship, see "Just Good Allies," *Economist*, 19–24 July 1981, p. 52. For a general analysis, see Dominique Moïsi, "Mitterrand's Foreign Policy: the Limits of Continuity," *Foreign Affairs* 61, no. 3 (America and the World 1982): 347–57.

17. For an analysis of Socialist economic policy and its turnaround, see Bela Balassa, "Une année de politique économique socialiste en France," *Commentaire* 5, no. 19: 415–28; Volkmar Lauber, *The Political Economy of France: From Pompidou to Mitterrand* (New York: Praeger, 1983), 173–79; and Stanley Hoffmann, "Mitterrand vs. France," *New York Review of Books*, 27 Sept. 1984, 52–53. For a rather bitter assessment of Socialist economic policy, see French economist Alfred Sauvy "Nouvelle politique économique: Premier bilan," in *Revue Politique et Parlementaire* no. 896 (January–February 1982): 28–35.

18. France's current account deficit narrowed from $12 billion in 1982 to $3.8 billion in 1983, while consumer price inflation fell from 11.8 percent to 9.6 percent. Various Socialist programs helped hold up employment initially, but the jobless rate rose sharply in 1984: to 9.7 percent from 8.3 percent in 1983 and 8.1 percent in 1982. *OECD Economic Surveys, France* (July 1984), 7, 30–44, 53–56; (July 1985), 33–40. On the lessons of limited economic autonomy for French Socialist programs, see "The Importance of International Economic Linkages," *OECD Economic Outlook*, no. 33 (July 1983): 16–21.

19. See Michael M. Harrison, *The Reluctant Ally: France and Atlantic Security*, 153–56.

20. Ibid., 182–84, 193–98.

21. The announcement of increased military collaboration under the 1963 treaty came on 22 October 1982. Both leaders warned against overestimating the consequences. Mitterrand excluded German participation in or financial support for the nuclear program. Kohl excluded any autonomous Franco-German strategy or denigration of the U.S. military role. See *International Herald Tribune*, 23–24 October 1982, p. 1. For subsequent progress, see n. 45. For the unimpressive results of earlier attempts, see Michael M. Harrison, *The Reluctant Ally: France and Atlantic Security*, 105–9.

22. For Mitterrand's speech of 20 January 1983, see *20 Jahre Deutsche-Französische Zusammenarbeit/ 20 Années de coopération Franco-Allemande*, Reihe Berichte und Dokumentation (Bonn: Presse und Informationamt der Bundesregierung, 1983). For French fears of West German neutralism, see *Europäisierung Europas*, "Zwischen Französischem Nuklearnationalismus und deutschem Nuklearpazifismus," ed. Claude Bourde and Alfred Mechtersheimer (Berlin: Verlag Europäische Perspektive, 1984), especially Michel Tatu's contribution, "Frankreich und die deutsche Friedensbewegung"; see also François-Georges Dreyfus, "Pacifisme et nationalisme en Allemagne Fédérale aujourd'hui," *Défense nationale* 38, no. 1 (January 1982): 7–22.

23. For SPD disappointment with Mitterrand's position, see "Les Socialistes allémands se démarquent des thèses de M. Mitterrand sur la sécurité européenne," *Le Monde*, 23–24 Jan. 1983, p. 1. Egon Bahr, a leading foreign policy strategist on the SPD's left wing questioned the viability of any alliance between nuclear and non-nuclear powers and criticized the domination the former exercise over the latter. Mitterrand's speech seemed to Bahr a symbol of nuclear hegemony. A year later, Bahr called for withdrawing all foreign-controlled nuclear weapons from the territory of non-nuclear countries. See "Atomare Klassenunterschied," in *Der Spiegel*, 13 Feb. 1984.

24. See, for example, French Socialist party foreign-policy expert Jacques Huntzinger, who would consider German nuclear weapons a legitimate *"casus belli."* "Défense de la France, sécurité de l'Europe," *Politique étrangère* 47, no. 2 (Summer 1983): 395–402.

25. Germany's geopolitical options are treated at length in David P. Calleo, *The German Problem Reconsidered* (Cambridge: Cambridge University Press, 1978), especially 166–69.

26. See "Exports," *NIMEXE Analytical Tables of Foreign Trade* 2 (Luxembourg: EEC Europe Statistic Office, 1984).

27. For Konrad Adenauer's insistence on a Western alliance over a neutralist reunification, see his early collection of speeches, *World Indivisible* (New York: Harper and Brothers, 1955), 49–104. For de Gaulle's pan-European vision, see chap. 4, n. 22. As vice chancellor and foreign minister, Willy Brandt laid out his views on *Ostpolitik*, reunification, and ties to the West in *A Peace Policy for Europe* (New York: Holt, Rinehart and Winston, 1969), especially 94–155. For examples of Chancellor Helmut Kohl's speeches before the Bundestag on the subject of reunification, see "State of the Nation in Divided Germany," *Statements and Speeches* (New York: German Information Center) 8, no. 4 (5 Mar. 1985); 9, no. 5 (18 Mar. 1986).

For a discussion of German Catholics' traditional "confederalist" and general European orientation, see Robert C. Dahlberg, *Heinrich Bruning, the Center Party, and Germany's "Middle Way"* (Washington, D.C.: Johns Hopkins School of Advanced International Studies, unpublished Ph.D. dissertation, 1983), 23–95. For an analysis of the importance of Catholic parties in the postwar choices of the Federal Republic, see Michael Stürmer, "Das industrielle Deutschland, von 1866 bis zur Gegenwart," in *Mitten in Europa, Deutsche Geschichte*, ed. Hartmut Boockmann (Berlin: Wolf Jobst Siedler Verlag, 1984), 366–409.

28. See Angela Stent, "The USSR and Germany," *Problems of Communism* 30, no. 5, (September–October 1981): 17–19, 22–24.

29. For an analysis of French interwar diplomacy toward the Soviets, see Arnold Wolfers, *Britain and France Between Two Wars* (New York: Harcourt and Brace, 1940), 76–94, 128–41; and Denis William Brogan, *The Development of Modern France* (London: H. Hamilton, 1940), 316–18, 396–99.

30. "[The Franco-Russian alliance,] though repeatedly betrayed and repudiated, remained no less in the natural order of things, as much in relation to the German menace as to the endeavors of Anglo-American hegemony." Charles de Gaulle, *Salvation*, 728. For Stalin's snub, see Alfred Grosser, *The Western Alliance, European-American Relations Since 1945* (New York: Vintage Books, 1982), 38–40. For an analysis of de Gaulle's views, see Michael M. Harrison, *The Reluctant Ally: France and Atlantic Security*, 68–70.

31. The basic rationale behind the French national deterrent is best developed in General Pierre Gallois's critique of the idea of extended deterrence in *Stratégie de l'age nucleaire* (Paris: Calmann-Levy, 1961), trans. as *The Balance of Terror: Strategy for the Nuclear Age* (Boston: Houghton Mifflin, 1961). Gallois stressed the equalizing power that nuclear weapons confer on a smaller power, if that power makes clear its absolute determination to defend its sovereignty even at the risk of nuclear annihilation. Thus, France needs only a large enough nuclear force to inflict unacceptable damage on an aggressor's population centers, regardless of any superiority in nuclear weapons that the aggressor enjoys. Gallois also argued that automatic retaliation was a safer doctrine for vacillating democracies than counterforce. The "actual value [of the French nuclear deterrent] was to serve as a semiautonomous trigger for the massive American strategic armory." See Harrison, *The Reluctant Ally*, 127. For a critique of this "trigger thesis," see also Lawrence Freedman, *The Evolution of Nuclear Strategy* (London: Macmillan Press/International Institute for Strategic Studies, 1983), 318–20. General André Beaufre's refinement of "multi-lateral deterrence," best expresses the real and practical doctrine defining France's nuclear role. Beaufre suggested that small independent forces, like France's, enhance deterrence by threatening an aggressor with the added risks from "multiple centers" of nuclear decision making. Beaufre develops his ideas in *Dissuasion et stratégie* (Paris: Armand Colin, 1964), trans. as *Deterrence and Strategy* (New York: Praeger, 1965). For a concise account of French doctrine and forces, see David S. Yost, "France's Deterrent Posture and Security in Europe, Part I: Capabilities and Doctrine," *Adelphi Paper*, no. 194 (London: International Institute for Strategic Studies, Winter 1984–85) and "Part II: Strategic and Arms Control Implications," *Adelphi Paper*, no. 195 (London: International Institute for Strategic Studies, Winter 1984–85). See also chap. 4.

32. See chap. 9, n. 40.

33. For details, see chap. 9, n. 36. For what new French tactical nuclear weapons imply for German defense and Franco-German strategic relations, see Robert Grant, "French Defense Policy and European Security," *Political Science Quarterly* 100, no. 3 (Fall 1985).

34. For a classic exposition of France as a nuclear-armed "sanctuaire," see General Lucien Poirier, *Essais de stratégie théorique* (Paris: Fondation Pour Les Études de Défense Nationale, 1982), especially 289–311. French defense policy assumed that any nonstrategic Soviet attack in Europe would aim first at Germany and thus engage American and German forces. French conventional forces in Germany would engage the enemy to determine whether the attack was an "aggression apparenté" (a frontier incident) or an "aggression caracterisé" (the first stage of an extensive penetration into Western Europe). The latter was to trigger the French tactical nuclear deterrent. By implication, in the former case, French forces would not join the battle. Michael M. Harrison, *The Reluctant Ally*, 128–29.

Under Valery Giscard d'Estaing, the French adopted a strategy of an "extended sanctuary" to include West Germany, but without any explicit extension of their nuclear umbrella. French officials continued to characterize the strategic nuclear force as "national"; willingness to use French tactical nuclear weapons in the forward battle for Germany was left ambiguous. See General Guy Méry, "Une Armée pourquoi faire et comment," *Défense nationale* 32, no. 6 (June 1976): 11–33; Michael M. Harrison, *The Reluctant Ally*, 191–204; and *French White Paper on National Defense* (New York: Ambassade de France, Service de Presse et d'Information, 1972).

Mitterrand's strategy has remained intentionally uncommitted. French nuclear weapons are not for a forward battle, and even French conventional participation is not automatic. See Chief of Staff General Jeannou Lacaze, "La politique militaire," *Défense nationale* 37, no. 11 (November 1981); and "Politique de défense et stratégie militaire de la France," *Défense nationale* 39, no. 6 (June 1983). Unofficial strategists have suggested emplacing nuclear weapons in Germany under a "double key" arrangement giving the Federal Republic a veto over their use. See Michel Tatu, *La bataille des euromissiles* (Paris: Éditions du Seuil, 1983), 48–50.

For a concise review of Mitterrand's strategy, see Robert S. Rudney, "Mitterrand's Defense Concepts: Some Unsocialist Remarks," *Strategic Review* 11, no. 2 (Spring 1983): 20–35; Michael Harrison and Simon Serfaty, "A Socialist France and Western Security" (Washington, D.C.: Johns Hopkins Foreign Policy Institute), 27–35; and David S. Yost, "France's Deterrent Posture and Security in Europe, Part I: Capabilities and Doctrine," 4–12, and "Part II: Strategic and Arms Control Implications," 2–32.

35. For French forces in "reserve for Europe," see David P. Calleo, *The Atlantic Fantasy* (Baltimore: Johns Hopkins University Press, 1970), 126–32. See also chap. 4.

36. See n. 31.

37. On 26 June 1974, the United States joined the other NATO members in a fourteen-point declaration recognizing French and British nuclear forces as "capable of playing a deterrent role of their own, contributing to the overall strengthening of the deterrence of the alliance." This was the first official recognition that the *force de dissuasion* contributed to the common security. See Alfred Grosser, *The Western Alliance*, 283, 284; and Michael M. Harrison, *The Reluctant Ally*, 183.

On American attitudes toward the French nuclear force, see also Samuel F. Wells, Jr., "The Mitterrand Challenge," *Foreign Policy*, no. 44 (Fall 1981): 57–69. Summaries of earlier and more critical views can be found in Wilfrid Kohl, *French Nuclear Diplomacy* (Princeton: Princeton University Press, 1971), 224–29, and Lawrence Freedman, *Evolution of Nuclear Strategy*, 303–24.

38. See Drew Middleton, "French Army's New Look Draws Praise," *New York Times*, 31 July 1984, p. A3; see also Stanley Hoffmann, "Gaullism by Any Other Name," in *Foreign Policy*, no. 57 (Winter 1984/85): 55.

39. See chap. 7, n. 21.

40. See Drew Middleton, "French Army's New Look Draws Praise," and Jack Anderson and Joseph Spear, "Vive la Méthode Française!" *Washington Post*, 16 July 1985, p. C11.

41. For the French economy's strong performance, see n. 3. For French trade, see Christopher Saunders, "Changes in the Distribution of World Production and Trade," in *National Industrial Strategies and the World Economy*, ed. John Pinder (Totowa, N.J.: Allanheld, Osmun, 1982), 22; and Bela Belassa, *European Economic Integration* (Amsterdam: North-Holland Publishing Company, 1975), 79–117.

42. Worries were constant in the popular press. See, for example, *L'Express*, 10–16 Feb. 1984, "Économie mondiale: La réprise pour qui?," and especially Michel Cicurel, "France: réalisme ou déclin?," Ibid., 22–23.

43. In October 1983, the Gaullist opposition leader Jacques Chirac (Prime Minister under Mitterrand in 1986) ambiguously broached the nuclear topic in Bonn by stressing the need for a European nuclear deterrent and for increased German participation in decision making at all levels of security matters. He later denied suggesting a German "finger on the nuclear trigger." See *Le Monde*, 20, 28 Oct. 1983; and 3 Dec. 1983. Numerous French analysts have gone farther. See, for example, René Foch, "Pour une sanctuarisation élargie," *Le Monde*, 11 Apr. 1984, p. 2; Michel Manel, *L'Europe sans défense?* (Paris: Berger-Levrault, 1982), 215–52; General Guy Méry, "Défense de la France et défense de l'Europe," *Défense nationale* 39, no. 1 (January 1983); and Jean-Paul Pigasse, *Le Bouclier d'Europe: Vers une autonomie militaire de la Communauté Européenne* (Paris: Éditions Seghers, 1982), especially 233–53. See also n. 35.

44. For German criticism, see n. 23. For the evolution of Mitterrand's attitude toward the Gaullist defense legacy, see n. 34.

45. At their October 1982 meeting, Mitterrand and Kohl created a joint military commission that meets every three months and includes several study groups, among them a nuclear group. See Marie-

Claude Smouts, "The External Policy of François Mitterrand," *International Affairs* 59, no. 2 (Spring 1983): 155–67. In February 1986, France and West Germany concluded an agreement. France promised to consult the Federal Republic before using tactical nuclear weapons on its soil. Kohl and Mitterrand directed French and German officers to draft detailed plans for using the *force d'action rapide* to defend West Germany. And the two countries announced additional joint maneuvers and training programs for their officers. Paul Lewis, "Paris-Bonn Military Accord Is Reached," *New York Times*, 2 Mar. 1986, p. 3. The commission's work also led to the 1984 initiatives to revive the Western European Union and the agreement for joint production of a combat helicopter. See Robert Grant, "French Defense Policy and European Security," 425. See also n. 47.

46. See chap. 9, n. 15.

47. In return for Germany's support for revival of the Western European Union (WEU) as a forum for discussing cooperative weapons production and defense policy, France pushed successfully for the removal of remaining restrictions (contained in the 1954 WEU Treaty) on German conventional rearmament. See Robert Grant, "French Defense Policy and European Security," 424–26. A most notable success in the area of joint weapons production was the May 1984 agreement by France and Germany to collaborate on the development of an antitank helicopter. On this and another fifty-odd Franco-German joint projects, see *Le Monde*, 30 May 1984, p. 1. A notable failure came roughly one year later when France and Spain pulled out of talks with West Germany, Britain, and Italy for joint production of a fighter aircraft. The failure stemmed from different conceptions of the fighter's mission and Franco-British rivalry over leadership in developing the plane. See "La France et l'Espagne refusent le project d'avion européen," *Le Monde*, 3 Aug. 1985, p. 1. For an analysis of the economic efficacy of such joint undertakings, see Keith Hartley, *NATO Arms Cooperation: A Study in Economics and Politics* (London: Allen and Unwin, 1983).

48. For initial European reactions to Reagan's SDI and Mitterrand's Eureka project, see chap. 5, n. 36. See also David Marsh, "Eureka emerges from its incubation with wide European support," *Financial Times*, 6 July 1985, p. 2.

49. See Paul Lewis, "France Approves Arms Plan Linked to European Allies," *New York Times*, 11 Apr. 1987, p. 3; and Pierre Servent, "M. Chirac se réjouit de l'unité des Français autour de leur défense," *Le Monde*, 10 Apr. 1987, p. 10.

Chapter 11: The Russian Role

1. For the uses of the Soviet threat in developing public support for U.S., European, and global economic programs, see Stephen D. Krasner, "United States Commercial and Monetary Policy: Unravelling the Paradox of External Strength and Internal Weakness," *Between Power and Plenty: Foreign Economic Policies of Advanced Industrial States*, ed. Peter J. Katzenstein (Madison: University of Wisconsin Press, 1978), 72–76.

2. See, for example, former Prime Minister Harold Macmillan's account of his visit to Moscow at the time of Khrushchev's Berlin ultimatum, *Riding the Storm, 1956–59* (London: Macmillan, 1971), 557–656.

3. See Archie Brown and George Schopflin, "The Challenge to Soviet Leadership: Effects in Eastern Europe," in *Eurocommunism: Myth or Reality?*, ed. P. Filo della Torre, E. Mortimer, and J. Storey (London: Penguin, 1979). See also Joan Barth Urban, "Moscow and the PCI in the 1970s: Kto Kovo?," in *Studies in Comparative Communism* 13, nos. 2, 3 (Summer/Autumn 1980).

4. See Johan Jorgen Holst, "Security as Mutual Education," in *Détente*, ed. G. R. Urban (New York: Universe Books, 1976), 123–24.

5. For detailed analyses of the legitimacy of various Eastern European governments, see *Political Legitimation in Communist States*, ed. T. Rigby and F. Feber (New York: St. Martin's Press, 1982).

6. Tension over U.S. use of Europe's NATO bases for supporting Israel was notorious during the October 1973 Arab-Israeli War. German bases were used without consultation; Spain, Greece, Turkey,

and Italy explicitly refused permission, and Britain insisted that its support be kept secret. See Alfred Grosser, *The Western Alliance*, 273–74.

7. The pipeline crisis of the early 1980s bore remarkable similarities to the 1962–66 German-Soviet oil pipeline embargo. See Angela Stent, *From Embargo to Ostpolitik: The Political Economy of West German-Soviet Relations 1955–80* (Cambridge: Cambridge University Press, 1981). See also chap. 5, n. 40, and chap. 10, n. 15.

8. See, for example, Colin Gray, *The Geopolitics of the Nuclear Era: Heartland, Rimlands and the Technological Revolution* (New York: Crane, Russak and Co., 1977), 67. See also the many writings of Richard Pipes: "Détente: Moscow's View," in *Soviet Strategy in Europe*, ed. Richard Pipes (New York: Crane, Russak and Co., 1976), "Why the Soviet Union Thinks It Could Fight and Win a Nuclear War," *Commentary* 64, no. 1 (July, 1977); and *US-Soviet Relations in the Era of Détente* (Boulder, Colo.: Westview Press, 1981).

For an interesting debate on this issue as well as on the overall nature of the Soviet Union and East-West relations, see George F. Kennan, "A Current Assessment of Soviet-American Relations," *Encounter* 50, no. 3 (March 1978); Richard Pipes, "Mr. 'X' Revises," *Encounter* 50, no. 4 (April 1978); and Leopold Labedz, "A Last Critique," *Encounter* 51, no. 3 (September 1978). See also, Paul H. Nitze, "Strategy in the 1980s," *Foreign Affairs* 59, no. 1 (Fall 1980).

9. Various Western schools of interpreting Soviet behavior have come in and out of fashion in the postwar era. The Soviet Union has always had its Western admirers, even in the Stalinist era; see Paul Hollander, *Political Pilgrims: Travels of Western Intellectuals to the Soviet Union, China and Cuba 1928–78* (New York: Cambridge University Press, 1980), 294–95. For a critique of seeing the Soviet Union as an outlaw state requiring a policy of perennial confrontation, see Seweryn Bialer, *Stalin's Successors: Leadership, Stability and Change in the Soviet Union* (New York: Cambridge University Press, 1980), 294–95. For "realist" analysis of the Soviets as antipathetic and dangerous, but not beyond the scope of traditional diplomacy, see George Kennan's views in chap. 3 passim. For the "revisionist" view that had Americans been more sensitive to Russian national interests, and themselves less aggressively ideological, the worst of the Cold War might have been prevented, see, for example, Gar Alperowitz, *Atomic Diplomacy: Hiroshima and Potsdam* (New York: Vintage Books, 1965); and Gabriel and Joyce Kolko, *The Limits of Power: The World and United States Foreign Policy 1945–54* (New York: Harper and Row, 1972). A further revisionist theory, popular with some political scientists and economists, has seen the exigencies of politico-economic "modernization" gradually "converging" national structures and practices in a common mold. For a summary and critique of the convergence theory, see Zbigniew Brzezinski and Samuel P. Huntington, *Political Power: USA/USSR* (New York: Penguin, 1977), 9–14.

10. There are as many views on the role of ideology in Soviet foreign policy as there are students of it. For some interesting views, see George F. Kennan, *The Nuclear Delusion* (New York: Pantheon Books, 1982), 75–101; E. P. Hoffman and F. J. Fleron, eds., *The Conduct of Soviet Foreign Policy* (London: Butterworths, 1971), pt. 3; and Karen Dawisha, "Soviet Ideology and Western Europe," in *Soviet Strategy Towards Western Europe*, ed. Edwina Moreton and Gerald Segal (London: George Allen and Unwin, 1984), 19–38. For a first-hand Soviet view, see Georgi A. Arbatov and Willem Oltmans, *The Soviet Viewpoint* (New York: Dodd, Mead and Co., 1983), 142–43. For discussions of the role played by revolutionary ideology, ideological competition with China, and traditional great-power interests in motivating the Soviet-sponsored Cuban intervention in Angola, see Joan Barth Urban, "The Soviets and the West European Communist Parties," in *Soviet Policy Toward Western Europe*, ed. Herbert J. Ellison (Seattle: University of Washington Press, 1983), 97; and "China's Impact," *Problems of Communism* 27, no. 2 (January–February 1978): 42–47. For a view of the Soviet Union as no more than a great military empire in the classic tradition, and therefore with classical national interests, see Edward N. Luttwak, *The Grand Strategy of the Soviet Union* (New York: St. Martin's Press, 1983).

11. For many in the West, Alexander Solzhenitsyn's *The Gulag Archipelago, 1918–1956* (New York: Harper and Row, 1973) either confirmed the worst of what they had long suspected or, especially in France, triggered a dramatic re-evaluation.

12. For a brilliant but controversial view about the militarization of Soviet society, see Cornelius

Castoriadis, *Devant la guerre* (Paris: Fayard, 1981). See also Jaques Rupnik, "From Party State to Army State," *The New Republic*, 5 Jan. 1982; E. Odom, "The Militarization of Soviet Society," *Problems of Communism* 25, no. 5 (September/October 1976), and Dimitri K. Simes, "The Military and Militarism in Soviet Society," *International Security* 6, no. 3 (Winter 1981/2).

13. See Herbert Romerstein, *Soviet Support for International Terrorism* (Washington, D.C.: The Foundation for Democratic Education, 1981). For a historical discussion of Russian involvement in overseas terrorism, see "From Azeff to Agca," *Survey* 27, no. 118/119 (Autumn/Winter 1983): 1–88.

14. On the economic pressures for openings to the West, see Abram Bergson, "Soviet Economic Perspectives: Toward a New Growth Model," *Problems of Communism* 22, no. 2 (March-April 1973): 1–9; and "The Soviet Economy: Domestic and International Issues," in *The Soviet Empire: Expansion and Détente*, ed. William E. Griffith (Lexington, Mass.: Lexington Books, 1976), especially 115–18.

Many astute Sovietologists, however, challenge the implied link between economic modernization and political democratization. See, for example, Jerry Hough and Merle Fainsod, *How the Soviet Union Is Governed* (Cambridge, Mass.: Harvard University Press, 1979), 285–93, 556–76. See also Timothy Colton, *The Dilemma of Reform in the Soviet Union* (New York: Council of Foreign Relations, 1984), 1–32. Colton, among others, points to the inherent pitfalls of partial reform.

15. An example of this neorevisionist argument can be found in Noam Chomsky's chapter, "The United States: From Greece to El Salvador," in *Superpowers in Collision: The New Cold War*, ed. Noam Chomsky, Jonathan Steele, John Gittings (London: Penguin, 1982), 20–43.

16. See, for an able defense of this "Eurorealist" view, Richard Lowenthal, "Dealing with Soviet Global Power," *Encounter* 50, no. 6 (June 1978).

17. See Seweryn Bialer, "The Soviet Union and the West in the 1980s: Détente, Containment or Confrontation?," *Orbis* 27, no. 1 (Spring 1983). For a discussion of the Reagan administration's ambiguous shift to a more moderate Soviet policy during the final year of Reagan's first term, see Leslie Gelb and Anthony Lake, "Four More Years: Diplomacy Restored?" in *Foreign Affairs* 63, no. 3 (America and the World 1984): 465–89.

18. See Archie Brown, "Gorbachev: New Man in the Kremlin," *Problems of Communism* 34, no. 3 (May-June 1985), 1–23.

19. Soviet military doctrine is another area of persistent debate and controversy in Western military and academic circles. For a Soviet view of this debate, see Georgi A. Arbatov and Willem Oltmans, *The Soviet Viewpoint*, 39–41. For a range of Western views of the "offensive" nature of Soviet defensive strategy, see Colonel Graham D. Vernon, *Soviet Options for War in Europe: Nuclear or Conventional?*, National Security Affairs Monograph (Washington, D.C.: National Defense University, 1979). For a discussion of the "standing start" blitzkrieg attack without prior mobilization, see General R. Close, *Europe without Defense?* (New York: Pergamon Press, 1979); a critique of this can be found in Les Aspin, "A Surprise Attack on NATO: Refocusing the Debate," *Congressional Record*, 7 Feb. 1977, 4911–14. See also General James H. Polk, "The North German Plain Attack Scenario: Threat or Illusion?," *Strategic Review* 8, no. 3 (Summer 1981). For more on the Soviet blitzkrieg argument, see Edward N. Luttwak, "The Operational Level of War," *International Security* 5, no. 3 (Winter 1980–81); and John J. Mearsheimer, "Why the Soviets Can't Win Quickly in Central Europe," *International Security* 7, no. 1 (Summer 1982). See also John J. Binder and Robert W. Clawson, "Warsaw Pact Ground Forces: Formations, Combat Doctrine and Capabilities," in *The Warsaw Pact: Political Purpose and Military Means*, ed. Robert W. Clawson and Lawrence S. Kaplan (Wilmington, Delaware: Scholarly Resources, 1982), 229–51.

20. The USSR bears 80–85 percent of the Warsaw Pact's total defense costs. See M. Checinski, "Poland's Military Burden," *Problems of Communism* 32, no. 3 (May-June 1983). See also *The Impact of International Economic Disturbances on the Soviet Union and Eastern Europe*, ed. Egon Neuberger and Laura d'Andrea Tyson (New York: Pergamon Press, 1980). By offering Eastern Europe preferential terms of trade, the Soviets are estimated to have transferred resources equivalent to almost $80 billion in 1980 dollars to Eastern Europe during the decade 1971–1980; see D. L. Bond, "CMEA Growth Projection for 1981–85 and Implication for Restricted Western Credits," NATO Economic Directorate, *The CMEA Five-Year Plans in a New Perspective: Planned and Non-Planned Economies*, Colloquium, Brussels, Mar. 31–2 Apr. 1982.

But many writers also reckon the political costs of losing its hegemonic position in Eastern Europe are prohibitive. See, for example, John Campbell, "Soviet Policy in Eastern Europe: An Overview," in *Soviet Policy in Eastern Europe*, ed. Sarah Terry (New Haven: Yale University Press, 1984), 13–18.

21. See David P. Calleo, *Europe's Future: The Grand Alternatives* (New York: W. W. Norton, 1967), 125–26.

22. It is far from obvious which German state exercises more leverage over the other. See Angela Stent, "The USSR and Germany," *Problems of Communism* 30, no. 5 (September–October 1981), 10–18.

23. Numerous writers note that failing to sustain and augment the improved consumption levels consistently promised would entail considerable political risk. See Robert Campbell, "The Economy," in *After Brezhnev*, ed. Robert F. Byrnes (Bloomington: Indiana University Press, 1983), 75. On the domestic political motives behind foreign grain purchases, see Adam Ulam, *Dangerous Relations, The Soviet Union in World Politics, 1970–82* (New York: Oxford University Press, 1984), 90–92. See also n. 14.

24. For studies of the effectiveness or ineffectiveness of Western economic sanctions and linkage policies, see T. Gustafsen, *Selling the Russians the Rope? Soviet Technology Policy and U.S. Export Controls* (Santa Monica, Cal.: Rand R-2649 ARPA, 1981); Philip Hanson, *Trade and Technology in Soviet-Western Relations* (New York: Columbia University Press, 1981); J. R. Mcintyre and R. R. Cupitt, "East-West Strategic Trade Control: Crumbling Consensus?," *Survey* 98 (Spring 1980); M. Mountain, "Technology Exports and National Security," *Foreign Policy* 32 (Fall 1978). On linkage, see Arthur Stein, "The Politics of Linkage," *World Politics* 33 (October 1980).

For Soviet disabilities as a trading partner, see Joseph Berliner and Franklyn Holzman, "The Soviet Economy: Domestic and International Issues," in *The Soviet Empire: Expansion and Détente*, 100–118.

25. On the decline of Soviet leadership and legitimacy, see Joan Barth Urban, "The Ties That Bind: West European Communists and the Communist States of Eastern Europe," in *The European Left: Italy, France, and Spain*, ed. W. Griffith (Lexington, Mass.: Lexington Books, 1979). For the fierce polemics between the Italian and Soviet Communist Parties after the declaration of martial law in Poland, see Urban, "The Soviets and the West European Communist Parties," 97–126.

26. See Angela Stent Yergin, "Soviet-West German Relations: Finlandization or Normalization," in *Soviet Foreign Policy Toward Western Europe*, ed. George Ginsburgs and Alvin Z. Rubinstein (New York: Praeger, 1978); Robert Legvold, "The Soviet Union and Western Europe," in *The Soviet Empire: Expansion and Détente*; and William E. Griffith, "The Soviets and Western Europe: An Overview," in *Soviet Policy Toward Western Europe*.

27. For U.S. late wartime and early postwar policy toward Eastern Europe, see Gier Lundestad, *American Non-Policy Towards Eastern Europe 1943–1947* (Oslo: Universitetsforlaget, 1978). On America's retreat from the rhetoric of "rolling back" Soviet domination over Eastern Europe, see chap. 3, n. 41. For later ideas of American economic engagement with the same Soviet-dominated regimes, see Seyom Brown, *The Faces of Power: Constancy and Change in United States Foreign Policy from Truman to Reagan* (New York: Columbia University Press, 1983), 259–77. For some of the dilemmas of current U.S. policy, see Jerry F. Hough, *The Polish Crisis: American Policy Options* (Washington, D.C.: Brookings Institution, 1982).

28. See Timothy Colton, *The Dilemma of Reform in the Soviet Union*, 1–17; Jerry Hough and Merle Fainsod, *How the Soviet Union Is Governed*, 285–93, 562–63, Seweryn Bialer, *Stalin's Successors: Leadership, Stability and Change in the Soviet Union* (New York: Cambridge University Press, 1980), 207–25; J. R. Azrael, "The Nationality Problem in the USSR: Domestic Pressures and Foreign Policy Constraints," in *The Domestic Context of Soviet Foreign Policy* (Boulder, Colo.: Westview Press, 1981), 139–53.

29. See Abram Bergson, "Soviet Economic Perspectives: Toward a New Growth Model"; Joseph Berliner and Franklyn Holzman, "The Soviet Economy: Domestic and International Issues"; Robert Campbell, "The Economy"; Alex Nove, *The Soviet Economic System* (London: Allen and Unwin, 2d ed., 1980), 124–53; Myron Rush, "Guns over Butter in Soviet Policy," *International Security* 7, no. 3 (Winter 1982–83); Boris Rumer, "Soviet Investment Policy: Unresolved Problems," *Problems of*

Communism 31, no. 5 (September–October 1982); Seweryn Bialer, *Stalin's Successors: Leadership, Stability and Change in the Soviet Union*, 294. See also Abram Bergson, "Soviet Economic Slowdown and the 1981–85 Plan," *Problems of Communism* 30, no. 3 (May-June 1981). See also nn. 14, 23.

30. See Celestine Bohlen, "Gorbachev Presses Changes," *The Washington Post*, 23 Feb. 1986, pp. A1, A23; and Gary Lee, "Soviet Congress Raises Hopes," *The Washington Post*, 24 Feb. 1986, pp. A13, A14.

31. See chap. 5, n. 37.

32. See Adam B. Ulam, *Dangerous Relations: The Soviet Union in World Politics, 1970–1982*, 32–51.

33. See chap. 5.

34. See chap. 8, n. 2 for George Liska's broad historical case for U.S.–Soviet "appeasement." For Soviet hints of interest in various forms of strategic cooperation, particularly against China, see Gerard Smith, *Doubletalk: The Story of the First Strategic Arms Limitation Talks* (New York: Doubleday, 1980), 141; and Adam Ulam, *Dangerous Relations*, 85.

35. For an example of the argument that French and British deterrent forces, once their modernizations are completed in the 1990s, will destabilize the strategic balance, invite preemptive strikes, and "fatally complicate the task of arms control," see George M. Seignious II and Jonathan Paul Yates, "Europe's Nuclear Superpowers," *Foreign Policy*, no. 55 (Summer 1984).

36. In 1985, France was credited with 172 independently targetable nuclear warheads and Britain with between 120 and 192 warheads that could be directed against 64 different targets. By contrast, the United States wields 10,174 independently targetable warheads, and the Soviets, 9,987. Institute for Strategic Studies, *The Military Balance 1985–1986*, 40, 46, 180.

37. For French doubts about an antimissile space shield, as envisioned in the U.S. Strategic Defense Initiative, see the interview with French Defense Minister Paul Quilès, "La defense spatiale ne rend pas caduque l'arme nucléaire," *Le Monde*, 18 Dec. 1985, p. 1.

38. See chap. 9.

39. See David S. Yost, "France's Deterrent Posture and Security in Europe, Part I: Capabilities and Doctrine," *Adelphi Paper*, no. 194 (Winter 1984/85), 18–23. Yost is not altogether definite about survivability of the premodernized French force against a worst-case Soviet first strike.

40. Before completing negotiations on the Non-Proliferation Treaty, the United States submitted a summary of NATO allies' questions and U.S. answers concerning Europe's nuclear defense. The interpretations included the statement that the treaty would not "bar succession by a new federated European state to the nuclear status of one of its members." The Soviet Union did not challenge the American interpretations. See *Arms Control and Disarmament Agreements, Texts and Histories of Negotiations* (Washington, D.C.: United States Arms Control and Disarmament Agency, 1982), 84–85.

41. On the Carter administration's refusal in SALT II negotiations to renounce the option of giving Western Europeans access to cruise missile technology, see Strobe Talbot, *Endgame: The Inside Story of SALT II* (New York: Harper and Row, 1980), 149–51. For the Reagan administration's consistent refusal to "compensate" the Soviets for French and British deterrents in the ill-fated U.S.–Soviet INF negotiations of 1979–83, see Talbot, *Deadly Gambits* (New York: Knopf, 1984), 24, 63, 85–113, 125–28, 161–62, 176, 182, 183, 192, 198–205.

42. See Lewis A. Dunn, *Controlling the Bomb: Nuclear Proliferation in the 1980s* (New Haven: Yale University Press, 1982), 13, 44–68. See also chap. 7, n. 26.

43. For the ratcheting effect of extended deterrence on the arms race, see Michel Tatu, *La bataille des euromissiles* (Paris: Éditions du Seuil, 1983), 60–61. Tatu notes Mitterrand's admission that U.S. Pershing missiles "respond to a disequilibrium of forces in Europe with a disequilibrium of forces in the world." SS-20s upset the European balance without directly menacing the United States. The NATO response, while redressing the balance in Europe, also posed a new, more dangerous threat to the Soviet homeland, since U.S. land-based missiles can now reach the Soviet Union in considerably less time than their Soviet counterparts can reach the United States.

INDEX

BEYOND AMERICAN HEGEMONY

DAVID P. CALLEO

In its current form as an American protectorate, the Western Alliance no longer serves
the interests of either the United States or our
European allies and cannot survive.

That is the controversial but inescapable conclusion of this pathbreaking new book. In a
sweeping historical analysis that is unique in
its brilliant integration of economic, military,
and geopolitical factors, one of this country's
foremost scholars in international relations
makes a well-nigh unanswerable case for a
more European-directed alliance. While
arguing that America and Europe continue to
need their alliance, David Calleo shows how
America's military hegemony in NATO is now
unnecessary and counterproductive. Only a
NATO led by the Europeans themselves can
resolve the growing problems of extended
nuclear deterrence, he maintains. And each
side's distinctive political interests in any case
limit NATO's utility as a forward base for
American power. Moreover, Calleo shows
how America's continuing struggle to sustain
an unneeded military hegemony in Europe
frustrates efforts to put our fiscal house in
order, with consequences that increasingly
erode the postwar world order, including the